Daughters of God,
Subordinates of Men

ALSO BY LESLY F. MASSEY

Women in the Church: Moving Toward Equality
(McFarland, 2002; softcover 2012)

*Women and the New Testament: An Analysis of Scripture
in Light of New Testament Era Culture*
(McFarland, 1989; softcover 2012)

Daughters of God, Subordinates of Men

Women and the Roots of Patriarchy in the New Testament

LESLY F. MASSEY

McFarland & Company, Inc., Publishers
Jefferson, North Carolina

LIBRARY OF CONGRESS CATALOGUING-IN-PUBLICATION DATA

Massey, Lesly F., 1946–
    Daughters of God, subordinates of men : women and the roots of patriarchy in the New Testament / Lesly F. Massey.
        p.   cm.
    Includes bibliographical references and index.

    ISBN 978-0-7864-9531-3 (softcover : acid free paper) ∞
    ISBN 978-1-4766-2143-2 (ebook)

    1. Women—History.   2. Women—Social conditions. 3. Women in the Bible.   4. Sex role—Religious aspects—Christianity.   I. Title.
HQ1127.M37 2015
305.409—dc23   2015034918

BRITISH LIBRARY CATALOGUING DATA ARE AVAILABLE

© 2015 Lesly F. Massey. All rights reserved

No part of this book may be reproduced or transmitted in any form or by any means, electronic or mechanical, including photocopying or recording, or by any information storage and retrieval system, without permission in writing from the publisher.

On the cover: artwork detail from *The Belvedere Madonna*, 1506, Raffaello S. Raphael (© 2015 PicturesNow)

Printed in the United States of America

McFarland & Company, Inc., Publishers
  Box 611, Jefferson, North Carolina 28640
    www.mcfarlandpub.com

Table of Contents

Preface   1

Introduction   5

ONE. Mesopotamia   15

TWO. Egypt   54

THREE. Judaism   83

FOUR. Greece   109

FIVE. Rome   147

SIX. Mystery Cults   177

Conclusions   197

Appendices:
    1. Periods of Ancient Mesopotamian History   215
    2. Periods of Ancient Egyptian History   217
    3. Key Events in Ancient Judaism   219
    4. Outline of Ancient Greek History   221
    5. Outline of Ancient Roman History   223

Chapter Notes   225

Bibliography   243

Index   251

Preface

It is ironic that this particular volume is the third book I have published concerning the status of women, rather than the first, since it deals with the cultural backgrounds that are more or less assumed in the other two. That makes it something akin to the prequel to *Star Wars*—the earlier story that is told later to answer questions as to where, when, and why. But feminist studies have advanced considerably since my own research began. My first McFarland publication was *Women and the New Testament*, 1989, essentially an exegesis of relevant New Testament texts but with the objective of demonstrating that the spirit and tone of the Gospel is contrary to the patriarchal models that have thrived in Christian tradition. That work included a critical discussion of Paul's statements in I Corinthians 11: 2–16, that the husband is head of the wife and any wife who prays or prophesies in the Christian assembly must wear a head covering to display her married status. Fresh perspectives on that text are included in this third work as well, noting that numerous scholars still see it as an enigma. I had wrestled with that text initially in 1973–74 in a master's thesis guided by Neil Lightfoot at Abilene Christian University. That thesis represents my earliest academic engagement with gender and feminist studies, which at the same time was my academic introduction to social and religious patriarchy.

The second volume, *Women in the Church: Moving Toward Equality*, 2002, is an analysis of the contrasting positions held by various Christian denominations on the status of women and the theological reasons for their position. This divergence is illustrated by two specific denominations—the Christian Church (Disciples of Christ) and the Churches of Christ, which have common roots in the nineteenth-century Stone-Campbell movement. The basis for their polarized posture on this topic is essentially different approaches to biblical interpretation, and in that regard the two denominations illustrate the church as a whole.

Only a few Christian denominations at the present time support true gender equity. The majority continue to defend traditional patriarchy, denying women leadership in church and insisting that the husband is rightfully the head of the family. Although female subordination is slowly being supplanted by more equitable social and moral ideologies, the fact that it still persists in many churches is evidence of the enormous strength of both tradition and perceived biblical authority. *Women in the Church: Moving Toward Equality* challenges traditional patriarchy, offering a sensible explanation for biblical statements on this topic, as well as a strategy for change for those churches willing to embrace gender equity.

Both of the above works are based on doctoral research done first under A.S. Geyser at the University of Witwatersrand and later under Viktor Bredenkamp at the University of Natal. I am grateful for the guidance of those noted scholars, as well as John De Gruchy, University of Cape Town, and Ursula King, University of Bristol, who served as examiners of my dissertation. I want to thank Jason Lamoreaux, professor at Texas A&M, and Carolyn Osiek, professor emerita of Brite Divinity School, who read all or portions of this third manuscript and offered helpful suggestions.

The present volume examines the status of women in the ancient cultures that form the backdrop for the early church and the New Testament. Typically, a brief mention of relevant backgrounds is included at the relevant text site in all thorough exegetical studies. However, a mere glimpse into the past hardly paints an accurate or impressive picture of the injustice women have suffered throughout history because of paradigms of patriarchy and male dominance, nor does it explain how such paradigms developed and how they came to be incorporated into Christian tradition. A close examination of the milieu in which New Testament documents were written reveals the extent to which ancient social customs influenced certain early Christian writers and the development of church tradition. A significant example is the link between slavery and female subordination in the house codes of Ephesians, Colossians, and I Peter.

In addition, the teachings of Jesus and his treatment of women can only be appreciated when examined against the backdrop of Judaism, especially the debates among rabbis on appropriate grounds for divorcing a wife, rabbinic and Mosaic laws that allowed the stoning of a woman caught in the act of adultery, laws that prohibited a menstruating woman from touching a male, norms that prohibited a pious Jew from conversing with or being touched by a woman he did not know, and laws that declared women essentially unsuitable for most forms of religious ritual and service.

Daughters of God, Subordinates of Men: Women and the Roots of Patriarchy in the New Testament suitably expresses the complex objectives of this work. The intent was first to state that women and men are equally the creation of God. Yet in every ancient culture women came to be the subordinates of men, not by divine design but as the result of social structures that emerged from the tendency of the strong to dominate the weak. Female subordination is rooted in the same complex principles that have resulted in slavery, military conquest, and social and political domination of one individual or one group over another. This work is about the status of women in ancient cultures, the complex meaning of womanhood in a male-dominated world, and how the patriarchal paradigm came to be included in various documents of the New Testament.

Certainly, Judaism and the concept of woman presented in the creation narrative is the most crucial component of New Testament backgrounds, in terms of shaping Christian tradition on the status of women and the meaning of womanhood. In fact, the seriousness of gender discrimination in Christian tradition is summarized in the indictment "And Adam was not the one deceived; it was the woman who was deceived and became a sinner" (I Timothy 2:14). And it is precisely this point of view that I challenge, with the hope that this volume offers support for further movement toward genuine gender equity in all churches and homes.

These three volumes together represent a personal journey, both academic and spiritual. As a male church minister in a conservative denomination when I began, publishing a critical study on this topic became a Rubicon crossing. It represented a definitive shift in theological perspective with no turning back. And along the way, as is evident to anyone reading all three works, I modified my position on certain points as I learned. One case in point is my earlier assumption of cult prostitution in various ancient cultures, which in recent decades has been challenged effectively by numerous scholars. But overall, the point from the first volume to the third, from beginning to end, is that female subordination is simply wrong and in conflict with the spirit of Christianity.

In the Christian Church (Disciples of Christ) for the past 25 years I have worked with numerous female scholars, ministers, elders, deacons, teachers, and ministry leaders whose faith, talent, and dedication to Christian service I respect immensely. In them, along with the strength and character of my wife, Margaret, and my daughters, Adrienne and Loren, I find ample evidence to support the theological position I have attempted to defend in these three books—full recognition and practice of gender equity in society, in the home, and in the church.

Introduction

Christianity faces an enormous dilemma with regard to the status of women. Despite significant political, social, and scientific advances, female subordination remains a powerful and resilient paradigm, both social and religious, in the predominant number of cultures today. Among Christians, the primary justification of patriarchy has been the story of Adam and Eve in the Hebrew Bible (Genesis 2–3) plus seven key New Testament texts[1] rooted in the notion that female subordination is the will and design of God. So it is abundantly clear that in most Christian denominations the major factor in preserving patriarchy is the authority of scripture.

In contrast, the academic community as a whole has come to recognize that there is no theological justification for the subordination of one gender to the other, whether in society, church, or home, and that the use of the Bible to defend patriarchy is an abuse of scripture. The individual documents that comprise the New Testament were written within a complex cosmopolitan environment in which patriarchy, along with other forms of human injustice, was taken for granted. Concerning specific texts that address relationships of husbands and wives, masters and slaves, and parents and children,[2] James Dunn writes that a problem is created "when we try to make the household codes into timeless rules which can be simply transposed across time to the present day without addition or subtraction."[3]

The Christian message includes the practice and promotion of virtues such as neighborly love, peace, tolerance, honesty, kindness, and justice, which have strong social, familial, and personal implications. While no New Testament writer, not even Jesus himself, ventures to describe a utopian society in total compliance with these noble principles, there can be no doubt that where such a message finds a foothold there is potential for the elevation of social ethics and standards. The spirit of the Gospel is clearly contrary to all forms of injustice—domination, persecution, racism, slavery, exploitation and abuse of the weak, and the subordination of women. And part of the calling of Christians is to live according to these noble principles, so as to positively influence the world.

Despite the incontestability of these principles, in nineteenth-century America many Christians defended slavery, because both the Hebrew Bible and the New Testament presuppose slavery as part of established culture. The same argument was made then, and continues to be made today, by traditionally oriented Christians in defense of the subordination of women. Ironically, slavery is now opposed by most Christians, despite the inconsistency of ignoring the texts about slavery and not those about women.

It must be recognized that New Testament documents did not appear in a vacuum. They were produced by individuals who lived in a very complex world, and who struggled with the pragmatics of interpreting the message of Jesus Christ to people of all religious, social, and ethnic backgrounds. Part of their challenge stemmed from a pressing eschatological expectation. Believing that the end was near, nothing else mattered as much as abandoning the trappings of the world in total devotion to their faith. Another factor was persecution, first from conservative Jews, and later from the Roman government. Following the example of the Apostle Paul, many chose a life of celibacy. For some, in fact, the obvious mode of serving God was asceticism. However, the majority maintained existing family structures and avenues of livelihood, while devoting as much time as possible to Christian service. As time went by, the intensity of that expectation diminished and Christian leaders set about to organize a church that would endure into an unknown future. Celibacy and asceticism were adapted to support evolving church polity. It would become a church with formal liturgy, hierarchy, and order. And unfortunately, it became a church where leaders vied for dominance—a church with an underlying agenda to acquire wealth and power, to enlarge its borders, and to control and manipulate both its people and its environment. Both tradition and sacred texts became essential implements of this agenda. One significant component was male dominance—husbands over wives and children, male priests over parishes, male bishops over priests, and in the West, the pope, the great father and vicar of Christ on earth, over all. The eastern churches developed a hierarchy of rival patriarchs.

A significant influence upon the church and the writers of various New Testament works is found in the cultures out of which Christianity emerged. An appreciation of the dilemma Christianity faces today with regard to traditional views of women, and indeed the ability to see biblical texts differently, must begin with an understanding of the *Sitz im Leben*, the life setting, of biblical literature. The world of Jesus and his early followers was cosmopolitan, with many interconnected and sometimes conflicting customs, traditions and religious beliefs. Some of the texts within the New Testament reflect the challenge of being Christian in that kind of world. Scholars commonly speak of the three worlds of the Apostle Paul, evangelist to the Gentiles and author of most of the works in the New Testament. He was first a Jew, trained as a rabbi under Gamaliel of Jerusalem. He was also a Roman citizen, freeborn in the city of Tarsus in Asia Minor. And, he was educated in the literature and culture of Hellenism, fluent in the Greek language. Like Saul of Tarsus, the church was born into these three worlds and its literature and doctrines were influenced by all of them.

However, the sociocultural background of Christianity reaches further back in time, and further outward geographically, than those three immediate worlds mentioned above. Beneath that immediate influence lay at least three millennia of cultural structure and development, with many legends, myths, and religious traditions from Mesopotamia, Egypt, and cultures of the Levant. There can be no doubt that this complex cultural milieu influenced the thinking of New Testament writers, and in turn left their mark on the developing church. It is that, and various specific elements of influence, that we seek to identify and understand in the present study.

Origin of Gender Roles

From the standpoint of anthropology, the status of women is a paradox throughout history. On the one hand, women often have been important and influential as social entities, the symbols of beauty and fertility, and the objects of male passion and pursuit. And there is ample evidence of occasional female rule, legal independence of women as a class, ownership of property, and freedom of religious expression. Theories concerning matriarchal societies have their roots in the work of Bronisław Malinowski, a Polish anthropologist who in the 1920s published studies of the indigenous cultures of the Trobriand Islands of Melanesia. There he found that the paternal role, as it is commonly understood, was not assumed by the husband, but he denied that this was a phase in transition from matriarchy to patriarchy and insisted that power still resided in an uncle or some other male figure in the clan.

Scholars today tend to agree that there is no real evidence of any matriarchal society, and from the dawn of human history patriarchy has been a firm social paradigm. In every culture there has occurred a distinct pattern of discrimination against women, resisting their recognition, denying them access to positions of meaningful authority, viewing them as weak and inferior to men, and relegating them to a status of subordination. In most ancient cultures, in fact, to be woman was to be possessed by, or dominated by, a male, either father, husband, or master, and therefore subordinate to males in general. In an introduction to a compendium of essays on the social status of women, Rosaldo states unreservedly:

We are heirs to a sociological tradition that treats women as essentially uninteresting and irrelevant, and accepts as necessary, natural, and hardly problematic the fact that, in every human culture, women are in some way subordinate to men.[4]

As yet, there is no firm agreement as to how and why gender role distinctions emerged in early human societies. No one denies various gender differences, and it seems plausible that in primitive cultures gender became the primary factor in determining who went out to hunt and who remained behind to care for the children. But over time, those role distinctions became more defined and complicated, leading to all-pervasive social paradigms of male domination and female subordination. Ortner suggests that in ancient cultures female biology, the domestic proclivity of woman, her closeness to nature, and her less assertive personality all combined to create a definition of woman as the second class. Thus, the ease with which woman has been associated with the productivity of the earth seems to have provided a rationale for female subordination in many ancient cultures.[5] She is part of nature, to be possessed, managed, and dominated by man.

Another rationale is found in ancient misconceptions about reproduction. In earliest human societies women were thought to have nothing to do with forming a child, but served only as a receptacle for male seed, sown in the womb. David and Vera Mace write:

> Ancient man knew nothing of the sperm and ovum. This knowledge belongs to the era of the microscope ... the seminal fluid was the substance that grew into the child.... But the seed was the man's seed and the child was the man's child. It was his ongoing spirit, his continuing life.... The woman could never be as important as the man any more than the soil could be as important as the seed. By her very nature she was secondary.... This is the very root of all the discrimination between man and woman.[6]

Still another factor is the great number of taboos that have surrounded menstruation, sexual intercourse, pregnancy, and childbirth, characterizing the female as a vessel of life, but also of impurity. Joan Morris suggests that this, "more than any other, has been the cause of the ostracizing of womankind—impeding them from participating in social, political, and religious meetings."[7]

Among these explanations, there is also the association of woman with evil. Ancient mythical females, such as Eve and Pandora, represent a deeply embedded social need to blame someone for the pain and misery in human existence. In some cultures, that remote connection with evil became dark and sinister, ever present in woman. Within the Judeo-Christian tradition, it was not enough to create Satan as the unseen tempter and deceiver; woman was made more or less Satan's consort, the one who left the door open for evil to enter, and at the same time the temptress who deceived man and caused him to sin. Of course, these ideas of blaming Eve and making the serpent into the devil are not inherent in the story, but are late Jewish and early Christian interpretations. Concerning this very notion in Christian history, Wagner writes:

> One of the most startling and lethal dimensions of the church's influence is the connection of the feminine to the diabolical, to the extent that late Jewish and early Christian thought virtually demonized women.[8]

Further, Wagner sees evidence in *The Apocryphal Book of Enoch* that Jews of the pre-Christian era believed that women learned the art of witchcraft from fallen angels. Enlarging on Genesis 6:1-2, a reference to the sons of God and daughters of men, the writer says that two hundred angels led by Samlazaz descended upon Mount Hermon, and from there they mingled with mortals:

> And all the others together with them took unto themselves wives, and each chose for himself one, and they began to go in unto them and to defile themselves with them, and they taught them charms and enchantments, and the cutting of roots, and made them acquainted with plants.[9]

Modern sociobiologists tend to explain gender role differences in terms of gene pools developed through natural selection, an evolutionary theory of gender role development.[10] Behavioral scientists favor the view that gender role differences are acquired after birth by means of cultural conditioning. This is commonly called socialization theory and is the springboard for neopsychoanalytic theory[11] and various feminist theories of gender role development.

In contrast with these science-based or enlightenment theories, most evangelical Christians and biblical literalists contend that gender roles, as well as the tension between genders, are traceable to the fall of humanity as recorded in Genesis 2-3. Along this line, Van Leeuwen says that theories such as evolutionary psychology have "no basis for sorting out what is created from what is fallen in human behavior."[12] This observation suggests that many Christians, perhaps even a majority, read the biblical creation stories as literal history, and therefore derive their major premise for understanding the cosmos and humanity. Against this, liberal feminists contend that regardless of humanity's long and sordid history, gender differences cannot continue to be a primary determinant of roles and status in society. Furthermore, the Adam and Eve myth cannot be read as literal history and biblical prescriptions based on it should not be transposed across time as divinely established paradigms.

It seems quite plausible that patriarchy as a social norm emerged from the basic pairing of male and female to produce offspring, and then extended upward and outward to society at large. The fact that human males characteristically are physically stronger and larger than females might suggest that male dominance occurred in prehistoric humanity as a matter of "superiority of the strongest and fittest." In many animal species, an alpha individual emerges in every group or family, and dominance is generally established by means of posturing, intimidation, aggression, or even cold brutality. In many species the dominant gender is female. However, in humans it seems likely that the original impetus for patriarchy was the tendency of males to dominate, control, and possess females. Then, once established, social models served to reinforce and justify that tendency.

Nonetheless, the resilience of the patriarchal paradigm, in all human cultures and over thousands of years, is remarkable. And while in the postmodern world, domination paradigms are slowly being supplanted by more noble social and moral ideologies, the fact that the subordination of women still persists is evidence of the enormous strength of both traditional structures and religious dogma. In fact, even in the present time biblical religion remains a key factor in resisting feminism and maintaining traditional patriarchy as a "God-ordained" order of relationships. Just as there is a difference between gender distinction and gender roles, there is also a difference between role distinction and dominance. And in every sphere of advanced human society we have come to recognize the necessity of controlling the urge to dominate, both on an individual and collective basis, in favor of broad-based systems rooted in tolerance, justice, and respect for human rights. For many cultures, this has become a self-evident truth and an essential paradigm. It has become evident also that other modern cultures, where women are dominated and prevented from contributing to the economy, tend to lag behind in development. In that regard also, abandoning ancient traditions is a matter of survival.

Modern Feminism

With all the advances in the modern and postmodern world, it is no surprise that the status of women has been among the most hotly debated and widely published topics. Modern feminism had its true beginnings in America, as the women's suffrage and the holiness revivalist movements in the early to mid–1800s. But at the root of that was the antislavery movement, in which women came to realize the similarity between their own plight and that of slaves. In July of 1848, the first feminist convention was held in Seneca Falls, New York. It was organized by Quaker women, of whom Lucretia Mott was a principal leader, with assistance from noted agnostic and activist Elizabeth Cady Stanton. Stanton's *American Declaration of Sentiment* became the touchstone for all later feminist movements and ultimately led to the great Emancipation Proclamation (1863) and women's right to vote (the Nineteenth Amendment, 1920).

Along with those significant socio-political advancements, during the same era a few Christian denominations chose to ordain women and declare their solidarity with the concept of gender equity. It is evident that the political reasons Stanton gave for the need for a corrective interpretation of the Bible were indeed valid, in particular that the Bible had been used for centuries to keep women in subjection.[13]

A hundred years later, a new surge of feminism arose that created fresh momentum toward social gender equity. Bahrani outlines three developmental waves of feminism, beginning with the socio-political movement of the 1960s.[14] This initial phase involved a push for social equality, combating androcentric bias, and establishing the presence of women in written history. While women's liberation spokeswoman Gloria Steinem received more publicity, groundbreaking academic work in the 1970s was done by scholars such as Sarah Pomeroy in the study of antiquities and in reconsideration of traditional paradigms.[15]

This gave impetus to a second wave of feminist scholarship that focused on gender reconstruction. It was here that the topic of ancient matriarchy was resurrected in an attempt to elevate respect for women in history. As far back as the mid–1800s, arguments had been made that the earliest human societies were ruled and dominated by women, and the term *matriarchate* was for a time defined in that manner.[16] Against that, the scholastic community soon agreed that there never has been a true matriarchy or an Amazonian society. In reality, most of those cultures which might seem so were either matrilineal, meaning that descendants were traced through the mother's blood line, or they were matrilocal, meaning that several generations of offspring resided around the home of a revered grandmother.[17] In most tribal societies the connection of women with the earth as sources of fecundity gave feminine symbols and goddesses certain prominence.[18] But in all of these cultures, males consistently maintained dominance. Even where the matriarchate was common, the prominence naturally assigned to women did not imply any real power, since they were considered among the possessions of the husband or father, and therefore little more than chattels.[19] Nevertheless, as Bahrani points out, second wave feminism "set out to expose the nature of patriarchy and female oppression and to establish women's (only) spaces."[20] The result was a significant step forward.

The third wave of academic feminism began in the mid–1980s and devoted itself primarily to forming fresh methods of reading and interpreting historical records. This wave, described by some as postfeminism, shifted away from what was perceived as the lives and wants of white middle-class Western women to the liberating concerns of women of the whole world. In recent years numerous new feminist perspectives have emerged in conjunction with liberation theology, including black feminist theology, all of great significance in awakening our collective world consciousness to the injustice of patriarchy and androcentricity.

McGrath explains that feminism represents a perception that religion in general has treated women as second-rate human beings.[21] Some post-Christian feminists have urged women to leave the "oppressive environment" of the church because Christianity is too biased to be salvaged. Others have suggested finding emancipation either in ancient goddess religions, or by the invention of new religions that provide women a meaningful role. However, mainstream Christian feminists have recognized the presence and influence of women throughout Christian history, and they have sought to reconstruct history to demonstrate that active presence and to reassess biblical texts in order to restore to women the recognition that has been edited out by male historians and clerics.

Elizabeth Schüssler Fiorenza, writing as a feminist historian, states two goals in her iconic work, *In Memory of Her* (1983): "to reconstruct early Christian history as women's history in order to ... reclaim this history as the history of women and men."

> The Bible is not just a historical collection of writings but also Holy Scripture, gospel, for Christians today. As such it informs not only theology but also the commitment of many women today. Yet as long as the stories and history of women in the beginning of early Christianity are not theologically conceptualized as an integral part of the proclamation of the gospel, biblical texts and traditions formulated and codified by men will remain oppressive to women.[22]

Present Objectives

The following study is neither a history of the ancient Near East nor a comprehensive survey of all relevant cultures. Rather, the focus is on how those cultures contributed to the image and status of women in the first Christian century, and also how those cultures influenced the writers whose doctrines are preserved in the New Testament. Patriarchy was a significant social paradigm in all the cultures of the ancient Near East. The general place of women is one expression of the basic values of those cultures and is woven into the earliest forms of religion and the earliest systems of law. Therefore, our task is to understand the ancient gender distinction between woman and man, and how male dominance and female subordination as social paradigms came to be part of the Christian tradition.

That process also contains four specific objectives. First, while Judaism was the primary vehicle that transported patriarchy into early Christian literature, it is undeniable that this paradigm and other related mores had their origins elsewhere. This study will illustrate that patriarchy, treasured by Jews and Christians as a divine institution within an ungodly world, was, in fact, assimilated into biblical doctrine from more ancient cultures.

Second, it will be demonstrated that New Testament writers lived within and presupposed various unjust social structures that were in place thousands of years before their time, and various texts concerning women reflect, rather than challenge, those traditions.

Third, sufficient evidence will emerge to support the conclusion that certain New Testament texts concerning women were written with the intent of advising Christians how best to live within their current social systems, although unjust and contrary to the ideals of Christian faith. The writers never imagined a world without hostility and oppression, and their challenge was to fulfill their purpose, mission, and calling as followers of Jesus Christ within an adverse world. The conviction was that individuals who lived by the principles of dominance and injustice might be won to Christ by means of the believers' virtue and willing compliance.

Fourth, this study will provide evidence that the social traditions which have held women in subjection within the Christian community have been perpetuated by a literalistic imposition, and therefore misapplication, of specific biblical texts against the overall thrust of the Christian message.

As various academic waves have developed in feminist studies, shifts in thinking did not result so much from the discovery of new documents and artefacts, but rather from a reassessment and reinterpretation of resources that for the most part were already available. This is a primary reason for this particular study. Most of the primary resources drawn upon here were already discovered, translated, and published a century ago, and while some details have been ignored by scholarship, others have been misinterpreted. The numerous issues that need reexamination include the origin of Jewish divorce laws, title inheritance by Egyptian princesses, cult prostitution in Babylonia and Greece, and the illusion of social freedom of women in ancient Rome.

The excitement of this particular volume lies in drawing together the research and expertise of many scholars in very specialized fields, including ancient linguistics, history, archaeology, cultural anthropology, sociology, biblical hermeneutics, and various areas of theology. In the introduction to her classic book *Goddesses, Whores, Wives and Slaves,* which dealt only with classical Greece and Rome, Sarah Pomeroy offers a caution about how ancient resources are interpreted. She says, "Women pervade nearly every genre of classical literature, yet often the bias of the author distorts the information."[23] This suggests that often modern scholarship is forced to look beneath and beyond the reports of ancient writers to discover truth.

Most of the available information from antiquity comes from men. It often represents social bias, is sometimes satirical and grossly exaggerated, illustrates a political agenda, contains hidden literary and poetic motifs, or is tainted with misogyny. In contrast, some historians, biographers, and orators provide sound and reliable information about the lives of women in antiquity. Some even support change in culture in order to elevate the status of women. And while evidence from artwork, sculpture, frescoes, and tomb inscriptions provide particular evidence of the daily lives and activities of women, very little comes from women themselves, and very little represents the actual perspectives, feelings, or beliefs of women. Therefore, in this present study, while drawing from a wide variety of resources, and while acknowledging various academic conclusions that have proved solid, it is also essential to challenge various faulty conclusions that have been taken for granted by scholars and clerics for decades.

The academic community is typically on the leading edge of enlightenment and social change and, certainly in the field of theology, far ahead of church laity. It is assumed, so it would seem, that ministers take what they have learned in seminary and translate it into concepts and terms meaningful to their congregants. That might not occur with more complex and challenging issues, simply because controversy tends to threaten stability at a congregational level and therefore jeopardizes the sustained livelihood of the minister. So, prudent ministers often choose to skirt around sensitive issues, or explain them in politically neutral terms so as not to make waves. As a result, shifts in thinking at the laity level occur perhaps decades after the academic community has moved on to new debates and new levels of understanding. In fact, in many church circles, the academic community is viewed scornfully as the enemy, having sold their spiritual birthright for the pottage of knowledge and vain sophistry. Nonetheless, we must be reminded of the role that intellectuals (both academic and cleric) have played in many social shifts and political movements over the centuries. And to their credit, truth and justice are always at the heart of academic debate.

Fiorenza makes a humorous comment concerning the complexity of some of her arguments. Friends who had read her manuscript suggested that the content of the first chapter might discourage readers who are not accustomed to such challenging and complex discussions. She responds that readers simply need to get up to speed.[24] Of course, her work is written primarily for serious academics, and therefore not one that would appeal to the average lay reader. With this present study comes the recognition that we stand on the shoulders of academic giants, and the intention is to assist lay readers in coming up to speed by offering challenging research in understandable terms and in a palatable format.

ONE

Mesopotamia

This study will begin with the status of woman in Mesopotamia because the Bible claims this region as the place of origins. The book of Genesis, assembled to provide an explanation of Israel's cultural and theological beginnings, describes a garden of paradise somewhere in the "land between rivers," mentioning specifically the Tigris and Euphrates, as the place from which humanity emerged. Genesis also includes stories of a great flood, towering ziggurats, and the dispersion of nations, all of which are identified with Mesopotamia.

The land between the Tigris and Euphrates Rivers is described by Bottéro as "the crowning glory of the ancient Near East."[1] Commonly recognized as the cradle of civilization, Mesopotamia is claimed to be the place of many discoveries and innovations: clothing, the wheel, agriculture, irrigation, livestock domestication, writing, walled cities, cuisine, law codes, social order, regulated economics, astronomy, mathematics, and so on.[2] Here also we find the earliest defined conceptions of deity, the earliest religious rituals, shrines and temples, and the most ancient stories of the creation and a great flood. As research and discovery continue, some of these claims may prove to be mythological rather than historical. But for now they stand, and their context includes glimpses into the earliest records of the place of woman in what is often termed "a man's world."

Interpreting Visual and Narrative Art

Bahrani's unique and very insightful work, *Women of Babylon*, is a study of art and its connection to concepts of femininity in ancient Mesopotamia.[3] One of the problems among scholars with regard to antiquities is how to interpret what is read and seen, and the two are equally difficult. One would think that ancient images would be relatively easy to understand, such as a body impaled on a pole, or a warrior running another man through with a

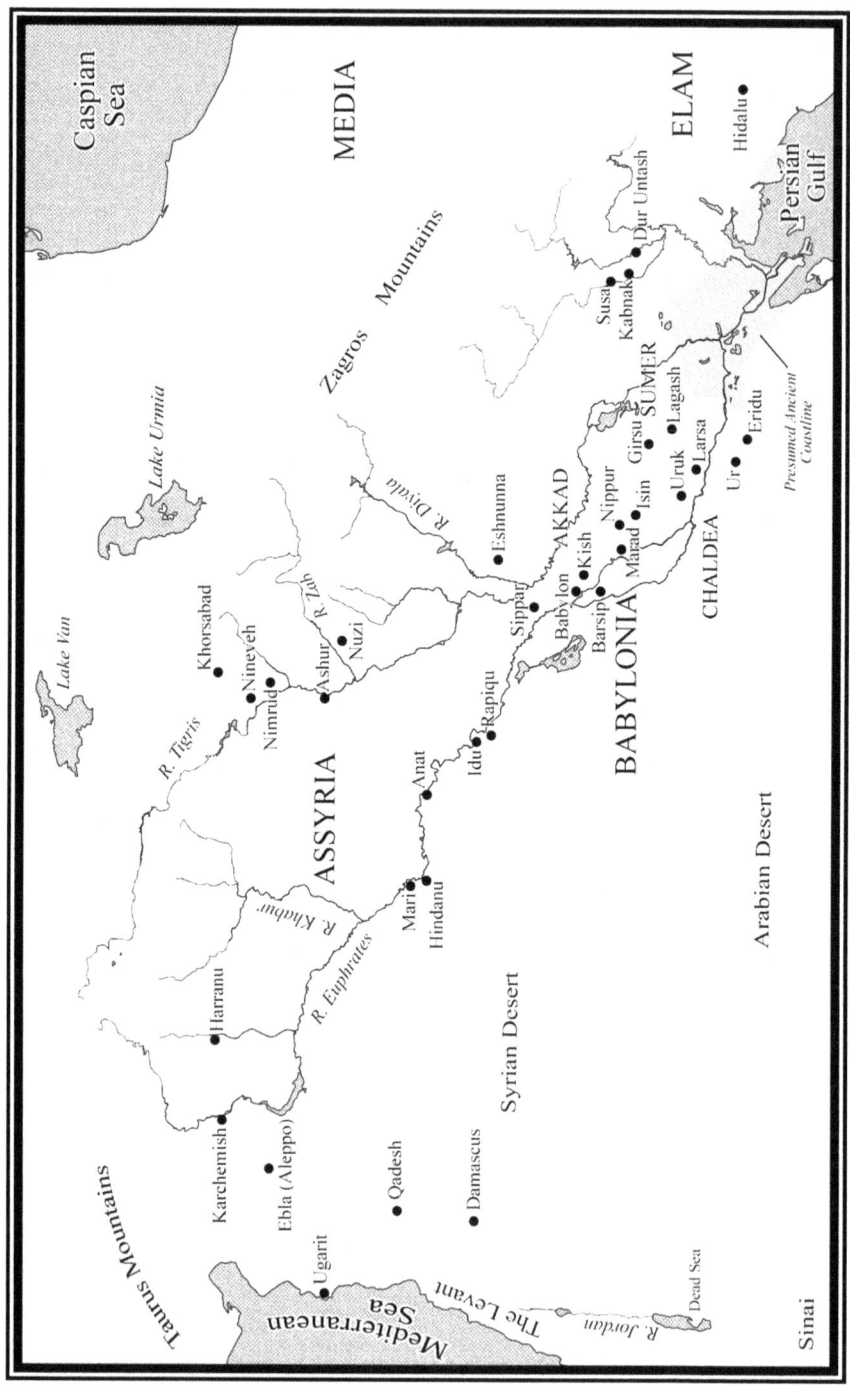

sword, or a woman giving birth, or a woman grinding wheat on a mortar. Likewise, a mythical god portrayed as the god of harvest simply represents the belief that the annual cycle of seasons, culminating in the gathering of grain for food, is a marvel initiated and nurtured by divine power. It is derived from the belief that all good things come by the beneficence of deity. But interpreting art, myth, and even factual records is not always that simple.

Bahrani says the traditional approach sometimes treats images as "subservient documents to the needs of archaeological chronologies, thus the focus is on iconographic taxonomies rather than style or composition." The methods are often too scientific, assigning meaning by the presence of a specific armband or headgear, or by a carving technique, rather than by semiotic issues and other aspects of visual analysis.

Concerning images of female deities, Bahrani dwells at length on Ishtar as a prime example of erroneous interpretation of glyptic art. One type of image is the armed goddess, commonly understood to be Ishtar. In some examples she is presented in a twisted profile, the legs marching forward, but the torso and face turned outward. This is not a full *en face* profile, but one that suggests that the image turns to the viewer, displaying her weapons as in similar images of male gods, whereby the image causes the viewer to stop, gaze, and recognize the power she possesses.

The other is the smaller image of a naked woman, often thought to be divine but having none of the traits or accoutrements associated with divinity. It commonly appears as a figurine or on terra-cotta plaques, on display before the public eye. And Bahrani says that this type of image was by design an "erotically charged site for the crystallisation of the male gaze."[4] Visual art as well as written language are cultural specific and must be interpreted with great care.

In her chapter entitled "Ishtar: The Embodiment of Tropes," Bahrani explores the cultural meaning embodied in the figure of Ishtar and the role she played within the whole culture of ancient Mesopotamia.[5] She is one of the best examples of the anthropomorphism of Mesopotamian gods, since she is enigmatic and capricious, at times ill-tempered, and prone to extremes. She is often angry and vindictive. She is the destroyer goddess and goddess of war, portrayed often with weapons in hand. However, she is also the goddess of love and fertility, the embodiment of tenderness, joy, familial love, charm, and grace. And along with this feminine side, she is portrayed sometimes as a sultry seductress.

Thorkild Jacobsen, in his book on religion in ancient Mesopotamia, includes examples of the contrasting image of Ishtar as seen in many myths

Opposite: Mesopotamia, cultures and domains (3200–500 BCE). Donald T. Massey (illustrator) and Lesly F. Massey, 2015.

18   Daughters of God, Subordinates of Men

and hymns. She is seductress and giver of great joy, but also the embodiment of pestilence and chaos:

> To pester, insult, deride, desecrate and to venerate is your domain, Inanna. Downheartedness, calamity, heartache and joy and good cheer is your domain, Inanna. Trembling affright, terror dazzling and glory is your domain, Inanna.[6]

Some have explained this remarkable duplicity as the result of the blending of the Sumerian Inanna with later Akkadian Ishtar. But all of her contradictory traits and elements of both love and violence appear in both mythical traditions. In one Sumerian myth, as a youth she was raped by her father's gardener. In the Akkadian version of the same story, she is the one who entices him, and when he resists she changes him into a frog. Jacobsen sees Ishtar as a blend of as many as five goddesses from all the cultures that came to form Mesopotamia: goddess of fertility and marriage, goddess of war, goddess of storms, morning and evening stars, and the divine harlot.[7] Some have argued that Ishtar's nature represents the opposition of masculine and feminine traits, leading to the conclusion among some scholars that this goddess was either bipolar, or bisexual, or even a hermaphrodite.[8]

Bahrani summarizes the symbolism of Ishtar as the "embodiment of tropes." One element of this is drawn from the work of Jacques Laean, who integrated Freudian psychoanalysis with structural semiology. Ishtar became the most prominent goddess in ancient Mesopotamia because she represented woman—the other gender, with no fixed position or genuine social value, employed in both art and literature as the symbol of alterity. Ishtar became a signifier that absorbs meanings and is associated with everything that is different from man. Laean suggested that what a culture excludes and marginalizes can become concentrated at the signifier.[9] Into Ishtar were poured all the male passions and ambitions, as well as male frustrations and fears. She is man's greatest allurement, yet the cause of all his problems and disappointments. The *Epic of Gilgamesh* contains numerous lines that suggest the male dilemma in dealing with feminine allurement.[10]

However, Bahrani discusses another very important possibility, summarized as "the power of the allure."[11] She points out that there is typically no clear distinction between male and female attire in Mesopotamia. Even the image of a long robe with an opening at the bottom exposing one leg, or with one shoulder revealed, are typical of both genders. However, a type of collar, or choker, as well a bracelets and other jewelry, are distinctly female. And in particular, a cross halter, separating the breasts, either worn on top of garments or alone, seems to specifically enhance the allurement of the female body. And the clinging garments of Ishtar appear to do the same.

One of the myths that has survived from both Sumerian and Akkadian cultures is "The Descent of Ishtar into the Netherworld."[12] Here Ishtar is portrayed as making a journey into the realm of the dead with the intent of extending her power. Upon her arrival, she is stopped at several gates. At each one, the goddess Ereshkigal instructs the gatekeeper to require Ishtar to remove an item of her garments. So, gate by gate, she undresses. First she removes her tiara, then her jewelry, and last her gown. Some scholars have suggested that this symbolizes her degradation before Ereshkigal. But in Mesopotamian literature, there is no indication of shame or degradation in nudity.

Another interpretation might be that as one comes into the world nude, so one departs. Thus, Ishtar was not allowed to take her finery or implements of power into the netherworld. Bahrani says that Ishtar's greatest component of power is sexual allurement, which also is "potentially destructive to mankind." The Babylonian version of this story dramatizes how the world above is impacted by the absence of Ishtar. Livestock cease to mate, and young men and women who would normally meet in the streets to engage in amorous play go to their own chambers, disinterested.[13] It may be that the principle of Ockham's razor applies here—the symbolism is quite simple. Inanna/Ashtar represents the libido of society, and without her, life will not continue. In the myth, the god Enlil has to find a solution. Ishtar is brought back to life, but to leave the underworld, a substitute must be found to take her place. She reclaims her garments and jewelry at each gate as she makes her way back to earth. There she finds that her lover Dumuzi, rather than mourning her demise, has taken over her throne. So she gives the minions of Erishkigal charge over him, and they drag him to his death.

Leick sees a difference between the mores of city life and that of the tribal and village communities. A poem called "Erra," from the late Babylonian period, describes the moral decadence of Mesopotamian cities, such as Uruk, "city of prostitutes, courtesans, and call-girls whom Ishtar deprived of husbands."[14]

Therefore, having already developed a solid patriarchal social structure, Mesopotamian culture came to defined its spectrum of realities in terms of its deities, but more specifically in terms of gender distinction. Order, law, stability, and development was represented as male. And conversely, the female represented allurement, mystery, life, unpredictability, conflict, war, destruction, chaos, and death. This was most elaborately illustrated by Ishtar, the woman.

Resources

We are indebted to the many archaeologists who devoted their lives to the discovery and excavation of lost ancient cities. Most people do not comprehend the challenge of this kind of endeavor, much less the tedious and often physically demanding work to unearth, clean and preserve, analyze, catalogue, photograph, and safely store artefacts for viewing and further study. Fictional characters like Indiana Jones (*Raiders of the Lost Ark*) and Rick O'Donnell (*The Mummy*) have glamorized the field of archaeology, while the scholars who have actually done such work remain essentially unknown and unrecognized by the public. And of course, the remarkable task of learning ancient symbols and languages and then accurately translating inscriptions and other written records into a modern language is the work of specialists whose gifts and dedication are likewise taken for granted. Of course, some early archaeologists were in truth, highly educated thieves searching for buried treasure. And many stole great artefacts from the cultures in which they were digging.

Deciphering cuneiform inscriptions retrieved from various sites in Mesopotamia began in the 1800s. The royal cemetery of Ur has yielded artefacts from as early as the dynasty of Akkad (2334–2154 BCE) and up to the reign of Nebuchadnezzar II (615–562 BCE). Excavations at Uruk produced the oldest texts, as well as countless inscriptions on cylinder seals, metal vessels, clay tablets, and pottery. The *Epic of Gilgamesh* is among the more prominent resources for understanding these cultures, having originated with the Sumerians and expanded in various forms by the Chaldeans and Assyrians. This is actually a collection of stories, the earliest versions dating as early as 2150 to 2000 BCE.

The greatest amount of information concerning the early Babylonian culture, including the status of women and the role of woman as a gender, comes from the Code of Hammurabi, dated around 1750 BCE.[15] Women had certain rights not found in most other ancient cultures, and even before the time of Hammurabi there were various laws that protected women from abuse, exploitation, and neglect. This famous law code is generally thought to be a compilation of various norms and standards established much earlier.[16] Even older is the Code of Ur-Nammu, written in Sumerian by the king of Ur on tablets and dating from about 2100 to 2050 BCE. The Laws of Eshnunna are from around 1930 BCE, and the codex of Lipit-Ishtar around 1870 BCE. Later codes include the Hittite laws, the Assyrian laws, and of course the Mosaic Law, all of which have various statutes pertaining to the behavior and treatment of women. Evidence suggests that most of the social paradigms were much the same, even with changes in dynastic rule, so these collections of laws are representative of the basic rules of life among all the peoples of this region.

Excavations in the Assyrian cities of Nineveh and Nimrud have yielded an abundance of clay tablets with intelligible inscriptions. The famous library of Ashurbanipal, King of Assyria (ruled 669–627 BCE), has provided significant literary resources, including the Assyrian laws, a major portion of the Gilgamesh epic, and the Enuma Elish,[17] which is the Babylonian creation myth.

Mention must be made of the works of Herodotus (484–425 BCE), a Greek historian born in Halicarnassus and called by Cicero "the Father of History." He visited Babylonia, among other places, and wrote his observations of daily life and customs there.[18] Both Herodotus and Diodorus of Sicily, a Greek writer in the first century BCE, wrote at length about a Babylonian queen named Semiramis. Her mystery is discussed below. However, there are enormous problems with the veracity of various reports of Herodotus, and that is part of the challenge of constructing an accurate picture of womanhood in ancient Mesopotamia.

Social Development

Evidence of occupation by large numbers of people in various parts of Mesopotamia dates to as early as 9000 BCE, and it must be recognized that developments took place over the course of millennia. Some, in fact, were the foundation for other more significant discoveries and developments. Agriculture and raising livestock developed long before the construction of walled cities. Pictographs developed before the formal emergence of writing and documented history.

Along with all of the cultural firsts in this region, the earliest records reveal a long-established patriarchal social structure with distinct gender roles. And, in this we discover a paradox. On the one hand, woman was clearly perceived as the mysterious and unpredictable other, with significant power. On the other hand, woman as a gender was understood to be inferior to man, and therefore held to a position of subordination, hardly more than a spectator in most of the significant events of community life.

From 3000 BCE onward, all or part of this region was ruled or controlled a series of Semitic cultures styled variously as Amorite, Akkadian, Chaldean, Assyrian, and Babylonian, among others, whose customs and cultural structures were very similar. Without a doubt, names and descriptors of these cultural groups are confusing. The term *Semitic*, for example, derived from the biblical name Shem, is commonly used in reference to a rather large language family centered in this region that includes Akkadian (Assyrian-Babylonian), Arabic, Aramaic/Syriac, Canaanite (Phoenician and Carthaginian), Chaldean, Hebrew, Ugaritic, and others. The same term has been used in reference to the collective cultures and ethnic groups that settled in Mesopotamia, as well as to groups that migrated back and forth between there and the Levant. This includes the Canaanites, as well as the Israelites, who are commonly called

Hebrews. There is general agreement that by the nineteenth century BCE, much of southern Mesopotamia was occupied by tribes from the northern Levant, identified as Amorites, who preferred a nomadic lifestyle and preferred sheepherding to agriculture. But the blending of cultures is attested by the fact that Amorite grain merchants eventually rose to prominence in several southern Mesopotamian city-states, including Babylon. In short, the various subcultures of the entire region called Mesopotamia were closely related and interconnected.

However, another culture lived in Mesopotamia; their language and ethnic origin was not Semitic. These people are called Sumerians. They entered southern Mesopotamia around 4000 BCE, and no one knows where they came from nor whether they migrated by foot or arrived in ships. Historian Eduard Meyer was the first to describe these people as very different from Semites. He characterized Assyrians as long-haired and bearded, with long heads, thick lips, and plump hooked noses. Artwork suggests that Sumerians, in contrast, were round-headed with thin lips, and the men were beardless, with shaved heads. Rather than the long embroidered robes of the Assyrians, the Sumerians wore simple skirts, or perhaps a longer wrap with a portion draped over one shoulder.[19]

In time the Sumerians were absorbed into the earlier Ubaidian and Semite inhabitants, but not before they left an indelible mark. The earliest recorded history of Mesopotamia is from Sumer. Their clay tablets dating from around 3200 BCE were first found at Uruk, a walled city whose ruins lie about 170 miles southeast of modern Baghdad and just east of the present Euphrates River. The texts found there are in archaic cuneiform, and are the oldest writing ever discovered. Sumerian precuneiform and Egyptian hieroglyphs are generally considered the earliest true writing systems, both emerging from protoliterate symbols by the middle of the fourth millennium BCE.

By 2900 BCE, Uruk had over fifty thousand residents and was the largest city anywhere. From excavations of numerous other Sumerian cities, such as Kish, Nippur, Lagash, Ur and Eridu, many beneficial artefacts have been retrieved that allow us a window to the earliest of developed cultures. The city of Ur, mentioned in Genesis as the home of Terah, father of Abraham, emerged out of a modest village around 3000 BCE and was continually inhabited until the early Roman era. With a port on the Euphrates estuary, it became a significant trade center. Roux says that the ruins of Ur are today "the most beautiful and eloquent in all Mesopotamia,"[20] particularly the temple complex with its impressive ziggurat.[21] Eridu, possibly the oldest although not the largest of Sumerian cities, was originally on the shore of the Persian Gulf at a time when sea levels were higher than today. Excavations there have yielded a cemetery, various temples, and also a ziggurat.

Recent archaeology has revealed still another culture even older than

One. Mesopotamia

the Ubaidians, Semites, and Sumerians, dating to the mid-sixth millennium BCE. This culture is called Samarra, and primary artefacts come from Tell es-Sawwan, located near the Tigris River north of modern Bagdad.[22] Inhabitants of this area were farmers and herdsmen who developed a rudimentary system to use flood waters to irrigate their fields. They also constructed a moat and wall around their towns. It appears that floods were common in this region from the most remote past, so great effort was made not only to survive the more devasting ones, but also to exploit the lesser ones to their advantage.

The Akkadians, Assyrians, and Eblaites were the first Semitic people to produce written records based on the cuneiform script developed by the Sumerians. The earliest writings in Akkadian date from around 2800 BCE. The Akkadian Empire (2335–2193 BCE), perhaps the first empire in history, was founded by Sargon. Under his able leadership, all of Mesopotamia came to be united under one rule and spread its cultural influence westward into Asia Minor (Anatolia-Turkey) and eastward into Persia (ancient Iran).

One of the more significant cities of ancient Mesopotamia is Nineveh, capital of the Neo-Assyrian Empire and for a time the largest city in the world. There is commonly accepted evidence that the area was settled as early as 6000 BCE, and it reached prominence by as early as 3000 BCE. The remains of Nineveh were discovered in the mid–1800s on the eastern bank of the Tigris River, across from the modern Mosul. The city walls measured about seven miles in circumference. Excavations there led to significant discoveries, such as the royal palace of Sargon II; the 70-room palace of Sennacherib, adorned with stunning bas-reliefs; and the palace and library of Ashurbanipal, with some 22,000 cuneiform clay tablets.

Perhaps the most famous Mesopotamian city is Babylon, the ruins located about 50 miles south of Bagdad. Several sources indicate the founding of Babylon around 2300 BCE, and it became an independent city-state in 1894 BCE under the leadership of an Amorite chieftain named Sumu-abum. Like other city-states in the region, from time to time old Babylon was dominated by other rulers, including the Assyrians. However, in the late seventh century BCE an alliance of Medes, Persians, Scythians, and Cimmerians brought an end to the Assyrian Empire, and a new Babylon emerged under the leadership of a Chaldean king named Nabopolasser. Babylon thus became the capital of the Neo-Babylonian Empire. Under Nebuchadnezzar II, there followed a new era of military conquest and architectural activity that made the city of Babylon one of the wonders of the ancient world. Students of antiquities are quite familiar with Babylon's impressive city walls, the legendary hanging gardens (their location and even existence remain a matter of dispute), the ornate Ishtar gate, and the Etemenanki ziggurat, all of which gave Nebuchadnezzar ample reason to boast.

It is important to keep in mind that nearly all the distinct cultures that occupied Mesopotamia were related, either in ethnicity or language, and the history of the region is best understood in terms of a series of dominating dynasties, the most prominent being the Sumerian, Akkadian, Assyrian, and Babylonian.

In her book *Mesopotamia: The Invention of the City*, Gwendolyn Leick surveys the region's history in terms of ten successive cities, beginning with the legendary Eridu, described as the Mesopotamian Eden, and ending with Babylon, the first great metropolis and depicted by biblical writers as the center of decadence and idolatry.[23] The numerous subcultures of Mesopotamia seem to have coexisted and blended over time. And, as a point of reference, the entire culture can be considered more or less contemporaneous with Egypt.

Royal Cemetery at Ur

During the 1920s, two of the most sensational archeological discoveries were the tomb of Tutankhamen in Egypt and the royal cemetery in Ur, in what is now southern Iraq. We do not know nearly as much about royal families in ancient Mesopotamia as we do about their contemporaries in Egypt. The difference is due largely to the nature of burials. In Egypt, pharaohs and their queens were embalmed and buried in tombs carved into bedrock beneath desert sands. Such an arid climate was key to their preservation. Lower Mesopotamia was an entirely different environment. Although surrounded by desert, the Tigris-Euphrates valley was prone to frequent floods, and the air in tomb enclosures remained humid. The result was quicker decomposition, regardless of how well they were embalmed.

The earliest probes into the ruins of Ur had actually begun in 1854, but were undertaken in full in 1922 with funding from the British Museum and the University of Pennsylvania. Sir Leonard Woolley was the director of the Ur project, which during the period between 1926 and 1932 included the royal cemetery. According to Roux, the 16 tombs found there fell into two categories.[24] First, there were six large areas that Woolley labeled "death pits." In these there were many corpses, and it was not always possible to determine the significance of one because of numerous secondary individuals, presumably sacrificed to accompany the deceased noble. These corpses were in such poor state that the gender could only be determined by the presence of jewelry. In some of these, inscriptions on cylinder seals or on metal vessels identified the primary corpse, such as Akalamdug, king of Ur, and his wife, Ashusikildingira. Inscriptions also identified a king named Meskalamdug, with no mention of a city, and his wife, Ninbanda. It was evident that these graves had been looted, since many artefacts were not in their original places.

One. Mesopotamia 25

One significant find was a corpse of a woman named Pu-abi (Akkadian for "word of my father") or Shubad (in Sumerian). She is described as *nin*, which means "priestess." She was evidently wealthy and of great importance, as indicated by the headdress, ornate lyre, and gold tableware buried with her. Surrounding her were the corpses of 5 soldiers and 23 female servants, all in fine attire. There was also an inscription to another woman named Hekunsig, priestess of the god Pabilsag, although she was not accompanied by such an entourage as Pu-abi.

Roux notes that the remarkable thing about all this is the predominance of women in these graves, as well as the fact that the so-called victims were not wretched slaves but people of significance in the royal household. Some of the male corpses appeared to be bodyguards, wearing leather helmets, with shields and lances either in their grasp or lying at their sides. Other corpses were possibly chariot drivers. Of the women, 4 were clearly harpists, and as many as 24 were royal servants, or "ladies-in-waiting," as some have described them, wearing either gold or silver ribbons in their hair. Roux says there were no indications that the victims were killed, but it seems rather that they voluntarily poisoned themselves and then lay down in orderly patterns to die. If this is the case, the reason would have been to express devotion to their mistress or master and to join them in the afterlife. Accepting that during this era many kings and queens were viewed either as gods or demigods, those who had served them for many years might deem them worthy of ultimate devotion.

Another explanation for this bizarre group burial is that all the corpses were royal substitutes, offered as some form of scapegoat to appease an angry god. And some scholars have said that this might represent the culmination of a sacred marriage ceremony, in which the king personified the god Dumuzi and had intercourse with a priestess who represented the goddess Ishtar (Inanna). However, there is no written suggestion that these ceremonies included either the death of the couple or a ritual burial. British archaeologist Moorey has suggested that the collective royal burials were specific to the city of Ur and were associated with the local moongod Nanna and his wife, Ningal, whose ceremonies were always led by a high priestess. Therefore, these early finds at Ur cannot be taken as a precedent for burial customs throughout Mesopotamia.

Leick argues against voluntary poisoning, but like Roux concludes that we simply do not yet know what happened in the death pits of Ur.[25] It is simply bizarre that this was our introduction to the people who lived in this remarkable era of history and whose culture represents the emergence of civilization. What we observe through this early and significant portal into Mesopotamia is that while both slavery and patriarchy were already well established, some women held positions of honor and significance. At the same time, it is evident that for the vast majority of women, life and status was defined in terms of servitude in a male-dominated world.

Women of Royalty

Among the benefits of this initial archaelogical discovery was the introduction to women of royal status in the earliest recorded and illustrated era of human history. And while there is very little of substance said about female royalty in any of the ancient cultures of Mesopotamia, there are a few later examples worthy of note. Addu-Guppi, the mother of Nabonidus, was a high cult official in the temple of the moon in Harran, the last seat of the Assyrian dynasty. Nabonidus renovated that temple, no doubt for the sake of his mother. And when she died in 547 BCE, he gave her the burial of a great dignitary and erected two stelae in Harran, with an inscription to summarize and eulogize her life. She appears to have been a member of the last royal family of Assyria, since the inscription mentions Ashurbanipal. She served some 68 years during the reigns of Nabopolassar, Nebuchadnezzar, Neriglissar, and her son Nabonitus. The inscription, written in the form of an autobiography, gives credit to the moon god Sin for giving to her (as a woman) an exalted position and fame throughout the land. She lived a 104 years and enjoyed good food and drink, a healthy body and happy mind, and saw great-great-grandchildren also grow up and live happily.[26] She was not totally unique in this kind of significance. There are records that Nebuchadnezzar appointed his daughter to the position of priestess of the moon god at Ur.[27]

Herodotus mentioned two notable queens in cultures before his time, Nitocris of Egypt and Semiramis of Mesopotamia, whose accomplishments he said rival those of many ancient kings.[28] This claim has presented a conundrum in that neither of these names appear in any of the royal records retrieved thus far. It would seem that somewhere names were confused and details were both embellished and conflated with other stories, obscuring the truth.

As reported by Diodorus, the legendary Semiramis was the daughter of the goddess Derceto and a handsome but nameless young mortal. She was born in the Philistine town of Ascalon on the Mediterranean coast, abandoned in a rocky deserted area, and nurtured by birds. She was then found by a shepherd named Simma, who named her and raised her in Syria. When she matured, the Assyrian governor Onnes saw her, fell in love, and took her away to Nineveh to be his wife. She proved to be highly intelligent and an astute advisor, so he enlisted her help in directing a military campaign in Bactriana. Ninus, the founding King of Nineveh, was so impressed with her that he offered Onnes one of his own daughters in trade. Onnes declined, resulting in threats by the king that pushed Onnes to suicide. Ninus then took Semiramis as his wife and queen. When Ninus died, the rule of the kingdom was passed to Semiramis. As the legend goes, she buried him in the palace of the kings and then set about to exceed his glory by building a city worthy of her own ability and ambition. It would be the city of Babylon. So her fame and power grew. And, according to Diodorus, she never remarried, but occasionally gave her favors to handsome young soldiers and then deposed of them to protect herself. Her travels included Media, Persia, and Egypt. Eventually, she attempted a military campaign in India and was defeated. At age 62, she handed over the rule of Assyria to her son Ninyas and then faded from history. The date of her reign would be placed somewhere between 890 and 650 BCE in neo-Assyria.

Roux explains that most of this story came from a Greek physician named Ctesias, who had moved from Asia Minor to Persia around 415 BCE and served Artaxerxes II as court physician. His writings have not survived, except in quotes by Photius in his *Bibliotheca*. But the surviving legend is full of anachronisms, and details are derived from the exploits of other genuine rulers. Therefore, there is no valid record of a queen named Semiramis.[29]

By the turn of the twentieth century, some scholars had decided that the true name of Semiramis was Sammuramat, identified in Nimrud inscriptions in association with Assyrian King Adad-nirari. That was apparently affirmed by the discovery of a stele in the ancient city of Assur identifying Sammuramat as lady of the palace and wife of Shamshi-adad, King of Assyria, mother of Adad-Nirari, and daughter-in-law of King Salmanasar. However, it was not until the work of Assyriologist Hildegarde Lewy that the mystery was solved. As summarized by Roux, the legend of Semiramis is an amalgam of traditions concerning two historic queens: Sammuramat, the warrior queen, and Naqia-Zakutu (Nitocris is a corruption of Naqia), who played a part in certain construction projects in Babylon after its partial destruction by Sennacherib in 689 BCE.

Therefore, the claims by later Greek writers of great queens in Mesopotamia are true in part. However, both of these women were anomalies in the deeply entrenched patriarchal structure of their culture. Their claim to fame was short lived and limited in scope. Furthermore, they do not represent the status of ordinary women in ancient Mesopotamia or any of its subcultures. For that, we must search further.

Status of Women

Zainab Bahrani supports the conclusion of numerous recent scholars that Mesopotamian art rarely depicts the daily life and routine activities of women. This is very different from Egyptian mortuary art, or later Greek and Roman art, in which women are engaged in daily chores, weaving, carrying water, or dressing and grooming their hair. The daily activities associated with womanhood were not the artistic or literary focus of the Mesopotamians, and the reason is likely more about genre than gender. It is simply a fact, recognized in both anthropology and in art history, that not all societies use art in the same way. Rather, as Bahrani observes:

> In Mesopotamia, both small-scale carvings and monumental arts made use of narrative imagery that included female figures. Rather than depict some truth about women's positions or roles in society, the women in these scenes are inserted into narratives that structure normative gendered behaviour, and are usually focused on masculinity. Depictions of female deities as well as non divine women appear in a variety of genres, but none of these scenes is solely an "image of a woman," the type of representation that can be thought to constitute a record of woman's life.[30]

Clearly, therefore, the primary focus of ancient Mesopotamian art and storytelling was to record the lives of men, in which women were somewhat involved but largely ignored. Therefore, lamentably, woman at this point in history was a construct woven into the fabric of a masculine narrative. Michelle Marcus writes about the exclusion of women from the monumental arts of ancient Mesopotamia and how that reflects the gender ideology in those cultures.[31]

In essence, there is a difference between the genuine place of women in that culture and the constructions of feminity that were employed as narrative devices. Examples can be found in the many Assyrian reliefs that adorned palace walls in the time of Ashurbanipal, who ruled from about 668 BCE to 627 BCE. In most illustrations, the king is with a company of soldiers in battle, or with nobles hunting, or engaging in some ritual or ceremony, but no women are present. And, admittedly, in many such situations women would not have been present. However, a contrasting depiction of the conquest of Babylon includes women among the captives. Slavery was a common and approved practice among the various cultures of ancient Mesopotamia, and in a male-dominated society female slaves were valuable property. So the point of the image was to display the prize of victory.

Another exception would be a scene in which the king reclines on a couch with the queen, Ashur-Sharrat, seated on a throne. They are drinking wine while fanned by a couple of female servants and entertained by female musicians, all in an atmosphere that is clearly one of relaxed celebration. The image seems to shout, "It is good to be the king!" Other than this, Bahrani says, "we are hard pressed to find an example of an Assyrian woman in the palace reliefs."[32] Those images that do exist are generally of foreign women, captured in battle along with men and equally degraded.

Megan Ciferelli draws attention to such images in bronze on the famous Gates of Balawat, an ancient Assyrian outpost near Nimrud. The gates were originally the entrance to the temple of Mamu, the god of dreams, and the images represent one of the Assyrian conquests, with guards escorting male and female captives. The women march with slightly raised skirts, which Ciferelli interprets as a ritual gesture of degradation.[33] Some have appealed to biblical references to "lifting the skirt" as a symbol of conquest. Bahrani rejects these interpretations, stating that "there is absolutely no similarity between the biblical traditions and those of ancient Mesopotamia."[34] While that assessment may be questionable, it seems equally plausible that women wearing long skirts would raise them with one hand in order to walk without stumbling. So, while too much can be read into the details of pictographs, the primary observation is that from early antiquity women were often captured in battle and taken as slaves—valuable, but hardly greater in value that the livestock with which they marched as the victors' prize.

Other scenes of battle display women standing at the top of city walls or marching with captives, beating their heads and tearing their hair, and they appear to be wailing in lament. This kind of expression of sorrow by women is also found in burial rituals. Some images illustrate women caring for and caressing children, or nursing infants. In a few they are portrayed giving water from a skin or flask to male workers or soldiers. But all these, in Bahrani's view, represent the construct of feminity in the Mesopotamian culture. Feminity, or womanhood, is defined as passive, submissive, and highly emotional; masculinity, or manhood, is defined as active, aggressive, and expressive when prompted by anger or sexual arousal, but otherwise generally dispassionate. Women are nurturers of children and supporters of the activities of men. And, contrary to suggestions by some, women in Mesopotamia were very much the possessions of men and the culture was fully and consummately patriarchal.[35] Therefore, artists did not portray the activities of women out of interest in them, but to make a statement about an event in the life of a king and his army, or the accomplishments of man, while women watched in awe and admiration.

Legal Rights

That said, it is also clear that women in Mesopotamia had a number of liberties not afforded women in certain other ancient cultures. They could engage in business, either on their own or in partnership. They could appear in law courts as witnesses or plaintiffs, lend money for interest, and buy and sell land and slaves at will.[36] When a woman moved into her husband's house, she brought with her a dowry that could include everything from clothes to servants and land. And if her husband died, she took all that with her, in addition to anything he might have given her as a gift.

Many of the long-standing customs and rules that were legitimized in the Code of Hammurabi served to protect women and provide them with certain legal rights. Keeping in mind that slavery was assumed by all these cultures, no doubt long before recorded history, certain laws served to regulate the treatment of both male and female slaves and indentured servants. For example, a husband had the right to sell himself, his wife, or children, into servitude to cover a debt, but the period was limited to three years.[37] A male or female slave could be given away for forced labor, and then subleased to a third party.[38] If a man tried to sell a female servant who had borne him children, he would have to refund the money and set her free.[39]

Some of the laws were written to protect women from abuse, and the enforcement of penalties and compensation would help to deter misconduct. For example, if judges determined that a man had slandered another man's wife unjustly, he would have a mark put on his forehead.[40] If a man was taken prisoner in war and left ample provisions to sustain his wife, she was obligated to stay in his home. If she left and moved into another man's house, she would be judicially condemned and thrown into the water to drown. If there were no provisions for her, she could leave his house and be another man's wife. If she did so, and bore that man children, and then her first husband came home, she would be obliged to return to her husband, but the children would remain with their father.[41] If a man abandoned his wife, she was free to go to another man and the first husband could not get her back.[42]

If a man were to strike a free-born woman so that she lost her unborn child, he was forced to pay her a prescribed amount as compensation.[43] If the woman died, the man's own daughter would be put to death as penalty.[44] However, the laws often betray the bias of male ownership. For example, if a man struck another man's female servant and she lost her unborn child, or she herself died, the attacker was compelled to compensate the owner.[45]

Inheritance

Inheritances from a husband's estate typically went to the wife or sons. For example, the Code of Hammurabi stipulates that if a father gave a present to his daughter, and then he died, the daughter was to receive a portion as a child from the paternal estate as long as she lived, but the estate actually belonged to her brothers.[46] Nonetheless, there can be no doubt that women in ancient Mesopotamia had certain legal rights concerning property ownership, including inheritances. The code prescribed that if a man deeded to his wife a parcel of land or a house, and then he died and his sons made no claim to the property, the mother could bequeath everything to a preferred son and leave nothing to the others.[47] Also, the woman's father had no claim to goods she inherited from her husband, even upon her death. The goods passed to her children.[48] However, if a woman died with no sons, the husband was entitled to a return of any bride price paid to her father, and her father was entitled to a return of her dowry.[49]

It seems that there was a social concern that daughters had the means of living if they did not marry, and only in special circumstances could a daughter truly inherit land or possessions. The code says that if either a "sister of a god or a prostitute" received a gift from her father, with a deed stating that she may dispose of it as she pleases, upon the father's death she had the right to leave her property to anyone she chose and her brothers could raise no claim to it.[50] This indicates that certain women were treated differently from the norm. It also seems odd that women with some religious designation would be coupled with prostitutes in this specific legislation. However, it should be noted that the topic of prostitution, specifically religious prostitution, has been challenged by recent scholarship, and the term "prostitute" in English translations of Sumerian and Akkadian documents may prove to be incorrect. That topic will be discussed later.

Further, the code says that if a "devoted woman or a prostitute" received from her father a dowry and a deed without a statement of her right to bequeath it as she pleases, when the father dies the brothers will control the property and provide her with a regular portion of corn, oil, and milk to live on. But the property belongs to her brothers.[51] The same would apply to a daughter whom the father devoted as a temple-maid or temple-virgin, or even as a "wife of Marduk."[52] Her care is assured while living, but she does not truly inherit property.

It is interesting also that the code made provisions for a daughter by a concubine. If she has a husband, she receives nothing from her father's estate. If she did not receive a dowry and her father had not arranged a husband, her brother was compelled to give her a dowry out of his inheritance and secure a husband for her.[53]

Marriage and the Home

In ancient Mesopotamian cultures, marriages were arranged by fathers, who also collected the bride-price, called the *tirhatu*.[54] A significant part of the marriage contract was the bride's gift, or marriage settlement, called the *nudunnu*.[55] Marriage is described as a male action of taking possession (*ahazu*) of a woman, just as he would capture a slave, land, or goods in battle. The husband was both lord and owner (*belu*) of his wife. If words were said in a ceremony, they amounted to nothing more than "I take you to be my wife," with the response "I take you as my husband."

If a bride and groom were young, the bride moved into the house of the groom's father and became part of his family. The father was the head and center of the family, even with grown sons. If the groom was older and independent, then the household into which the bride moved was his. The system was consummately patriarchal.

Herodotus offers a report that raises questions concerning the relationship of slavery and marriage. His observations have been challenged by some, as we shall note later concerning cult prostitution. However, a visit to the slave market, or even the auction of brides for a negotiable price, seems simple enough to understand, had the venerable historian asked someone to explain what was taking place. Perhaps he did not. This is his report:

> Of their customs, whereof I shall now proceed to give an account, the following (which I understand belongs to them in common with the Illyrian tribe of the Eneti) is the wisest in my judgment. Once a year in each village the maidens of age to marry were collected all together into one place; while the men stood round them in a circle. Then a herald called up the damsels one by one, and offered them for sale. He began with the most beautiful. When she was sold for no small sum of money, he offered for sale the one who came next to her in beauty. All of them were sold to be wives. The richest of the Babylonians who wished to wed bid against each other for the loveliest maidens, while the humbler wife-seekers, who were indifferent about beauty, took the more homely damsels with marriage-portions. For the custom was that when the herald had gone through the whole number of the beautiful damsels, he should then call up the ugliest—a cripple, if there chanced to be one—and offer her to the men, asking who would agree to take her with the smallest marriage-portion. And the man who offered to take the smallest sum had her assigned to him. The marriage-portions were furnished by the money paid for the beautiful damsels, and thus the fairer maidens portioned out the uglier. No one was allowed to give his daughter in marriage to the man of his choice, nor might any one carry away the damsel whom he had purchased without finding bail really and truly to make her his wife; if, however, it turned out that they did not agree, the money might be paid back. All who liked might come even from distant villages and bid for the women. This was the best of all their customs, but it has now fallen into disuse. They have lately hit upon a very different plan to save their maidens from violence, and prevent their being torn from them and carried to distant cities, which is to bring up their daughters to be courtesans. This is now done by all the poorer of the common people, who since the conquest have been maltreated by their lords, and have had ruin brought upon their families.[56]

It appears that monogamy was the general rule of marriage, but with certain variables and contingencies. A wife could offer her maidservant to her husband, and it was acceptable for him to have children by her.[57] The term *concubine* is generally applied, indicating that a servant's status thus shifted and sexual intercourse with the husband was approved by the wife. However, he was not permitted by law to then take a second wife. If his wife was barren, he could take a second wife, but her status was not equal to the first wife. Nor could a servant who bore the husband children assume equalty with the wife. If a servant was given to the husband but bore him no children, the wife could sell her for money.[58]

A young bride was expected to be a virgin. A letter recovered in Mari expresses the expectations and commitment of a young woman identified as the "wife of Sin-Iddinam."

> Before Sin-Iddinam took me I had agreed with the wish of father and son. When Sin-Iddinam had departed from his house, the son of Askudum sent me a message "I want to take you." He kissed my lips; he touched my vagina—his penis did not enter my vagina. Thus I said, I will not sin against Sin-Iddinam.[59]

In the home, the wife was the mistress of her dowry provided from her father's estate. But her husband was the lord of the wife as he was the lord of his slaves, cattle, sheep, fields and grain.[60] A woman in Mesopotamian culture was destined to a cycle of fixed roles. Gula, the patron goddess of medicine and healing, describes in a hymn the typical stages in a woman's life: "I am daughter, I am bride, I am spouse, I am housekeeper."[61] Bottéro summarizes the duties of the homebound wife in Mesopotamia as "milling flour, cooking, or preparing culinary specialties, spinning or weaving."[62]

Chastity was expected of a wife, and generally morality was viewed with a bias in favor of men.[63] The Code of Hammurabi allowed a man to take a second wife if his first wife was gravely ill. But he could not divorce her and was obligated to support her financially until her death. She had the liberty to leave and return to her father's house. If so, the husband was obliged to return her dowry and let her go.[64] If a man took a wife, but then had no intercourse with her, she was not truly his wife and was free to be married to another.[65]

There is also evidence that the veiling practice began in ancient Mesopotamia, although customs varied with places and times. It is unclear whether the veil covered the head only, or also covered the face. The custom took place in the presence of the bride's parents, and the Assyrian laws (1500 BCE) indicate that the veil was a symbol of the husband's property rights over the wife.[66] These laws also prescribed which women could and could not wear a veil in public. A married woman had to be veiled, but a concubine could only be veiled if in the company of the primary wife when outside the home. If a man wanted to veil a concubine, he could do so before five or six friends. However, a prostitute was forbidden to wear a veil and thereby pretend to be married. It she did so, she could be seized, brought before the palace court, and whipped.[67]

Some of the laws were intended to protect the interests of the father of the bride. For example, if he had been given a bride-price and then the suitor changed his mind, the father was allowed to keep whatever he was given. If the father of the bride changed his mind, he was obligated to return the bride-price undiminished.[68] Some marriage arrangements included protection for the wife from creditors, except for debts she had incurred before marriage.[69] However, if both contracted a debt with a merchant, both were obligated for payment.

There were numerous other specific laws that controlled how estates were to be divided among children when multiple wives were involved. For example, should a man die after having been married with children and the first wife had died, and then married again and had more children and the second wife died, the sons could claim shares of the father's belongings, but the dowries of their mothers went to their specific children. And one law prescribed how money should be set apart from an estate to provide a bride-price for a minor son not old enough to take a wife.[70] Further laws set out how estates were to be divided when children were born to multiple women, including female servants.[71]

So, while most of us think that modern laws on divorce settlements and child support are complex, it appears that it was equally so in ancient Mesopotamia.

Sex and Sexuality

It is evident that many scholars have misinterpreted the sexual imagery in Mesopotamian art. Among the numerous examples, mention should be made of clay figurines dating from the Neolithic Period, commonly dubbed "mother goddess." They typically have truncated arms and legs and faceless heads, but enlarged breasts and pubic area, and have been thought by some to represent the center of worship and cultural unity in some type of matriarchal society. These interpretations have been rejected by modern scholarship. Similar misinterpretation has occurred with regard to copulation images on terra-cotta plaques dating from the second millennium BCE. Women in scenes depicting sexual intercourse often have been identified as prostitutes, when in fact there is no reason for such an assumption. Bahrani says, "It is an unfortunate situation that any woman engaged in a sexual act in either visual or textual context is labelled a prostitute."[72] An example is a rather famous and provocative image dating from about 2000 BCE that is on display in the Louvre Museum. It represents a couple engaged in intercourse, the male approaching from behind. They are standing, and the female is at the same time drinking beer. She is not drinking from a flask held in the hand, nor from a wineskin. Rather she is pictured sucking a long curved tube from a jar on the floor. To the modern Western observer, this appears obscene in several dimensions. But in the Mesopotamian society, this was a portrayal of something natural and commonplace.[73] Further, it is more likely to represent a husband and wife than a stranger and a prostitute.

The same is true of nude images of goddesses, such as Ishtar, that are incorrectly assumed to represent her association with the temple cult. The fact is that sexuality was more openly portrayed in Mesopotamian art than in the modern West, without the distinction between aesthetic art and pornography. However, there is overwhelming evidence that images of female nudity were powerful in ancient Mesopotamian cultures, associated with the allurement (*kuzbu*) of sexuality. From all we can gather, it seems that free love was practiced among the Mesopotamians with little if any shame or guilt. There is ample reason to think that women were allowed to and expected to enjoy sexual activity with the same passion as men. Bottéro provides examples of rather sultry love poetry and letters found in abundance at numerous sites. He summarizes what appears to be the prevailing sense concerning sexual pleasure:

> Why on earth should one feel demeaned or diminished in the eyes of the gods, practicing it in whatever way one pleased, always provided ... that no third party was harmed or that one was not infringing any of the customary prohibitions which controlled daily life.[74]

Bahrani states that there are more written texts about sexuality and the experience of sex in Mesopotamian literature than among all the writings from Egypt and Greece. In early Sumerian script the symbols for male (*gis*) and female (*sal*) were a penis and a pubic triangle, and these became the standard gender icons in cuneiform. Both Akkadian and Sumerian literature make reference to the vulva and penis explicitly, without any social requirement of euphemism. Furthermore, for the Mesopotamians there was no distinction between aesthetic art and pornography as in the modern West. They did not consider graphic images of sexual activity as vulgar or immoral. Nakedness is portrayed openly without embarrassment, and no Sumerian or Akkadian text discovered thus far has any derogatory reference to nakedness. Bahrani adds that "it is noteworthy that there was no word that compares to the English word "naked" or "nude." The Akkadian term *eru* that has been so translated actually means "destitute," with no connotation of revealing private and secret parts of the body to one's shame.[75] Clothing was a symbol of status and wealth, and nakedness in public indicated poverty. But female nakedness in art was an open display of beauty and sensuality. As a side note, Bottéro writes that in all the extant texts from Mesopotamia, no mention has been found of oral sex, whether fellatio or cunnilingus, whereas the practice is well documented in Egypt.

Medicine, Health and Childbirth

Most of the "medicine" in ancient Mesopotamia involved primitive magic, such as potions, talismans, and incantations, particularly in the area of gynecology.[76] Medical texts do not elaborate on contraceptives, except the use of stones either to conceive or not to conceive. But these were merely a string of beads, a magical charm worn around the neck, rather than a bona fide contraceptive device or potion. There are also a few implications that anal intercourse was practiced simply to avoid pregnancy, even by temple priestesses.

Images of childbirth indicate that a woman in labor would wear a small image of the god Pazuzu to ward off the evil of the goddess Lamashtu, who was believed to come into the chambers of a pregnant woman and kill the fetus. Similar beliefs exist today in various cultures, for example, small demonic spirits that come around one's bed at night with the intent of mischief. But Lamashtu was especially sinister in that she fed on infants and small children. She was depicted as a hybrid, with a hairy body, the head of a lioness, ears of a donkey, and the feet of a bird with sharp talons.

There are extant texts about various forms of venereal disease or milder infections, which would have resulted from sexual intercourse with an infected partner. These are stated from a male perspective, mentioning discharge from the penis, pain, and other symptoms. Likewise, certain texts describe an ailment we would call "love sickness," when the patient constantly clears his throat, walks around talking to himself, and suffers sleeplessness and loss of appetite.[77] But these also are from a male perspective, illustrating the bizarre nature of erotic attraction. This raises a question as to whether all erotic poetry in Mesopotamia was in fact produced by males, including those suggesting a female perspective.

As in most, if not all, ancient cultures the role of midwives in Mesopotamia was significant. Gula (also Ninkarrak, or Ninisinna, "Lady of Isin") was the goddess of healing and midwifery, and associated with the city of Isin, the center of medicine and healing. Jane McIntosh says that a midwife commonly assisted women through pregnancy, birth, and recovery. It is also evident that medicinal practices were closely tied to "magic." Ill health was commonly associated with the will of a deity, the work of a malevolent spirit, or a magical spell by an enemy. Mothers were protected by amulets to ward off the attempt of Lamashtu to cause miscarriage, death of the infant, or sickness and death of the mother.[78]

Adultery

Despite a remarkable openness to sexual relations, there were clearly defined boundaries for the conduct of wives, and adultery was a serious

One. Mesopotamia 37

offense. The Code of Hammurabi included numerous laws in this regard. If a man's wife was caught in the act of adultery, both she and her lover could be tied and thrown into the water to drown. The husband had the right to forgive, but he received no condemnation if he did not.[79] If a man violated a betrothed woman who was a virgin, still residing in her father's house, he was put to death and the woman was not accountable.[80]

The code also states that if a wife was accused of adultery, but not caught in the act, she could be put to the "river test." Dating from the Sumerian period as early as 2300 BCE, this method of determining guilt or innocence is often called the "the water ordeal."[81] Bertrand Lafont offers a lengthy analysis. This ordeal involved being thrown into the river and forced to swim, on the irrational assumption of divine intervention should the accused be innocent. In a culture virtually surrounded by flowing water, rivers were seen as sacred, inhabited by a divine presence. If the wife was indeed guilty, it was assumed that the gods would simply allow her to drown. If she survived, it was then assumed that the gods intervened and gave her strength to swim. In the latter case, the husband could take her back without further punishment. Lafont says that appealing to the supernatural to decide guilt or innocence "is common to many religions and areas of civilization."[82]

An example is found in Hebrew scripture, in the form of drinking "bitter waters" (Numbers 5:11–31). And various dunking methods were used by the medieval church in Europe as a test for heresy, as well as the Puritans during the witch hunts of the sixteenth and seventeenth centuries. But the existence of such a test in Mesopotamia is evidence of some form of law and justice, rather than the free reign of unsubstantiated vengeance and retaliation. No one could be condemned without proof, even if that proof was irrational and misguided. Further, it indicates a deep cultural religiousness, evident in the belief that deities had an interest in the normal lives of individuals and a willingness to participate when invoked. Although no mention is made of any specific deities in connection with this ordeal, a few had relevant domains and attributes: Nanshe, goddesss of justice; Enbilulu, god of rivers and canals; Mandanu, god of divine judgment.

Much of the data concerning "the ordeal" comes from letters by Meptum, governor of a province south of Mari, written to King Zimri-Lim (1775–1760 BCE). The town of Hit, on the banks of the Euphrates, was the most popular place for these ordeals, and people traveled far to witness them. It seems that the ordeal bore both liturgical and ceremonial elements. A vigil took place on the preceding evening. Then before the event, the accused uttered ritual formulas and the charges were read, along with reasons for resorting to the ordeal. Lafont says that there are two primary aspects to this ordeal that must be noted. One is that it was not always the accused who was subjected to the test. Often it was another person, even a group of champions. Second, the test was not just a matter of swimming the flowing river, but it had to be done carrying a weight, even the size of a millstone. In reading various accounts, it appears that these tests became sporting events, and masters might select a team made up of aged and weak individuals, obviously less likely to survive, so that the accused could not be vindicated.

One report from Meptum involves the ordeal imposed on a female servant of a queen, wife of king Yarkab-Addu, in a region called Zalmaqqum. She was accused of using sorcery and betraying palace secrets. However, in recounting the story Meptum raises certain unanswered questions, suggesting that the servant knew too much and her ordeal was arranged to conceal an affair by the queen. The ordeal served its purpose. The servant drowned. No deities intervened.

Part of the judicial process that Lafont terms "irrational" was the swearing of an oath, which in itself was a form of ordeal intended to prevent lies. The oath, in one form or another, still survives in most modern judicial systems, despite the fact that perjury happens frequently. It is also noteworthy that from the outset, such laws in Mesopotamia were biased in favor of men. While both men and women could be subjected to the ordeal, most subjects appear to have been women. The charges that warranted such were adultery, sorcery, and treason, crimes of which women were commonly accused.

According to the Medio-Assyrian laws (around 1400 BCE), mutilation was an appropriate punishment for an adulterous wife and her lover. This could include cutting off the wife's nose and castrating the man.[83] Some of the laws indicate that marital infidelity and related ruthless actions were common, and legislation served not only to deal with complex cases but also as a measure to deter misconduct. For example, one law states that if a woman conspired with a man to murder their two spouses so they could marry each other, both of them would be impaled. A man found guilty of incest would be exiled. A man caught having intercourse with his daughter-in-law would be sentenced to death by drowning. If the son had not yet had intercourse with her, she would be compensated for all she brought into the father's house and released to marry someone else. A mother and son who committed incest could be burned to death.[84]

Divorce

Divorce was accomplished simply by a husband's verbal repudiation of a wife, although he was obligated to return her dowry and provide sufficient resources, whether money, goods, or property, in order to help raise any children she bore to him. This applied even if she were a servant or slave, and not considered his wife. When the children reached adulthood, the wife was to be granted an inheritance equal to that of a son, and she would be free to marry someone else. If there had been no bride-price, the husband was still obligated to give her a mina of gold as compensation.[85]

In contrast, if a wife wanted to leave her husband's house, but she was found guilty of creating debt and causing damage, the husband could dismiss her with no financial obligation. He also had the right to keep her as a servant and marry someone else. If a woman was neglected or mistreated by her husband, and she offered evidence before judges, she could take her dowry and return to her father's house. But if she was found guilty of ruining her husband's house, she could be sentenced to death by drowning.[86]

Professions

There were very few true professions for women in ancient Mesopotamia. Generally speaking, women were not afforded the privilege of education, so female copyists, scribes, court chroniclers, or authors were very few. One such exception was Enheduanna, *en*-priestess (high priestess) of the Akkadian moon god Sin (Sumerian *Nanna-Suen*) and thought to be the daughter of King Sargon. She wrote two famous prayers to Ishtar, the goddess of love and war, and therefore is remembered as one of the earliest authors from ancient Mesopotamia, perhaps the first on record. In a hymn called *The Indictment of Nana*, she described how she was forced from her noble office and banished from Ur.

> Truly I had entered my holy giparu at your behest,
> I, the high priestess, I Enheduanna!
> I carried the ritual basket, I intoned the acclaim.
> But now I am placed in the lepers' ward
> I, even I can no longer live with you!
> They approach the light of day,
> The light is obscured about me,
> The shadows approach the light of day,
> It is covered with a sandstorm.
> My melliflous mouth is cast into confusion.
> My choicest features are turned to dust.[87]

There is also evidence that royal wives were often commissioned to write poetry, and therefore it is likely that education was available to women of their station, if they wanted it. But that was not the case for ordinary women. Those who had failed as wives, either being divorced or departing by choice, were naturally relegated to what may be termed "pleasure professions," including entertainers, such as singers and dancers, tavern servers, and prostitutes. As noted earlier, there is debate as to just what term in either Sumerian or

Akkadian meant "prostitute." Assante says that the terms *kar.kid* and *harimtu* have been commonly translated "prostitute," but in fact refer to a single woman not under the authority of a male, such as a father or husband.[88] This also means that portions of the Code of Hammurabi have been misunderstood, because of the translation "prostitute" where something else was meant.

Nevertheless, it is generally accepted that prostitution was common and was the natural option for some women needing an income. In the famous *Epic of Gilgamesh* there are lines that describe how, in a fitful dream while stricken with fever, Enkidu attributes all his misfortunes to prostitutes. The following lines are pieced together from various versions (Assyrian, Hittite, Chaldea):

Never will you build a happy home. Never will you be introduced into the harem.
Beer froth will stain your fair bossom, and drunks will splash vomit over your finery.
You will live in the streets and your home will be the shade of the walls. Drunks and sots will thrash you as they please.[89]

Thus, the everyday life of a woman in ancient Mesopotamia was nothing glamorous, particularly if she was under the stigma of "nonwife." However, considering that the majority of women were either slaves, free servants, or of the poorer class, work was the routine of daily life. Leick speaks of the role that women and children played in the textile industry during the third dynasty of Ur (2113–2029 BCE). With a centralized economy and a competent administration, the state developed a monopoly in the production of items in demand, including woolen and linen cloth. The northern valleys became the locus of raising livestock, primarily cattle. Fishing and agriculture emerged as a significant component of that economy. Much of the work was performed by men, but as is observed in less developed countries today, women did more than their share of manual labor.[90]

Religion

As a whole, the various cultures of Mesopotamia were polytheistic, and their many deities, like the later Greco-Roman pantheon, were both male and female and were highly anthropomorphic. According to their broad mythology, the gods created humanity to serve them but freed them when they became too burdensome and frustrating. Being constructs, the deities of Mesopotamia were very much like the humans who created them. Typically a male god had a wife and together they produced offspring who in turn were deities with special attributes. In general, both male and female deities were prone to envy, jealousy, and rage; they were lustful and engaged in relationships with each other and with mortals. Some, more than others, were capricious and duplistic, displaying both good and evil traits to the extreme.

Van de Mieroop says that a fundamental ideology of Mesopotamia was that each city was the dwelling place of a particular god or goddess. Nanna resided at Ur, Inanna (Ishtar) at Uruk, Enlil at Nippur, and so on. And the temple complex in each walled city was a place to collect and distribute agricultural resources, because it was believed that the gods received them as gifts from the people and then redistributed them to the people.[91] No doubt this ideology developed further into the belief that each specific creative and productive human skill was a gift of the gods. Hence over time, lesser gods emerged with areas of specialty corresponding to those skills. Enki (Ea) was god of intelligence and crafts. Nabu was god of wisdom and writing. Nanshe was goddess of social justice and prophecy. Ninurta was the god of agriculture, and as champion of the gods he was seen as the source of youthful vigor. Shamash (Utu) was the god of the sun, justice, and patron of travellers. Sin (Nanna) was god of the moon. Tammuz (Dumuzi) was god of food and vegetation.

It is clear also that deities changed and developed with culture, and each god and goddess took on different roles to serve the interests and needs of their subjects, who were in fact their creators. The different names by which each was known reflect the development and blending of various subcultures in Mesopotamia, even the absorption of Sumerian deities by Semitic cultures. At the top of the Mesopotamian pantheon was Anu (An), said to be the most ancient and therefore the father of the gods. He also was god of heaven and the sky. In the city of Uruk in particular, the ziggurat of An towered above the city, symbolizing both the protection and care given by An, as well as patriarchal authority.[92]

Enlil (Anshur) was the god of the wind, the supreme ruler of earth and humanity, and consort of Ninlil, goddess of the air. Sumerian myth also tells how Enlil raped and impregnated the young goddess Ninlil. Perhaps the moral conscience of the Mesopotamians is revealed in this myth, in that the other gods were disgusted by Enlil's wanton behavior and banished him.[93] Ninlil is also known as Sud (in Assyrian, Mulliltu).

Ereshkigal was goddess of the underworld (realm of the dead) and wife of Nergal, the god of war and plague. Although Enlil was selected as chief of the Assyrian deities, Ashur became the principal god of the city Ashur, and Nineveh became an important religious center for worship of the goddess Ishtar. Marduk (Bel) was the patron god of Babylon and head of the Babylonian pantheon. Ninhursag (also called Mami, Belet-Ili, Ki, Ninmah, Nintu, or Aruru) was the earth and mother goddess.

No doubt the most famous of Mesopotamian deities is the Sumerian Inanna, known later as Ishtar. Mythology claims her to be the daughter of the god An. In art, Ishtar is portrayed in various guises as both the goddess of love and goddess of war and destruction. The modern fascination with Ishtar appears related to the legends of lurid sexual practices and the sexual language of many hymns associated with her cult. In ancient lore she is portrayed as having many lovers, her first being Dumuzi (Tammuz in Akkadian), whose divine persona is thought to have developed from some heroized ruler in prehistoric times. However, interpreting Ishtar has become a great enigma for scholars of antiquities, as stated at the beginning of this chapter. She is an almost inexplicable paradox. Over the course of time she came to be associated with numerous Near Eastern goddesses, such as Astarte, Anat, Asherah and Ashteroth. So, in thinking of religion in Mesopotamia, it is important to remember that Ishtar represented various conflicts within the social mind of Mesopotamian culture.

It is clear that religion was largely involved with the celebration of royalty and leadership, and very early the tradition developed that the current ruler was considered a mediator between the gods and humans. Perceived as either a god or in communion with the gods, the king was revered, along with the royal family. They represented life and order, bestowed by the gods. While the king and his family were well and in control, the gods were happy and the future of the community was secure. A king was overthrown because the gods were unhappy, or because the gods decreed it for reasons known only to the gods. By means of rituals, the cultures of Mesopotamia reenacted the interests and actions of the gods. In Ashur, for example, Adad-nirari I prepared a guest room in the palace for visits by the gods. Some kings, like Sennacharib, built a special house outside the city walls and transported idols there for a festival. This represented a gathering of the gods for celebration. Some kings also constructed gardens for the gods to enjoy a casual outing.

Bottéro writes that the mythical love affairs of Inanna and Dumuzi were celebrated annually by a reenactment of a night of lovemaking between the king and a priestess of the temple. This custom developed early, and Leick points out that Shulgi, the king of Ur (2094–2047), was praised for his skills in lovemaking as Inanna's mythical consort.[94] Excavations at Uruk have produced evidence of such a relationship between the King Shu-Sin and a woman named Kubatum (c. 2030 BCE). Special songs and poetry were composed for such occasions, some resembling the style and language of the biblical book called Song of Solomon.[95] The relationships of the gods were featured in many ceremonies. A couple portraying a god and goddess would reenact a divine wedding around their cult statues.

> Bathed, perfumed, splendidly arrayed, then carried with great pomp to a room in the temple known as the nuptial chamber, they spent some time side by side, supposedly consummating their union, which was celebrated by banquets and rejoicings of the whole populace gathered around them.[96]

The Uruk Vase is an alabaster vessel discovered in the Inanna temple at Uruk, dating to around 3300 BCE. It is carved in low relief with five registers of images that represent this marriage ritual. Bahrani says that there is no textual description of this ritual from the Uruk period, but it is attested in other times and evidence is certain for actual copulation between the goddess (represented by a temple priestess) and the king.[97] The ritual mating of the gods seems to represent the mystical force that brought new life each year and the growth of crops after the winter season. Therefore, it represented the fucundity of the gods that give life to the earth, and it was intended to assure the people of another bountiful season.

Some rituals were performed by priests, in particular the slaughter and offering of animals to the gods, and the *en*-priest (the high priest) supervised their work. This practice was common among ancient cultures, not just in Mesopotamia. However, there was also a special role for women. Some served as priestesses, and traceable to the rule of Sargon the Great (2340–2284 BCE) there was an *entu* (or an *en*-priestess) who served in a more elevated capacity.

Sargon is credited with founding Akkad, clearly the first supraregional political state in the ancient Near East.[98] From an obscure background, Sargon's inscriptions give no reference to paternal ancestors. Various legends survive about the identity of his father, suggesting that he was a gardener promoted to cupbearer to king Ur-Zababa. However, an intriguing version from Babylonian tablets gives attention to his mother, whom he describes as a high-ranking religious official:

Sargon, the mighty king, king of Akkad am I.
My mother was an *en*-priestess, my father I never knew.
My father's brother inhabits the highlands.
My city is Azupiranu, which lies on the bank of the Euphrates.
She conceived me, my *en*-priestess mother, in concealment she gave me birth,
Set me in a wicker basket, with bitumen made the opening watertight.
She cast me down into the river from which I could not ascend.
The river bore me up, to Aqqi the water drawer it brought me.
Aqqi the water drawer, when lowering his bucket, did lift me up.
Aqqi the water drawer did raise me as his adopted son.
Aqqi the water drawer did set me to his gardening.
While I was still a gardener, Ishtar did grow fond of me,
and ... I did reign as king.[99]

Adjacent to the zigurrat in Ur there was a building called the Gipar, which represented an important component of that city's religion. This was the residence of the *en*-priestess and her entourage of servants and assistants. It was amply equipped with kitchen, storage, and sleeping quarters, and included courtyards and reception rooms. Here also was a room called the *cella*, where stood a statue of the goddess Ningal, also a resident of the Gipar. The duties of the *en*-priestess included praying for the well-being of the king, and thus serving as a mediator between the gods and the leader of her people. Women who served in this role include Enheduanna, who was succeeded by Enme-Nannar, daughter of king Naram-Sin. Leick says that there were periods when the Gipar fell into disuse, but it was revived. The last revival was during the reign of Nabonidus (555–539 BCE), when his daughter Ennigaldinanna served as the last known *en*-priestess.[100]

There were other dimensions to Mesopotamian religion not pertaining to the celebration or worship of the gods. At some point, it became important to know what the gods were thinking, or what the gods had planned, in order for the king and the people to prepare. The library of Ashurbanipal in Nineveh included some three hundred tablets containing omens, intended to predict the future based on observations of details in the physical world. Omens could be found in almost anything, from flights of birds, to the color of a sheep's liver, to the behavior of a house cat. Such information was very important to the king, in order to stay healthy, prepare for battle, or to defend himself against a traitor. So, a new component of religion developed, called divination; it was performed by an *asipu*, or seer.

The *Enuma Anu Enlil*, dating to around 1600 BCE, is the earliest collection of astronomical omens, developed from the belief that planetary alignments, comets, and eclipses held the secrets to the future and could be interpreted as to their application to national and political affairs.[101] For all these omens there were prayers and incantations to change the minds of the gods, should the signs not bode well. It is obvious that anyone who had knowledge and skill in these new areas of religion also held a degree of power within the circle of leadership. From this, no doubt, developed the concept of prophecy, in which someone might become the mouthpiece of a god. And, as we might expect, the secrets, wisdom, and knowledge were primarily held by men. A woman could not be trusted with such knowledge or power.

The Maqlû Texts contain a series of Akkadian incantations dating from possibly 1000 BCE, many of which are antisorcery rituals. As in other ancient cultures, once there developed a belief in benevolent and malevolent gods whose will was played out in the lives of humans, there also developed a belief in spirits sent up from the realm of the dead to perform sinister tasks, and from that arose the concept of demons who could possess a human body. Knowledge of celestial and terrestrial omens evolved into knowledge of rituals and encantations to manipulate the material elements, and to control spirits and demons. And when sickness fell upon a family, or when crops failed, it was surmised that a sorcerer had cast a spell, drawing demonic power into the mortal realm. So counterspells had to be devised. The eight tablets contain nearly a hundred rituals and incantations, with directions for a ceremony performed one night each year in the month of Abu (July/August). It was believed that during that season spirits moved to and from the netherworld and were most vulnerable to spells to control them or send them back to their source.[102]

So, from seers and prophets arose diviners, and from diviners arose sorcerers, and so the beliefs and practices evolved. While most of the seers in ancient Mesopotamia were men, as time went by women also came to participate in divination. And as this role shifted from royal advisors to agents of evil, so also the role tended to involve women even more. This, it would seem, is also part of the devolution of the cultural view of womanhood and the demonization of women, not only in Mesopotamia but other ancient cultures as well.

Consecrated Women

It is clear that in ancient Mesopotamia there were certain classes or groups of women who engaged in religious practices and were treated differently from the norm. Dating as early as the reign of Immerum in Sippur (1880–1845 BCE) there were women called the *naditu,* who were pledged to a god and lived together in a sort of convent called a *gagum* adjacent to a temple. The term *naditu* is Akkadian for "left fallow" and indicates that they were consecrated virgins, or at least had never birthed a child.[103] Their lives were overseen by a superintendent. They were not part of the temple cult, but rather often engaged in business or a craft. Some of the *naditu* imported goods, others bought and sold slaves or other merchandise, and others owned farm lands and supervised their own workers. They appear to have been among the merchants (*tamkaru*) responsible for driving the economy, and whose activities were regulated by law to curb fraud.[104] Nonetheless, they were highly revered and highly influential within their immediate society. The Code of Hammurabi said that a "sister of a god" could neither operate a tavern nor enter a tavern to drink, on pain of death.[105] Anyone who slandered a "sister of a god" would be marked.[106] The *naditu* were all from wealthy families, even the daughters of kings and nobles. Goods bequeathed to them were in their control as long as they lived, but were returned to the family after death. To have a daughter living in the *gagum* seems to have been a mark of prestige. The primary religious duty of the *naditu,* it seems, was to pray for the health and well-being of their fathers, and to make offerings twice each day. This is very similar to the role of various priestesses whose duty, already discussed, was to pray on behalf of the king. The *naditu* were also expected to take part in religious festivals and processions. And there can be no doubt that they contributed significantly to the local economy by their active engagement in business. They were educated, literate, and some were trained as scribes. Amat-Mamu served as a scribe for 40 years. However, as Leick words it, "the *naditu* lived their lives in social limbo, grown up yet childless, dissociated from the paternal family yet loosely integrated into the household of the god,"[107] a station that was almost meaningless except for the prestige it brought to the family.

Another category of woman whose role was both religious and socially significant was the *qadishtu*, who worked in conjunction with a midwife in assisting birth, provided her house for childbirth, and performed purification rituals. The term is very similar to the Hebrew *qedesha*, and the Semitic root suggests the concept of "holy" and "set apart." There are numerous examples of such women in Sumer, where they are described by the equivalent term *nu.gig*. These women seem consistently to be part of the upper strata of society, even members of royalty, and were often married. Westenholtz sees the *qadishtu* as among various classes of women set apart for very special religious and social service roles; they had a special relationship to a male deity, and their sexuality was regulated, either by marriage or celibacy.[108] From all this, it is evident that in ancient Mesopotamia, there were significant roles for women in religion and society that somehow represented the mystery, power, and divine connection of womanhood to the gods.

Cult Prostitution

There can be no doubt that prostitution in some form existed in ancient Mesopotamia. But for many years it has been claimed that Mesopotamia was also home to various forms of sacred prostitution, based in part on a report from Herodotus concerning practices in Babylon:

> The Babylonians have one most shameful custom. Every woman born in the country must once in her life go and sit down in the precinct of Venus, and there consort with a stranger. Many of the wealthier sort, who are too proud to mix with the others, drive in covered carriages to the precinct, followed by a goodly train of attendants, and there take their station. But the larger number seat themselves within the holy enclosure with wreaths of string about their heads—and here there is always a great crowd, some coming and others going; lines of cord mark out paths in all directions the women, and the strangers pass along them to make their choice. A woman who has once taken her seat is not allowed to return home till one of the strangers throws a silver coin into her lap, and takes her with him beyond the holy ground. When he throws the coin he says these words: "The goddess Mylitta prosper thee." (Venus is called Mylitta by the Assyrians.) The silver coin may be of any size; it cannot be refused, for that is forbidden by the law, since once thrown it is sacred. The woman goes with the first man who throws her money, and rejects

no one. When she has gone with him, and so satisfied the goddess, she returns home, and from that time forth no gift however great will prevail with her. Such of the women as are tall and beautiful are soon released, but others who are ugly have to stay a long time before they can fulfil the law. Some have waited three or four years in the precinct. A custom very much like this is found also in certain parts of the island of Cyprus.[109]

Many scholars have challenged Herodotus and the implications of this report. Afonso says that it is "lurid and misleading," for certainly not all women would succumb to such a tradition.[110] So also says Bottéro: "The good Herodotus was mistaken," no doubt seeing so many women there he thought it to be the duty of every woman once in her lifetime.[111] But such doubts have not deterred the common and widespread assumption by scholars that any woman described in Mesopotamian records as a priestesss, or mentioned in connection with a temple or any ritual practice, must have been a "cult prostitute."[112] Numerous documents join three categories of women in a way that appears to connect them to a religious cult. For example, the Erra Epic, dating from the late Babylonian period, refers to the city of Uruk as the home of Anu and Ishtar, the city of *kerzertus, shamhatus*, and *harimtus*, "whom Ishtar deprived of husbands and called her own."[113] These terms commonly have been translated "prostitutes, courtesans, and call girls," when in fact there is no evidence to suggest those connotations. The same is true of the term *ishtaritu*, clearly associated with the cult of Ishtar, but with little evidence that temple duties included prostitution.

The most valuable recent studies on this topic include Julia Assante's study of the *kar.kid/harimtu*,[114] and a work by Stephanie Budin entitled *The Myth of Sacred Prostitution in Antiquity*. Accepting that prostitution is by definition the sale of sex, or more precisely sexual intercourse in exchange for money or goods, Budin states categorically that "sacred prostitution never existed in the ancient Near East or Mediterranean."[115] She contends that until 1985, seven terms in Mesopotamian cuneiform records were commonly translated "cult prostitute." They areas follows, first the Sumerian followed by the Akkadian equivalent in parentheses: *nin.dingir* (*entu ugbabtum*); *nu.gig* (*ishtaritu* or *qadishtu*); *mi.suhur.la* (*kezertu*); *nu.bar* (*kulmashitu*); *lukur* (*naditu*); and *shamhatu*.[116] Of these we have already discussed the *en*-priestess, the *naditu*, and *qadishu*, and it is clear that none of these categories of women could be termed "cult prostitute." They were various categories and types of priestesses, women who performed significant tasks in the cult and worshiped specific deities, but they did not engage in intercourse for money.

Of the other terms, Budin demonstrates that there is not enough evidence to classify their activities as prostitution, although the precise nature of their lives and roles in religion is not clearly known. But the problem is that most of the translations of key documents, such as the Code of Hammurabi, use the term "prostitute" in places where terms like "votary," "devotee," "priestess," "or dedicated virgin" would have been more accurate and appropriate. The result is that the myth of ancient cult prostitution has been perpetuated by means of incorrect translation of terms in various ancient languages.

Arguing specifically against Assante, Silver says that by denying that any of the terms previously translated "prostitute" could actually mean "sex for money," Assante has eradicated prostitution from religious cults as well as from the whole Mesopotamian culture. Silver contends that there is ample evidence that not only did prostitution exist, but for women who found themselves outside the security of attachment to some male, whether husband or father, prostitution was a viable means of survival. He also contends that such funds were an essential part of the economics of the temple and religious cult.[117]

So, if not cult prostitution, what is this report from Herodotus all about? His classic work, *The Histories*, is a detailed account of the conflict between the Greeks and Persians between 430 and 424 BCE, including scattered discussion of various cultures. Herodotus writes in remarkable detail, and much of what he describes is corroborated by other historical sources, but numerous ancient writers criticized Herodotus for his grossly inaccurate reports. Budin explains that Herodotus inserted into his work descriptions that were grossly inaccurate, but neither mistaken nor intentionally misleading. On the contrary, he employed a literary device called inversion to contrast life in Greece with the rest of the nations. His purpose was to defend and extol Greek culture as superior to all other cultures. The report above, concerning a one-time service as a temple prostitute with a "foreigner," is a construct, as is the description of young women sold on the auction to unknown husbands. A thorough reading of his work makes that obvious. Herodotus creates an exaggerated contrast between the noble cultural mores of the Greeks and the insanely illogical practices he attributes to non–Greeks. His primary tools are women and sexuality, arguing that Greek men control their women, keeping them at home and undefiled, whereas women in other cultures are out of control and sexually polluted.

Budin sites numerous examples of this inversion device, as well as implausible claims concerning the sexual conduct of women in other cultures.[118] Concerning the Lydians, Herodotus says that young women of the working class earn money for their dowries as prostitutes, and give themselves away in marriage.[119] Of the Egyptians, he claims that women go to the market and keep shop while their husbands stay at home and weave; men carry burdens on their heads, while women carry them on their shoulders; men urinate sitting down, but their women do it standing up, and so on.[120] In India, he says, men and women copulate in the open like cattle.[121] Concerning northern Agathyrsi (a region in modern Romania), Herodotus says that women are held and used in common so that all the men may be brothers with no jealousy.[122] In Sarmatia (located in what is now Ukraine and Southern Russia), he says, a woman cannot marry until she has killed a male enemy in battle, and those who do not often grow old and die single.[123] And, concerning a tribe living by Lake Tritonis in North Africa, he reports that there are no married couples and women are common property of all the men.[124] All of this is inaccurate.

Budin is certain that the model for the inversion device of Herodotus, particularly the example in VOLUME I, section 199, is the Greek women's ritual enacted in the Thesmophoria, held in honor of the goddess Demeter and her daughter Persephone.[125] Therefore, Herodotus creates images of a defeated Babylonia that are the opposite of all the standards and mores of Greece. Budin summarizes as follows:

> The image of all local women penetrated by foreigners, desecrated, yet compliant, accepting money for their services as demanded by the gods, must ultimately have served as a harsh lesson on the vicissitudes of fortune and divinity and the wages of war and defeat for its Greek audience.[126]

Over the course of centuries, numerous writers drew from Herodotus, either re-creating his fictional images of cult prostitution as literary devices, or assuming them to be factual. This would include *Syrian Goddess*, written by Lucian of Samosata (CE 125–180), in which he describes women engaged in a ritual to the god Adonis in Byblos.

> The women who refuse to be shaved have to submit to the following penalty, viz., to stand for the space of an entire day in readiness to expose their persons for hire. The place of hire is open to none but foreigners, and out of the proceeds of the traffic of these women a sacrifice to Aphrodite is paid.[127]

Budin is emphatic that this description of what is assumed to be "sacred prostitution" is fictional, a notion that "drifted up in Herodotus' wake."[128] So, while the concept of cult prostitution is commonly assumed by many historians and scholars of antiquities, there is every reason to think that such was never really the case. The women thought to be "cult prostitutes" were, in fact, priestesses serving in numerous capacities. Some were recruits to enact or actually engage in ritual intercourse with kings, and some many have offered themselves in prostitution, but it was never the kind of "cult prostitution" that has been suggested.

Great Myths

The Mesopotamian story of creation is called the *Enuma Elish*, from the opening words "when in the height." Leonard King, in the introduction to his 1902 classic *The Seven Tablets of Creation*, writes:

The poem embodies the beliefs of the Babylonians and Assyrians concerning the origin of the universe; it describes the coming forth of the gods from chaos, and tells the story of how the forces of disorder, represented by the primeval water gods Apsû and Tiamat, were overthrown by Ea and Marduk respectively, and how Marduk, after completing the triumph of the gods over chaos, proceeded to create the world and man.[129]

Besides the *Enuma Elish*, there are other versions of the creation that assume the world that the Mesopotamians knew, and explain how things came to be as they are. The following is King's translation of the creation by the Babylonian god Marduk:

Of the holy house, the house of the gods, the habitation had not been made. All lands were sea. At that time there was a movement in the sea; Then was Eridu made, and E-sagil was built, E-sagil, where in the midst of the Deep the god Lugal-dul-azaga dwelleth; The city of Babylon was built, and E-sagil was finished. The gods, the Anunnaki, he created at one time. The holy city, the dwelling, of their hearts' desire, they proclaimed supreme. Marduk laid a reed upon the face of the waters, He formed dust and poured it out beside the reed. That he might cause the gods to dwell in the habitation of their hearts' desire, He formed mankind. The goddess Aruru together with him created the seed of mankind. The beasts of the field and living creatures in the field he formed. He created the Tigris and the Euphrates, and he set them in their place; their names he declared in goodly fashion. The grass, the rush of the marsh, the reed, and the forest he created, the green herb of the field he created, the lands, the marshes, and the swamps; The wild cow and her young, the wild calf; the ewe and her young, the lamb of the fold; Plantations and forests; The he-goat and the mountain-goat ... him. The Lord Marduk laid in a dam by the side of the sea, ... a swamp, he made a marsh, ... he brought into existence. [Reeds he form]ed, trees he created; ... he made in their place. [Bricks he laid], buildings he set up; [Houses he made], cities he built; [Cities he made], creatures he created. [Nippur he made], E-kur he built; [Erech he made, E-an]a he built.[130]

Leick begins *Mesopotamia: The Invention of the City* with a quote from this story, commenting that the city called Eridu is essentially the Mesopotamian version of Eden. She writes, "Just like the marsh dwellers of southern Iraq, who still build their huts on floating islands of reed, the god spreads mud upon a reed frame to fashion a platform. From this primordial, rather flimsy basis, the cities and their temples take their beginning. Henceforth the gods take up residence on earth and live in cities."[131] Thus, the Mesopotamians saw their own world as the whole world. They could see the sun and moon and stars above, but they did not understand them. Every great component of their world was a deity—the ocean, the river, the land, the sky, the luminaries above. They were unaware of lands or peoples beyond their vision or travel.

Ancient Mesopotamia also produced a number of flood myths, and the hero was known by various names; Utnapishtim in the Gilgamesh epic, Ziusudra in the Sumerian version (both names mean "he who found life"), and Atra-hasis ("very wise") in the Babylonian version. In all the accounts, the great flood was sent by the god Enlil, but the Babylonian version adds that the primary reason for this harsh decision was the noise and clamor made by humans, thus robbing the gods of peace and quiet. Enlil attempts to reduce their numbers by famine and disease, but this does not work. So Enlil decides to send a flood. The god Enki intercedes, by instructing the "wise man" of Shuruppak how to survive. He enlists the services of ship builders and feeds them well while they work. The boat is complete in a week, and when the rains come and the rivers rise, Atra-hasis and his family and all the workers get on board. Many people die, and he can see bodies floating like dead fish in the water. When the boat settles, he sends out a dove, a swallow, and a raven, to test whether the waters have receded. They all survive and life returns. Atra-hasis and his wife are given eternal life and a new dwelling place at the edge of land. In this story also we can see the role of religious myth to explain how things came to be the way they are. Leick writes:

> The message of the flood-heroes and the eponymous sage Shuruppak is that the most lasting achievements of urban civilization are not buildings and walls, since they can be swept away and turned into ruins and fields; and not power, since the gods control all destiny, but knowledge and humility.[132]

There is within the flood stories a subtle explanation for the development of the class of women known as the *naditu*. According to this myth, the mother goddess is instructed to create new people, but Enki has a plan to limit the population. Certain women are forbidden to bear children, and some will be unable to bear children. In addition, the infant mortality rate is elevated by assigning a child-snatching demon to patrol the land and kill as many newborn infants as possible.

Feminine Mystique and Power

It is neither in the creation or flood stories that we find the most significant definition of womanhood in Mesopotamia. Bottéro writes that despite the restrictions and domination by a male-oriented culture, a Mesopotamian woman had two reliable trump cards by which she could stand up to her husband, father, or entire society of male overlords: one was her feminity, and the other her "personality, spirit and character."[133] In 1949, Joseph Campbell wrote about the symbolism of femininity in the *Epic of Gilgamesh*.[134] Woman represents wisdom and power, as well as temptation and ruin. In the language of mythology, a woman represents all that can be known and experienced, and in this great epic, the hero's quest is both for knowledge and fulfillment. Intercourse with a woman is a connection with the Mother-Goddess and with all the wonder of the cosmos. The woman represents life, and the hero is the master and possessor of life. There are two mortal women in the epic who convey learning and wisdom. The first is Shamhat, who is sent to tame the wild man, Enkidu, by going into the wilderness where she lies naked to attract his interest. For seven days Enkidu remains erect and has intercourse with her repeatedly. It is by this experience that the animalistic Enkidu is awakened to a higher nature and becomes civilized.

After the death of Enkidu, Gilgamesh wanders in search of immortality. He encounters the second significant woman, the tavern keeper named Shiduri. She explains that the realities of life are quite simple; the gods have decreed that people are born, they live, then they die. And while alive, they should live for enjoyment. Gilgamesh rejects her advice and continues his quest.

The third female figure in the epic is Ishtar. When Gilgamesh returns victorious over Humbaba, she descends to visit him in Uruk and begs him to marry her, promising to give him wealth, a prosperous kingdom, and respect by everyone. But the noble king rejects her. He sees her as a temptress who has had many lovers, but is never satisfied with any of them, and a deceiver who makes many promises of love that end in disappointment:

> Gilgamesh opened his mouth and answered the glorious Ishtar: "If I take you in marriage, what gifts can I give in return? What ointments and clothing for your body? I would gladly give you bread and all sorts of food fit for a god. I would give you wine to drink fit for a queen. I would pour out barley to stuff your granary; but as for making you my wife—that I will not. How would it go with me? Your lovers have found you like a brazier which smoulders in the cold, a back door which keeps out neither squall of wind nor storm, a castle which crushes the garrison, pitch which blackens the bearer, a water-skin that chafes the carrier, a stone which falls from the parapet, a battering-ram turned back from the enemy, a sandal that trips the wearer. Which of your lovers did you ever love forever? What shepherd of yours has pleased you for all time? Listen to me while I tell the tale of your lovers."[135]

Summary

Glasgow's claims of a matriarchate and extraordinary political leadership by women in this region as early as 3000 BCE are extravagant and lacking in evidence.[136] In reality, the status of woman in ancient Mesopotamia is a paradox. Legally, women were persons of rights, but at the same time, clearly in every society and subculture that represents ancient Mesopotamia, women were held to a station of subordination and control by man.[137] There is reason

One. Mesopotamia

to believe that women in Sumer had a higher status than those in the later Semitic culture. In ancient Mesopotamia we find the earliest records of women in subordination to a social structure of patriarchy. It does not explain this structure as ordained by the gods, but expresses itself in very complex constructs of divine nature. In daily life a woman was relegated to the possession of some man, unless she did not fit into the common social structure. In that case, she had to find a place. But she remains, in some way, subordinate.

Therefore, while Mesopotamia is no doubt the birthplace of civilization, with Egypt and India following close on its heels, our knowledge of this remarkable stage in human development is limited. But overall, we can see a culture in which female subordination was already clearly defined, and the complex perception of women's status and role in society is expressed in the image of the goddess Ishtar. Lerner summarizes in these terms:

> The Code of Hammurabi marks the beginning of the patriarchal family as an aspect of state power. It reflected a class society in which women's status depended on the male family head's social status and property.[138]

Leick concludes that "to some extent the descriptive epithets of Mesopotamian goddesses reveal the cultural perception of women and their role in ancient society."[139] Woman is wonderful, mysterious, and the object of male passion and intrigue. But she is also capricious, unpredictable, and capable of incredible destruction. So to allay male fears, she is kept in control and under careful scrutiny. These are the earliest images on record of the status of women and what it means to be woman.

Two

Egypt

The scope of ancient Egyptian history spans more than three thousand years, from the earliest records to the first Christian century. We know little of the pre-Egyptian period, except that it involved the slow developing Naqada culture, marked by intermittent tribal conflict and dominance by leaders like Iry-Hor, Ka, and the so-called Scorpion King(s). However, Egyptian history is typically measured from around 3050 BCE, in the time of Narmer (also called Menes), who is credited with unifying Upper and Lower Egypt and founding the first ruling dynasty. From this time forward, there occurred a series of stable dynasties broken by periods of instability, including invasion and domination by other kingdoms or empires.

The Old Kingdom includes the famous Khufu, who was responsible for the construction of the Great Pyramid of Giza and the Sphinx, which remain prominent among the wonders of the ancient world. The second intermediate period saw a division of Egypt, with invading Hyksos kings ruling the Nile Delta and the northern region while Egyptian kings ruled the south from Thebes. The New Kingdom includes a period of conflict with the Hittites, culminating with the battle of Kadesh in 1274 BCE, as well as the famous Eighteenth Dynasty of rulers, such as Thutmose III and his wife Hatshepsut, Amenhotep IV (Akhenaten) and his wife Nefertiti, and Tutankhamen. The Nineteenth Dynasty coincides roughly with the biblical story of the Exodus of the Hebrews, led by Moses, and their eventual invasion of Canaan under the leadership of Joshua. Most scholars conclude that Rameses II was the pharaoh of the Exodus. Following that is the late period, which coincides with the Babylonian and Persian Empires. Then during the Classical era, Egypt was under the rule of larger empires, first the Persians, followed by the Greeks, and then the Romans. During the latter period of Roman rule, Christianity was born.

In the enthusiasm of early archaeology in the nineteenth century, many of Egypt's discoveries ended up in museums of other countries. Nonetheless, Egypt today offers visitors a breathtaking experience, from the pyramids of

Giza to the Valley of the Kings. The Cairo Museum is currently home to the largest collection of treasures of ancient Egypt, scheduled to be relocated to the Grand Egyptian Museum in Giza in 2015. Among the lesser but still impressive collections of Egyptian artefacts are those housed at the British Museum in London, the Ägyptisches Museum in Berlin, Petrie Museum of Egyptian Archaeology in London, Musée du Louvre in Paris, and the Museum of Fine Arts in Boston.

The language of ancient Egypt went through an evolution, roughly parallel to the dynasties. The first four phases were all written in hieroglyphs, the famous picture-writing typically carved into stone, as well as a cursive form called hieratic that was written in ink on papyrus. The languages of these periods are called Archaic Egyptian (before 2600 BCE, the language of the early dynastic period); Old Egyptian (2686–2181 BCE, the language of the Old Kingdom); Middle Egyptian (2055–1650 BCE), which lasted through the early Eighteenth Dynasty until the Amarna period (1353 BCE), and on into the fourth Christian century as a literary language; and then Late Egyptian (1069–700). Another language called Demotic developed around the seventh century BCE and was used into the fifth Christian century. Coptic emerged in the first century CE, and was common in and around Egypt until the seventeenth century. Even a brief synopsis of Egyptian history seems complex, but it helps to demonstrate the enormous task of archaeologists and linguists in interpreting the vast amount of data that has been retrieved from beneath the rocks and desert sands. The Egyptians left written records in the form of inscriptions in temples and tombs and on majestic stelae, some providing lists of rulers with records of their exploits, accomplishments, and conquests. Temple reliefs and inscriptions have provided little assistance in reconstructing the secular elements of ancient Egyptian culture. However, tombs have proved a much better resource, in that pictographs and inscriptions often illustrate elements of the home life of the deceased, as well as dress, hair styles, and jewelry.[1]

Among the most valuable sources is the Palermo Stone, which records key events from the first five dynasties.[2] The Tell Amarna tablets are also a valuable resource, and at that site was discovered the iconic bust of Queen Nefertiti. There are also thousands of scarab amulets bearing inscriptions, both commemorative and honorary, as well as countless fragments of papyri and ostraca, especially from the Greco-Roman era.

Another significant source of information is the body of reports from classical writers, such as the Greek historian Hecataeus of Miletus, who visited Egypt before 476 BCE. Herodotus of Halicarnassus also visited around 450 BCE, but he may not have seen much beyond the Greek city of Naucratis. Diodorus Siculus, also a Greek historian whose work spanned 30 years during the reigns of Julius and Augustus, offers glimpses into Egyptian life just before the birth

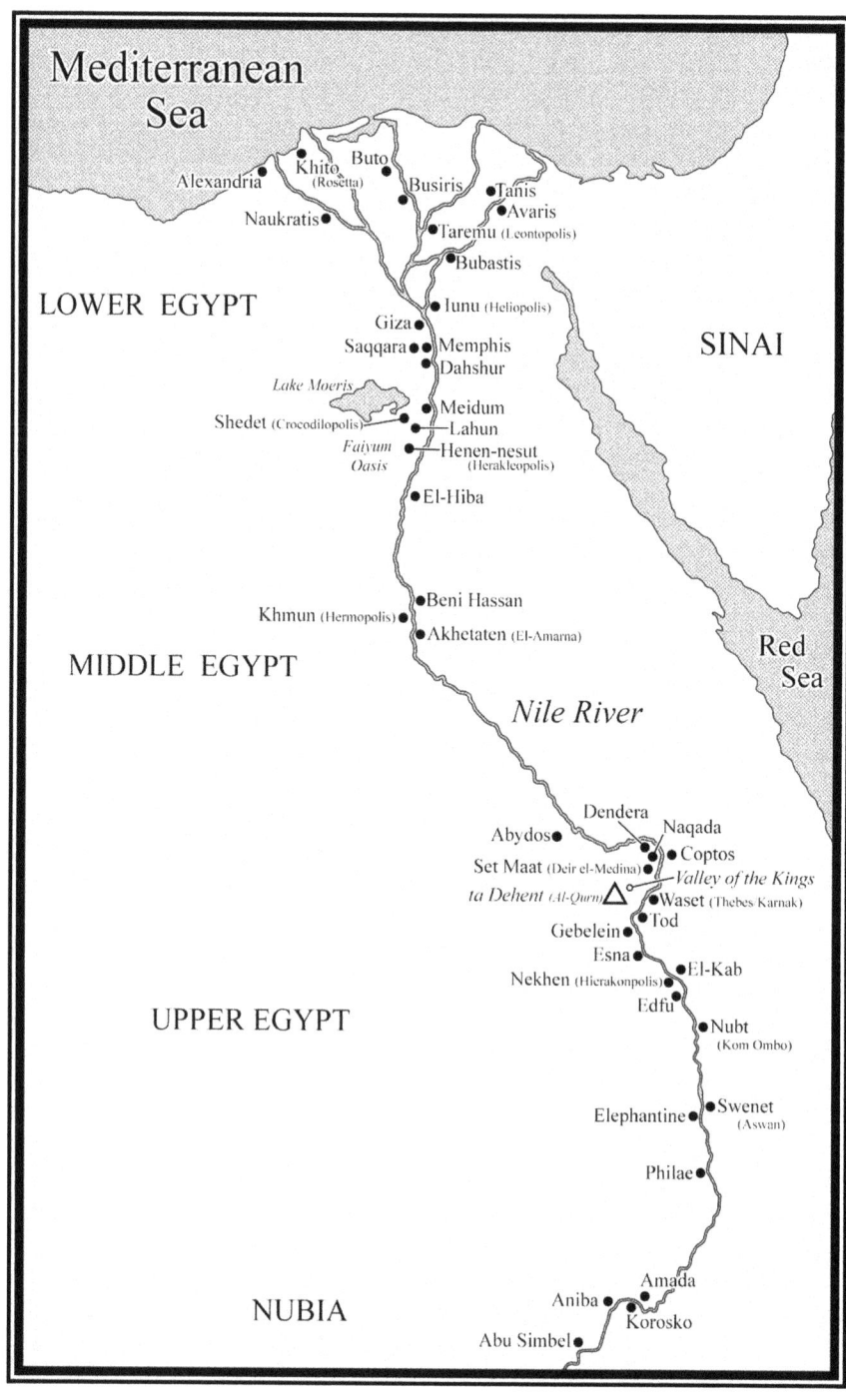

Two. Egypt

of Jesus of Nazareth. And certainly valuable are the works of Strabo, a scholar from Amaseia in Pontus, who visited Egypt in 24 BCE. His alleged purpose was to see Aelius Gallus, a friend and Roman prefect. But while there, Strabo took careful note of what he saw and then sailed up the Nile to Kush and eventually visited Ethiopia as well. His famous *Geography* includes a significant section on Egypt. And then, of course, there is Manetho, the Egyptian priest of the third century BCE whose history called *Aegyptiaca* provides insights into the dynastic divisions of Egyptian antiquity. Cyril Aldred points out that the Egyptians did not have the same concept of history as do modern Western academics, and often we have to learn either by reading between the lines or by trimming excess in order to reconstruct reality.[3] Most of what we know pertains to Egyptian royalty, but there are a few resources that shed light on life among the lower working class as well.

Our primary interest in this study is to determine Egyptian influences on the Hebrews, and in turn the writings of earliest Christianity, however subtle and remote that influence may be. Therefore, information gleaned from the Hebrew Bible is important. There we find certain evidence of interaction between the Hebrews and Egyptians over a span of several hundred years. According to Genesis, the first specific contact with Egypt was by Abram, later known as Abraham, the patriarch from whom the Hebrews descended. During his migration from Mesopotamia he settled for a time in Haran, and then passed through Canaan and southward to the Negev, and then into Egypt. He soon returned to Canaan where he and his immediate descendants remained. The story recounted in Genesis suggests that during his brief time in Egypt, Abraham feared that the Egyptians might kill him to take his "beautiful" wife. So he asked her to say that she was his sister. Consequently, some of the nobles presented her to the pharaoh, no doubt thinking that she was available for marriage. She was "taken into pharaoh's house" and Abraham was given considerable goods, including sheep, oxen, donkeys, camels, and both male and female servants. After an outbreak of some sort of sickness, the nature of which is not clear, the king concluded that this woman was married and he had been deceived. He reprimanded Abraham and sent him away.[4]

According to Genesis 41–50, Joseph, the great-grandson of Abraham, was sold by his own brothers to Midianite traders, who then sold him to an Egyptian named Potiphar. Through an intriguing series of events Joseph became an official in the Egyptian court, supervising storage of grain. He was renamed Zaphenath-paneah, and married an Egyptian woman named Asenath, who is described as the daughter of Potiphera, priest of On (Genesis

Opposite: Egypt, cities and significant sites of the dynastic period (3000–350 BCE). Donald T. Massey (illustrator) and Lesly F. Massey, 2015.

41–50). Eventually, during a period of famine, Joseph's family came to Egypt looking for food. After a tearful reunion with his brothers, Joseph arranged for the entire family to settle in Goshen in the northeast segment of the Nile Delta. There the Israelites, as they came to be known, enjoyed the hospitality of Egypt until a new ruler came to power who "did not know Joseph." According to Exodus, they subsequently found themselves in forced servitude.[5]

The Jewish Haggadah equates the name Potiphar with Potiphera, who became Joseph's father-in-law. On is also called Heliopolis, so according to this account Potiphar was a priest of the sun god Ra (sometimes written Re).[6] Scholars often point out that in this context the name Potiphar is anachronistic. It is associated with high officials, but it is not found in records until the Twentieth Dynasty. It is derived from *pa-dice-pu-Re*, "one given by the sun god Ra."

A problem arises in dating these events, since no solid archaeological evidence has been found to corroborate the biblical claim of a Hebrew settlement in Goshen, or a long period of slavery by the Egyptians. The traditional Jewish date of the Exodus is 1313 BCE, which would place their sojourn in Egypt beginning before 1700 BCE, a very long time to live in another country without some measure of evidence. Certain inscriptions, dating from 1350 to 1230 BCE, indicate that it was customary for officials to allow Bedouin from Canaan and Sinai to penetrate the fringes of the delta region during hard times.[7] Among such people, the Hapiru have been equated by some with the Hebrew (later called Israelites), although more recent scholarship calls this into question. The earliest mention of a people called Israel is the victory stela of Merneptah from his mortuary temple in Thebes. The stela celebrates his victory over Libyans and sea peoples in the fifth year of his reign (1209 BCE), and mentions three Canaanite cities conquered: Ashkelon, Gezer, and Yenoam. It also says "Israel is wasted without seed," and the hieroglyphics suggest that Israel was at that time a people, but with neither an established city nor a country.[8]

Remains have been identified of both Pithom and Raamses, mentioned in Exodus 1:11 as storage cities constructed by Hebrew labor. A third such city is mentioned in the Septuagint, called On (believed to be Heliopolis). However, the Septuagint calls them "fortified cities" rather than "storage cities." Archaeologists have discovered that the name Pithom (from the Egyptian *pr-itm*, also called Heroonopolis in Greek) was associated with two separate sites. In the late 1800s, Edouard Naville and Flinders Petrie searched for the ruins of Pithom, eventually identifying the site Tell-el-Maskhuta, located at the eastern edge of Wadi Tumilat. Later, another site, Tell-el-Retabeh, was located some eight miles west of Tell-el-Maskhuta. At this site were found a group of granite statues representing Rameses II, with various inscriptions identifying the Temple of Atum as well as a city wall and storage

Two. Egypt   59

buildings, and the remains of bricks made without straw. Their initial conclusion was that this was the Rameses mentioned in Exodus. Other scholars, including Allen Gardiner, Kenneth Kitchen, and W.F. Albright argued that it was in fact Pithom.

It was then determined that the designation *pr-itm* fit both sites, and that the earlier site at Tell-el-Retabeh had been abandoned and relocated to Tell-el-Maskhuta. More recent excavations at Tell el-Maskhuta suggest a settlement there in the eighteenth and seventeenth centuries BCE, associated with the Hyksos rulers.[9] Confusion in locating these sites was in part due to changes in various branches of the Nile River over many centuries, causing archaeologists to search in the wrong places. Eventually, the Pi-Rameses remains were found at Qantir, some 30 kilometers south of Tanis. Tell el-Dab'a, another 2 kilometers further south, was identified as the Hyksos capital Avaris.

Despite the vast archeological treasures of ancient Egypt already discovered, research and debate continues on numerous specific issues. It remains difficult to know to what degree the Land of the Nile might have influenced Judaism, and then indirectly Christianity. More will be said about this in the section on Judaism. However, we must acknowledge this great culture as a significant part of the backdrop for the New Testament, and certainly part of the foundation of the patriarchal social system inherited by Christianity.

Female Divinity

Scholars vary their starting points in discussing Egyptian culture, but in the present study the concept of female divinity is a good introduction to the status of Egyptian women in general, and the meaning of womanhood. Acknowledging that the realm of the divine is a human construct, from the earliest time Egyptian culture was expressed to some degree in their concepts of divinity, and in time those concepts served to perpetuate cultural norms. Egyptian accounts of the creation did not describe a willful act of a preexisting and eternal God, as in Judeo-Christian tradition. It was more along the lines of a spontaneous disbursement of matter into many specific forms out of the lifeless sea called Nu, but each major city had its own variation of the myth.

In Hermopolis, for example, the belief was that there were eight deities: Nu and his female consort Naunet were the water of the primordial sea; Huh and Hauhet were the infinity of the Nu; Kuk and Kauket were the darkness in Nu; and Amun and Amaunet were the hidden nature in Nu. The males were pictured as frogs and the females as snakes.

In Heliopolis, the creation was attributed to Atum, a deity closely associated with Ra. Atum was seen as the inert potential in Nu. Atum was self-created, and therefore the source of all the elements and forces in the world. By masturbation, Atum then produced Shu (air) and his sister Tefnut (water). The hand of Atum (later identified with Hathor, goddess of sexuality) represented the female principle inherent within himself that helped bring forth the seed that became Shu and Tefnut. This pair then produced Geb (earth) and Nut (sky), who essentially defined the boundaries of the cosmos as the Egyptians understood it. Nut produced four children, who represented the forces of life: Osiris, god of fertility and regeneration; Isis, goddess of motherhood; Set, the god of male sexuality; and Nephthys, the female counterpart of Set.

The Memphis version centered on Ptah, the patron god of craftsmen, and thus made creation an intelligent project with both design and purpose. And the version in Thebes made Amun the hidden force behind all things, and therefore the supreme god with all others an extension of himself. In all these myths, the ultimate source was male, but male and female principles combined to give life and perpetuate the cycle. Therefore, the female deity became essential for life, and she both represents and nurtures a significant part of subsequent Egyptian culture.

Among those deities is Isis, who represented the ideal wife and mother. Isis was the sister and consort of Osiris, the god of the dead. According to myth, Osiris was murdered by his brother Set. In grief, Isis searched for his body until she found him and then brought him back to life. By her brother Osiris, she then conceived and bore a son named Horus. Fearing the vengeful nature of Set, she hid the child in the marsh of Khemmis, in the Nile Delta. Through this story, Isis became the embodiment of motherhood and protector of children. She also was invoked in funerary proceedings, in the hopes for a resurrection such as that of Osiris.[10]

Hathor was the goddess of female sexuality and fertility. She was invoked as the protector of women in childbirth, and upon death to provide rebirth into the afterlife. Hathor also represented the perceived duplicity in women. As the goddess of music, dance, and intoxication she was a temptress, a goddess of seduction. Her more capricious side functioned, along with Mut, Tefnut and Sakhmet, as the eye of Ra.

With time and association with other cultures, the Egyptian pantheon blended with other gods and goddesses. Horus, the falcon god, became the patron of the Egyptian king. Set, the slayer of Osiris, abandoned the head of a greyhound for a human head and assumed the garb of the Canaanite god Baal. His consort was no longer Isis but Anath. Ashtarte, the famous Semitic goddess of fertility, also found a place in the Egyptian pantheon. Other female deities in Egypt include Taweret, represented as a hippopotamus with certain feline features. She was especially revered by women during pregnancy. Heget was the frog goddess of birth. Sekhmet was the lion goddess. Wadjit was the cobra, symbol of Lower Egypt. Nekhbet was the vulture, symbol of Upper Egypt.

Religion

Herodotus regarded the Egyptians to have been the most scrupulously religious people of all mankind.[11] This large and curious diversity of deities, in many ways different from the Greco-Roman pantheon, were revered by the Egyptians as the owners of the universe, aware of all human endeavors and capable of intervention. But how these deities were represented, and how they were worshiped, seems to have evolved and shifted constantly over the centuries. Hathor came to be depicted as a cow, or a buffalo cow in earliest artefacts. Isis became the patron deity of the year. Some authorities see her as the same as Sopdit, associated with the dog star, Sirius, whose festival began the New Year. Murray and others claim that Isis, Sopdit, and Hathor became so intermingled in Egyptian legend that it is impossible to distinguish them.[12]

A papyrus vignette in the Cairo Museum portrays Isitemheb, a woman of nobility, paying homage to a crocodile, no doubt seen as host to the god Sobek.[13] The city of Fayyum, the Greek Crocodilopolis, was the center of Sobek worship. Likewise, Bubastis was the center of cat worship, revolving around the goddess Bastet, mistress of love and matters of femininity and fashion, and whom Aldred describes as "the universal mother."[14] Each temple had officials, such as the superintendent who was usually the high priest also, and the chief reader (lector). Blackman says that high priests of large temples not only represented the needs of the people to their deities, but also wielded significant political power.[15]

Both men and women could offer prayers to deities, which typically were for humble blessings rather than for power or wealth. Since some of the deities were female, it was natural for certain cults to have only female devotees.[16] There were also a variety of ways women participated in rituals, including the honorable station of priestess and prophetess. As early as the Old Kingdom, women participated in temple rituals in various ways. Each temple had a troupe of female singers who shook the sistra and crotals as they sang songs to the gods. These women usually lived at home, rather than at the temples, and their services were only required at certain times.

However, a special role, best described as "priestess," emerged in cults devoted to goddesses such as Hathor and Neith. These women could be married or single, and in earlier dynasties came only from the upper class. By the New Kingdom, wives or daughters of artisans could find employment serving deities in their various temples. Married priestesses were often accompanied by their husbands while making sacrifices and offerings. There were also higher orders of women, called the *Khenerit*, who resided at the temple.

Another significant religious role has been identified the "god's wife." It seems that this title or position emerged from an earlier role called *duat netjer*, or "divine adoratrice," which arose in the Eighteenth Dynasty and at first may have been only an honorary position given to the queen. But in time it developed into an active role in the temple rituals of Amun, including assisting the priest in lighting a brazier with a firebrand, offering a meal to the gods and praising them with raised arms, and joining a troupe of priests and attendants in ritual purification by washing in the sacred lake of the temple. In the Eighteenth Dynasty there was a distinction between the attire of the queen as priestess and as royalty. Later, the priestly attire shifted to royal, and the role of god's wife shifted from queen to king's daughter. Robins also points out that the role was confined to the area of Thebes. Part of her role was to pacify Amun to avert divine anger, and also to stimulate him as "god's hand," so that he would maintain fecundity in the world.[17] This association is subtle, but it represents the cultural perception that woman's role in life was, at least in part, to please and sexually gratify a man.

Most priests and priestesses were part-time, and did not have social or political influence. However, in the cult of Hathor there were priestesses of various ranks, including the equivalent of high priest (*hmt ntr*). In the Fourth Dynasty of the Old Kingdom, Queen Meresankh III, who was the granddaughter of Kheops (Khufu) and wife of Khephren, is recognized in tomb inscriptions as high priestess of the god Thoth.

One of the significant functions of such priestesses was to impersonate the character or nature of the deities as part of a temple ceremony. For example, when a priestess of Hathor danced in a temple service, she would try to portray the graciousness associated with this deity. Watterson says that in funerary ceremonies two female mourners might impersonate the goddesses Isis and Nephthys as a pair of birds (specifically kites), because according to legend they had assumed this form when they searched for the body of the murdered Osiris.[18]

Prophetesses were also common in Egypt, and as such made pronouncements which greatly affected the course of history. Among them was Arthryte, daughter of Rameses II. Also, the Pelluciae of Amun were a body of priestesses who made divine pronouncements and are thought by some to be responsible for much of the literature of their day. Contrary to the norm, some women were educated. Penthelia, who was a priestess of Phta, the god of fire in Memphis, has been credited by some historians with the material later comprising the Homerian works known as *Iliad* and *Odyssey*. While not many have subscribed to this theory, it represents a wide academic respect for her unusual talent and influence.

One other note on Egyptian religion should be made here concerning Amenhotep IV, also known as Akhenaten (the Greek form of his royal name is Amenophis). He was a pharaoh of the Eighteenth Dynasty who ruled for 17 years and died around 1336 BCE. He is especially noted for abandoning traditional Egyptian polytheism and introducing a form of worship centered on the sun god Aten. This new worship has been considered by some to be a form of monotheism. He compared Aten to the sun, shining much brighter than the stars and therefore superior to the traditional gods. His departure from the old religion was not accepted, and after his death he was discredited as disloyal to Egypt's tradition.

Female Royalty

Since the office of ruler was considered divine, anyone who ascended to such a position took on certain attributes that were essential to the very life and existence of Egypt, as a country and as a culture. Thus, the recognition of a new king was celebrated by means of rites and rituals, and was taken very seriously. As Robins words it, "the king stood between the divine and human worlds, acting as the point of contact and mediator."[19] Since all variations of the creation stories began with a male deity, the role of king was reserved for males only. In general, it can be said that Egyptian queens were the objects of public envy and adoration and often the pride of their kings, but they enjoyed the status of royalty without true political power. There were several exceptions, and most of them were during the Eighteenth Dynasty. It should be noted that by this time Egyptian kings were often polygamous, and one of the wives typically would be called the "king's principal wife."[20]

Ahmose I is considered to be the founder of the Eighteenth Dynasty. But when he came to power, Kamose had ruled the middle portion of Egypt from Thebes, while Hyksos rulers controlled the northern delta region and also Nubia to the south. It was Kamose who initiated battle, and records indicate that he managed to expel these foreign rulers and recapture territory. But it is his successor, Ahmose I, who receives credit. It is possible that when he succeeded Kamose, Ahmose was young and his mother Ahhotep assumed various duties until he was capable of demonstrating true leadership. In gratitude he recorded on a stela at Karnak an inscription praising her as one who protected and reunited Egypt.[21]

Ahmose married Ahmose Nefertari, who was the daughter of his brother Kamose, and therefore his niece, although some historians have concluded that she was his sister. Among Egyptian rulers, marrying sisters was a common practice. As a queen, Ahmose Nefertari appears to have been as important

64   Daughters of God, Subordinates of Men

as her mother-in-law. She was mother to Amenhotep I, who followed Ahmose as pharaoh. A stela in the temple of Amun at Karnak records that Ahmose bestowed upon her the title of "wife of Amun." She held a priestly office in the cult of Amun at Thebes. Records make it clear that over the years she assisted Ahmose in many projects, and she lived on after her husband and son Amenhotep I. His successor, Thutmose I, respected her position, and upon her death honored her with an epitaph suggesting that the god's wife, Ahmose Nefertari, flew to heaven and was united with the god.[22]

Another significant queen during the Eighteenth Dynasty was Hatshepsut, half-sister of Thutmose II. She was therefore the principal wife and wife of the god. When Thutmose II died, he was succeeded by his only son, Thutmose III, born of a concubine named Aset. It appears that he was young, and therefore Hatshepsut ascended to power over the son, and was recognized as ruler over Egypt. At some point in the official reign of Thutmose III, Hatshepsut took on the title and masculine garb of a king and was depicted standing next to Thutmose III. According to Robins, this status required that Hatshepsut abandon the title and office of god's wife, and she therefore passed it to her daughter Neferura, her only child of record by Thutmose II.[23] It appears that this was necessary in order for the king to have a royal female present during certain ceremonies.

During the reign of Hatshepsut, she established peaceful international relationships, restored worship to temples that had fallen into disuse under the Hyksos, and completed construction of the temple of Deir el Bahri, decorating its walls with scenes depicting her claimed divine origin. In one inscription Hatshepsut specifically mentions restoring the worship of the god Ra.[24] Reliefs that decorate the colonnades of this lavish temple commemorate many of Hatshepsut's accomplishments. Of significance is her trading expedition to Punt, in Africa. Although the quest was for myrrh, she also brought back gold, ivory, and live apes. The reliefs show myrrh trees with the root balls encased in baskets. Despite all these accomplishments, Hatshepsut lived and ruled in a patriarchal world and there was resistance to the notion of female political power. After her death, her name was struck from lists of rulers.[25]

The same temple illustrates that Thutmose III proved to be an able military commander and an avid builder. Today the famous obelisk of Thutmose III, carved from red granite from Aswan, stands in the Sultanahmet Square in Istanbul, Turkey. It is called the Obelisk of Theodosius, because it was moved to Constantinople by the Emperor Theodosius in 390 CE. Each of its four faces has a single central column of inscription, celebrating the victory of Thutmose III on the banks of the Euphrates in 1450 BCE.

Tiy, the queen of Amenhotep III, came from humble backgrounds but was truly honored by her husband and her son, who would rule as Akhenaten.

The vast lake near the funerary temple of Thebes, of which remains only the famous Colossi of Memnon, was constructed for her enjoyment. Sayce describes her as a woman of strong character, evidenced by her influence over her son when he became the king. She also displayed strong influence by introducing the cult of Aten.[26] Most images of Egyptian rulers bear no distinctive facial features and are identified only by titles or surrounding details. Tiy, on the contrary, is identified with a distinctive downturned mouth. Her name appears on numerous scarabs, and during her reign for the first time a queen was depicted with the emblems of Hathor in her insignia. But she, like Hatshepsut, found little support in elevating the social and political power of women as a class in Egypt.

Nefertiti was another prominent queen, whose iconic bust with unique crown was discovered at Amarna. No other queen was so frequently commemorated in Egyptian art. She was the wife of Akhenaten (originally Amenhotep IV), son of Tiy. Besides turning to a new religion centered on the sun god Aten, Akhenaten also built a new capital city in the desert of Middle Egypt, calling it Akhetaten (the horizon of Aten). Robins points out that various stelae from household altars depict the queen seated with the king beneath the disk of Aten, forming a triad similar to triads of deities common in traditional Egyptian religion.[27] Additionally, Nefertiti played a special religious role in that common people could offer prayers directly to her. She is depicted in various garments and crowns, including those of king.

The last years of Akhenaten's reign and the role of Nefertiti during those years are the subject of scholastic debate. There is evidence of other women in Akhenaten's royal family. One was named Kiya, much loved by the king, although her titles were mysteriously removed from records and replaced by those of the king's daughters Meretaten and Ankhesenpaaten. The term Mitanni (or Mitannian) has been associated with a wife of Akhenaten, but it is possible that Nefertiti was a princess from Mitanni and the name refers to her. But it seems that Akhenaten also married certain princesses from Babylonia. Unlike Nefertiti, these are not memorialized with titles and inscriptions.

Watterson echoes a century of claims that a principal means of male ascension to the throne was by marriage to a royal heiress.[28] She says that while title and civic status typically traced through the father, property and lineage in Egyptian families commonly was traced through the mother, particularly in royal families. An Egyptian male would describe himself as the descendant of his mother, rather than his father; for example Ahmose, son of Abana. And while Egyptian kings commonly married foreign princesses, they would not arrange a marriage between an Egyptian princess and a foreign noble, since that might allow her offspring to lay claim to power in Egypt through her line.

Robins contends that this assertion is without supportive evidence. In the Eighteenth Dynasty, with which this theory is usually connected, there is no example of a pharaoh ascending to power by marriage to a royal princess. Some of the queens of the Eighteenth Dynasty have the title "king's daughter" and others do not. "It is enough," Robins says, "that the principal wives of Thutmose III, Amenhotep II, and Amenhotep III were all of nonroyal origins."[29]

However, there is evidence that some kings married their sisters or half-sisters and even had children by them. This was rare, and certainly not practiced among common Egyptians. In fact, it may have been done by certain kings simply to identify with the gods, who were in myth characterized by incestuous relationships.

We know nothing about how and why some kings chose a principal wife of nonroyal background. It is quite plausible that kings came in contact with many daughters of lesser nobles, advisors, and military commanders. There is evidence from a tomb in the Valley of the Kings that this was the case with Tiy, consort of Amenhotep III. Her father Yuya appears to have been a charioteer, and her mother, Tjuyu, held numerous titles. Anen, brother to Tiy, was a priest at the temple of Amun in Thebes. So, the family was significant, even if not from a line of kings.

There is also evidence of certain kings marrying their own daughters. An example is Satamun, the daughter of Amenhotep III and Tiy. She was described as "king's wife," even while her mother was still alive. It is possible that something like this also occurred with Akhenaten and his daughters Meretaten and Ankhesenpaaten. In the next dynasty, Rameses II had three daughters, Bint-Anath, Meritamun, and Nebettawy, who were called his "principal wives." Robins points out that the fact that children were born to some of these relationships, when no other male is mentioned as possible father, discounts the suggestion by some that the titles of "king's wife" and "principal-wife" were somehow honorary, or represented royal status, with no implication of sexual involvement.[30] It is noteworthy also that some kings married foreign princesses for the purpose of political alliance and international diplomacy.[31] This was a common practice in many ancient cultures.

Social and Legal Status

It is quite clear that the status of women in ancient Egypt was considerably more elevated than most other ancient cultures. Women were able to go about through city streets and in the countryside with faces and heads unveiled, particularly unlike women in Greece. Herodotus was bewildered by the contrast. But he reports that many customs among the Greeks that to him seemed natural and proper were reversed in Egypt. As previously noted, he may have misunderstood or exaggerated what he saw, but he said that "women attend the market and are employed in trade, while men stay at home and do the weaving."[32]

Evidence suggests that women freely visited the markets, engaged in business transactions, and invested their own resources in property at will.[33] Many sculptures and wall paintings depict women with their husbands, counting livestock, supervising workers, observing craftsmen, inspecting workers in fields, selling merchandise in the market, and attending banquets with their husbands.

Egyptian women were considered to be the legal equals of men, although as in Mesopotamia, women's rights seem to be more related to class than gender. An Egyptian woman was considered legally independent, not under the hand of a man, whether married or not, and could act on her own behalf. She had full legal capacity, or *capax*. She could be a partner in legal contracts, she could bring action against an offender in court, she could witness legal documents, she could be executrix of wills, she could give herself in marriage, she could legally adopt children, and she could buy, sell, or rent property, in her own right and name. And she could apply profits to other investments.

Parkinson's careful report on legal documents from the Middle Kingdom includes the will of an official named Ankhreni, who apparently had no immediate family and willed his property to his brother Wah, who was a priest. During the reign of the next king, Amenemhat IV, Wah made a will, specifying that the property, all goods, and three servants that his brother had left him would upon his death be given to his wife Sheftu (also called Teti). The will provided that Sheftu had the right to pass on any portion of those goods to children she might bear to Wah, and assured her of unchallenged accommodation in rooms constructed by Ankhreni for Wah, as well a place of burial in Wah's tomb.[34]

A papyrus fragment from Thebes, from the Thirteenth Dynasty, gives evidence of the legal rights of a woman to appeal to the courts if she had a serious claim. In this document, a man reports that his daughter, named Tihenut, sued him for wrongdoing. She claimed that he had taken several servants, who were a gift from her own husband, and then gave them to his new wife and children. Tihenut, understandably, wanted them back.[35]

During the reign of Rameses II (1304–1238 BCE), there was a court case concerning ownership of a portion of land. The suit was lodged by a scribe of the Temple of Ptah in Memphis named Mose, and over the course of time involved a woman named Wernero, her son Huy, and eventually Huy's widow Nebnofret. The details of both the trial and a later appeal are recorded in hieroglyphics on the wall of Mose's tomb at Sakkara. While the last portion of the inscription is lost and the final outcome unknown, Watterson says that is gives confirmation that "women could own land, could act as trustees, could initiate court actions and be held to be as competent in a law court as men."[36]

Most of the extant legal documents from the New Kingdom come from Deir el-Medina, and they clearly demonstrate the legal equality of women.

> Not only could women inherit, own, and dispose of property in their own right, they could enter into business deals, and they could go to court as plaintiff, defendant, or witness, on equal footing with men. In contrast to some cultures, a male guardian was not required to act for them.[37]

Women were also legally responsible for their own actions, in terms of business and social ethics. If a woman was accused of theft, slander, fraud, or nonpayment of a debt, she could be brought before the court, and if found guilty she would receive the same punishment as a man. That might be a beating, a monetary fine, or forced labor.

Even during the Ptolemaic period, when Egypt was under the rule of Greek kings, there is evidence that women appealed to Egyptian laws and customs, rather than to those of the Greeks.[38] An example is Apollonia (Egyptian name, Senmonthis), who lived in Pathyris around 150 BCE. She was the daughter of a soldier, and at about age 20 she married a cavalry officer named Dryton. He had a son from a previous marriage, but in time Apollonia gave him five daughters. Over the span of two decades, Dryton wrote and amended his will several times. At first, Apollonia was included along with her daughters and Dryton's son. In his final will, the inheritance assigned to Apollonia and her remaining two daughters was downgraded to a meager monthly ration of wheat, oil, and 200 drachmas, to continue for four years only, provided she remained at home and kept herself chaste. A very detailed account of her life is preserved in a papyrus document.[39] Apollonia was a woman of means and business acumen, and she eventually went to court to protect her assets and those of her sisters and daughters from greedy and ruthless relatives.

These illustrations of legal equality do not discount the insecurity and injustice suffered by women of the poorer class. Widows were especially vulnerable to exploitation, and many were as disadvantaged as in other ancient cultures. The *Instructions of Amenemope* from the New Kingdom warns against oppressing and exploiting widows.[40] This particular work, likely composed during the Ramesside period (1300–1075 BCE), contains 30 sections of wisdom, essentially advice for daily life. It is attributed to the scribe Amenemope, son of Kanakht, as a legacy for his own son.[41] The New Kingdom has been characterized as "the age of personal piety," and a collection of wisdom such as this was likely to assist the common people in coping with difficult social and economic circumstances. This work has been of particular interest to modern scholars because of its similarity to biblical wisdom literature, and even the precepts in the Law of Moses.

Marriage and the Home

Marriage, setting up a household, and raising children appear to have been among the typical ambitions of Egyptian men and women. The sage Ptahhotep (c. 2345–2181 BCE) advised his pupils to take a wife and set up house in due time.[42] He adds, "Love your wife passionately, as is proper. Fill her belly, clothe her back. Soothe her body with perfumed oil. Gladden her heart as long as you live, for she is a fertile field for her lord. Never contend with her in court, and keep her from gaining the upper hand."[43]

Robins gives special attention to a register of workers in a village at Deir el-Medina, dating as early as 1550 BCE, which compares to a modern census in that it list occupants house by house and defines a group as a man, wife (*hemet*) and children. This would support the general conclusion that among the common Egyptian population, monogamy was the basic pattern of marriage.

Marriages in ancient Egypt were typically arranged by the household heads. However, there is ample evidence of romance, courtship, and lasting love in marriage. Among the many surviving examples of love poetry, there are these lines from a husband about his wife:

> If I kiss her and her lips are open,
> Then I am drunk even without beer.
> My sister has come, my heart is overjoyed
> As I open my arms to embrace her.
> My heart pulsates within me
> Like a red fish in its pond.
> Oh night go on forever,
> Now that my queen has come.[44]

It appears common for couples to refer to each other as "brother and sister," symbolic of their love and affection, and therefore there may have been exaggerated reports of incest in Egyptian society.[45] Marriage between full brother and sister occurred, especially among royalty, but even this was rare. Marriage between half-brother and sister seems more common and acceptable. There is a story of a love relationship between Neneferkaptah and Ahwere, the son and daughter of pharaoh Merneptah, who wanted to marry. The king was reluctant, not on moral grounds or a violation of social propriety, but because he preferred arranging marriages for both of them with the children of important military commanders. But when Ahwere became ill from prolonged unhappiness, her father gave in.[46]

The formalities of marriage in ancient Egypt were limited. Little is known of any specific ceremony, but some have suggested that the couple might enter the temple of a principal god to offer a sacrifice and receive a blessing. However, evidence suggests that being married was based simply on the intention by a man and woman to make a life together, and this was formalized by the wife moving into the house of the husband. Watterson points out that until the Twenty-Third Dynasty, a girl was customarily given in marriage by her father, the last documented occasion of that being a papyrus record from 548 BCE. After that, the custom was for the man to say, "I take you as my wife."[47] In the case of Ahwere and Neneferkaptah, mentioned above, the bride later reported that she entered her husband's house and became his wife.

A bride was expected to bring a dowry into the marriage. As indicated by an ostracon found at Thebes, the marriage settlement was contracted on the basis of two-thirds investment by the groom and one-third by the bride. In Ahwere's case, her father issued a command that all kinds of beautiful things be given to her to take with her to her new home, and it was so.

The one legal formality of marriage that should be noted was a contract or "marriage settlement," known only from the seventh century forward. Whether rich or poor, couples were not required to have a ceremony or appear before an official. A wedding was considered to be a private and personal matter. However, there were formalities concerning financial obligations, ownership of property, and control of various possessions and assets. In order to protect both parties in the event of a future conflict, property and financial contributions had to be documented with specific conditions stated and agreed upon. The "marriage settlement" required the date, name of the husband and wife, names of parents of both, the husband's occupation, the name of the scribe, names of witnesses (which by the Ptolemaic period had grown to 16), followed by all stated details and conditions, including terms of divorce. In this document, the husband also stated his gift (*shep en sehemet*) to the wife, a practice that probably had its origin in the bride-price, common in ancient cultures and still practiced in some cultures today. Pestman provides a detailed summary of all these proceedings.[48]

Robins also discusses the varied meaning of the concept of "wife" from as early as the Old Kingdom. The word for husband is *hi*, but the term is rarely found on inscriptions, simply because in any sort of familial context the male is assumed to be the husband. However, the common term for wife is *hemet*, used also as early as the Old Kingdom. During the Eighteenth Dynasty it was often replaced by the word *senet*, which also means "sister," although the primary word remained *hemet*. The term *hebsut* was also used in places, although it specifically means "concubine," and in some records a woman is called both *hemet* and *hebsut*, meaning that she was a servant who had become a wife. Some have suggested that *hebsut* was used in reference to a second wife after the death of the first. But the term is rare, and there are too many examples of *hemet* used where multiple living wives are obvious.

Two. Egypt

Diodorus spoke critically of the comparative power of Egyptian women in these matters, stating that "the wife lords it over the husband as in the deed about maintenance, and men agreeing to obey the wife in everything." But Diodorus made a few incorrect assessments, such as his claim that with the exception of priests, all Egyptian men practiced polygamy. He may have based that on some of the rulers.[49] Perhaps he, like Herodotus, distorted reality somewhat as a literary device. But it cannot be denied that there have been numerous errors made by modern scholars, who simply drew incorrect conclusions from data they read or images they observed. Over the past century, scholars generally believed that royal succession, as well as general inheritance, was fixed in the female line.[50] Robins argues convincingly that there is no evidence to support this claim.[51] Monogamy seems to be the norm in Egypt as far back as can be traced, although there were exceptions to this also. It is evident that by the New Kingdom, Egyptian kings had harems, and by the Thirteenth Dynasty one woman was considered to be the principal wife. By the Eighteenth Dynasty, the harem was divided into those of royal lineage and those not, with the legitimate wife being the mother of the king's heirs.[52]

Montet observes that Egyptian "painters and sculptors have left an attractive picture of the Egyptian family."[53] Families are often portrayed with the father and mother holding hands while their children gather closely around. A famous pictograph has Akhenaten and Nefertiti sitting casually facing each other, the queen holding two of their daughters, one on her knee, while the king cradles and kisses the third.[54]

In contrast, some Egyptian literature reveals a great deal of infidelity and immorality on the part of men and women, and paints an unflattering picture of women. They are described by some as frivolous, flirtatious and unreliable, incapable of keeping a secret, untruthful and spiteful, as well as naturally unfaithful. The sage Ptahhotep, in discord with his recommendation of marriage, spoke of women in general as the epitome of sin and an endless source of mischief, while men were described as faithful, affectionate, and devoted.[55] In this, we see a hint of misogyny in a specific individual, but beyond that there is evidence of the tendency in antiquity to demonize and blame woman as a gender for the problems of the world.

Upper-class women had an easy life in many respects. As "mistress of the house" (*nebet per*) such a wife might have had no chores except to manage servants. In the *Tale of the Two Brothers,* Bata's wife "sat in his house while he spent the day hunting desert game."[56] But the importance of raising children would naturally mean that a fertile wife might be pregnant or nursing most of the time over the course of several years. Some also used the services of wet nurses, so even the task of nursing infants was at least shared. Watterson notes that in the New Kingdom, men often served in wealthy homes as cooks, weavers and launderers. This is the impression given by the biblical story of Joseph's seduction and the false accusations made against him by the wife of Potiphar.[57] Likewise, Anpou, the elder of two brothers in an ancient Egyptian legend, was the husband of a lecherous wife who attempted to seduce his younger brother, Bata. When her affections were refused, she made accusations against the younger brother that resulted in her husband's rage and harsh reaction. However, when he later discovered the truth, he killed his wife and threw her body to the dogs.[58]

Adultery by a wife was considered to be a serious crime against her husband and could be punishable by death, either by knife or by fire.[59] Men, however, were not under such a threat and had liberty to engage in relationships with concubines if their desire was not gratified in marriage. A husband was permitted to beat his wife with a stick, and a brother could so beat his sister for the purpose of discipline and instruction. But if a man went too far with this treatment and inflicted injury, he could be taken before the court, and if found guilty of abuse he could be punished by a beating or a fine. In general, marriage disputes, including adultery, were considered to be domestic matters, of no interest to the state. A woman who committed adultery could be denied her financial rights. Documents from Deir el-Medina suggest that while such matters were brought before officials for adjudication, the greatest danger for a man having intercourse with a married woman was the retaliation of the aggrieved husband.[60] In the *Instruction of Any* this warning is offered to men:

> Beware of a woman who is a stranger,
> One not known in her town;
> Do not stare at her when she goes by,
> Do not know her carnally.
> A deep water whose course is unknown,
> Such is a woman away from her husband.
> "I am pretty" she tells you daily,
> When she has no witnesses;
> She is ready to ensnare you,
> A great deadly crime when it is heard.[61]

Divorce could be initiated by either the husband or wife with a simple declaration of repudiation. At no time in Egyptian history was divorce viewed with social disapproval. Yet, no matter how simple divorce may have seemed, it often carried with it financial burdens and serious family conflicts. Besides adultery, common grounds for divorce included the apparent inability of a wife to bear children, failure to produce a son, or simply the husband's displeasure with the wife and his interest in another woman. It appears that as a man ascended in power or status, he might divorce the wife of his youth and marry someone of higher social standing, or someone who might prove advantageous to his ambitions. An Egyptian wife might divorce her husband for either physical or emotional mistreatment. There is no evidence of any social disadvantage or disapproval of divorce, either for a man or woman. There was no stigma attached to being divorced.

Financial burdens typically rested on males, either for the support of multiple wives, or payment to a divorced wife as he had agreed to in the marriage contract. But since these matters were not truly legitimate, nothing could be done to force payment. And the burden on females would be finding a means of survival if they had no independent income or property. Also, as neither marriage nor divorce was a legal matter, so also children were neither legitimate nor illegitimate. The primary issue was inheritance of wealth or title from those who had it to bestow.

Motherhood

The *Instruction of Any* advises young men:
> Take a wife while you are young,
> That she make a son for you;
> She should bear for you while you are youthful.
> It is proper to make people.
> Happy is the man whose people are many;
> He is saluted on account of his progeny.[62]

This suggests that among Egyptians, the "mistress of the house" was considered to be a fertile field in which the "lord of the house" sowed his seed, not just for pleasure but in order to produce children. Since women who did not get pregnant failed to fulfill their primary purpose in marriage, they were in danger of being divorced. Fertility, therefore, was something for which married women prayed continually. Sites such as Deir el-Medina and Amarna have yielded clear evidence that households commonly had a shrine where individual members or the family as a whole might worship their favorite deities and petition for specific favors. Some household deities, including Hathor, Bes, and Tawreret, were associated with fertility and childbirth. A variety of small figurines, some of females with the pubic area accented by a triangle, represented one mode of petitioning deities for the ability to bear children. And, as we might expect, some couples died childless despite their fervent prayers, such as the scribe Ramose and his wife Mutemwia. There is evidence also that some childless couples chose to adopt, although little is known of the process.

Robins discusses at length the Egyptian understanding of menstruation and conception; they knew that a missed period might be an indication of pregnancy. However, she points out that among the numerous tests for pregnancy,

74   Daughters of God, Subordinates of Men

other than taking the pulse and examining the breasts, few seem scientifically viable. The same was true of determining the gender of a fetus. And despite the common desire for producing children, there were occasions when pregnancy was not wanted. There are a few texts containing prescriptions for contraceptives, and some may have proved effective, such as various substances or mixtures used intravaginally.[63] Others, however, seem unlikely preventatives and may have resulted in injury or infections.

Childbirth is rarely depicted in Egyptian art, but there are sufficient images to illustrate that the common posture for delivery was squatting on two large bricks. Lichtheim includes a text in which a man compares his chastisement by the goddess Meresger to "squatting on bricks like a woman in labor."[64] The story of Rudjedet, from the Middle Kingdom, depicts the miraculous birth of the first three kings of their dynasty. Details reveal that spells and incantations were used to assist the mother with pain and to invoke divine protection and good health for both mother and child. Suckling infants is a more common image, further illustrating the value Egyptians placed on having children. The *Instruction of Any* assumes that a mother might nurse a child for as long as three years.[65] One scribe in the New Kingdom compares the joy of his work to a mother's joy in "giving birth, when her heart knows no distaste; she nurses her son continually; her breast is in his mouth every day."[66] Many images and paintings depict mothers or wet nurses suckling babies, as well as lactating mothers expressing milk from one uncovered breast, probably for the purpose of mixing it with other substances to make a more robust meal for an infant. Various papyri have survived that offer medicinal formulas using mother's milk combined with other ingredients, some even to help a baby sleep. As in numerous other ancient cultures, rudimentary medicine was commonly used in conjunction with magical incantations and prayer. Should the outcome be positive, whether the cause was natural or supernatural could never be determined but was a matter of belief.

Domestic Life

Upper-class dwellings in ancient Egypt were quite spacious and ornate, with comfortable bed chambers, dining areas, reception rooms, and numerous work and storage rooms. There was commonly a kitchen, granary, bakery, brewery, weaving room, carpenter's shop, animal stalls, and a butchery. If space was available there would be one or more courtyards, an area for a vegetable garden or orchard, and perhaps also a private well.

A few housing and settlement sites have been excavated from the Middle and New Kingdoms that shed light on the lives of non-elite, or worker class Egyptians. Barry J. Kemp has published a number of books and papers on these findings, particularly on dwellings at Amarna.[67] The city of Amarna was constructed by Akhenaten on virgin land on the east bank of the Nile in Middle Egypt, and the site was only occupied for 20 years. Akhenaten also moved the royal burial site from Thebes to Amarna, and another workmen's housing village was constructed further east for that project. Still another such village was discovered at Deir el-Medina, on the west bank near Thebes, constructed to accommodate workers who built the royal tombs in the Valley of the Kings. Houses in these sites varied in size, perhaps depending on the status of the workers. Models recovered from various tombs reveal much about how these workers lived.

The town of Kahun was built to house workers for the pyramid complex of Senusret II (1877–1870 BCE). Kahun had the largest houses of such construction sites, comparable to those described above. At Amarna, houses of officials were like those of Kahun, but they had larger grounds enclosed behind a wall. The main house was surrounded by other buildings for special purposes, like those mentioned above. There were also stalls designated for spinning and weaving, and somewhere on the grounds there was a vegetable garden and a well.

The workers' dwellings at Amarna were not nearly so large, measuring only about 15 by 30 feet each. The presence of feeding troughs in some buildings indicates perhaps that animal stalls were scattered among the dwellings. Sunk into the floor of some dwellings was a limestone mortar for grinding grain. A common feature of the houses was a raised brick border on one or two walls of a room, thought to be a sleeping area. In the lower portion of the floor, there was a pottery hearth for heating the room on cold nights. Niches in the wall were for placing small lamps. Some houses had staircases running up to the roof, a logical place for an oven and additional living quarters.

There is also evidence that sizable families lived in these relatively small quarters. House-by-house registries from Deir el-Medina reveal that these accommodated some single workers, but also couples with no children and couples with as many as four children. While this might be considered crowded by modern Western standards, it is quite normal by the standards of millions in developing countries even today.

Without a doubt, the majority of the population in ancient Egypt was poor. Both men and women of the lower class (*fellahin*) made a living by hard work. We have noted already the fact that wealthy and noble classes made use of lower-class workers, as well as slaves, to do the many chores essential in running a large household. For the majority, routine chores were about personal and family survival, and the three basic occupations that fed all of Egypt were farming, herding, and fishing.

The wives and daughters of poor farmers, herdsmen, and fishermen had roles to play that were essential for the entire family to live. They are not depicted harvesting grain, but following harvesters, gathering fallen ears in baskets, or bringing water for the workers. They are often portrayed winnowing grain and grinding. They are not pictured trapping birds, but beating to frighten birds toward snares. And perhaps here, we have to rely on customs among the poor in today's Egypt to surmise how they lived in antiquity. Some things have changed very little.

Most of the arable land in Egypt was along the Nile River. The regularity of flooding, the rich silt left behind, and the predictability of the climate, combined to make the Nile valley a fertile and productive belt cutting through the desert. There farmers thrived. Even when droughts scorched the earth in other Mediterranean lands, Egypt usually had plenty. Fields were crowded with grain and fruit, and every family enjoyed good wine from bountiful vineyards. There were only a couple of periods in Egypt's history when severe drought impacted the whole economy.

The Nile also teemed with fish and was a source of livelihood for many fishermen. Today over a hundred species of fish are considered native to the Nile. The Egyptians are credited with the development of the fish hook, commonly dated to the Twelfth Dynasty (1991–1778 BCE), but Flinders Petrie identified a barbed copper fish hook dating even earlier. These simple fishermen used fishing line made of twisted flax or linen fibers. They also used dragnets and basket traps. We have to consider the possibility that many Semites who visited Egypt, or lived on the fringes of Egypt for a time, learned from them as well. We have no reason to think that Bedouins, commonly identified as wandering traders and shepherds, would spontaneously develop the art of fishing in Lake Gennesaret. It is more likely that they learned from the Egyptians, or from Canaanites who had learned from the Egyptians.[68]

Winifred Blackman, an anthropologist who in the 1920s lived for long periods in the villages of Upper Egypt, reported that this region produced a conservative people who, despite the influence of invading powers and new religions like Christianity and Islam, retained to a remarkable degree many of their ancient customs, beliefs and methods, "practically unchanged from ancient times."[69] She offered descriptions of life in peasant villages: women caring for children, along with their work methods, rites of passage, magic, and superstitions. Of course, most of the heavier types of labor, as well as carpentry, metal work, masonry, and transport, belonged to the men. But there is ample evidence from numerous sources that such work as baking, weaving, basket making, spinning, harvesting, grinding grain, and even caring for livestock were usually done by women.[70] Working on her knees, a woman would grind grain on a stone mortar, which was typically sunk into the floor to prevent movement. Grasping a larger stone, heavy enough to grind by its own weight, she would pull and push it over the grain, back and forth on top of the mortar, until the grain was pulverized and reduced to course flour. From this flour also a woman might separate a measure to brew beer, as suggested in the story of the "Eloquent Peasant" from the Middle Kingdom.[71] Paintings depict women as weavers, operating simple horizontal looms in shops and along city streets. And, it was not uncommon for a wealthy individual to have as many 20 or 30 servants working looms in a large room adjacent to the house, no doubt as a profitable business.

Robins says that market scenes were not common in tombs, but the tomb of Ipy in Deir el-Medina has a scene of a boat docked along the riverbank. The boat is carrying grain, and porters leave the boat with bags of grain while others return with empty bags. Women are seated on the shore with baskets, and appear to be engaged in either trade or sale of such commodities as fish, bread, and vegetables. There is evidence for a system by which traders (*shuty*), who were the servants of either temples or wealthy individuals, traveled up and down the river trading goods. Kemp indicates that there is no evidence of independent river traders. This was all done by servants, on behalf of their owner-masters.[72]

Among pastoral tribes, as it remains today in primitive and developing cultures, women walked long distances to draw water and find firewood. They also cooked and washed clothes in whatever water was available, usually in a river or wadi. They also tended sheep and goats.[73] As Watterson appropriately states, a peasant Egyptian woman in antiquity, "like her modern sister, led a hard life of menial toil which was interrupted, but only briefly, at regular intervals for the incessant bearing of children."[74] Life expectancy was short, compared even to women in developing cultures today.

Occupations and Professions

It is quite evident that women in ancient Egypt were not afforded much opportunity for education. Certainly the ability to read and write was key to filling any meaningful position in bureaucracy, whether by inheritance or promotion by stellar ability, and that was by rule limited to males. Basic education, therefore, was essentially training to be a scribe (*sesh*). Ward reports that the feminine form of that term occurs occasionally in the Middle Kingdom, and illustrations in the tomb of Aashit at Deir el-Bahri include a woman described as a *seshet*. However, not all scholars agree that in such cases it means a "female scribe."[75] Robins says that the appearance of this term along with one that means "hairdresser" might suggest a job such as cosmetician.[76]

It seems likely that many royal and elite families would allow daughters access to scribal training, and then apply their literacy for writing letters and keeping family records. But there is no evidence that such skills resulted in females ascending to positions within bureaucracy. Nonetheless, there is ample evidence that women filled many positions of authority in ancient Egypt, although typically within the structure of a royal or elite family. Fischer provides evidence from the Old Kingdom of women holding official administrative titles, including steward in charge of food supplies, or supervising weaving, entertainers, and tenant property.[77]

Apart from all this, six professions can be identified that were very common for women in Egyptian antiquity. The difference is that what we are calling "professions" suggest that someone paid a fee for their services. There were no possibilities of ascending to the profession of scribe, governor, treasurer, advisor, military commander, or teacher. These were all roles of power and influence, of which a woman was unworthy. Therefore, the professions that can be identified were priestess (already discussed in connection with religion), midwife, nursemaid, mourner, musician, and dancer.

In every community a common duty of certain women was that of midwifery. There may have been schools of some sort to train midwives in various temples, but most midwives would have learned only by experience and would have been assisted by local women or female family members. More advanced medical training was reserved for males, and some doctors specialized in female diseases, but not obstetrics. And, of course, all of the knowledge was very rudimentary and laced with traditional beliefs and practices that had little true medicinal value. In this environment, midwives were held in high esteem. They existed during the period of Hebrew bondage in Egypt, and according to Exodus 1:16, they were ordered to kill male Hebrew infants at birth in order to control the population.

The Westcar Papyrus includes a story about midwifery.[78] It is the last in a series and very different from the other stories. Rededjet is a fictitious character, about to give birth to three sons. Ra orders the goddesses Isis, Nephthys, Meskhenet, Hiked and Khnum to come to her aid. They disguise themselves as musicians and hurry to her house. Acting as midwives, they assist Rededjet in the difficult birth of triplets. Each child is strong and healthy, with limbs covered in gold and wearing headdresses of lapis lazuli. The triplets are destined to be kings. The plot of the story develops around the maidservant who has a quarrel with her mistress. After a beating by her mistress, the servant flees, vowing to report the matter to the king. On the way, she meets her brother and tells the story to him. Displeased, he also beats her. Then as she makes her way along the banks of the river, she is devoured by a crocodile. The story, no doubt, had a meaning in its own time that escapes our understanding.[79]

In ancient Egypt, the mortality rate of mothers giving birth was high. Some also were unable to nurse their own babies, and the services of other lactating women were enlisted. Nursing and caring for the children of wealthy families is reminiscent of the biblical story of the baby Moses, found by the daughter of the Pharaoh, who then procured the services of a Hebrew woman.[80] Wet nurses were highly influential in the lives of children they had nursed. It may have been that after weaning, they continued to offer care for some time. The story of Moses is an example (Exodus 2:1–10). Because of the royal edict to kill Hebrew babies, Moses' mother hid him in a basket when he was three months old, set afloat along the shores of the Nile. The daughter of the Pharaoh found him. And on the advice of a Hebrew girl, who happened to be Moses' sister Miriam, his own mother was recruited to nurse him.

It is also evident that some officials married women who served as royal wet nurses, no doubt because of their relationship with the king and royal family. At Thebes, many tombs have been found and carefully studied. One is that of Amenemhab, a military commander who served both Thutmose III and Amenhotep II. On his tomb, his wife is depicted nursing a young prince. Similarly, the tomb of Kenamun displays his wife as nursemaid to a royal child, identified as Amenhotep II.

Another career in ancient Egypt was professional mourning, also common in other ancient cultures and one specifically available to women. A family with financial means would hire mourners to stand outside the house while a body was being mummified, or to follow the procession to burial. Mourners customarily wailed with considerable volume, holding their arms aloft, swaying from side to side. They also tossed dirt in the air and onto their heads, tore their garments, and even scratched their faces to the point of bleeding.

Women also found a livelihood in music. Walls of Old Kingdom tombs are adorned with depictions of normative life, and music was among the activities associated with both religious ceremonies and secular occasions. The Westcar Papyrus includes a story about a group of female deities who disguise themselves as itinerant musicians, giving evidence that such was not uncommon in real life. Instruments included a variety of flutes and both single and double pipe (much like a clarinet and oboe). One called the *arghul* in Arabic is still used today in Egypt and other countries, especially to accompany belly dancing. It is a single reed and double pipe instrument, with one pipe used for melody.

There were at least two varieties of harps, one made with a bow shape and the other with an angled form. Many of these instruments were imported from other cultures. The angular harp and the lyre are believed to have come from Asia Minor. Watterson mentions that there are only a few pictographs of the lyre in Egypt, the earliest being on the wall of the tomb of Khnumhotep at Beni Hasan (from the Middle Kingdom). It is played by an Asiatic bedouin. It seems not to have gained popularity. The lute, in contrast, was very popular. Some were made entirely of wood. Others had a wooden neck with a sound

80   Daughters of God, Subordinates of Men

box made of a tortoise shell. These appeared during the New Kingdom, with as many as three strings; the neck had a series of frets. Percussion instruments included a variety of rattles, clappers, tambourines, and even necklaces that made various noises with rhythmic movement of the body. There have survived images of women using all such instruments, clapping hands and snapping fingers to keep time.

Women also found opportunities as professional dancers and entertainers. Watterson mentions a depiction from the tomb of Werirenptah at Sakkara, possibly as early as the Fifth Dynasty, and now housed in the British Museum. It includes a group of male musicians and singers, as well as a group of female dancers and singers.[81] We know nothing of the actual form of dancing during this era, but some dancers are depicted holding items in their hands, such a mirror or hoop, and some appear to be juggling balls. This might have been more comparable to a modern circus, where acrobatic performers entertained to music.

What is called belly dancing today has ancient roots, and was among the earliest forms of erotic dancing. It is doubtful that it began in Egypt, but we have every reason to think that it was performed there quite early. There are no pictographs of women dressed in the same manner as traditional belly dancers, but it may have begun differently. Juvenal and Martial describe dancers from Asia Minor and other places using undulating movements, playing castanets, and sinking to the floor with quivering thighs.[82]

Most would assume that prostitution would be listed here also, since it is commonly termed the world's "oldest profession" and is found in most ancient cultures. However, as Watterson points out, there is very little evidence of prostitution in ancient Egypt.

Common and Forced Labor

Robins notes that statute labor, later in Europe called corvée labor, was unpaid labor imposed by the state on lower classes, for work on public projects.[83] The obligation of such labor by tenant farmers on private estates has been widespread throughout history. It is traceable to the beginnings of civilization as a form of taxation, when subjects simply had nothing else to give except their time and physical labor. In ancient Egypt, from as early as the Old Kingdom, pharaohs imposed statute labor to help with government projects, such as flood control along the Nile, and the construction of pyramids, temples, quarries, canals, and roads. This obligation for each individual was for a limited period of time, perhaps only a few days each year. The Amarna letters include one text from Biridiya of Megiddo dealing with provision of statute workers. It is evident that both men and women were obligated under this system, but it is not clear what kinds of work were assigned to women. It is likely that all the forms of manual labor mentioned above could apply in this case.

Dress and Grooming

Egyptians were much concerned with cleanliness. They customarily washed several times each day, not only on getting out of bed but after meals as well. Women maintained a wide range of toilet preparations, both for hygienic purposes and as beauty aids. The climate required regular treatment for bodily freshness, and a mixture of turpentine, incense, and scent served as a suitable rubbing compound. Other personal deodorants were available as well. A variety of treatments were known to the Egyptians for smoothing facial blemishes, removing superfluous body hair, removing wrinkles, and encouraging lustrous hair growth. The eyes were painted with special concoctions, black for liner and pastels for shade, much like those used later by the Romans. The classic almond shape for eye makeup was characteristic of Egyptian men and women for many centuries, and is depicted in both paintings and sculpture.

Women's garments in ancient Egypt were much the same as those worn by men, consisting of a fine shift under a white transparent pleated robe gathered over the left breast (leaving the right uncovered), open below the belt and falling to the feet. Fringed sleeves left the forearms exposed, displaying lavish bracelets and rings on several fingers. The poorer classes dressed more modestly and for comfort in working. Men often only a loincloth while working. Professional female musicians are depicted in long transparent robes, or as often in the nude, yet wearing a few pieces of jewelry. Young servant girls appear to have displayed their naked bodies to both master and guest.

Wealthy and royal women had their hair dressed by servants. Poorer wives attended to their own hair, but in each case the task was completed with pride. Both genders cut their hair short, or shaved it completely and substituted wigs, either short with rows of curled locks, or a single long bob swept back to display the ears. In the Middle Kingdom a fuller type of wig became the fashion, cut off squarely over the breasts, or parted in back and falling forward over the shoulders into plaits. Such wigs served more than a decorative purpose. The hot and humid climate in the northern delta and along the Nile made naturally long hair very uncomfortable and unmanageable. The substitution of wigs for natural hair was therefore common, but not necessarily a social requirement. During the Eighteenth Dynasty it was fashionable for men and women to go about with shaved and uncovered heads.[84]

Summary

The status of Egyptian women up to the Ptolemaic Dynasty seems to be that of respect, charm, and at times exultation. But after that, through Greek and Roman influence, their station was somewhat demoted. They actually lost many of their legal rights during the reign of Amans II (570–526 BCE), and by the beginning of the Christian era their lives were similar to those of women in other Mediterranean countries influenced by Rome.[85]

Tension exists among scholars, especially those of the early twentieth century compared to more recent times, concerning the assignment of domestic duties. This illustrates the problem of data interpretation. Petrie, writing nearly a century ago, concluded that classical resources are fairly reliable for establishing customs in ancient Egypt, simply because customs have not changed much between then and now, despite the influence of Christianity and Islam.[86] Wilkinson says that domestic roles were always similar to other Near Eastern cultures, but acknowledges that certain changes occurred, such as lessening restrictions as a result of Roman influence.[87] However, we have noted certain changes from one dynasty to the next, shifts in terminology and variations in the definition of marriage, monogamy, and polygamy within the same society, but varying from one class to another. In all this, generally speaking throughout Egyptian antiquity, title and power belonged to men. While having certain legal freedoms denied to women in other ancient cultures, in general Egyptian women were always under the control of men. And, despite the elevated status of women and occasional power wielded by queens, male dominance was carefully guarded.

Three

Judaism

Womanhood in Judaism during the centuries prior to the birth of Christianity is a challenge to determine and define, for a number of reasons. First, the information obtained from the Hebrew Bible (Tanakh) spans many centuries, and there are significant shifts and variations in custom from the era of the patriarchs to the restoration period of Ezra and Nehemiah and beyond. Second, the opinions of the rabbis, upon whom we must depend for most information related to the fourth century BCE onwards, differ widely regarding the place of women in Jewish culture. Third, because they developed before they were recorded during and after the second Christian century, there is uncertainty about the age of some views, regulations, and customs. Since even rabbinical writings contain many anachronisms, care must be taken not to assign customs from a late period to a more ancient one. Without caution, rabbinical doctrines from as late as Constantine might be read mistakenly back into the time of the Hasmonaeans. There were, in fact, significant changes in Jewish culture during the period from the Babylonian Exile to the third Christian century. Furthermore, we have reason to believe that centuries earlier the Hebrew culture that emerged from Egypt was significantly different from that of the patriarchs. It is very likely that some of the customs and theology attributed to the patriarchs in Genesis was read back into ancient legends centuries after the fact. Despite these challenges, it is essential to try to reconstruct a reasonably accurate picture of the prevalent attitude toward women and the meaning of womanhood during this significant phase of history, and how that might have impacted early Christians and various New Testament documents.

Resources

The Hebrew Bible includes the same books as the Christian Old Testament, although in a different arrangement and grouping. The name Tanakh is an acronym from the three traditional divisions: the Torah (Law, or the

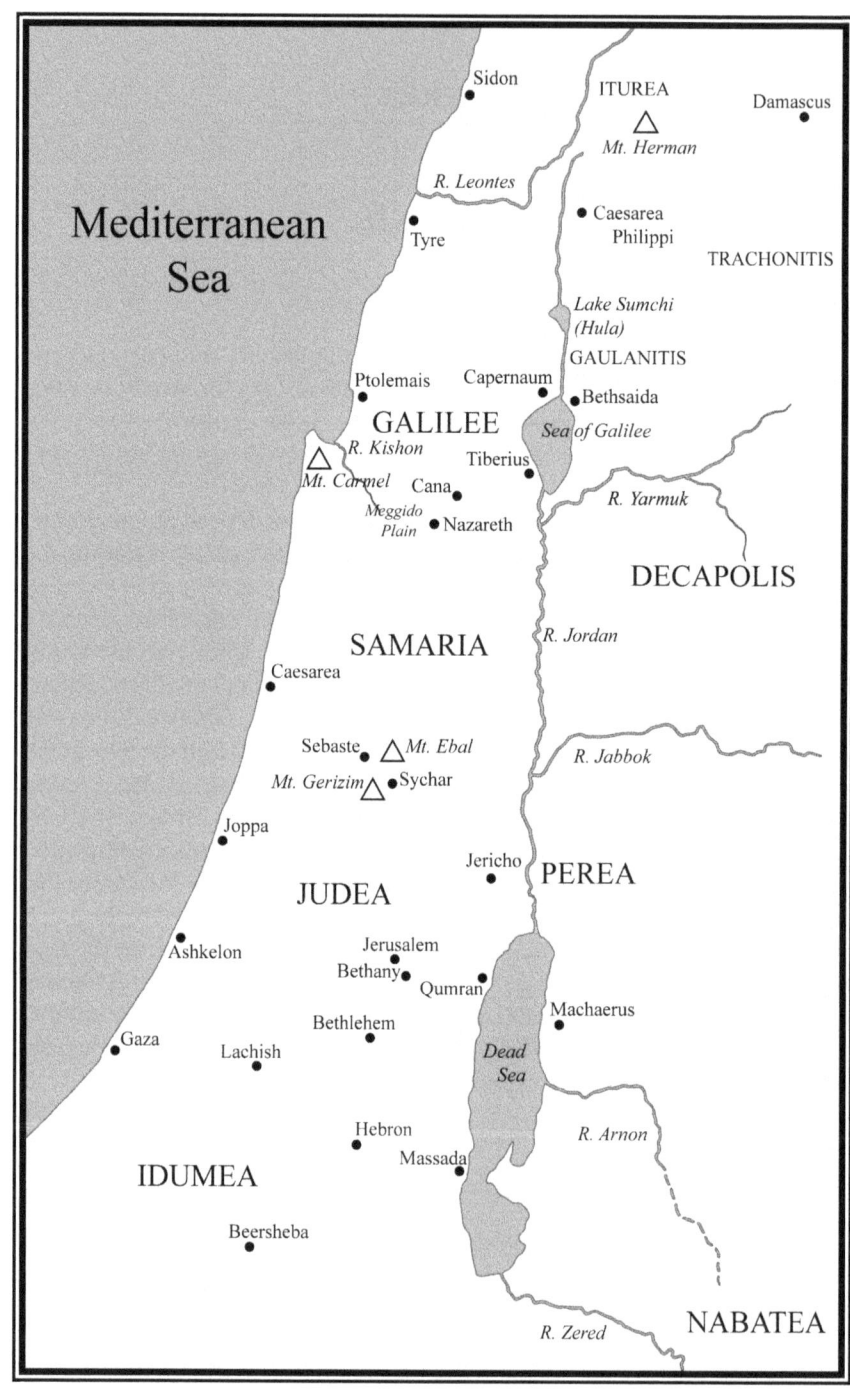

Five Books of Moses), the Nevi'im (Prophets) and the Ketuvim (Writings). According to the Talmud, most of the contents of the Tanakh were compiled by the Great Synagogue by 450 BCE and have since remained unchanged.[1] It may be that the process of agreeing upon a fixed collection of works, called canonization, stretched from 200 BCE to 200 CE. Nonetheless, the traditional collection is the same as those in the Septuagint, the Greek translation of the Tanakh, which was commonly read in the synagogues of the Diaspora within two centuries before Christ, and typically was the version quoted by New Testament writers.

The Jewish Apocrypha are a collection of writings that were not accepted into the Tanakh, but have great value in determining events and customs during the four centuries before Christ. Until the third century CE, various apocryphal books were quoted by rabbis in Palestine. However, over time the apocrypha fell out of use in Judaism and were preserved through the Middle Ages only by Christians. They still are included in the Roman Catholic Bible, but do not appear in versions accepted by most Protestants.

The best source for the traditions which survived the Babylonian captivity, and those which developed after that event, is the large collection of rabbinic literature produced from the first century CE onwards, and perhaps the Qumran texts and apocryphal literature, which date as early as the third century BCE. Much of Jewish tradition was transmitted orally for generations, being instructed by those regarded as learned in the law and prophets. By the time these regulations came to be written, their origin and purpose had been forgotten, a problem for modern scholars who wish to determine precisely what beliefs were predominant in the early and middle first century. Generally, the reports of all such witnesses are lumped together to produce a composite picture representing Judaism from 300 BCE to 400 CE. However, it is evident that the Mishnah was compiled no earlier than 200 CE from the arguments of four generations of rabbis, and the Jerusalem and Babylonian versions of the Talmud grew out of the Mishnah and were compiled over a period from the third to fourth centuries and from the fifth to sixth centuries CE, respectively.[2]

The Talmud includes 63 tractates, the central text of rabbinic Judaism. There are two components: the Mishnah, a written compendium of the oral law, and the Gemara (completed around 500 CE), a collection of commentaries on the oral rabbinic law and the Tanakh. The Mishnah consists of six orders, a third of which is called the Nashim and is especially important to the status of women. The Nashim consists of seven tractates:

Opposite: **Palestine, first century CE. Donald T. Massey (illustrator) and Lesly F. Massey, 2015.**

86   Daughters of God, Subordinates of Men

1. Yebamoth pertains to the levirate marriage, the mandated marriage of a widow to her brother-in-law, derived from Deuteronomy 25:5–10.
2. Ketubo deals with the Ketubah, essentially the prenuptial agreement for marriage, as well as topics such as virginity and various marital obligations.
3. Nedarim deals with marital vows and their legal consequences.
4. Nazir pertains to the details of the Nazirite vow and related abstinance.
5. Sotah pertains to the ritual testing of a woman suspected of adultery, derived from Numbers 5, as well as other rituals, blessings and cursings.
6. Gittin deals with divorce and related documents.
7. Kiddushin deals with betrothal (engagement and the initial stages of marriage), as well as laws of lineage.

Last, the Midrash (plural Midrashim) is the body of homiletic stories told by Jewish rabbis to explain passages in the scriptures, but going beyond the primary religious, legal, and moral teachings. There are two types of Midrashim. The *midrash aggada* is essentially a form of storytelling that explores ethics and values in nonlegal texts of the Tanakh. In contrast, the *midrash halakha* focuses on Jewish law and practice for the purpose of clarification. The earliest of the Midrashim are from about 400 CE and are too late to have had an influence on the New Testament.

A significant Jewish leader in the early first Christian century is Babylonian Rabbi Hillel, who came to Jerusalem around 30 BCE and died there in 20 CE. Although there is disagreement about the dates, his work coincided with the reigns of Augustus Caesar and Herod the Great, and therefore the birth of Jesus of Nazareth. His more conservative and stricter contemporary was Rabbi Shammai (50 BCE–30 CE), with whom Hillel vied for power in the Sanhedrin. Their schools (or houses) were known as Beth Hillel and Beth Shammai, and it is said that they disagreed on more than three hundred religious issues. Among the more notorious differences were who should be allowed to study the Torah,[3] whether small lies are justifiable,[4] the order of candle lighting during the celebration of Hanukkah,[5] and the acceptable grounds for divorce.[6]

While all these resources have been freely available to Christian scholars, much of the contents is complicated. The work of modern Jewish scholars has proved invaluable in both analysis and interpretation. While many presuppose encyclopedias to be a secondary resource, the *Encyclopedia Judaica* is of first-rate academic depth and quality. There are also independent works, such as Rachel Biale's *Women in Jewish Law*,[7] that offer a major contribution to the modern study of the status of women in ancient Judaism.

The Creation Stories

The story of the creation in Genesis is the root of all Jewish beliefs concerning women's secondary and inferior nature, and in turn becomes the foundation for certain Christian beliefs, primarily through references by the Apostle Paul or later paulinists. In recent history, Christians have read these stories as literal history, and many still view the Bible as a whole as divinely inspired and without error. With regard to Genesis in particular, reliablity is questionable because of many anachronisms, duplications, and conflicts. For example, in Genesis Terah's home is referred to as Ur of the Chaldees.[8] Archaeologists are in agreement that the Chaldees did not enter southern Mesopotamia until around 1000 BCE, which means that the writer of this account lived during or after the time of Solomon. And the statement "before any king reigned over Israel" (36:31) reveals that the writer lived after the Israelites had kings, and possibly before they split into two kingdoms.[9] Therefore, certain data from the writer's own time were unconsciously written back into stories of earlier times.

However, the origin and purpose of the creation narrative in Jewish literature, as well as the distinction between the two accounts in Genesis, simply cannot be ignored. The first account in Genesis 1 speaks of the appearance of mankind, or humanity, including the female. This is generally considered to be of priestly origin, not completed until after the temple era, perhaps the final form even postexilic, when weekly liturgy followed a lunar calendar and the entire people became feminine in relation to Yahweh.[10] Man and woman could at that time be presented as sexually polarized within the oneness of mankind (Adam) without playing on the reversal of their value or status which followed the Fall.[11]

Genesis 2:7–22 contains the Yahwist tradition, focusing on the institutions of family and society and deriving its creation and paradise material from ancient mythology.[12] It portrays the male being created first, and the female fashioned from one of his ribs. Adam is made from the dust of the ground, his name *(ha adam)* suggesting perhaps the redness of clay. God's observation that it is not good for man to be alone is presented as an afterthought, certainly unworthy of an omniscient God, and a rather degrading view of woman is presented in that Eve was made only after Adam failed to find a suitable companion among all the animals.

The second account of creation also describes the woman as a "helper" *(ezer)* for the man. Traditionally this expression has been thought to suggest an inferior assistant, a mate or partner, with the adjectival term *neged* meaning "suitable," "fitting," or "for the benefit of." The two terms together are translated "help meet" in the Authorized Version, which has been in Christian tradition a quaint name for man's inferior and subordinate sidekick. But the term *ezer* appears 21 times in the Tanakh, of which 16 refer to a superordinate source of help, God specifically, and never suggests the concept of a secondary assistant.[13] The expression actually conveys the idea of a presence like the man, a reflection of himself, and one with whom he can relate.[14] This is definitely suggested in Adam's response upon seeing her, that she is "bone of my bones and flesh of my flesh."[15] Rosenzweig argues effectively that *neged* also means "equal," in no way suggesting secondary or subordinate in character.[16] But as far as can be determined, the view that male and female were created simultaneously as partners, opposites designed to complement each other, never found credence among the Hebrews in spite of the implications of the first chapter of Genesis.

The term *ishah* is merely the feminine of *ish*, and does not necessarily imply that woman was taken "out of" man as suggested in Genesis 2:23. This represents an infusion of later thinking, similar to the Platonic myth of Eros in which, according to Barnhouse and Homes, the sexual attraction carries with it a memory of distressful tearing apart.[17] Tavard concludes also that the Yahwist writer portrays his Ishah-Eve in opposition to the feminine idols of the Canaanites, displaying a consciousness of fertility symbols and the submission to the lordship of the husband. He speaks in favor of her pristine vocation of completion and perfection, and man's complement.[18] Upon this fanciful and highly symbolic account, the rabbis developed elaborate doctrines about human nature. They typically explained Eve's origin in the following fashion:

> God said: I will not create her from the head that she should not hold up her head too proudly: nor from the eye that she should not be a coquette: nor from the ear that she should not be an eavesdropper: nor from the mouth that she should not be too talkative: nor from the heart that she should not be too jealous: nor from the hand that she should not be too acquisitive: nor from the foot that she should not be a gadabout: but from a part of the body which is hidden that she should be modest.[19]

Many rabbis added their views that it was all to no effect, since women are basically greedy, lazy, jealous, and garrulous. Some thought of women as compulsive eavesdroppers. So, while they felt compelled to take the rib story literally, the rabbis could not help but suspect that somewhere in the process God made some kind of error, either in production or in design.

Modern scholarship is forced to view critically a literal interpretation of the Adam and Eve story,[20] and the difference between the first and second creation account in Genesis is highly significant to the study of female subjection in later Christian tradition.[21] The two accounts may be no older than the monarchy, although conservatives believe them to be totally Mosaic in authorship. After 400 BCE, the two accounts came to be seen as one, with woman appearing to be an instrument of procreation, the source of sin, and the bearer of a curse. Their appearance together might indicate an imperception of their original significance giving rise to misinterpretation, which is represented it seems by the common gender disparity among Jews in Jesus's day.

Tavard sees the two as reflecting the influence of two contradictory traditions. The latter was nourished by other cultures, degenerate and inferior, while the former reflected the positive order to which the Hebrew society hoped to return in the Messianic era.[22] One rabbinic tradition saw the first account as an androgynous form of humanity, meaning that the original being was dual in sexuality.[23] Adam's observation that Eve is "bone of my bone and flesh of my flesh" is intensified by his conclusion inserted by the Yahwist that man will "leave father and mother and cleave to his wife, and the two will become one flesh,"[24] a view of women which was more elevated than later Judaism allowed. But looking at his own culture, the Yahwist could only attempt to explain how things came to be as they are, and he reconstructed a prelapsarian order, a paradisiacal society with conditions the reverse of his postlapsarian world. Conditions after the Fall, as they were observed in the writer's own and in surrounding cultures, demanded some explanation. A woman's painful and degraded lot in life is suitably explained as a curse resulting from her sin. This includes all naturally unpleasant aspects of feminity, especially pain in childbirth, as well as the consignment to a subordinate station under the husband and her generally inferior social status.[25]

The phrase "your desire shall be for your husband" is puzzling, although it seems to imply the writer's observation that despite the unpleasantness of her lot in life a woman typically yearns for a personal relationship with a man, and has a sexual appetite which may be acceptably satisfied by her husband only.[26] Some suggest that it means she will not be permitted to initiate sexual activity, but only respond to her husband's desires. Others have suggested that it simply means that she will have a desire for sexual intercourse, despite the unpleasantness of pregnancy and the pain of childbirth.[27]

In her discussion of the woman's exemption from certain portions of the mitzvot, Biale sees a strong tension between two views of women, appearing in the creation narrative in the form of a rivalry between God and the husband. On the one hand, God represents a fundamental ethical position that men and women are of equal moral, physical and spiritual value, with no stratification endorsed. On the other, Biale says:

> The husband represents an attitude grounded in daily life and social reality, where there are distinctions of religion, class, learning, and of course gender. Women are inferior to men in economic power, social standing, legal rights, and religious role and importance.[28]

Therefore, in one account woman is created in the image of God as man's equal. In the other, she is created solely to meet man's needs.

Early Hebrew Culture

The stories in Genesis about the patriarchs reflect a mixture of Babylonian and Bedouin traits. Abram, later called Abraham, was a wealthy nomad originating from Ur Kasdim (Ur of the Chaldees) in southern Mesopotamia. It appears that he was young when his father Terah migrated from there to Haran, a trade center in upper Mesopotamia, which we know from the famous Ebla Tablets[29] dating fom 2250 to 2500 BCE. Joshua says to the Israelites, "Long ago your ancestors, including Terah the father of Abraham and Nahor, lived beyond the Euphrates River and worshiped other gods" (Joshua 24:2). So, while Abraham's ancestry traces to polytheistic Ur, his immediate roots were in Haran in northern Syria. The region of this Haran is referred to variously as *Paddan Aram* and *Aram Naharaim*. Genesis 27:43 makes Haran the home of Isaac's wife Rebekah, and their son Jacob spent 20 years in Haran working for his uncle Laban (Genesis 31:38–41). It has been mentioned earlier that Semites migrated back and forth between the Levant and Mesopotamia, and it may be that the family of Terah came from somewhere else and did not remain long in Ur. Their Bedouin customs do not match those of the settled cultures of Mesopotamia.

Also, we should note that the mention of the Chaldees in Genesis 11:31 is an anachronism, since it is well established that the Chaldees did not occupy that region until the ninth century BCE, nearly a thousand years after the time of Abraham. Porten writes that we learn from the royal archives of Mari that these were patriarchal societies, and the Nuzi documents provide a picture of the family life and household laws of that era. There is also evidence of some degree of blend of Semitic and Hurrian societies in Haran from the eighteenth century onward, and that matches roughly the time Abram lived there, before migrating southward.[30]

We have to assume that among the early Hebrews polygamy, or more accurately polygyny, was common in various forms. Although one wife was regarded by the husband as his "beloved," she had to share his affection with other wives and concubines. Slavery also was an integral part of Hebrew life and was permissible under the Law of Moses.[31] As was typical of Bedouins of the Near and Middle East, each wife and maid had her own tent and her own possessions.

Sarah is a good example of a typical wife in patriarchal Bedouin cultures. She is idealized by the Christian writer of I Peter in extolling the virtues of a Christian woman, but her character is shaped by customs that predate Christianity by nearly two thousand years.[32] Her story reflects the shame of childlessness among Semitic women, and that it was perfectly acceptable in their culture for a female servant to bear children on behalf of a legitimate wife.[33] But through all her struggles, Sarah was an obedient wife, revering and honoring her husband from her subordinate station.

Three. Judaism   91

A certain amount of helpful information can be gleaned also from stories of Isaac and his son Jacob.[34] The former married Rebekah, who was procured for him by a servant who travelled back to Haran to search among Abraham's own relatives for just the right young woman. This story also reflects the ancient belief that mate selection, at least for certain special people, is orchestrated by deity. The story of Jacob, one of Isaac's two sons, illustrates polygyny. He married sisters Leah and Rachel, daughters of Laban. He was required to work for seven years to cover the bride-price of each. It seems that among these early Hebrews a woman had no part in the selection of a husband, although she could refuse a marriage proposal. She was more or less the property of her father and dared not disobey him. As in other early cultures of Near Eastern antiquity, women among these nomadic peoples were subordinate to men as a class and were generally responsible for drawing water, tending sheep, cooking, and caring for children. From Jacob's two wives and two concubines, twelve sons and one daughter were born, all while Jacob still lived in the region of Haran.[35] The daughter, Dinah, was raped and then avenged by her brothers, and is listed among those who moved to Egypt at Joseph's invitation (Genesis 46:15). Other than that, she plays no remarkable role in the birth of a nation. By that time, Joseph has married an Egyptian woman, and his two sons Manasseh and Ephraim were both born in Egypt (Genesis 41:50–52).

It is important here to note the actual origins of these people, and the terms identifying them. The word "semite" comes from the name Shem, one of the sons of Noah, and only in recent centuries has been used to describe a group of nations and tribes with similar languages, including Mesopotamians, Syrians, Canaanites, and Israelites. The term *Habiru* (also *Hapiru* and *Apiru*) was used by the Egyptians and others to describe a smaller group within and among the semitic peoples, but the term appears to signify social level rather than ethnicity.[36] Porten points out that it describes a people spread all over the region, in and around Canaan, who "lived on the margin and under the protection of societies whose laws did not apply to them."[37] Redmount agrees, stating that the term Habiru had no common ethnic affiliations, and that the people it describes led a marginal and sometimes lawless existence on the fringes of settled society. From various ancient sources we can conclude that these people were thought of variously as nomads, vagabonds, shepherds, and sometimes marauders, outlaws, mercenaries, and slaves.[38] In time it came to describe the Israelites, and is so used by the writer(s) of Genesis in retrospect (39:17, 40:15, 41:12). It also came to describe the language of the Israelites, and today classical Hebrew is affiliated with Chaldee in academic lexicons and grammatical texts. The earliest written forms were in cuneiform.

Porten writes that the first waves of western Semites arrived in Egypt by the nineteenth century BCE and eventually declined in numbers under pressure of Indo-Europeans and Hurrians who invaded Mesopotamia, Syria, and Palestine.[39] Among them were the Hyksos, and their similarity to the Israelites is evidenced by royal names like Yaqob-har. The family of Jacob was allowed to enter Egypt and settle because the Hyksos rulers at that time were of simliar ethnicity. The Hyksos domination of the delta region of Egypt ended in 1570 BCE, which also brought to an end the era of the Israelite patriarchs.

We have noted earlier the connection the Hebrews had with the Egyptians, briefly by the patriarch Abraham himself, and more significantly with Joseph, who advanced to a position of "superintendant of granaries" and married an Egyptian woman named Asenath. We have also noted that as yet there is no solid archaeological evidence to support the claim of a 430 year sojourn of Hebrews in Goshen (Exodus 12:40). But biblical archaeologists over the past century have built a case for this occurring during the Hyksos rule from their capital in Avaris in the eastern delta region.

Moses had considerable acquaintance with Egyptian culture also, but for a different reason. According to Exodus, Moses was born at a time when the relationship between the Hebrews and their hosts had changed to one of forced servitude. This likely corresponds to the ouster of the Hyksos kings and the return of Egyptian rule in the Nile delta region. The biblical description is that a pharaoh rose to power who did not know Joseph, and saw the massive numbers of Hebrews in the land as a danger to his rule. So he ordered male babies killed, to reduce the numbers and the threat. Jochebad, the mother of Moses, hid him in a basket (ark) which she set afloat among the reeds at the edge of the Nile. He was found by the daughter of the Pharaoh, who saw that he was Hebrew. His sister Miriam, who was watching from a distance, volunteered to find a Hebrew wet nurse for him. As discussed earlier, this was a common practice. She procured the services of his own mother. When he was weaned, he was brought to the Pharaoh's daughter, who named him Moses and raised him as a prince in the king's household. Nothing is said of the nature of his upbringing or education, but it can be assumed that he learned to write and was well informed in history, politics, and military science. He also knew that he was Hebrew. And one day, years later, he saw an Egyptian beating one of his fellow Hebrews, and in anger he killed the Egyptian. In time the Pharaoh learned of this event, and determined to have Moses killed. But Moses fled to Midian and lived there for the next 40 years. It was there that he was called by God to deliver the Israelites from their servitude in Egypt.[40]

The Israelites who left Egypt under the leadership of Moses were not the only Habiru who had some connections with and reliance upon Egypt. Nonetheless, with the Exodus, there is a major change in the nature of their culture, and soon they would have a recognizable distinction from other

Three. Judaism   93

Semites and Habiru. Archaeologists have struggled to agree on the date of such events, and which pharaoh might have been the antagonist in the Exodus saga. Most Egyptologists and biblical archaeologists have settled on a later date for the Exodus, concluding that Seti I (1308–1290 BCE) was the ruler who initiated the oppression of the Hebrews after Joseph's death, and Rameses II (1290–1224) was the pharaoh of the Exodus.[41] Others have argued for an earlier Exodus date of 1446 BCE, insisting that the pharaoh who killed the baby boys at the time of Moses' birth was Amenhotep I (1532–1511). By this reckoning, the princess who adopted Moses was Hatshepsut, and the pharaoh of the Exodus was Thutmoses III. The motivation for this earlier date of the Exodus is to harmonize archaeological data with biblical chronology, assuming literal accuracy of the biblical record.[42] Porten, a Jewish scholar writing for *Encyclopedia Judaica*, freely admits that "there are gaps and inaccuracies in the chronological and genealogical data in the Bible which are, moreover, mutually contradictory."[43] The 480 years from the Exodus to Solomon (I Kings 6:1) actually represents 12 generations, which would be considerably less time. Likewise, the 430 years of Egyptian bondage (Exodus 12:41) represents the four generations from Jacob to Moses, also significantly less time.

Van de Mieroop discusses the link between Moses and the Egyptian ruler Akhenaten. Some have asserted that during Moses' time among Egyptian royalty, he was inspired by the concept of monotheism Akhanaten presented in the cult of Aten. Unlike other Egyptian dieties, Aten was never represented as either human or animal. Van de Mieroop says that the great hymn to Aten resembles Psalm 104, which declares him to be the creator of all things, like whom there is no other. Sigmund Freud, infamous in some Christian circles, in his last published work called *Moses and Monotheism*, suggested that Moses was part of Akhenaten's court and during his time in Midian reshaped Aten into the creator God.[44] That may seem far-fetched, but we have to consider that several generations of life in Egypt must have shaped the Israelite culture in some way. And the stories of the great patriarchs recorded in Genesis were not written until long after the time of Moses. They were based on oral legends and myths and were likely reshaped in light of a new theology of their leader and the experience of the Exodus. If that is true, the stories of the patriarchs become another example of anachronism in Genesis, since they likely would have had the same beliefs as other Semites in that region, and both monotheism and ritual circumcision were inserted into their legends much later.

After the Exodus from Egypt and the establishment of the Law of Moses, Israelite customs took a form that was preserved with little variation until the Babylonian captivity, a period of approximately nine hundred years. What defined their culture from that time forward is the religious cult with a holy place, first a tabernacle and later a temple, as well as a priesthood, and clearly defined prescriptions for life and worship. These are presented in the other four books of the Pentateuch, namely Exodus, Leviticus, Numbers, and Deuteronomy. While traditionally these are called the books of Moses, and are commonly assumed to have been written by Moses, their origin is uncertain. It was previously thought that the book of Genesis was of at least three sources, called the Yahwist, Elohist, and priestly sources. In recent decades scholars have concluded that the initial composition can be identified as Yahwist, drawing from separate traditional stories about patriarchs, adding genealogies, itineraries and the "promise" motif to create a unified whole. The sections on prehistory were drawn from Greek and Mesopotamian sources, editing them to fit the current theology. This was subsequently expanded into the final edition by editors of the priestly source. The final version, along with the book of Deuteronomy, dates no earlier than the Restoration period, in the time of Ezra and Nehemiah. Thus, on the one end, Genesis attributes a theology to the patriarchs that developed after and as a result of the Mosaic Law code. On the other end, Deuteronomy provides a refined and expanded version of certain details of the Torah and elaborates the concept of covenant, reflecting the current interpretation of events over previous nine centuries.[45]

The stories included in the Hebrew Bible tell of a number of women who greatly influenced the history of Israel. Some of them are exceptional cases and reflect very little of the life typical of Hebrew women. Examples include Miriam, the sister of Moses and Aaron, a prophetess who led in worship and national triumph after the crossing of the Red Sea,[46] and Deborah, a prophetess who served as a military leader and judged Israel after the conquest of Canaan.[47]

Other stories portray the more normative life of women, of which Ruth is a prime example. Ruth was a Moabitess who lived in the time of the Judges and entered Judah with Naomi, her mother-in-law, after the deaths of their husbands in Moab. The account bearing her name gives insights into the gleaning customs of Palestianian farming communities, methods of matchmaking, the social manners of virtuous women of the era, and the contract of levirate marriages, to be discussed later.[48] More significant, this short story illustrates the plight of widows, old or young, and the fact that without some attachment to a male a woman faced life as a beggar. In negotiating a marriage between her daughter-in-law and the appropriate kinsman, Boaz, Naomi played a role that was a matter of survival for both of them.

Hannah also seems to typify women of her culture. She is best known for her earnest prayers to God for a son and her dedication in fulfilling the promise that he would be trained in the service of Yahweh.[49] From her brief story it can be learned that during the close of the rule of the Judges polygynous marriages were still contracted by Israelites, perhaps usually because of the barrenness of the first wife. It can be seen also that women were permitted to enter the holy shrines, such as Shiloh, to offer sacrifice and pray aloud. Biale offers Hannah's prayer as an example of supplicative prayers in which women were not exempt, as were the Shema, the morning and evening prayers, and the prayer after meals, according to the later Mishnah and commentaries on the mitzvah.[50]

Some biblical passages reflect general disdain for tyrant queens such as Jezebel and Athaliah, as well as for prostitutes, witches, false prophetesses, adulteresses, and nagging wives.[51] In contrast, there are numerous proverbs that reflect the love, devotion, and wisdom that typified mothers in the ancient community of Israel.[52] Proverbs 31:10–31 is famous as a description of the ultimate "worthy woman." This, however, is something of an enigma. The entire section is presented as the advice of King Lemuel, as taught him by his mother. It begins with the mother's encouragement not to cloud his mind by much drinking or to waste his energy on women. It is logical that the section on the worthy wife is also from Lemuel's mother, although commonly read as if written by a husband. Since there is no other reference to Lemuel, and since the Proverbs as a collection are attributed to Solomon, many have assumed that Lemuel is Solomon. The name simply means "belongs to God." It is not clear whether the section in question is a description of a real woman (the king's wife), or possibly an idealistic description of "the perfect wife," a woman who does everything while her husband sits idle at the gates with the elders. In fact, some scholars think that the writer (whoever it may have been) was being cynical, expressing dismay that such a woman cannot be found anywhere. If these were words of advice from Solomon's mother, Bathsheba, perhaps they were expressed in opposition to his collection of many wives and concubines.[53] Perhaps these words were her self-praise, in contrast with all those women who had led Solomon's heart away from God.

It is clear that the woman described here does not fit the stereotypical wife and mother in ancient Israel. This woman is obviously wealthy, in this context a queen, in charge of servants, and clearly more independent than would be the typical woman of her day. However, modern readers commonly take this passage as a description of the ideal woman, and therefore a model for female behavior and character in any culture and time. She is the woman, the wife, the mother, who has endless responsibilities, yet remains cheerfully and compliantly devoted to God and to her husband.

Social and Legal Status

It appears that Jews living in times closer to the emergence of Christianity maintained practices similar to their Gentile contemporaries with regard to the confinement of their women to the home. The Jews generally believed that restriction to the house was one of the ten curses placed upon Eve for her part in the fall of mankind, and it needed to be perpetuated.[54] It is interesting that the same passage in the Torah was never interpreted to restrict all Jewish males to farm labor. In any case, in their subjected position, Jewish women commanded a measure of dignity, although their social activities were strictly controlled. Pious Jews avoided familiarity with married women so as not to arouse suspicion of wrong intentions. For this reason a man was to refrain from conversing with women in the street, even with his wife, daughter or sister, and women were to conduct themselves with modesty and sobriety at all times.[55] It must be noted, however, that the emergence of such puritanical norms very likely resulted from a period, or very long periods, of prolific adultery and unchastity, even on the part of religious leaders, so that ultimately any conversation with a woman in public was a valid cause of suspicion. These attitudes help us to understand why Jesus was criticized for conversing with or being touched by women, particularly those of ill repute.[56]

A woman living in Jewish Palestine had practically no means of independent support. She had to be either a wife, a daughter, or a slave, and therefore bound to a man as some type of dependent.[57] In the cities there were certain exceptions, but even there in order for a woman to be a shopkeeper she had to be set up in business and supervised by her husband.[58] Legally, a girl was under the control of her father until she was 12½ years old. During these years the father could make claim to anything the girl earned, found, or was given.[59] This made each daughter an asset to a man's estate and a potential source of future income. Jewish women had few areas of legal self-assertion. A girl more than 12½ years old had the right to give herself in marriage, as could a widow, if no one had made arrangements on her behalf. Beyond this, the legal powers of women were virtually nonexistent. In Palestine, women were not even recognized as legal witnesses in courts of law. While this is nowhere suggested in the Tanakh, it clearly developed before the first Christian century. Josephus says: "But let not the testimony of women be admitted, on account of the levity and boldness of her sex."[60]

Marriage

A very ancient belief in Judaism was that marriage was a divine concept, that marriage partners were arranged by divine providence, and that each marriage was to be regarded as sacred because it consisted of a divine contract.[61] Therefore, it appears that every person, no matter how insignificant in the social hierarchy, was thought to fulfill an important role in the divine scheme of history simply by marrying and rearing children.

Over a long period, the Jewish rabbis favored early marriages. One rabbi commented that a man who had not married by the age of 20 spent all his days in sin, or at least in the thought of sin.[62] Marriage was considered a natural law and the command to "be fruitful and multiply" was understood to apply to every man.[63] Such a command was not applied to women, but from a practical standpoint there were no careers for women that compared with marriage and motherhood. Biale says that marriage was central to ancient Jewish society and everything seems to hang on it: social status, economic gains and stability, personal fulfilment, sexual satisfaction, and biological continuity.[64]

Marriages were usually arranged by the parents or by an outside party known as a matchmaker (*shadchan*).[65] The father was expected to find his son a wife and his daughter a husband. When such a partner was found, agreement had to be given by both the prospective bride and groom, but for the bride it was more a matter of acquiescence. If she did not agree to the mariage, she had to protest vigorously. Otherwise, her silence was taken as consent. A woman whose marriage was contracted while she was a minor might later exercise her right of refusal and be set free from the marriage without a bill of divorcement.

Biale points out that virtually nothing is known about words said or how a wedding ceremony might have been conducted in early Judaism. Before a couple were married there was a formal betrothal, a process called "acquiring" a wife. A female could be given in betrothal while she was still in her girlhood (*naarah*), which ended at the age of twelve years, six months and a day.[66] A man and woman were legally married with the formal act of betrothal, for at this point the projected marriage had been approved by all and the financial preliminaries had been settled by the families.[67] Sexual relations with another party during this period was considered adultery.[68] The Kiddushim specifies that a woman was acquired in one of three ways: money, or object of worth (*perutah*); deed (*shtar*); or intercourse (*bi'ah*). By that act, a man would set aside his wife and forbid her to all other men.[69] Although betrothal by intercourse or money was permitted by both Tenakh and Mishnah, it seems that later rabbis endeavored to suppress such practices and insist on more formal arrangements.

After the Mishnaic period, betrothal was preceded by an engagement (*shiddukhin*), and marriage was completed with a contract (*ketubah*) that specified the financial and legal obligations assumed by a husband toward his wife.[70] The *ketubah* required a husband to work to support and provide for the needs of his wife. But the wife also had considerable responsibility in fulfilling the marriage contract. The *ketubah is* vivid in its description of the domestic duties of the wife, varying with the number of servants she brought with her.[71] Her duties as a wife were also defined in terms of sexual relations.[72]

With the exception of intercourse during menstruation, a man could do with his wife whatever might please him. Her job, if she brought no dowry into the marriage, was to spin, weave, grind, bake, wash, cook, nurse and care for children, and make the bed. If she brought a servant into the marriage, or the means to buy one, she was exempt from grinding, baking and washing. If she brought two servants, she was also exempt from cooking and caring for her children. If she brought three servants, she was also exempt from working wool and making the bed. If she brought four, she was allowed to sit idle and do nothing.[73]

Virginity was expected in a bride, although such was not always the case. The Hebrew term *bethula* is the closest synonym of the English word "virgin." Rebekah is so described in Genesis 24:16; "a virgin, neither had any man known her." But probably the meaning of the term is simply "a young woman, a girl." The "tokens of virginity" were customarily returned to the father's house as evidence of satisfaction with her purity.[74] A woman who tried to pass for a virgin when she was not was considered to have "played the whore," and sinned against her father's house.[75] The rape of a virgin in ancient Israel was treated according to the circumstances. If she was betrothed, and the alleged rape occurred in the city where she could cry for help, both she and the male were stoned to death. If she was not betrothed, the offender had to pay her father and then marry her.[76] It is evident that the crime was not considered on moral grounds, but a violation of the rights and property of the male to whom she belonged, either father or husband.

Not all marriages were ideal, and numerous sources reveal the intense unhappiness of husbands whose wives were contentious, ill-tempered, and ungodly.[77] Jesus ben Sirach, in spite of his occasional positive comments concerning women, has been characterized a misogynist because of statements such as the following:

> A man will endure any wound but the heart's wound, and any malice but a woman's.... No head so venomous as a viper's, nor any anger like a woman's. Better share thy home with a lion and serpent both, than with an ill woman's company.[78]

Concerning polygyny, Mosaic and rabbinical laws present certain contradictions. Deuteronomy 21:15 suggests at least a tolerance of plural wives, no doubt reflecting practices among the ancient patriarchs, while later Judaism and the whole of Tannaite literature presuppose a monogamous society. Deuteronomy 17:17, which opposes a king collecting wives, appears to have arisen in the time of David and Solomon. However, nothing is ever said against it by the prophets of the day or by the court chroniclers. Moore suggests that the economic situation of the general population and the burden of the *ketubah* acted as a natural check on plural marriages.[79] But other scholars maintain that mankind in general has become dissuaded from polygamy by higher moral principles. Caverno speaks of polygamy as a great moral evil, impying that the numerous cases among ancient figures is an inexplicable violation of a higher norm. Abraham, he states, "was in the toils of polygamy, and it brought pain and retribution."[80]

All this considered, it is evident that the earliest Hebrew patriarchs, who are revered in Christian tradition as great men of faith, lived according to moral standards which are beneath those of both Jewish and Christian tradition.

Levirate Marriage

With the levirate marriage, from the Latin *levir* ("husband's brother"), early Judaism made provision for the perpetuation of family names, even when males died before siring children. The law also provided some means of reducing the number of unsupported widows. One category of widow was called a *yevamah*, a woman whose husband died without producing children. This law appears in Deuteronomy and states that in such a case, his surviving brother, called the *yabam*, was obligated to take her as his wife and give her children in the name of the deceased brother.[81] This arrangement is implied in the story of Onan, who married his brother's wife and used her for sex without allowing her to get pregnant.[82] And the levirate law is part of the intriguing plot in the story of Ruth. However, it contradicts laws in Leviticus that forbid a man to marry his brother's wife.[83] And it seems more like a postexilic amendment, devised to assist in the repopulation of Judah during its critical time of reconstruction. Nevertheless, the law is known in Jesus's day and is implied in the question posed by a group of Sadducees about the concept of resurrection of the dead.[84]

Another category of widow is the *agunah*, a woman whose marriage has ended or has been suspended because of the death or disappearance of her husband, and there is no valid way of attesting his fate. Biale discusses at length this very common and tragic circumstance for women in ancient Israel.[85] She suggests that for many women, the only solution was cohabitation, meaning to live with a man without benefit of legal marriage and the *ketubah*. Although not Jewish, the Samaritan woman encountered by Jesus at the well of Sychar may have chosen her specific mode of life out of desperation. Whether she was divorced or widowed is not stated, but only that the one she was now with was not her husband.[86] This too adds to our understanding of the plight of widows in Jerusalem during the early years of the church (Acts 6:1), as well as the circumstances that prompted the discussion of widows in I Timothy 5.

Adultery and Promiscuity

A problem which has persisted through the history of Judaism, as in virtually every culture, is that of adultery. In the Hebrew Bible adultery is expressed by the term *na'aph*, which is understood to be the illegitimate sexual intercourse of a woman with a man other than her husband.[87] It was categorically prohibited by the Torah, was punishable by death even in the time of Christ, and was generally considered by the Jews to be a grave sin against God. Guilty persons were amenable to the extreme penalty only when taken in the very act of adultery, and even the rabbis indicate the difficulty of obtaining such legal evidence. In cases of suspicion on the part of the husband, the accused wife had to undergo an ordeal of bitter waters, taken from Deuteronomy 5, to test her innocence. It is interesting that the apocryphal Christian work known as the *Protevangelium of James* claims that when it became known that Mary, the mother of Jesus, was found pregnant, both she and Joseph were required by the priests to submit to the bitter water ordeal to test their innocence. This practice dates from centuries earlier, but still may have been practiced in certain places.[88]

According to the Mishnah this practice was abolished by Johanan ben Zakkai sometime after 70 CE, on the grounds that men who usually stood in judgment over accused women were themselves not above the suspicion of immorality.[89] Perhaps even this admission is an understatement, for unchastity among Jewish men is common throughout ancient history. Such a double standard does appear to be consistent with the patriarchal system, however, and for this reason we might conclude that the form of adultery which they typically condemned is that involving a married woman, whereas sexual relations between a married man and an unmarried woman constituted an offense of a lesser category.[90]

Biale says that the law allows a man to engage in sexual relations with a wife and concubines, but the wife was restricted to relations with her husband only.[91] However, an unmarried and unbetrothed woman (called a *penuyah*) was as free to engage in sexual relations as any male, although the Halakah indicates that such behavior was considered promiscuity (*zenut*), a rather broad term that might even include adultery.

Lesbianism (called *mesolelot*) was known in ancient Judaism and was frowned upon. Homosexuality is among numerous sexual transgressions discussed in Leviticus 18 and 20 and described as an abhorrence (*to'evah*). Yet, it was thought by most rabbis that this was not the same degree of impropriety as intercourse with a male, because, so they assumed, there was no penetration in lesbian lovemaking.

In all this there is a gross discrimination against women, which no doubt was regarded by Jewish males as perfectly fair and logical. David and Vera

Mace suggest that the primary reason for such a double standard was the notion that the womb was sanctified soil for planting male seed. A wife who committed adultery betrayed her husband in the gravest possible manner, in that "the womb in which he planted his seed must not be contaminated by alien seed."[92] The man's situation, however, was entirely different in that he, being the bearer of the seed, could plant it wherever he chose, and he regarded all his children legitimate regardless of the womb in which they were nurtured.

Prostitution

The term *zonah* appears in both the Tanakh and the Halakhah and is generally translated "prostitute." But this, too, was debated among the rabbis and may have described any woman whose behavior was promiscuous, including adultery.[93] Afonso says that prostitution was an "accepted though deprecated" element of urban and rural life in ancient Judaism.[94] The term *zonah* often appears in the Hebrew Bible metaphorically, depicting Israel's unfaithfulness to God through idolatry.[95] In some instances, prostitution is mentioned as commonplace, with no written condemnation. References to Tamar's temporary harlotry and Rahab's profession include no moral judgment.[96] Samson's visits to a harlot in Gaza blend into the rest of his picturesque life, as if harmonious with local custom. And it would seem that during Israel's monarchy, harlots had legal recourse to the king's court to settle disputes, just as any other individuals.[97] Other texts, however, denounce prostitution as a shameful profession and sin against God. Israelites were not to prostitute their daughters, on penalty of flogging.[98] And priests were forbidden to marry such women. A priest's daughter who "played the whore" was to be executed by fire.[99] For a girl to engage in intercourse before marriage, and then to marry as a virgin, was regarded as "playing the whore" and thereby bringing reproach on the family and the nation of Israel.[100] Therefore, giving one's daughter to a man without benefit of marriage was a great evil in that it could lead to a community filled with bastards.

Despite opposition, prostitution seems to have thrived in ancient Jewish society. In preexilic Palestine, harlots could be encountered in streets and squares, accosting male passersby and soliciting business with alluring behavior and smooth talk. They bathed in public pools and entertained, both at home and in banquets, with music and singing. Their advances were dangers against which the wise sages warned naive young men.[101]

Talmudic writers express different opinions concerning prostitution, especially in the application of biblical texts to their own day. For example, while Deuteronomy 23:18–19 denounces prostitution and forbids the use of its revenue for paying religious vows, it was the opinion of R. Judah ha-Nasi that it was only forbidden to those for whom intercourse was a transgression, and the wages of unmarried prostitutes were acceptable for temple dues. According to Herr, some rabbis argued that money from a prostitute was acceptable, but not material goods.[102] In spite of all the differences of opinion and wrangling over terms and definitions, rabbis generally condemned all association with public prostitution, warning against approaching a harlot's door, and advising those who desired a sound reputation to avoid the harlot's market.[103]

The subject of cult prostitution is a current debate among scholars. In the past it was believed to exist in ancient Israel, as it has been claimed with regard to Babylonia and Greece. English translations of Deuteronomy 23:17–19 read "temple prostitute," and it is clearly denounced. It appears also that the periodic expulsion of harlots during the Divided Kingdom was related to their association with idolatry.[104] However, the term *kedesha* appears only four times in the Tanakh, and is defined as "consecrated woman" by Oesterley and Robinson.[105] These texts may pertain to having sex with women who worked in the temple but were not in fact prostitutes. According to II Maccabees 6:4, Antiochus Epiphanes introduced cult prostitutes into the Jerusalem Temple, outraging Jewish nationalists and contributing to the rise of the Maccabean Revolt in 167 BCE.[106] A fuller discussion of this debate is included in the next chapter.

Divorce

Jewish divorce laws had their origin in Deuteronomy 24:1–2. Concerning this passage some Jewish scholars conclude that the practice of divorce is presupposed, there being no law or record of the institution of divorce in the Old Testament.[107] Other passages allude to the practice but are unclear concerning the details.[108] In later times it became necessary to obtain the wife's consent before a divorce could be secured, unless she had given extreme cause for the action, but during and prior to the first Christian century such was unnecessary. The rule at that time was: "The man that divorces is not like to the woman that is divorced; for a woman is put away with her consent or without it, but a husband can put away his wife with only his own consent."[109] So, it appears that at one time in history divorce was effected simply by a verbal repudiation, although later it was necessary to appear before the court to make the act truly legal.

During the first Christian century there was considerable contention among the rabbis over the expression "unseemly thing" (*ervat davar*) in Deuteronomy 24:1–2. Sometimes translated "indecency," this was the only stated grounds in the Torah for divorcing a wife. The school of Shammai held that the only legitimate grounds for divorce was unchastity.[110] The school of Hillel, however, extended the phrase to include less serious faults, even the scorching of food. A century later later R. Akiva said that a man could divorce his wife even if he finds someone more attractive.[111] Regardless of the reasons, in general the right of males to divorce their wives was taken for granted.[112] The advice of Jesus ben Sirach expresses a callous attitude toward women: "If she go not as you would have her go, cut her off and give her a bill of divorce."[113] A woman was not allowed to divorce her husband under Jewish law, but there is evidence that under certain circumstances a woman could argue her case before the law courts and compel him to grant her a bill of divorcement, even against his will.[114] Grounds for such action included impotence, denial of conjugal rights, physical ailments, abusive treatment, or a nasty occupation, such as tanning.[115]

The Synoptic Gospels report that Jesus of Nazareth was drawn into this debate, but their reports of what he said differ.[116] Matthew reports Jesus siding with Shammai by offering the concession "except for fornication." Neither Luke's nor Mark's version has an exception. And Mark 10:12 is unique, being the only mention of the possibility of a woman divorcing her husband, which may suggest the writer's accommodation of Roman customs. It is interesting that Matthew and Mark don't agree as to whether this law came from God or Moses. All three Synoptics have Jesus stating that remarriage after divorce is tantamount to adultery.

There were occasions in Jewish history in which women sent their husbands bills of divorcement, although this violated tradition and the implications of law. Salome, sister of Herod the Great, so divorced Costobarus, and Herodias, the woman responsible for the death of John the Baptist, so divorced Philip the half brother of Herod Antipas, whom she subsequently married. Both cases were denounced by Josephus as unlawful.[117]

The strongest deterrent to divorce was the *ketubah*, which included various clauses assuring the wife of financial benefits payable out of the husband's estate in the event of divorce.[118] However, certain types of misconduct on the part of the wife were considered a just cause for nonpayment of the *ketubah*, and for this reason Jewish males were very interested in the technical definitions pertinent to divorce, realizing that frequent and unjustified divorce could prove extremely costly. This also helps explain why many Jews wanted to interpret the "unseemly thing" of Deuteronomy 24 to include much more than sexual infidelity. In so doing they were not only justifying the repudiation of an unwanted wife for trivial causes, but were also establishing legal defaults to warrant exemption from payment of her support.

Education

In ancient Israel there was little concern for any kind of formal education other than religious, and up to the second century BCE even this was limited to adults.[119] Under the influence of Hellenism, the Jews became aware of the value of elementary education, and schools were established in the synagogues, both inside and outside Palestine, for boys from the age of six.[120] Jesus ben Sirach, whose work began in the late third century BCE, is credited with introducing tuition-free education, and in his day private study sessions were often conducted in the homes of more capable students. Toward the end of the second century BCE, Simeon ben Shetah inaugurated the first system of community-supported public education, at which time the traditional sage began to give way to the scholastic instructor, or rabbi.[121]

From the earliest times the common opinion was that a woman had no need for formal education or technical instruction in the Torah. Her subordinate social and economic status required only the skills that could be learned from her mother by observation and imitation in the informal atmosphere of the home. Especially in rural communities, most girls were trained in weaving and cooking, midwifery, attending flocks, harvesting, singing, professional mourning and the usual skills related to marriage and motherhood. These are all skills demonstrated among women in the Tanakh. Beyond this, instruction was limited to the oral traditions of Israel's religious heritage and the principles of monotheism. In time divergent opinions developed among the rabbis concerning the need for and the approach to female education, and the question was hotly debated during the tannaic period. Eliezer ben Hyrcanus is representative of the view which ultimately prevailed: "There is no wisdom in a woman except with the distaff." The same rabbi stated on one occasion, "If a man gives his daughter knowledge of the Law, it is as though he taught her lechery."[122]

Others, however, seemed very favorable toward the education of women, at least for those who showed exceptional ability. Ben Azzai taught that a father had a responsibility to instruct his daughter in the Torah, and various statements in the Mishnah imply that many rabbis held a similar position.[123] Women were exempt from the "command" to study the Torah, although some rabbis permitted them to do so, but in general they were considered to lack the authority to instruct their children in technical or scholarly matters. This responsibility belonged exclusively to the fathers and rabbis.[124] Both women and unmarried men were excluded from formal teaching positions, and the Gemara explains that this restriction was because of the fathers and mothers. It may be that since the children were conducted to school by their parents, the restriction served to guard against immorality between a parent and teacher. It is also possible, however, that such restrictions were enforced out of social respect for the age and status of parenthood. A single man was possibly regarded as less qualified, and less suitable in a sense, to instruct children than the children's own mothers. Another woman was less suitable than the children's own mothers and certainly less than their fathers. But a married man who was also a scholar commanded both the respect and authority to serve in the stead of the parents as instructor of their children. Therefore, no woman or single man could fill this role. This rationale is clearly part of the complex paradigm of father rule and male superiority that existed in varying forms in other ancient cultures, and which would find its way into Christian tradition as well.

Although the education of women was viewed with increasing toleration by the first Christian century, advanced scholarship among females was rare. Learning to read was an initial complication, requiring a knowledge of ancient Hebrew and sufficient funds to obtain copies of the scriptures. This limited higher education to the wealthy, and also generally excluded women. Among the few exceptions were the maid servants of the patriarch Judah, around 165–200 CE, who were well enough instructed in classical Hebrew to comment on even rare terms in Scripture.[125]

Instruction of women in the Mishnah was even more rare, although by the second century CE it was at least acceptable in some rabbinic circles. Bereriah, wife of R. Meir and daughter of R. Hanina ben Teradion, is reported to have offered frequent correction in interpretation, as well as other opinions on literary questions, all of which were accepted without hesitation by her husband and other rabbis.[126] One might conclude, therefore, that by the first century CE the doors of education were opening to Jewish women, although most rabbis considered female scholarship exceptional and not strictly in keeping with feminine roles.

Religion

The rites and devotions in ancient Judaism were always conducted by men. A general rule was that women observed all negative ordinances, regardless of time, and participated in the rituals of sacrificial worship, although under supervision.[127] But women, slaves, and minors were exempt from reciting the Shema, wearing phylacteries, and all positions of religious leadership. As a rule, they were exempt from ritual prayer, Torah reading, and the study of the Torah. In short, women were excluded from every ordinance and ritual which depended upon a set time of year, month or day.[128] Maahs, who contends that the position of the Tenakh on the status of women is ambivalent, stresses that in the cultus of Israel, gender roles are not as rigidly defined as one might expect. Quoting Gerstenberger, he argues that what a woman could do was "a pragmatic and not a theoretical affair."[129]

Dating to the earliest Jewish laws, there were indeed certain regulations that pertained to women exclusively, due to physiology or domestic responsibility.[130] For example, a woman's atonement was incomplete after her menstrual discharge and after childbirth until she brought the necessary offering for purification.[131] There were also special ordinances pertaining to the sorceress, the wife incriminated under the Law of Jealousy, the daughter of a priest, and any woman making a vow. Beyond these, the balance of Israel's religious laws either excluded women explicitly, included them implicitly, or permitted their participation without constraint. Vos gives an exhaustive treatment of Old Testament regulations concerning women in worship, but the work does not deal with the more dramatic developments following the Babylonian Exile, which have greater relevance to early Christianity.[132]

In the restored temple women were permitted, although not required, to attend the three annual festivals; the feast of unleavened bread, the feast of weeks and the feast of tabernacles, all of which had been established in the Torah.[133] The proceedings were observed by women from the upper galleries around three sides of the women's court. This area was within the sacred precincts but was separate from the sacred enclosure in which the sacrifical worship took place, and from which women were prohibited.[134]

Women were required to make sacrifices, free-will offerings, thanks offerings, and offerings to complete vows, any of which could be after the order of a burnt offering or peace offering. However, since a woman could not come into the inner court to lay hands on the offering according to the sacrificial law, the question arose whether to dispense with that part of the rite in women's sacrifices.[135] In some cases the sacrifice was brought out into the women's court so the devotee could lay hands on it. It seems, however, that this procedure was more for the appeasement of discontent women than a compliance with regulations.[136]

The establishment of synagogue worship and the changes in custom following the Diaspora required certain modifications of the religious status of women, and there are a few hints that women enjoyed somewhat more involvment in synagogue worship than in the ancient temple. Rabbis allowed women to recite the Tefillah, as well as the benediction after meals, and were under the law of the Mezuzah. Although women were not included among the members of the synagogue, they were allowed to read publicly from the synagogue lessons, but not from the Torah.[137]

Considering the stricter norms of earlier times, one wonders if even a synagogue reading would have been tolerated by most rabbis. If it ever was permissible theoretically, the women were probably expected to decline any token opportunity to read. A tomb inscription from Smyrna, possibly dating from the second century CE, suggests that a wealthy woman named Rufina served as *archisynagogos* (director) of the synagogue there.[138] Sir William Ramsay, speaking of the changes in custom throughout Asia under Greek and Roman influence, alludes to this inscription, but he adds that the issue has been exaggerated by historians.[139]

Another custom, which has been the subject of considerable debate, is the separation of men and women in the synagogue assembly. Concerning unfounded claims to this effect, Strack says that "neither Old Testament nor New nor earlier Jewish tradition knows of a separate part of the synagogue for women; the passage so often cited from Philo is the much later *De Vita Contemplativa*."[140] It appears that the synagogue only came under such an arrangement in the fourth century CE by two rabbinical school leaders, Abaji and Raba.[141]

While the Tanakh might be ambivalent concerning the theoretical status of women, in mainstream Judaism there is an unmistakable bias in favor of men. Philo, of the early first century, clearly regarded women to be socially and spiritually inferior, depraved by nature, the initiators of sin and perversity.[142] While it can be said that the frequent grouping together of "women, slaves and minors" in rabbinic literature was purely for the purpose of liturgic exemption, one cannot avoid the impression that women were generally regarded as second-class human beings. This becomes an important consideration for Christians in the attempt to understand the household codes that have been used to support patriarchy as a component of Christian dogma.[143] The prayer of R. Jehuda in the Talmud is commonly quoted to illustrate the degradation of women in the eyes of the rabbis:

> R. Judah taught three things that a man should say every day: "Blessed be God; 1. for not creating me a pagan; 2. nor foolish; 3. nor a woman." He should thank God for not having been created a pagan, for he would be little esteemed, according to this verse (Isa. 40:17): "All nations before him are as nothing"; for not being a fool, because the fool feels no fear of sin; and finally, for not being a woman, because they are not subject to all the precepts of religion.[144]

It is important to note, as does Fiorenza, that this is not a misogynist statement, but rather a prayer of gratitude for male privilege.

Menstruation

Jewish law declared a menstruant woman as a *niddah*, meaning "one who is ostracized." This complex law is rooted in Leviticus 15, which deals with various bodily emissions that were considered to render an individual impure, whether male or female, and whether the emission was normal or the rusult of some disease or infection. These laws required a fixed time before the individual could be declared pure. In the early days of Israel's cult, offerings had to be brought to the entrance to the tabernacle, and priests would declare him or her clean.

The taboo on contact with a menstruating woman was more serious because of the fear of blood. There was also a distinction between impurity during normal menstruation and that associated with a longer discharge of blood. Biale explains that these laws rested in two different contexts: laws of purity and impurity, and laws on sexual prohibitions.[145] The former had the purpose of excluding a contaminated person from the divine residence, in Jerusalem meaning the temple. Anyone touched by a contaminated woman therefore would be considered impure and unfit to enter the temple, or to perform various rituals there. This, of course, ranged in history from the days of the tabernacle to the destruction of Herod's temple in 70 CE. There was a different application of these laws in areas of the Diaspora where the focus of religion had shifted to the synagogue. And generally after that time, the taboo of *niddah* shifted to matters of sexual intercourse and health. However, in a culture where religion was practiced primarily by males, and where religious purity carried great significance, being defiled by intimate contact with a woman, or even by the touch of her hand, was a matter of great concern. This fact is significant in New Testament studies, particularly with the apparent disregard Jesus had for many traditional taboos. He conversed openly with women he did not know and was not disturbed by their touch.

Summary

Woman in ancient Judaism was clearly viewed as subordinate to man, and in terms of creation a "divine afterthought." No amount of apologetics can alter or cover the fact that the rabbinic attitude and that of Jewish men in general up to the first century was clearly discriminatory and biased.[146] Women in general were considered to be physically, intellectually, and spiritually inferior to men, designed by God for pleasure and procreation. But by reason of their ceremonially impure bodies, they were ontologically unsuitable for direct spiritual ministry in worship.

Four

Greece

When it was published in 1975, Sarah Pomeroy's classic work *Goddesses, Whores, Wives, and Slaves* was on the leading edge of the feminist reassessment of women in antiquity. Focusing on classical Greece and Rome, Pomeroy warns in her introduction that care must be taken in drawing conclusions from ancient literature written by men. Some of the heroines of Bronze Age Greek tragedy do not represent the lives of ordinary women, but rather reflect the attitudes and fantasies of the male writers. The same is true of Homer, or whoever wrote the tales attributed to him. Some writers were clearly misogynists, Hesiod perhaps the most prominent example. Prose writers, in Pomeroy's view, often paint a truer picture of ordinary women. However, we now understand that some historians, such as Herodotus, intentionally distorted facts as a literary device. So, like investigators at a crime scene, modern historians are obligated to sift carefully through evidence to distinguish fact from fiction. The challenge is to discover the genuine nature of women's lives when the details have been ignored, distorted, or intentionally undisclosed, and to correctly interpret those ancient artistic, dramatic, historical, and legislative images of womanhood.

Sufficient writers in ancient Greece speak on the subject of women to demonstrate patriarchal and androcentric structures that doubtless had developed long before their time. Xenophon explained gender role distinction in Greek law and custom as following the natural order of things designed by deity. The outdoor and public world is assigned to men, and private interior matters are assigned to women.[1] Thus in the opinion of some Greeks, the sad saga of female subordination and debasement was justified and essential, based on woman's own nature and the will of the gods.

However, the stereotype of the quiet, secluded, and subordinate Greek wife is not accurate at all times and places. Pomeroy shares the optimism of recent feminist scholars that critical reexamination of evidence will result in a clearer and more accurate image of the role and status of women in antiquity

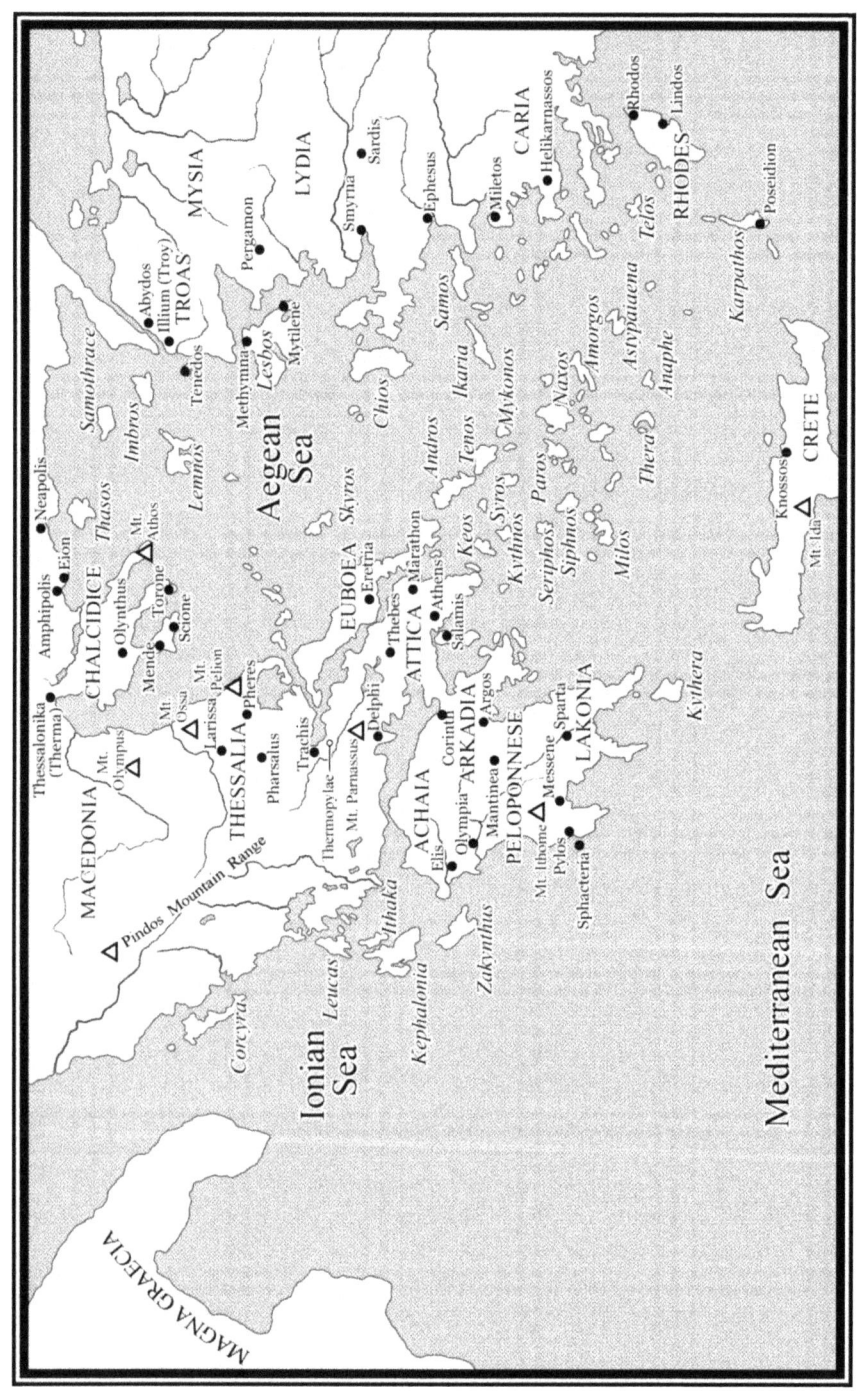

and will also contribute to the resolution of contemporary problems between men and women.[2] That is certainly part of our present objective.

Female Deities

As in certain other cultures, the meaning assigned to womanhood in ancient Greece is evident in religious mythology. Acknowledging that gods and goddesses are human constructs intended to provide explanation and order to both cosmos and society, we find in Hesiod's *Theogony* the earliest Greek portrayal of divine evolution.[3] Thought to have lived between 750 and 650 BCE, Hesiod may have drawn from older Babylonian, Mycenaean, and Hittite myths to create his own stories of the origins, nature, and activities of gods and goddesses. Nonetheless, he undoubtedly portrayed female deities according to his perception of women in his own surroundings.

As do most other ancient creation myths, *Theogony* begins with an image of a primordial abyss containing the essential elements out of which the cosmos and all living things would emerge. The first generation of deities began with the goddess Gaia (from *Ge*, earth), then Tartarus (cavelike underworld), with Erebus (darkness between earth and underworld), Eros (reproductive desire), and Nyx (night). Then Erebus and Nyx produced Aether (the upper atmosphere) and Hemera (day). From Gaia came Uranus (sky), Ourea (mountains), and Pontus (sea). Then Gaia and Uranus mated to produce twelve Titans,[4] no doubt divine personifications of certain notable figures in earlier Greek history or legend. They also produced powerful creatures that included three cyclopes (Brontes, Steropes, and Arges) and three Hecatonchires (hundred-hands), whose names were Kottos (the furious one), Briareos (the vigorous one), and Gyges (the large-limbed one).

Hesiod describes how a second generation of deities was produced. Repulsed by the Hecatonchires, Uranus hid them away in the underworld. Gaia was outraged by his action and recruited the Titans to punish their father. Only Cronus responded, and with a sickle provided by his mother he castrated Uranus. Drops of blood on the ground, along with the testicles that he threw into the sea, then produced more children. One was Aphrodite, described in some myths as the daughter of Uranus and the goddess Thalassa, but here emerging from the substance of Uranus alone.

A third generation of deities was born of very complex relationships among the previous deities. Cronus gained control of the cosmos, although Uranus and Gaia were confident that one of his children would overthrow

Opposite: Greece and vicinity, fifth century BCE. Donald T. Massey (illustrator) and Lesly F. Massey, 2015.

him. When he married Rhea, his sister and fellow Titan, Cronus swallowed each of the children she birthed in order to safeguard his continued power. They were Hestia, Demeter, Hera, Hades, Poseidon, and Zeus. However, Rhea pleaded with Gaia and Uranus to help her save Zeus by sending her to Crete to give birth, and by giving Cronus a huge stone to swallow instead of the child. After his birth, Gaia hid Zeus in a cave beneath the Aegean Mountains. Then somehow tricked by Gaia, Cronus regurgitated his other five children, who allied with Zeus in a war against the Titans for control of the cosmos. The Hecatonchires were rescued by Zeus and assisted in defeating the opposing divine forces.

Zeus ultimately produced 19 other children from various mothers. They were all daughters and all virgins. The first three were born of Themis (Right), and their names are Eunomia (Order), Eirene (Peace), and Dike (Justice). Blundell interprets this as suggesting that the violence and injustice of the previous rule were left behind, in favor of a peaceful and enlightened government where the female principle is governed by patriarchy. In Pomeroy's view, Hesiod outlines a progression from divine matriarchy to patriarchy, and with it a shift from "female-dominated generations characterized by natural, earthy emotional qualities to the superior and rational monarchy of Olympian Zeus."[5] Hesiod's reason, no doubt, was to state his own opinion of womanhood, but more significantly, to explain in myth how woman had come to her state of subordination. This is not to suggest that Hesiod knew of a time when human societies were matriarchal, but only that he viewed woman's subordinate status as justified and essential, and perhaps degraded from her primordial state.

Reminiscent of the biblical story of Eve, the Greek myth of Pandora blames woman for all the ills of the world. Hesiod offered his version of the Pandora myth in *Works and Days*.[6] He suggested that Pandora was the first woman created by the deities, who bequeathed to her certain gifts. Among them, and clearly viewed as sinister, was the gift of seduction. These gifts were held in a jar (*pithos*) which, when opened by Pandora out of mere curiosity, released all kinds of evil into the world, ranging from disease to the drudgery of work. Aristophanes echoes the power of this myth by describing women as "a plague, the source of all evils to man."[7] Hesiod definitely saw in women all the woes of humanity.

> But when he had made the beautiful evil to be the price for the blessing, he brought her out, delighting in the finery which the bright-eyed daughter of a mighty father had given her, to the place where the other gods and men were. And wonder took hold of the deathless gods and mortal men when they saw that which was sheer guile, not to be withstood by men. For from her is the race of women and female kind: of her is the deadly race and tribe of women who live amongst mortal men to their great trouble, no helpmeets in hateful

poverty, but only in wealth. And as in thatched hives bees feed the drones whose nature is to do mischief—by day and throughout the day until the sun goes down the bees are busy and lay the white combs, while the drones stay at home in the covered skeps and reap the toil of others into their own bellies— even so Zeus who thunders on high made women to be an evil to mortal men, with a nature to do evil.[8]

From this demeaning description of women in general, Hesiod moves to brighter days with the victorious Olympians in charge of the world. There is certainly irony in his inclusion of six chief goddesses in the ultimate generation of Greek deities: Athena, Artemis, Hestia, Aphrodite, Hera, and Demeter. Despite the fact that they serve under the governance of Zeus, the chief of the gods, they all are important to Greek culture and have many powers that impact the lives of mortals. In this, Hesiod may have intended a patronizing element to soften the indignity and injustice of woman's subjugation. But that station is very clear in the myths.

Sue Blundell offers a thorough assessment of the attributes and roles of these goddesses in Greek antiquity.[9] There is irony also in that three of the six are portrayed as virgins, while male Olympians are typically sexually active, and four of the female deities are portrayed as active outside the home in matters typically associated with men. This indicates the complex and almost contradictory view of womanhood in Hesiod's time. On the one hand woman is strong, attractive, skilled, and her sexuality is mysteriously intriguing and irresistible. She is intelligent, abounding in earthy wisdom, and the giver of life. On the other hand, she is inferior to males in physical strength. She is unstable and untrustworthy, and there is something about her sexuality that is sinister, ugly, and threatening. The importance of virginity in certain female deities clearly stands in juxtaposition to the primary purpose and role of woman in ordinary Greek society, as dutiful and loyal wife, and also bountiful and nurturing mother.

The first of these Olympian goddesses is Athena, portrayed by Hesiod as having no mother, but produced by Zeus alone.[10] Athena is best known in connection with her patron city Athens, and her virginity was honored in the name of the temple where she was worshipped, the Parthenon (from *parthenos*, virgin). She is commonly depicted as somewhat androgynous, having both feminine and masculine attributes. One descriptor was Athena Ergana (the worker woman), associated with handcrafts, olive oil production, and other common but important industries on which the entire culture depended. She was also thought of as the founder of the textile industry in Greece, celebrated in a quadrennial festival called the Panathenaea.

A second and more common representation of Athena was that of warrior goddess. She is often portrayed dressed in armor and carrying weapons. In this capacity she intervened to assist Achilles in defeating the Trojan Hector in their mano a mano confrontation, and she also guided Odysseus in war against the Trojans and in his legendary exploits as he made his way home to Ithaca.[11] Associated with this is her role of mentor and encourager (*kourotrophos*) of young men. Neither Achilles nor Odysseus was a unique protégé of Athena. Blundell summarizes:

> For Jason she constructs the *Argo* in which he sails off in quest of the golden fleece. Bellerophon is presented by the goddess with a golden bridle, so that he can tame the winged horse Pegasus. When Perseus cuts off the head of the Gorgon Medusa, it is Athena who guides his hand. Above all, Heracles, the archetypal hero, is able to rely on the goddess as his mentor and helpmate in many of his labors.[12]

Wisdom, described by the term *sophia* and symbolized by the owl, is also a significant attribute of Athena. But it is interesting to note that this concept shifted during or after the time of Aristotle. In preclassical Greece, wisdom was associated with the knowledge and skills of trades. The wife of Zeus was named Metis, a term which described knowledge and counsel in crafts, perhaps even sorcery. Later emphasis shifted to a philosophical concept of wisdom, and so the role of Athena slowly evolved from knowledge of trades and crafts to philosophical understanding of life and social structure.

The goddess Artemis, also a virgin, was the twin sister of Apollo, born to Zeus and Leto. From childhood, so it was imagined, Artemis was inclined to the outdoors. In maturity she became a huntress and was described as "sister of the archer god, a maiden who delights in arrows, who grew up with Apollo."[13] But it is Hera, her stepmother, who calls her "a lion among women," adding that Zeus gave her permission to kill at will.[14] In one portion of her myth, it is said that Artemis and Apollo united to bring punishment upon a mortal named Niobe, because the woman boasted that she had produced more children than Leto, the mother of the twin deities. So, armed with bow and arrow, Apollo killed her six sons while Artemis killed her six daughters. Another example of the destructive nature of Artemis is that she persuades Agamemnon to sacrifice his daughter Iphigenia in order to gain favorable winds for his attack of Troy.

There is reason to think that the destructive tendencies portrayed in Artemis might relate to the ancient practice of human sacrifice. Pausanias discusses a place named Limnaeum, associated with the worship of Artemis, where there once was a wooden image. It was stolen by Orestes and Iphigenia, and the Lacedaemonians claimed that it was then brought to their land. The image carried with it power to drive people insane, incite violence, and spread disease. Because of this, an oracle was given to stain the altar with human blood, choosing a victim by casting lots. However, Pausanias explains as follows:

Lycurgus changed the custom to a scourging of the lads, and so in this way the altar is stained with human blood. By them stands the priestess, holding the wooden image. Now it is small and light, but if ever the scourgers spare the lash because of a lad's beauty or high rank, then at once the priestess finds the image grows so heavy that she can hardly carry it. She lays the blame on the scourgers, and says that it is their fault that she is being weighed down. So the image ever since the sacrifices in the Tauric land keeps its fondness for human blood. They call it not only Orthia, but also Lygodesma (willow-bound), because it was found in a thicket of willows, and the encircling willow made the image stand upright.[15]

So, it would seem that Artemis portrayed a sinister side of womanhood, the tendency to initiate quarrels, to lash out in anger, and to exact revenge by blood.

Hestia is commonly known as the goddess of the hearth. She, like the typical Greek wife, stayed at home to keep the fires burning. Ironically, Hestia is also portrayed as a virgin. According to myth, she was courted by both Apollo and Poseidon, but she refused their advances. Then touching the head of Zeus, she made a vow to remain forever a virgin.[16] Zeus rewarded her commitment to purity with a place of honor in the home. In this she became a partial role model for all Greek women, remaining mostly at home attending to domestic responsibilities. So, by not venturing into the arena of male activities, Hestia seems rather dull. Perhaps this also explains why little about her is included in mythology. Of course, her virginity is a contradiction to that role, but it serves as a symbol of perpetual purity and her resistance to the advances of other males.

There is a certain tension in Greek culture, in that women are the keepers of the home but are also somewhat domestically transient. They leave the home of the father or guardian and relocate to the home of a husband. In that, the role of wife as keeper of the hearth and home seems rather unsettled. Only in the image of Hestia is there added to the home a sense of permanence. She represented solidarity and support, as well as stability and security, both at home and in the community.[17]

Hera is the sister of Zeus, but myth portrays her as the wife and queen of Zeus. They have two daughters, Hebe and Ilithyia, who are relatively insignificant as goddesses. Of their two sons, Ares is an ill-tempered war god. The other, Hephaestus, is born lame. Hera is not a good mother. She is ashamed of Hephaestus and throws him into the sea. He survives and in an underwater grotto he learns the trade of blacksmith, which he uses vengefully against his uncaring mother. Homer also portrays Hera as nagging and controlling. Upon learning that Zeus has produced a child (Athena) without her body as a vessel, she retaliates by producing the serpent-creature Typhoeus.[18]

One of the strangest things about the Hera myth is that each year her virginity was restored by bathing in a spring called Canathus, located near Nauplion, a ritual recorded by Pausanias.[19] This might represent the importance of sexual purity and fidelity, expected in all Greek wives. It may also represent the expectation by Greek husbands that wives keep their bodies clean and healthy.

Hera was prominent in Greek society as the goddess of weddings and marriage, being particularly revered by young women. She assisted in preparing for the marriage ceremony, and in uniting the couple. Aristophanes records a chorus of prayers offered to her.[20] Pausanias describes the temple dedicated to Hera and a quadrennial festival at Olympia in her honor, in which young women participated in foot races. They wore short tunics with the right shoulder and breast exposed.[21]

And any authority or power seen in her is derived from her husband: Homer states through Aphrodite that honor must indeed be given to a goddess who reclines in the arms of Zeus, the greatest of the Greek gods.[22] Hera represents the paradigm of subordination of Greek wives, for no matter how glamorous or powerful she may appear or how honored she may be in religious ritual, any appearance of authority is within the system of male dominance. Also, the tension between Zeus and Hera represents the common attitude of Greek men toward wives and motherhood.

Aphrodite is perhaps the best known of all female Greek deities. According to Hesiod, when Cronus castrated his father and threw the genitals into the sea, a white foam appeared, out of which arose the beautiful Aphrodite. She floated slowly on the waters until she arrived at Cyprus, where her role among mortals began.[23] Hence, she is sometimes called "the Cyprian."[24] Aphrodite, like the Mesopotamian Ashtarte (Isis), is the goddess of love and sexuality. Her consort and companion is Eros (sexual desire). With this desire being significant in primitive human society, the influence of Aphrodite traces to the most ancient roots of Greek culture. However, Aphrodite is not portrayed as a loyal and adoring wife. She is sexually promiscuous and adulterous. She is initially married to the blacksmith Hephaestus, but has affairs with the gods Hermes and Ares, as well as mortals like Anchises and Adonis. It is Aphrodite who encourages the relationship of Paris and Helen that leads to the Greek war with Troy.

The Adonis myth tells us something of the nature of Aphrodite. She falls in love with him when he is still a child, and to protect him she consigns him to the care of Persephone in the underworld. When Persephone later refuses to let him go, Aphrodite makes an appeal to Zeus, who like the wise Solomon of Israel is forced to make a difficult decision. Similar to assigning joint custody of a child in a modern domestic dispute, Zeus divides the annual residence of Adonis into thirds; one part with Aphrodite, one with Persephone, and the third to be spent alone.

Some might conclude that the Adonis myth symbolizes the annual death and revival of vegetation in regular cycles. The name Adonis is derived from the western Semitic term *Adon*, meaning "lord." However, associated rituals seem void of celebration of love, marriage, or renewed life. The Adonia, a festival celebrated primarily by Greek women, centered on mourning for the dead Adonis. As part of the ritual, women would place in soil certain plants with short lives. When they sprouted and then withered, mourning would follow. Another festival held primarily in Alexandria involved a wedding of Aphrodite and Adonis, followed by a ritual of grief while the image of Adonis was cast into the sea. These seem to point to an underlying fear of something lost, perhaps even the male fear of female sexuality. In all this there is represented a perspective that Greek women are prone to infidelity and must be guarded carefully. Aphrodite is good at sex, and very alluring, but she is neither a devoted wife nor a loving and nurturing mother. She has the power and inclination to create chaos and to destroy marriages, families, and nations.[25]

The sixth female Olympian is Demeter, her name derived from the Greek word for mother (*meter*). Although she is often described as "the mother goddess" or "the goddess of the harvest," the scope of Demeter's importance to the Greeks was much broader. She presided over the sacred law as well as the cycle of life and death. Her connection to the earth was not the control of vegetation, but the human role in cultivating the earth, planting, and harvesting grain. Among the earlier myths about her is the Homeric "Hymn to Demeter," dating perhaps to the seventh century BCE. The writer describes how Persephone, Demeter's daughter, was picking flowers one day when she was abducted by the god Hades and carried down to the underworld. Demeter spent several days wandering the earth by torchlight, searching for her daughter. Eventually she learned that this happened by the consent of Zeus, and that Persephone was now the bride of Hades. In anger, Demeter left Mount Olympus to live among mortals and used her power to prevent the growth of grain. A great famine resulted, and efforts by Zeus to placate her failed. Eventually, the god Hermes was sent to the underworld to negotiate the return of Persephone. According to the "Hymn to Demeter," the result was much like the myth of Adonis: time had to be shared between two realms.[26] The blooming of flowers in spring, therefore, indicates the presence of Persephone with her mother again.[27] Over time, the myths concerning Demeter and Persephone were altered and grew, eventually being associated with the birth of the Eleusinian Mysteries celebrated in September, just before planting season. This will be discussed in another section.

The symbolic and metaphorical meaning of Demeter and Persephone have attracted the interest of psychologists such as Carl Jung, who suggested that the two deities represent two distinct phases in a woman's life, maidenhood and motherhood, each connected to the other and extending forward and backward. Together they represent something like immortality, and the role of womanhood in providing continued life to the community.[28] Blundell sees rather a negative implication for a young woman living at that time. It might suggest that leaving home to become a wife is something of a death experience, which at least holds the potential for a new sense of life and personal identity.[29]

In short, the gods and goddesses of ancient Greece represent both the most beautiful and the most fearful elements of the cosmos, and also the most noble and the most sinister characteristics in humanity. Pollux (second century CE), a Greek scholar and rhetorician from Naukratis in Egypt, describes the gods of the Greek pantheon as

> above the heavens, in the heavens, on the earth, in the sea, underground, guarding the hearth, guarding the city, ancestral, of the clan or kin, of the market, of the harvest, of the camp, propitious, who turn away evil, who make free from trouble, who cleanse and purify, who put to flight, saviors who bestow security, who attend birth, betrothal, and wedding, and protect the grape.[30]

But apart from all the wonder and vast scope of the alleged role of Greek deities in the cosmos, we must recognize that a significant underlying theme in the myths is a defense of patriarchy.

Homeric Literature

The earliest description of Greek customs appears in Homer's *Iliad* and *Odyssey*, dated no earlier than the ninth century BCE but contextually reaching back to the late Bronze Age. This period is also called the archaic period, or pre-classical era, ending around 500 BCE. The identity of Homer is still a mystery, and some question his very existence. There is certainly debate concerning the accuracy of his tales about Midos, Knossos, and the Trojans. The works of Homer appear to be a development of numerous tales and legends, consolidated perhaps by one writer. Pomeroy says that Homer was illiterate, and his stories were passed on orally for generations before they were written in the sixth century.[31] Whether by Homer or someone else, these works came to be revered by the Greeks in the classical period, and today are perhaps the most famous of all ancient Greek literature. Like the goddesses of Hesiod's mythology, the women of the *Iliad* and *Odyssey* are fictional and serve primarily as literary devices. Little about the lives of ordinary women can be gleaned from Homer's tales, but they are significant as reflections of prevailing attitudes toward womanhood.

The *Iliad* is commonly said to be about the Trojan War, but it is really about the rage of Achilles, leader of the Myrmidon contingent and the greatest Greek hero in that war. The narrative begins nine years after the start of the war, as the Achaeans raid a Trojan-allied town and capture two women, Chryseis and Briseis. Agamemnon, commander of the Achaean army, takes Chryseis as his prize and Achilles claims Briseis. Chryses, a Trojan priest of Apollo, offers the Greeks wealth for the return of his daughter Chryseis. Although the Greek army finds this offer appealing, Agamemnon refuses. Chryses prays for the intervention of Apollo, to which the god responds with a plague within the Greek army. After nine days, Achilles calls an assembly to push for a solution. Under pressure, Agamemnon agrees to return Chryseis to her father, but also decides to take as compensation Briseis, who is the prize and property of Achilles. Angered, Achilles declares that he and his men will no longer fight for Agamemnon, but will go home. Odysseus, hero of the second great Homeric epic, takes a ship and brings Chryseis to her father, whereupon Apollo ends the plague. Between the two captive girls, the only one who displays any measure of personality is Briseis, who mourns the death of Patroclus because he was kind to her.

However, the woman who features most prominently in the *Iliad* is Helen. She is the wife of Menelaus, king of Mycenaean Sparta and brother to Agamemnon. And while it is claimed that she was abducted, she actually left Menelaus willingly and resolutely to be with Paris, young prince of Troy. However, her personality is portrayed as capricious and ambivalent, and without a doubt she is the cause of the war. Once the Greeks have landed on Trojan shores, Helen taunts Paris to fight to keep her, although she points out that he will probably be killed.[32] To the writer of this epic, she clearly represents a perception that women possess a mystical allurement, and with it the capacity to bring misery into a household and to incite war between nations by inflaming the passions of rival mortals. A scene at the Scaean gate illustrates the point. Iris, the messenger goddess, comes to Helen in the form of Laodice, the most beautiful of the daughters of Priam, king of Troy. She informs Helen that the war between the Greek and Trojan soldiers has come to a halt, and Paris and Menelaus are preparing to fight. Helen's heart turns from her love for Paris to longing for her husband, Menelaus. She dons a veil, and in tears hurries down to the Scaean gate in the company of two servants. There Priam sits with the elders, too old to fight but full of conversation, like cicadas singing in a tree. When they see Helen approaching, they whisper to each other.

> No one could blame Trojans and Greeks for suffering so long for a woman's sake. She is fearfully like the immortal goddesses. All the same, and lovely as she is, let her sail home and not stay here, a scourge to us and our children after us.[33]

Andromache, wife of Hector, also has a significant role in this protracted story, and one that paints a picture of womanhood with greater character and wisdom than Helen. Yet it is clear that her personal identity is defined primarily by her relationship to men—father, brothers, and husband. After the first engagement with the Greek army, she runs to meet Hector at the city gates and pleads with him not to return to battle. She has lost her own parents as well as seven brothers over the course of time, and she begs him not to make her a widow and her child an orphan.[34] So, her role in the story, along with Hector's mother Hecabe, is to provide the tension of restraint for the sake of her own needs and the security of the family and home. Her distress is evident: men do what men do often for reasons that seem less than trivial, often at great expense, and with very little possible gain.

Women in the *Odyssey* occupy a more prominent position than those of the *Iliad*, and have stronger personalities. However, their power is often negative and malevolent. This tale is about the hero Odysseus and his long journey home to Ithaca after the war with Troy. He encounters several females along the way who pose something of a threat, either physical or moral. He is introduced sitting on the beach, having spent seven years on an island belonging to the nymph Calypso, who is obsessed with winning his love. He has lost his ship and all his crew and is trapped on the island. During this time his wife Penelope and his son, prince Telemachus, are at home in Ithaca, warding off suitors and trying to maintain order and stability.

In time, Zeus sends Hermes to rescue Odysseus from Calypso. She is persuaded to permit Odysseus to build a new ship and depart. The hero sets sail, but the sea god Poseidon causes a storm to wreck his ship. Athena intervenes, and Odysseus lands at Scheria, home of the Phaeacians, where he is found by the princess Nausicaa and is welcomed by the king and queen. They have heard of his exploits at Troy and promise to assist him in his journey home if he will tell them about his adventures. So, Odysseus spends the night describing the events that brought him to Calypso's island. His story includes the events in the land of the Lotus Eaters, his battle with a Cyclops, and his affair with the witch Circe, who turns his men into swine. He also recounts their temptation by the deadly Sirens, his journey into Hades to consult the prophet Tiresias, and his fight with the sea monster Scylla.[35]

Blundell discusses the explicit sexual imagery in portions of this story, especially with Calypso and Circe—the reduction of men to animals, or to impotence once naked, the irresistible allurement of the Sirens, and the forcible assertion of masculinity that changes the woman's damaging passion into positive and supportive love. Even the young Nausicaa is attracted to Odysseus, and at least for a time she is a temptation, which the hero resists before continuing his journey homeward.[36]

While the focus of Homeric literature is the endeavors and exploits of men, women play significant roles. They are typically treated with respect and occupy positions of honor. In fact, it would seem that women were virtually venerated in Homer's time, although the honors related directly to their beauty and feminine charm. There is also evidence in Homeric literature of a bride-price (*hedna*), a relic from much earlier times.[37] Pomeroy suggests that one of the factors that contributed to the female image in this era was that there were more women than men. While male children were preferred, and female infants often exposed, it is possible that the number of men who died in battle created this gender disproportion.[38]

Already during this era the natural confinement of women to the home in rearing young, gathering medicinal plants, supervising the household, tending and training animals, all blended to create an aura of respect, as if women were closer to nature than men. Nowhere in Homeric literature does there occur any rude or abusive treatment of women as a class. Single women felt free to mingle with young men in public places, to attend dances and banquets, and to meet their sweethearts for amorous play without fear of social reprimand.

However, most of the females in Homer's stories are wives and daughters of tribal chieftains and do not fairly represent the status of women in general.[39] And these women, who in reality were a few highly respected females in a male-dominated society, are the only supportive evidence offered for matriarchy during this era.[40] Nevertheless, women of Homeric Greece appear to have enjoyed a degree of honor and respect not commonly reported in later times.[41] Odysseus says of his relationship with Penelope:

> There is no finer, greater gift in the world than that when a man and woman possess their home together, two minds, two hearts, that work as one. Despair to their enemies, a joy to all their friends, their own best claim to glory.[42]

Transition to the Polis

From the days of Homer and Hesiod to the classical age, a great change occurred in the status of Greek women. Several factors may have contributed to their rapid degradation. Initial changes in Greek polity were brought about by laws enacted in Athens. Draco is credited with the first constitution of Athens (c. 621 BCE) and various laws, such as the death penalty for certain crimes and the sale of a debtor into slavery.

Eva Cantarella argues that one Draconian law in particular defined the prevalent Greek attitude toward women, that being the law of adultery (*moicheia*). This law allowed the killing of a man who had sexual relations with another man's wife, but the wife was not killed. Rather, she was treated as one violated, a victim, even if she had consented to intercourse and thus demonstrated her inability to know right from wrong. Also, she was considered to have been defiled or corrupted (*moicheutheisa*) by this relationship, and therefore she was subject to repudiation by her husband.[43] This, it seems, defined woman both as irresponsible and therefore in need of supervision, and the property of her husband, to be dispensed with if no longer suitable.

According to Plutarch, Solon later repealed all of Draco's laws except those relating to homicide.[44] From one standpoint the laws made a positive contribution to the future of humanity, in that his concept of equality among citizens provided a basis for the development of democracy. But the two principal flaws in Solon's design were the division of society into slave and citizen classes, and an official advocacy of the subordination of women.[45]

A by-product of his government was an increasing interest in warfare and conquest. Once the Greeks discovered and developed metal alloys and manufactured implements, they turned warfare into a profitable business. Dorians destroyed the remaining peaceful civilization of Aegean peoples and began exploits in surrounding areas. During this period, aged tribal chieftains gave way to young and vigorous warrior-politicians. The former were more interested in the defense of local property, which included their women. The latter had visions of expanded borders and new conquests. As they returned from exploits in Miletus and Sardis, having established contact with the Persians who had invaded Ionia, they brought new views of the role and station of women and the meaning of womanhood. It may be that men saw something advantageous in the Asiatic idea of the harem and so were prompted to follow their own pleasures without criticism from mothers, sisters, or wives.

Some viewed women a little above cattle, each with her own intriguing but inferior traits. Simonides of Amorgos divided women pedantically into ten categories, each represented by an animal and each intentionally degrading: the daughter of a sow, the fox-woman, the busy bee, the proud mare, the daughter of a barking bitch, and such like.[46]

During the transition to the classical era, the family group (*oikos*) became the essential basic unit of the larger social structure, the city (*polis*). If there had been any matrilocal and matrilineal practices in earlier Greek societies, during this time they gave way to patriarchal monogamy, with the legitimate wife reduced to an agent of procreation. Married men commonly engaged in relationships with other women, but wives were expected to be faithful to their husbands. Other women were considered to be objects of male pleasure and amusement.[47] The essential status of the wife shifted to one of ignorance, seclusion, silence, and inactivity.

The legal status of Greek women can be stated concisely. As a natural result of the social norms which held women to their lives of seclusion and dependence, the law regarded them as minors all their lives, with no more civil authority than a child.[48] Every female was under the legal care of a guardian, and at the death of her husband a son assumed the role. The male in this role was called lord (*kyrios*) of the household.[49] He was the head in terms of authority and guardian in terms of financial support and protection. No woman could conduct any kind of legal transaction, and anything done by a male upon the advice of a woman was legally invalid.[50] Plutarch indicates that a woman had the right to bring charges against her husband for adultery, by entering a writ of divorce.[51] Otherwise, women in the vicinity of Athens were legal nonentities.

Naturally, such censorious regulations as those of Draco and Solon did not affect the entire Greek culture but were limited to upper classes and city dwellers. Athens is commonly taken as normative for all of Greece, because we have so much more information about it. However, there is ample reason to conclude that the poorer rural communities remained traditionally linked to the unrestrained Homeric days. Dio Chrysostom reports concerning a village in Euboea, in central Greece, that the women freely associated with the men, sat at the same tables at meals beside their own husbands, and freely talked and joked, even with strangers.[52]

Classical Era

Classical Greece is characterized by significant restrictions placed on women, except within a limited circle of friends. In general, the average Greek wife of the leisured classes led an existence hardly acknowledged outside the home. It is certain that women married young, and throughout their lives they had little contact with men other than their own husbands. Hesiod suggested that the right age for a man to marry was about 30, while that of his bride should be about five years after puberty. As a result, each female was very limited in social experience and judged the entire male population by the features and mannerisms of her husband. Plutarch (46–120 CE) relates that Hiero, a tyrant of Syracuse in the fifth century BCE, was once rebuked by a friend for his foul breath. He in turn scolded his wife for not informing him. She replied, "I supposed that all men smelled that way."[53]

Wealthy men were away from home more than not, and when at home they generally lived in quarters separate from their wives, called the *andron*. Husbands and wives ate together, if there were no male guests, but respectable wives occupied themselves elsewhere during banquets and when the husband entertained visitors.[54] Woman's quarters, called the *gynaeconitis*, were off limits to males. Simon incurred the wrath of Lysias for forcing his way into the ladies' apartments in a certain quarter of Athens. Lysias mentions that his niece and his sister had become so well ordered and conservative from life in the *gynaeconitis* that they were ashamed to be seen even by their own kinsmen.[55]

The Greeks regarded women to have been designed by the deities to remain indoors, while men were designed for outdoor life.[56] Both were bound to live according to nature's design or bear the penalty. Therefore, a wife seldom left the house. If such an occasion became a necessity, the husband's permission was sought and she remained in the company of a female servant. Consequently, men conducted most of the marketing along with other forms of business. Occasionally, female slaves were sent on errands, but usually only *hetaerae*, a category of prostitute to be discussed later, and freed-women of the lowest class appeared in the market place.[57] The extremely secluded lives of young girls naturally made them very modest and submissive wives. Aristophanes indicates that among certain classes even married women would shrink back and blush if seen at the window by a passing man.[58]

In some centers, activities of women were regulated by a board of censors. Phylarchus speaks of a sunset curfew enforced in Syracuse and various travel restrictions placed on females, which clearly were not merely for their protection.

> Phylarchus, in the twenty-fifth book of his History ... having said that there was a law at Syracuse, that the women should not wear golden ornaments, nor garments embroidered with flowers, nor robes with purple borders, unless they admitted that they were public prostitutes; and that there was another law, that a man should not adorn his person, nor wear any extraordinarily handsome robes, different from the rest of the citizens, unless he meant to confess that he was an adulterer and a profligate: and also, that a freewoman was not to walk abroad when the sun had set, unless she was going to commit adultery; and even by day they were not allowed to go out without the leave of the regulators of the women, and without one female servant following them.[59]

There were exceptions to these stereotypical reports. Plutarch indicates that women did frequent the festivities associated with weddings and funerals, and they had liberty to participate in religious devotions, even the mysteries.[60] But he also tells a story about Theano, thought to be the wife and student of philosopher Pythagoras, whose arm was accidentally exposed while putting on her cloak. And she commented that her arm was not for public view.[61]

Attitudes varied considerably with locality throughout Greek history. Lefkowitz and Fant say that the social institutions and discipline of the Spartan (Lacedaemonian) state existed for a single purpose: "to protect the state by maintaining the best fighting force in the world, and both its male and female citizens were involved in achieving that aim."[62] After their defeat by Sparta in the Peloponnesian War, the Athenians had great respect for the Spartan constitution and the laws enacted by Lycurgus. But they had difficulty in understanding the different social norms. Visiting Athenians were left goggle-eyed from the free association between Spartan boys and girls and the participation of Spartan girls in various forms of athletics. Cantarella says that Spartan women were considered to have liberal sexual habits, no doubt due to their upbringing outside the home, in the *stadia* and *palaestrae*, which in the view of Plato and Aristotle contributed to the demise of Sparta.[63] Euripides reports that these brash young ladies wore clothes that exposed the thigh, took part in athletic events, and even wrestled with male competitors.[64] Lydia also had customs incongruous with the conservative standards of Attic Greece.[65] Strabo indicates that both Lydian and Armenian girls typically spent a period of their early womanhood in cult prostitution, although this has been challenged by recent scholarship.[66]

Typically, elite Greek women knew little beyond their secluded and stifled existence. If liberation had been afforded them, most might not have been able to cope. Plato actually favored communal meals for mixed groups, as suggested in his proposals for the ideal state, but he recognized that such would be difficult to impose on women so acclimated to subjection.

> How then shall anyone attempt, without being laughed at, actually to compel women to take food and drink publicly and exposed to the view of all? The female sex would more readily endure anything than this; accustomed as they are to live a retired and private life, women will use every means to resist being led out into the light, and they will prove much too strong for the lawgiver. So that elsewhere, as I have said, women would not so much as listen to mention of their rights without shrieks of indignation.[67]

Little had changed four centuries later when Cornelius Nepos contrasted liberated Roman women with the shy and secluded Greeks.

> A great many things in our customs are decent, which are thought scandalous among them. For which of the Romans is ashamed to bring his wife to a feast? Or whose wife has not the first room in the house; for she is neither admitted into a feast, unless of relations, nor sits but in the inner parts of the house, which is called the women's quarters, where no one comes, unless allied to her by near relation.[68]

Plutarch indicates some degree of improvement in attitudes toward women, but still within the context of marital subordination. He instructs that while a husband is away, a virtuous woman should stay at home and hide herself, but when she has opportunity to be in his company she should be very visible. Further, he recommends that she restrict her friends to those of her husband.[69] Therefore, by the middle of the first Christian century, the social activities of Greek women were less restricted than a few centuries earlier, but we cannot deny that it may have varied from one community to another.

Another matter of concern to Greek writers is whether women should be permitted any degree of free speech. Plutarch boldly expressed his opinion that a woman should be quiet, or at least express her opinions through her husband.

> Pheidiea made Aphrodite of the Eleans with one foot on the tortoise to typify womankind staying at home and keeping silence. A woman ought to do her talking either to her husband or through her husband, and she should not feel aggrieved if, like the flute player, she makes a more impressive sound through a tongue not her own.[70]

There were some who held the opinion that women should not only refrain from engaging in conversation with men, but should never be the subject of one either. Thucydides said that such would be the ideal woman.[71] Plutarch, who gives much attention to the subject of feminine virtue, can only fault the opinion of Thucydides in part. He asserts that a woman with a good name is very worthy of public knowledge and discussion, in that her virtuous life is a standard for all.[72]

Women in Greek Drama

The great Greek playwrights rose to fame in the classical era, and all those whose works have survived were Athenians. The tragedies were written between the early and late fifth century BCE. Aeschylus was born in 525 BCE in the town of Eleusis, near Athens. He produced as many as 90 plays, of which seven have survived. The greatest is a trilogy entitled *Oresteia*, set during and after the Trojan War and involving some of Homer's characters. In the first, called *Agamemnon*, the king's wife, Clytemnestra, takes charge of Argos with masculine aplomb while he is away fighting against Troy. She also selects Agamemnon's cousin Aegisthus as her lover, thus exhibiting the same sexual assertiveness as the male heroes of Greek legend. And when Agamemnon finally returns home, she murders him in order to maintain control of the city. The second play of the trilogy, *The Libation Bearers*, is about Orestes, the son of Agamemnon and Clytemnestra, who returns to find his father dead and his rightful rule seized by his cold-hearted mother. So, encouraged by Apollo to avenge his father's murder, he kills both his mother and her lover. In the third play of the trilogy, *The Eumenides*, Orestes goes before Athena and 11 other judges at the Areopagus to determine whether his actions were justified. He is acquitted and returns to Argos as ruler. The females in this saga also include the Erinyes (the Furies), a troupe of goddesses of vengeance who torment Orestes until he is acquitted, and then once he is in power they offer their energy in his support.

In the tragedy called *Antigone*, by Sophocles, the primary character is the daughter of King Creon, ruler of Thebes. Her brothers have both died, leading opposite sides in civil war. Creon has decided that Eteocles will be honored and the body of Polyneices will be left unburied on the battlefield. Although she is warned by her sister Ismene not to do so, Antigone defies Creon's decision by performing funeral rites for Polyneices. Creon declares that by her action she has usurped his position of man. So, as punishment he has her walled up in an underground chamber. There she takes her own life.[73]

Euripides is known for plays in which women are portrayed as passionate and violent. One is called *Medea*. Her husband Jason repudiates Medea in order to marry princess Glauce, daughter of Creon, who in this drama is King of Corinth. Medea pours out her bitterness and anger, declaring that a woman's lot in life is most wretched. To punish Jason, she then murders the princess and the king, as well as her own children. Hereby, she takes on the vengeful role common to the male Greek heroes, dangerous to her enemies but loyal to her friends.[74]

Other plays by Euripides represent heroines as devoted and self-sacrificial. His last play before his death in 406 BCE, called *Iphigeneia in Aulis*, has Agamemnon willing to sacrifice his eldest daughter Iphigeneia to the goddess Artemis, whom he has slighted, in order to allow his troops to set sail and engage in war against Troy. Although Achilles is prepared to defend her, Iphigeneia sees her life as a small sacrifice compared to the honor of Greek soldiers. She says, "One man is more worthy to look at light than ten thousand women."[75] In *Electra*, the sister of Orestes is the one who displays the traits of a hero. And the principal character in *Alcestis* is portrayed as the ideal wife, noble in character, faithful to her husband, and a reliable manager of the *oikos*.

Of the comedies by Aristophanes, three are totally about the lives and activities of women. *Lysistrata* was first performed in 411 BCE in Athens. It was about a woman who organized Athenian women in a mission to end the Peloponnesian War. They initiate the process by withholding sexual favors from their husbands and lovers, simply to gain attention. Then they storm the acropolis and take control of the treasury, hoping to block finances for the war. *Thesmophoriazusae* was also first performed in 411 BCE and was based on a real festival held in Athens on the Pnyx, a hill about one kilometer west of the Acropolis designated for the gathering of women to discuss and decide political matters. In the play a man dresses as a female to intrude and spy on the secret activities there. *Women in the Assembly* is about a group of women who infiltrate a meeting dressed in men's clothes. These plays all touch on the connection and continuity of *polis* and *oikos*, the relationship between matters of the home and matters of society. They also demonstrate the intense emotions inflamed when private matters are made public. However, like other Greek literature, these have an underlying objective that speaks the perspective of the male authors. Aristophanes suggests that women are prone to take matters too far, not only to upset social order and break the law, but to defy the decrees of the gods.

It is evident that several writers championed the cause of female elevation, in opposition to almost violent defense of the status quo by their male contemporaries. Xenophon, a contemporary of Plato, applauds the character of Aspasia with regard to the duties of wives. And Aristophanes, in the play *Women in the Assembly*, portrays the female gender as demanding and certainly deserving better social conditions.[76] It might be that these and other spokesmen flourishing in the late fifth and early fourth centuries were awakened to the plight of women by the works of Euripides, less than half a century earlier (around 485–405 BCE). Bonnard takes special note of how Euripides agitated the whole of Athens by his strong expression of sympathy for the tragic reality of female subjection:

> In the eyes of his contemporaries Euripides paid a heavy price for not respecting Pericles' dictatorial instruction: "Silence regarding women, silence about their virtues, silence about their misfortune." Euripides felt too keenly for them to be silent.[77]

Euripides, in his play *The Trojan Women*, has Andromache saying that a major scandal for women is not staying at home. This suggests some degree of seclusion and hardship for a noble woman, who was expected more than others to conform to these rules. After the death of her husband, Hector, and the murder of her son Astyanax, she became the concubine of Neoptolemus and bore him a child. No doubt Euripides felt a sense of accomplishment when, in his old age, younger thinkers picked up his chant and women themselves demonstrated for greater social recognition. Subsequently, female subordination in Greece continued throughout the rest of the classical age and into the first Christian century, with the exception of the elite who enjoyed certain measures of liberation under the syncretic culture of Rome.

Women in the View of Philosophers

Of the many Greek philosophers whose names are known, only a few are prominent in their scope of influence and fewer still spoke on the topic of womanhood and the status of women in society. Among the earliest groups, the Pythagorans were primarily mathematicians who followed the proposals of Pythagorus of Samos (c. 570–495 BCE). They produced a "Table of Opposites" that we know through Aristotle.[78] The table included male and female listed among pairs of antithetical principles in the cosmos, such as light and darkness, right and wrong, good and evil. Prior to that, there was not much discussion of gender issues.

In the fifth century BCE there arose certain itinerant teachers known as sophists, who discussed, among many other issues, whether certain social structures were natural or social in nature. This included the status of women. Among them were Protagoras, Gorgias, Prodicus, Hippias, Thrasymachus, and others, who are known primarily through their opponents Plato and Aristotle. Socrates (469–399 BCE), generally considered to be the father of Western philosophy, is also known only through the dialogues of Plato and Xenophon and the plays of Aristophanes. His dialectic method of inquiry, known as the Socratic method, was primarily applied to the examination of significant moral concepts, such as justice. This method seems to have involved asking questions in order to find answers and is the basis for the modern scientific method.

However, more significant to this study is the *Republic*, by Plato (427–347 BCE), a student of Socrates. Plato's hypothesis that the human soul was once in a better place and now lives in a fallen world has been seen by some as a source for early Christian teaching. The *Republic* includes the earliest philosophical treatment of gender issues as part of the ideal state, and the concepts presented are attributed to Socrates, beginning with a dialogue about the meaning and essence of justice. The work presents the idea of a class system, comprised of rulers, soldiers, and workers, with the first two categories serving as "guardians" of the city (*polis*). Among the guardians, women would be considered the equals of men, including education and training, although the assertion was made that males will prove superior in most skills. This structure is designed to improve the state, not to elevate the status of women, and under this system women must make their behavior approximate to that of men. In dialogue with an interlocutor Glaucon, Plato's brother, Socrates proposes education for women that includes music, gymnastics, and the art of war. It is acknowledged that women have different aptitudes and skills, just as do men, and it is not possible to assign them all equal tasks. In this system procreation will be regulated, and children born at the same time will all be called brothers and sisters, and in this way guardians of the state will share wives and children in common. It is proposed also that the role of mothering will be eliminated, presumably recruiting nursemaids from the working class. Despite all the significant structural changes proposed in the *Republic*, clearly patriarchal terminology is used concerning familial relationships, such as "possession and use" of wives and children, and the role of the husband over them as a "guard of a flock."[79] In Plato's *Laws*, written shortly before his death, the visions of the *Republic* are refined somewhat and include a return to more traditional family structure, as well as the archaic concept of arranged marriages.[80]

Aristotle (384–322 BCE) was a student of Plato for some 20 years, but his ultimate views on the nature and roles of women differed from those proposed by Plato. In his *Politics*, Aristotle outlined three relationships of dominance in the traditional home (*oikos*) that compare with accepted political authority. One is the relationship between master and slave, which he describes as tyranny because it exists for the benefit of the master. The second is the relationship of father to children, which he compares to a monarchy because it provides essential care and protection to the weak and defenseless. The third is the relationship of husband to wife, which is political, a permanent relationship of assigned roles where the husband is the authority over the wife. He believed that women differ from men in their psychological traits as well as social and physical competencies. Men possess the ability to command and govern, but women are innately subordinate and submissive. Aristotle saw males and females as complementing each other in terms of their contribution to a home, but in general the tasks associated with that relationship, especially the roles of ruling and compliance, are gender specific. He did acknowledge the need for female education, but he saw that as to the benefit of the state and not something that would change their traditional domestic role.[81]

From the Hellenistic era there is a treatise, probably written by a neopythagorean but attributed to Plato's mother, Perictione, who some claimed to have been a disciple of Pythagoras. The treatise offers advice to young women about how to live: a harmonious woman should be endowed with wisdom and self-control; devoted to her husband, children, and household; resist temptation to engage in affairs; live for her husband and not her own interests; avoid wearing excessive make-up, perfume, or seductive clothing; endure all unpleasant or harsh traits of her husband and adopt his thinking rather than developing thoughts of her own; revere the gods; obey all laws and institutions; and respect her parents. Above all she must guard and care for her marriage, for everything depends on this. If her husband thinks something is sweet, or sour, she should agree. Otherwise, she will be out of harmony with her entire world.[82]

Probably the most significant contribution the Greeks made to Christian tradition, as far as the status of women is concerned, was the Aristotelian political structure of rulers and subjects at every level of society, from household to state. This submission and domination ethos became a significant factor in Pauline theology. On the one hand it appears to have roots in the Jewish concept of female subordination, but some modern feminists see it as having crept into Christianity from Hellenistic sources.[83]

Marriage and Home

The Greeks considered procreation a duty to the gods, to the state, and to their ancestors, in order to produce a succession of worshippers, citizens, and family heirs. The production of children, therefore, was the primary purpose of marriage, and every man felt obliged to fulfill his obligation. Xenophon says, "We obviously select for wives the women who will bear us the best children, and then marry them to raise a family."[84] Paternal selection of a bride for the son was also the norm.[85] Girls were commonly given in marriage between the ages of 15 and 17, although for a male, 18 was considered very young to be married.[86] Xenophon indicates that some women were employed as professional matchmakers, which in fact amounted to the negotiation of business deals between families.[87] Girls were often consigned to men they had never met and were not consulted as to inclination or preference.[88] Plutarch says it was customary for a father to choose a bride for his son, perhaps years before the appropriate time for their marriage and one whom he had never seen.[89] However, it is likely that even these customs varied with geography and social strata. Dio Chrysostom gives a picture of courtship among the respectable poor, and it seems that the boy and girl had a freedom of association that could allow for the development of true love.[90] He contrasts that with the nature of weddings among the wealthy, with scrutiny of property and pedigree, dowries, promises and deception, contracts, and of course, the conflicts and drama at the wedding itself.[91]

There is reason to believe that efforts to maintain, or to enhance, social status through marriage served to destroy general appreciation for marital fidelity among Greek nobility. Such marriages were characterized by indifference, coldness and discontent. Xenophon said that in his day there was no one with whom a husband conversed less than his wife.[92] Four centuries later Plutarch observed the failures in the Greek marriage system and advocated a far more serious and solemn approach. In his *Advice to the Bride and Groom,* Plutarch stated that marriage should be entered upon because of love, and he encouraged every couple to develop companionship in order to achieve the ideal marriage state.[93] He also encouraged wives to exercise the simple and common attributes which create a bond of love, such as conversation, character and companionship, for marriage should be an intimate union. Those who marry for dowry, or even for the purpose of having children, are just business partners.

Despite the appearance of Plutarch as an idealist and champion of women's elevation, he clearly advocated the subordination of wives to their husbands:

> If they subordinate themselves to their husbands, they are commended, but if they want to have control, they cut a sorrier figure than the subjects of their control. And control ought to be exercised by the man over the woman, not as the owner has control of a piece of property but, as the soul controls the body, by entering into her feelings and being knit to her by good will. As, therefore, it is possible to exercise care over the body without being a slave to its pleasures

and desires, so it is possible to govern a wife, and at the same time to delight and gratify her.[94]

Here Plutarch makes his point sternly and dispassionately, that women should be almost void of personality and individuality, reflecting only the emotions and opinions of their husbands. This also suggests that husbands should understand the feelings of wives, not out of genuine empathy, but as a means of control. In other places, he expresses himself with an air of poetic charm:

> Whenever two notes are sounded in accord, the tune is carried by the bass; and in like manner every activity in the virtuous household is carried on by both parties in agreement, but discloses the husband's leadership and preference.[95]

Yet, however his manner of expression varies, this philosopher and statesman was adamant that wives should never try to dominate their husbands. Regardless of superior intelligence or knowledge, value of dowry or depth of charm, the wife's role in marriage could only be one of subordination.[96] Ironically, the very discussion is evidence that some women did dominate their husbands.

The household duties of a Greek wife were the sort to be expected under the circumstances of her social status. The system theoretically demanded strict obedience to the husband as the head of the household.[97] The wife, as the principal ward of her husband, was placed in charge of all household management, including all moveable objects in the household, the servants, and the children.[98] Although the Greeks recognized children as the offspring and the responsibility of both parents, the mothers were delegated the task of child supervision. The concept of "community of property" seems to have existed in some areas of Greece, but Plutarch says that the property should be *thought* to belong to the husband.[99] He recommended the pooling of all resources into a common fund, with the husband as the chief executive and the wife as general manager. Xenophon observed that there is probably no one to whom a husband would commit a greater number of significant affairs than to his wife.[100] In practice, the Greek wife was the mistress of her husband's home and served in every capacity from business manager to family nurse. In wealthy households the wife controlled a large force of servants, male and female, each responsible to the lady for instructions. In poorer communities, both urban and rural, the wife did her own chores, assisted only by her children.

Marital fidelity was generally enforced to the advantage of the husband. A wife who was found guilty of adultery was therefore guilty of a civil injury to the husband, whereas an adulterous husband was typically not liable for civil discipline. In fact, such an offense would not bring any form of disgrace upon the husband. Both married and single men had sexual relations with hetaerae, and it appears that wives expected their husbands to have an occasional affair. The danger was doing so with a married woman, whose husband would not be so tolerant or understanding. The law left the punishment of a wife's lover to the discretion of the husband, and if they were caught in the act, the offender might be killed, with no legal repercussions.[101] Otherwise, severe punishment might be enjoined by the court, such as a fine and monetary compensation to the wronged husband. The wife was never executed, but the husband was compelled to divorce her.

Some have claimed that an adulterous woman in Greece was branded with infamy, and at least in Athens, anyone who married such a woman was disfranchised.[102] Plutarch relates the ordeal of an adulterous woman in Cumae, an Italian city founded by Euboean Greeks in the eighth century BCE. She was ceremoniously brought into the marketplace and before the critical eyes of the entire city led about on a donkey. From that moment, she was disgraced by the nickname "donkey rider."[103] Obviously, such was not a sufficient deterrent, since adultery was rife. Women found a variety of ways to delude even suspicious husbands. It was easy to enlist the aid of a trusted female servant, tutor, nurse, or even mother, to carry messages, make arrangements for secret meetings, and unlatch the door to allow the lover entrance.[104] Dio Chrysostom, writing in the first Christian century, indicates that bribes were often paid for this sort of assistance, and to assure secrecy. He further suggests that such infidelity was increasing during his time.[105] Such a comment is no surprise, since most cultures all through history have had their "doomsday" prophets who viewed contemporary conditions with anxiety and lament.

Despite the dearth of love and fidelity in many marriages, the security of a home and husband was a coveted possession to most Greek women. Married women were often torn between the desire for true love and companionship and the need for security in marriage. For this reason, they took great care to avoid separation and divorce. The simple village and rural life lent itself to greater marital stability. Lower classes were less concerned with dowry, competition, and seclusion of wives to the home. Companionship between husbands and wives appears more common, both in labor and household chores, as well as education, or lack of it, and basic purpose in life. For a variety of reasons, lower class and rural husbands appeared less inclined to visit brothels or engage in affairs, perhaps because of limited financial resources. The wives, in turn, being more occupied with domestic chores and confident of their husbands' devotion, were less inclined to engage in affairs.

The two primary causes for divorce in classical Greece were adultery and barrenness.[106] Dio reports that women who knew they were barren could secure unwanted babies to rear as their own, thereby safeguarding their marriages.[107] That kind of chicanery seems implausible, unless the husband was away most of the time. But desperate people are sometimes forced to do desperate things.

Education

According to Xenophon, young girls in Greece were encouraged to see, hear, and say as little as possible. This is doubtless the practical result of various social restrictions placed upon women by tradition, but there seems to be little to suggest that the Greeks officially opposed the education of women. The same writer reported a conversation between Socrates and Antisthenes, who were watching a young girl entertain banquet guests by tossing hoops in the air and catching them. Socrates said:

> It is apparent that the talent of women is not at all inferior to that of men though they are wanting in bodily vigor and strength, so that whosoever of you has a wife, let him teach her with confidence whatsoever he would wish her to know.[108]

Antisthenes suggested, no doubt sarcastically, that Socrates should so instruct his own wife Xanthippe (meaning "yellow horse"), for she is one of the most difficult women in the world. Socrates responded that one who wishes to excel in horsemanship does not choose a well-mannered horse, but one of high spirits, for if he can master that horse he can master any. Thus, he selected an obstinate wife, because if he can endure her, he can endure all the others.[109] This was no doubt a jibe at Antisthenes, but Socrates made it at his wife's expense.

Throughout Greek history there were certain advocates of higher education for women, including Cleobulus, of the seventh century, Pythagoras, of the sixth century, and Plato, of the fourth century BCE, although we have noted earlier that Plato saw women as intellectually and spiritually inferior.[110] Plutarch, representing the first Christian century, also supported female education, though he encouraged husbands to carry out the instruction. In fact, he thought it rather noble for a woman to consider her husband her guide, philosopher, and teacher.[111] While relatively few women attained any degree of scholarship, Plutarch recognized that educational advancement of women was to the advantage of the entire society. However, he thought that if they were not allowed to do so, "left to themselves, they would conceive many untoward ideas, low designs, and emotion."[112]

The first evidence of such was Sappho, born around 612 BCE, famous as a poet of the Island of Lesbos. Virtually every detail of her history is questionable, but there is little doubt as to her fame as a writer and champion of women's elevation. The Alexandrians listed her among nine great lyric poets of Greece. There is evidence that her mother was called Cleïs, and that she had a daughter by the same name.[113] Many believe that young girls flocked to her from all parts of Greece to learn poetry in a sorority devoted to Aphrodite, the Graces, and the Muses. They returned to their homes with a love of poetry and intellectual pursuits and encouraged other women in scholastic endeavors. All subsequent intellectual attainments by Greek women are commonly attributed to the influence of Sappho. However, Bonnard and others are convinced that her true objective was to teach girls the art of living and being women in a man's world. Her intentions were never to motivate women toward science, philosophy, or politics.[114] There is reason to think that she also taught women the arts of lovemaking. Blundell offers a lengthy discussion of the connection of Sappho with homosexuality and the etymology of the term *lesbian*, which originally may have suggested the performance of fellatio on a male.[115]

Other examples of literate women in classical and preclassical Greece include: the daughter of Thucydides, who composed the eighth book of her father's history of the Peloponnesian War; Plutarch's circle of students, including Clea and Eurydice; Nicobule, who wrote a history of Alexander the Great; Aganice, daughter of Hegetor of Thessaly, who studied astrology; Agnodice, who studied medicine disguised as a man and revealed herself when qualified to practice; Aspasia, who practiced medicine in the fourth century BCE, acquiring fame as a surgeon; and Antiochis, who practiced medicine in the third century, specializing in salves and plaster cures.[116] In the Hellenistic era there was also a poet named Erinna, from the Dorian island of Telos. Her poem "The Distaff" expresses lament at the death of a woman named Baucis, who was her dear friend.[117]

Religion

It was once thought that the old Greek religion began in mythology, and the cultic rituals and songs evolved from the exploits of legendary heroes and their contact with the gods. It is now evident that the myths presupposed the cult, and the cult was rooted in the life of the family and clan.[118] Myth, therefore, was created to explain beliefs and practices. Pollux describes how people worshipped these deities. They would come to the shrines in their best clothing, call up or call down the presence of the gods, pray with hands raised, ask favors, make offerings and sacrifices, sing songs and paeans, burn incense, hang up garlands, and make drink offerings.[119]

There were various kinds of religious rituals. The simplest were practiced in the home. Because of the connection of womanhood with the home, which was the core of the society, women naturally participated in and even led many rituals that were part of family life, such as the premeal offerings of thanksgiving to Hestia. This was also a sacred place for a new bride to be welcomed into a house and for a new baby to be celebrated. In many Greek city-states, like Athens, there was a city hall (*prytaneion*) with a city hearth representing civic unity.

Despite the strict seclusion of Greek women during the classical era, throughout recorded history they were permitted to take part in public religious activities uninhibited and unveiled. Around 250 BCE, Herondas recorded his observation of two women who visited the temple of Asclepius, the God of healing, to make an offering. They were not timid as they waited at the gate among a crowd of visitors and walked about the grounds admiring the artwork. They conversed freely with one another and the priest, and prayed aloud to a number of gods.[120]

There were also rituals connected with death, including the preparation of a body for burial and mourning. These rituals were commonly performed by women. However, laws instituted by Solon restricted some of these activities, suggesting that in the archaic era funeral rituals had become excessive. So, after Solon, mourning processions and gatherings were limited to older women. There were also limits to the volume of offerings placed at a tomb, and women who were not related to the deceased were not allowed to visit a tomb after interment. Blundell suggests that a possible reason for these regulations was to curtail ostentatious displays by those of wealth. But there is reason also to conclude that on occasion intense mourning had been used by women to fuel retaliation for murder. Therefore, legislation targeted those who would use a funeral to initiate a feud or a riot.[121]

Male priests typically supervised in rituals to male deities, while priestesses performed the same role in worship of female deities. The assistants who actually slaughtered animals for sacrifice were male. Of course, technically speaking, in Athens religious cult was part of the state, and was therefore controlled by men. But in terms of public rites and rituals, religion was the one arena that provided women full access. And, to be discussed later, there developed a variety of cults that were unofficial and not subject to the patriarchal norms.

One of the primary cults in which women participated was the Olympian Athena. The priestess of Athena Polias played a significant role in local politics and could speak with authority as a representative of Athena.[122] Shrines at Dodona and Delphi had a very special kind of priestess, called the Pythia, who served as an oracle of the gods. It appears that the sanctuary of Apollo at Delphi was the most significant, and the Pythia might be consulted by leading officials on significant political matters.[123] In Athens, the position of priestess was considered to be a public office, the only such position held by a woman. The Great Panathenaea was the most significant of the state festivals, and it was officiated by the priestess. According to Herodotus, when Athens was about to be besieged by the Persians in 480 BCE, the priestess interpreted an omen that led to the city's evacuation.[124]

Prostitution

An intriguing feature of the social status of women in ancient Greece is a concept of prostitution peculiar to that culture. Greek women were divided into two basic categories. The first comprised all respectable wives and maidens who were classified legally as "citizen-women." As early as the sixth century BCE, prostitution came to be sanctioned and was regarded as an essential and permanent institution in Greek society.[125]

Several factors contributed to this phenomenon. First is the Greek appreciation for all manner of beauty, as perhaps evidenced by their art. The standards of seclusion enforced upon Greek wives and daughters naturally hampered any display of feminine beauty. Courtesans, therefore, came to serve as the acceptable avenue of displaying openly beauty and glamour. A second factor was the Greek attitude toward "strangers," or noncitizens.[126] In Athens particularly, citizens were concerned for protecting the purity of Greek blood in every family lineage, and for this reason marriages with noncitizen women were outlawed. In Sparta such women were not allowed even residence within the city.

Third, and related to the above, there developed a paradoxical attitude among Greek men, in that while they insisted on confining their wives to the home, they also enjoyed female company on walks, at banquets, in the markets and on business engagements. Since no social restraints were attached to the activities of "strangers," these women made ideal companions in all activities not suitable for wives. Men were willing to pay for this company, and as one would expect the relationships usually included sexual intimacy. This role was rather profitable, and offered some degree of security to those women not privileged to contract marriages with men of the citizen class.

Other forms of prostitution are well documented. These factors combine to create a complex system of prostitution almost as significant to Greek culture as the institution of marriage. There can be little doubt about the influence of this system upon the early church in the Gentile world, both in its definition of sexual immorality and its concept of marital fidelity. Several New Testament texts have been commonly read against the backdrop of prostitution and relationships with hetaerae, particularly Paul's letters to the church in Corinth.[127] However, it seems that Paul's use of the word *porneia* refers to any kind of illicit sexual relationship, or sex outside the commitment of marriage and against the moral standards embraced by a true believer and follower of Jesus Christ. The noun *porne* describes woman who engages in sex for monetary reward.

In general the attitude toward prostitution in Greece was one of acceptance as an essential part of the culture, as in most of the ancient world. Plutarch advises the wife of an incontinent man to be tolerant if he engages in an occasional affair. But both Plutarch and Dio Chrysostom speak out strongly against immorality as if they recognized extramarital intercourse to be a violation of higher principles.[128] But there seems to be no distinction between sex with prostitutes, hetaerae, or another man's wife, except that taking another man's wife was an affront to his honor.

It seems that all prostitutes in ancient Greece could be termed *hetaerae*, regardless of social class or sphere of activity. However, there are at least three specific categories. The lowest class was primarily slaves brought into the country by the state to serve in public brothels (*dicteria*). Essentially, the term *porne* referred to a common whore, meaning one who engaged in sexual intercourse for money. Houses of prostitution were supervised by city inspectors, and all revenue went to the state. The regulations of Solon in Athens were designed to preserve public order and decency by confining brothels to certain quarters of the city, and in many places that continued for centuries. Prostitutes were compelled to wear distinctive dress, and they were forbidden to participate in religious activities.

Thus, it is clear that this form of prostitution was both legal and common in various centers of ancient Greece, although in the eyes of certain writers this represented an undesirable element of their culture. Dio Chrysostom, writing in the first Christian century, indicates that the practice had become a serious social problem.[129] According to Athenaeus, the tyrant of Syracuse named Hieronymous took a prostitute named Peitho out of a public brothel and made her his queen, much to the disgust of the public.[130]

Hetaerae

Commonly translated "courtesan," the term *hetaerae* describes a large category of prostitutes who were professional companions or escorts. Athenaeus provides many intriguing insights into the lives of Greek women, including the hetaerae.[131] They can appropriately be called prostitutes because their livelihood was from individuals in exchange for services that may or may not have included sex. Some of these were slaves, owned and trained by procuresses who operated much like a modern pimp and received the bulk of the money earned. However, the nature of the training was more than sexual. The hetaerae were typically educated, schooled in art, dancing, literature and any grace that might make them appealing to men of wealth and refinement.

Such men, whose wives were typically secluded to the home, would gladly pay for the companionship of an attractive female while in the company of friends, at banquets, or just walking through the streets. Besides their beauty and solicited affection, their refinement made them more engaging in conversation. Aspasia, companion to Pericles after his separation from his wife, is thought by some to have been of this class.[132] She was a foreigner, from the Ionian Greek city of Miletus. But she was highly gifted and intelligent and became a noted figure in Athenian society.

The most numerous of hetaerae were freed women, slaves who had acquired freedom and operated independently with complete social liberty. These women were usually highly educated, enterprising, and were considered ruthless in their pursuit of wealth and prestige. They often preyed on young and inexperienced males, inviting them to banquets, engaging in drinking bouts, and entertaining them in every seductive way to eventually obtain money. Among these were the *auletrides,* young women who entertained at banquets with singing, dancing, and flute playing. Parties often included an auction in which *auletrides* were sold for the night to the highest bidder.[133]

The highest stratum of the hetaerae were those who were freeborn. Some were Ionians, drawn to wealth and affluence, and others were divorcees and unsupported widows who turned to prostitution in order to maintain the status to which they were accustomed. Some did so just to survive. However, all free women who were known to solicit this kind of income forfeited citizenship and had to remain unmarried. But once having chosen this course, few cared about marriage or citizenship, since they seemed to exert a significant influence as art critics, political commentators, and students of philosophy, poetry and oratory. They were called the "learned" hetaerae, and were comparable to modern upper class call girls. Their company and their favors came at a high price, and many became wealthy, owning imported garments, priceless jewelry, and large estates, and commanding numbers of servants.

It is also noteworthy that hetaerae, as well as dancers and prostitutes, could be readily identified on the streets by their garments. Hetaerae wore more garments than the average married woman, but finer, fancier, and showy; and they were also noted for elaborate gold ornaments. The fabric of their clothes was often transparent, like fine silk. Seneca said that hetaerae wore garments so sheer that they were exposed as much as if totally naked.[134] Respectable married women, characterized by seclusion and confinement to the home, had to wear a head covering whenever in public. Often referred to as veiling, in Greece this was accomplished by drawing one portion of the outer garment over the head. This was a symbol of her relationship to her husband.[135] For hetaerae, even the head coverings were transparent.

Cult Prostitution

The concept of cult (sacred, or temple) prostitution has been taken for granted among modern scholars and historians, based on numerous reports by ancient writers.[136] By definition, this is prostitution associated primarily with a religious cult, which in Greece would be the cult of Aphrodite, the goddess of fertility. Thus it has been claimed that men engaged in sexual intercourse with temple harlots as an act of religious devotion.[137] Strabo is often quoted as saying that there were a thousand cult prostitutes in Corinth alone.[138] However, as noted earlier with regard to the report of Herodotus,[139] recent historians have challenged the concept of cult prostitution as unfounded. Stephanie Budin's *The Myth of Sacred Prostitution in Antiquity* is a thorough and important study of this topic.[140] Budin effectively demonstrates that cult prostitution, meaning the offering of sexual intercourse by a woman for money that was then donated to a deity or a temple, did not exist in the ancient world. This myth, she says, is based upon a combination of misunderstanding and misrepresentation, both on the part of certain ancient writers and modern scholars.

Many are convinced that Herodotus was the origin of this myth, and his report concerning practices in Babylon were then echoed by other ancient writers such as Lucian of Samosata and the author of the apocryphal letter of Jeremiah. However, the claim of such an institution in Greece traces to Pindar, a lyric poet from Thebes whose life spanned the late sixth to the midfifth century BCE. A pertinent portion of his work called *The Servants of Peitho, Fragment 122*, is quoted by Chamaeleon of Heraclea in his work called *On Pindar*, and then preserved by Athenaeus. Although a few lines are missing, the meaning is clear.

> You girls who welcome many guests as servants of Peitho in sumptuous Corinth; you who burn the pale tears of green incense, while often in thought you fly upwards toward the mother of loves, Aphrodite Ourania— to you she grants that free of reproach and, o children, in couches of pleasure, you are to harvest the fruit of soft youth! With necessity all is good.... But I do wonder what the lords of the Isthmos will say as I contrive a beginning like this to my honey-sweet *skolion*, a companion to women shared. Gold will reveal a pure touchstone.... Lady of Cyprus, here to your grove Xenophon leads grazing girls, a hundred-limbed herd, rejoicing at prayers fulfilled.[141]

Budin says that a *skolion*, which is what Pinder calls this particular poem, was a drinking song, either sung or recited at a *symposion*, a gathering of upper-class male citizens in the company of hetaerae, for the purpose of celebration of sports victory or theatrical success. While a portion of his theme is sex, and it seems evident that the companions are prostitutes, there is nothing to suggest association with a religious ceremony or offering. Athenaeus

Four. Greece

cites Chamaeleon as saying that whenever the city prayed to Aphrodite about major events, such as when the Greeks defended themselves against Persian invasion, they included as many hetaerae as possible in offering prayers and attending the sacrifices. This, supported by other sources, only suggests the role of hetaerae as temple servants, but does not suggest prostitution or sexual activity of any kind.[142]

The same is true of the report of Strabo, which has been the primary source for countless claims of cult prostitution in Corinth. A Greek born in the Roman province of Pontus around 60 BCE, Strabo became a significant geographer and historian. His tours of various regions are dated from 40 to 20 BCE, and his *Geography* was completed around 7 BCE. Strabo discusses "cult prostitution" only twice, the first drawing from the report of Herodotus pertaining to Babylon, which he appears not to trust. The second is about the Armenian cult of Anaitis, in which he actually uses the verb *porneuein*, and the report also resembles that of Herodotus. In all other references, including Corinth, Strabo describes activities which pertain to various roles in a religious cult but have nothing to do with sacred prostitution.[143] The pertinent segment of Strabo's report on Corinth reads:

> The temple of Aphrodite was so wealthy that it possessed more than a thousand hierodules, *hetaerae*, for both men and women to offer to the goddess. And because of them the city was visited often and enriched by the multitudes. For ship captains freely wasted all their money, and therefore the proverb: "Not for every man is the voyage to Corinth."

Budin points out certain anachronisms in Strabo's report, including the fact that he references a time when the temple of Aphrodite was larger and wealthier, and he mentions a number of rulers before his time who impacted the city either positively or negatively. It is clear that he visited Corinth, but it is not clear that he witnessed what he describes here. Budin also points out that Strabo's use of the word *hierodule*, which literally means "temple servant" is a term that had fallen out of use by Strabo's time, and which has been mistranslated countless times by modern scholars as "temple prostitute" or "sacred prostitute."

In Egypt during the Hellenistic period a hierodule was defined as a paid cult servant exempt from taxes and corvée labor. The hierodules of Boubastis may have had other duties, but they are described in a letter to Zenon as the keepers of the sacred cats. Financial records of the public games at Oxyrhyncus include hierodules among various workers, such as shakers, herald, and trumpeter.[144] The use of the term in Anatolia dates back to the Bronze Age when religious servants lived on sacred land (*hiera khora*) and all were under the authority of a high priest. It is ironic that Strabo himself gives testimony of as many as 6,000 hierodules under the supervision of Arkhelaos the priest, appointed by Pompey.[145]

142 Daughters of God, Subordinates of Men

The third example is a slave dedicated by his or her owner to a deity as a form of manumission, thus becoming a hierodule. An inscription from one Kloinizoas of Lycia indicates the donation of two female slaves (*paidiskas*) named Akierous and Apionitheis.[146] This carried with it protection and financial support for the hierodule, but also the benefit for the former owner as a donation to the deity. All evidence suggests that a hierodule was a servant of the temple, either male or female, who performed specific duties that included assisting the priest with sacrifices and offerings, lighting lamps, playing music and singing, caring for sacred animals, caring for sacred grounds, and so on. But there is nothing in his report that suggests cult prostitution in any form.

Macedonia

Special attention must be given to two areas in Greece where the classic subordination and seclusion of women was challenged. One is the region known as Macedonia, to the north of the Roman province of Achaia. The ancient kingdom of Macedonia lay to the northeast of Greece in the central Balkan peninsula between the Adriatic and Aegean Seas. The actual origin of the Macedonians is questioned, although the preponderance of evidence indicates an affinity with the Hellenic race to the south. The history of Macedonia is largely that of the royal family, which claimed to be Greek and traced its descent back to Perdiccas.[147] With time, they blended with the native Illyrians, and natural barriers segregated them from their kinsmen to the south so that their cultural development took a divergent path.[148] Several great kings did much to consolidate the various Macedonian tribes into a stable military unit, but it was not until the rule of Philip II, beginning in 357 BCE, that Macedon emerged as a formidable European power. Under his direction, the Hellenic states united into a Greco-Macedonian campaign against the Persians. After Philip's assassination, his son Alexander fulfilled this ambition by building an empire, ruled by a Macedonian and united by "all things Greek." This policy called Hellenism, which included language, architecture, art, literature, athletics and philosophy, was such a pervasive and cohesive force that well into the first Christian century and beyond, koine (common) Greek was the primary language of the Roman Empire. In Palestine, many Jews were known as Hellenists because they shifted from traditional Judaism to a form that embraced Greek culture. The shift from the Greek classical era to a Hellenistic world brought many changes, including the status of women both in household and society, depending, of course, on class and location.

After the breakdown of barriers between Macedonia and Greece during the time of Philip of Macedon, women of the north retained the traditional social freedom suggested in Homeric literature. Carroll describes them as a succession of "proud and haughty princesses" who had royal rights and privileges, wealth, political power and social independence. Some could muster a veritable army with their own resources and address them with fiery speeches. They were bold enough to make proposals of marriage to men, and they dispensed with their rivals with "sinister coolness and cruelty."[149]

Pomeroy describes several powerful queens who resemble the character of Clytemnestra of Homeric legend, eliminating rivals and killing husbands in order to gain political control or to assure ascendency for a son.[150] One was Olympias, the mother of Alexander. Plutarch wrote that she was enthusiastically involved in the cult of Dionysus, and the fact that her pet snake often stretched out next to her in bed tended to quench Philip's passion for her.[151] Olympias was blamed for Philip's murder, although at the time she was in exile.

Another such queen was Laodice, the first wife of Seleucid King Antiochus II. He repudiated her in order to contract a diplomatic marriage with Berenice, daughter of Ptolemy II Philadelphus, but later returned to live with Laodice. Ptolemy was outraged, but it was Laodice who took desperate measures to assure succession of her son Seleucus. She poisoned Antiochus, and also arranged the murder of Berenice and her infant son. Retaliation by Ptolemy III, brother of Berenice, led to the Third Syrian War (246–241 BCE).

During Alexander's Hellenization process, it seems that the people of Macedonia took on some of the refinement of Greece without sacrificing the contrasting independence of women. But after the battle of Pydna (168 BCE) when the Romans gained control of Macedonia, the status of women was enhanced even further, extending into the early Christian era.[152] Among the earliest of modern archaeological discoveries were numerous memorial inscriptions suggesting that Macedonian women were capable of supplementing their husbands' income by various means, ranging from wages in common labor to returns from business investments. Some women were held in high esteem by civic organizations, and upon their death were honored with tributes on elaborate tombstones.[153]

Further evidence for this is seen in the Lukan account of Paul's evangelism, where large numbers of women in Macedonia converted to Christianity. In the city of Philippi, Paul finds and converts a group of women led by Lydia, a purple dye merchant of considerable prestige. In Thessalonica, his converts include "many leading women" and in Berea he finds "Greek women of noble status."[154]

Alexandria

The principal Greek center in Egypt was Alexandria. Ptolemy I Soter, one of Alexander's generals and the first in a line of Ptolemaic rulers in Egypt,

144 Daughters of God, Subordinates of Men

strongly influenced the reshaping of Egyptian society. Alexandria was rivaled only by Athens as a Mediterranean axis for Hellenism, and consequently Greek became the official language, along with Bohairic in most of Lower Egypt. Various Coptic dialects, such as Sahidic, Fayyumic, and Memphitic, prevailed in regions along the Nile from Thebes southward. But even these dialects came to be written in Greek characters early in the Christian era.

Women in the Ptolemaic dynasty, like those in earlier Egyptian history, occupied a station of marked influence with few of the restrictions of their contemporaries in Achaia.[155] One powerful queen of this era was Arsinoe II, who was both the sister and wife of Ptolemy II. She ruled at his side until her death in 270 BCE, and was the first Egyptian queen to have her portrait engraved with her husband on coins. Following the ruthless methods of Olympias and Laodice, at the beginning of her reign she had all her rivals executed.

Perhaps the most famous Egyptian queen during the Hellenistic era was Cleopatra VII, who inherited the throne at age 17. Julius Caesar intervened to settle a dispute between Cleopatra and her younger brother Ptolemy XIII. She gave birth to a son, claiming Caesar to be the father, and later lived with him in Rome until his assassination in 44 BCE. She is remembered most for her relationship with Marc Antony and the power she attained through political alliance with Rome. After her death in 40 BCE, Egypt fell under Roman authority and for the second time saw the colonization of foreigners among its population. Subsequent cultural blending was completely to the advantage of Egyptian women, especially those of Alexandria.

Women in Greek Art

Along with the shifts in the status of women in the classical era, there was also a shift in how women were depicted in art. In the archaic period males were the focus of art, and it was common to portray them nude, sometimes called "heroic" nudity. In contrast, during this era women were portrayed fully clothed. Primary evidence comes from a large number of stone figures of young women (*korai*) and young men (*kouroi*) appearing after 650 BCE, exhibited for public view, particularly in cemeteries and in religious sanctuaries.[156]

Reasons for this contrast in imagery are difficult to assess. Blundell suggests that nude images of males might suggest the social acceptance of homosexuality among Greek males. It is more likely that it represents the pride early Greeks had in male strength and agility, and is also connected to the fact that from the earliest records Greek males participated in athletics nude. Thucydides suggested that male nudity in athletics was one of many practices that demonstrated advanced Greek thinking, as compared to the customs of barbarians.[157] Kenneth Clark, in his classic study of nudity in art, suggests that the male nude represents a sense of "human wholeness," which would imply also that at the time woman was considered somehow "incomplete."[158] Based on the different positioning of the arms and legs in statues of this era, Blundell concludes that

> the ideological significance of the *korai* figures can perhaps be summed up very simply. Women should be nubile but modestly draped, they should stay in one place, and they should be fertile.[159]

The classical era of Greece saw marked shifts in the portrayal of women in art. Women were often portrayed nude, and many paintings were erotic in nature. Some artists represented females in sheer clothing that revealed form. What influenced those shifts is difficult to determine. We know that Plato suggested that in the ideal state, women should also engage in athletic training and do so in the nude.[160] But it seems rather that the art of that era represents changing social perspectives and a greater acknowledgement of female sexuality. Since many of the nude images after the early fourth century were called Aphrodites, portraying the goddess preparing to bathe, it seems that the imagery represents two motifs: acceptance that the female body was sexually attractive, but at the same time interpreting woman as the embodiment of certain social and religious ideals. Pomeroy suggests that during this era there was a more open acknowledgement of female erotic impulses and need for sexual gratification. Women in Greek art during this era were often sexually suggestive, even explicit, as opposed to the "heroic" nature of male nudes.[161] So, the abundance of nude images in classical Greece were not really about the Greek fascination with the human body, but symbolic of the shifting views in Greek culture concerning the meaning of male and female.

There is no consistency in the artistic portrayal of women in routine life or in religious activities, except that the typical Greek wife has her hair pinned up, but uncovered. Virgin goddesses commonly are portrayed with a drape over the head. One of the Pythia at the Delphic Oracle is also depicted with her head covered as she gives a reading to an enquirer.[162]

Summary

The ideal of womanhood in ancient Greece is generally marked by seclusion, ignorance and subjugation. This was especially so in the cities of the province of Achaia. Mythology, especially seen in the writings of Hesiod, serves as both explanation and justification for how things were in Greek culture, and the female deities represent various aspects of the male views and fears, in some cases hatred, of woman. The application of Freudian analysis to Greek mythology has led some to conclude that the roles assigned to female deities served to express and to deal with the male fear of woman and motherhood. This also represents the social tension in Greek culture concerning gender identity and roles.

Women of respectable poorer classes and of isolated rural communities enjoyed a slightly greater degree of respect and freedom, more closely resembling the station represented fictionally in the works of Homer. There were pronounced exceptions to the rule of seclusion, such as warrior princesses in ancient Sparta, the hetaerae in the late classical era, women in northern Egypt during the Ptolemaic period, and business women in Macedonia in the Roman era. Occasional outcries against gender inequity found little sympathy, and the visions of an ideal state expressed in Plato's *Republic* never materialized. But various characteristics of Roman rule diminished the structures of the old Greek city-state and the laws initiated by Draco and Solon.

By the first Christian century, Greek women suffered enough male dominance to find appealing the sense of freedom available in the mystery cults, but they also had enough social independence to choose their own religious practices, even if their husbands did not participate. Female education was becoming more common and acceptable, and marriage was becoming more defined as a relationship of love, respect, and devotion.

Five

Rome

The date for the founding of Rome is usually set at 753 BCE, celebrated on April 21 with the Festival of Pales, goddess of shepherds. Two separate myths have blended to become one national saga. One is the story of the twins Romulus and Remus, purported to be sons of Rhea Silvia and the war god Mars. Abandoned at birth, they were fed and nurtured by a she-wolf until they were found by a shepherd named Faustulus who, with his wife Acca Larentia, raised the boys as their own. Another version is that Acca Larentia was in fact a prostitute. Eva Cantarella suggests a connection of this with the she-wolf legend, since the term *lupa* was sometimes used to describe a prostitute.[1] In either case, the twins would grow up to be warriors with a mission to defeat their great-uncle Amulius, who had overthrown Silvia's father Numitor as ruler of pre-Roman society. They were successful, but after a quarrel Romulus killed his brother and ruled alone.

The other myth is based on Virgil's epic *Aeneid,* which tells the story of how the Trojan prince Aeneas came to Italy. There his people blended with the local population to produce a line of kings of Alba Longa. Generations later, King Procas became the father of brothers Numitor and Amulius. When Numitor inherited rule, Amulius rebelled and had his brother imprisoned. Rhea Silvia in this myth is not the mother of twin brothers, but Numitor's virgin daughter, subsequently forced by Amulius to become a Vestal priestess. So in both myths, there is the motif of familial conflict, rivalry, and ambition for power from Rome's earliest days.

The ancient Roman Empire has been described as the "goddess of the earth and of its people, without a peer or second."[2] The actual history of Rome reveals the astonishing transition of a state of backward farming villages into a vast empire spreading outward from the central metropolis, and encompassing most of Europe, Asia Minor, the Levant, and North Africa. Developing slightly behind the Greeks, the emergence point for Rome seems to be the end of the second Punic War (201 BCE), when armies returned home from foreign centers with immense luxuries and the Roman population

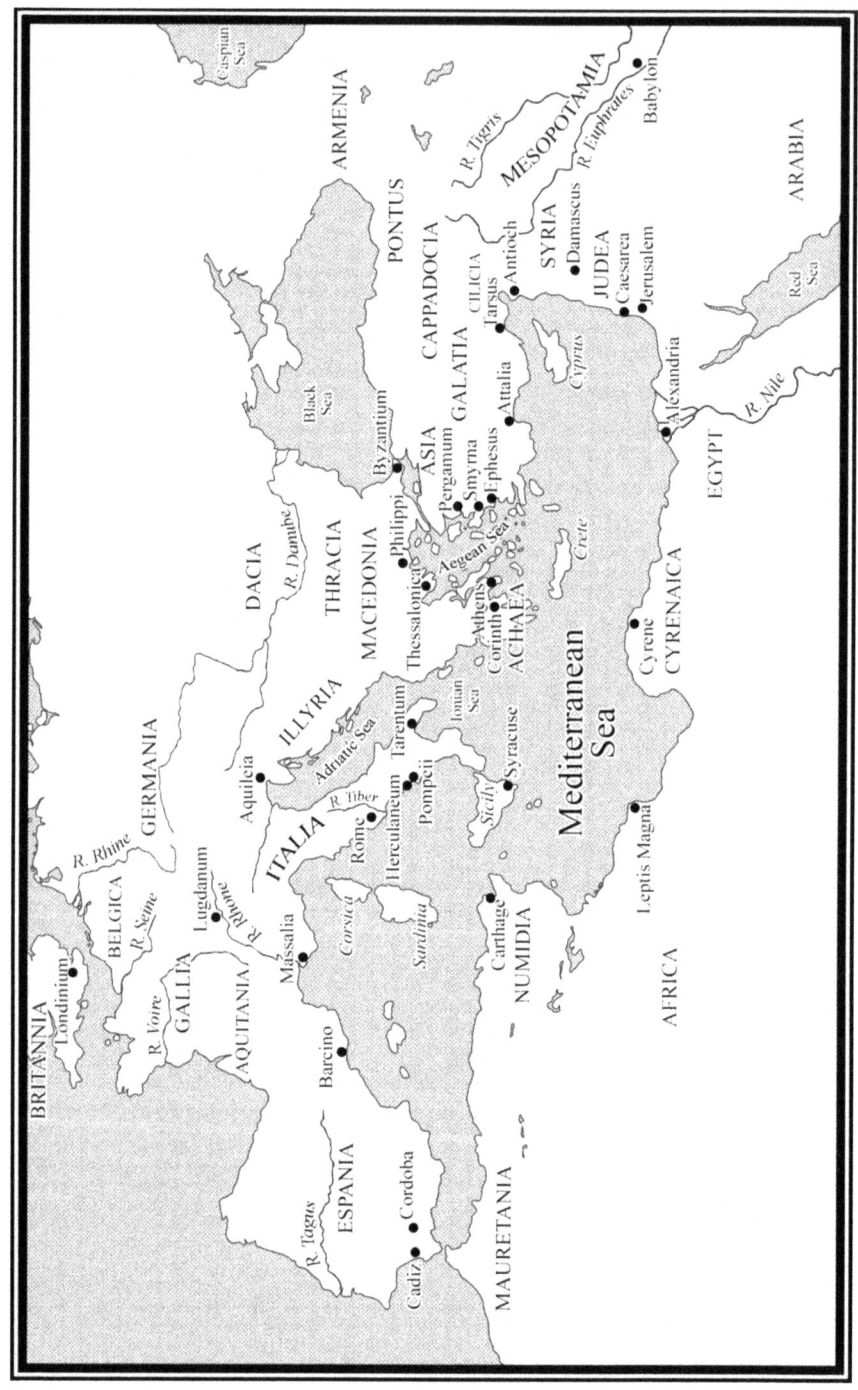

began to develop a taste for the exotic. Livy describes those times in these words:

> For the beginnings of foreign luxury were introduced into the City by the army from Asia. They for the first time imported into Rome couches of bronze, valuable robes for coverlets, tapestries and other products of the loom, and what at that time was considered luxurious furniture—tables with one pedestal and sideboards. Then female players of the lute and the harp and other festal delights of entertainment were made adjuncts to banquets; the banquets themselves, moreover, began to be planned with both greater care and greater expense. At that time the cook, to the ancient Romans the most worthless of slaves, both in their judgment of values and in the use they made of him, began to have value, and what had been merely a necessary service came to be regarded as an art. Yet those things which were then looked upon as remarkable were hardly even the germs of the luxury to come.[3]

However, according to Appian the transition began with the ruling class taking over small farms, either by purchase or by force, and making serfs of the lower classes. The indigenous Italian population was left poor and unemployed, and subsequently became the proletariat of the cities.[4] The result was that within a century a relatively small state of farmers was converted into a powerful oligarchy of wealthy landowners, merchants, and bankers, with a large class of poor workers at the bottom. An upheaval of social standards and cultural paradigms is to be expected under these circumstances. After the destruction of Carthage in 146 BCE there was a feeling of security throughout Roman society, having overpowered their only real threat to domination of the Mediterranean world. The general sense was that those in the Roman upper class could now relax and give themselves over to pleasure in a secure Republic.

Otto Kiefer, reviewing ancient history from within war-torn Europe around 1940, states that the greatest effect of such change was in the lives of Roman women.

> The old organization of family, with all its restrictions on individual freedom through the predominating *patria potestas*, was bound to break up—although it had guaranteed a certain limited standard of manners and morals. No one can wonder at its dissolution.... When an entire economic epoch is breaking up, it is impossible for women not to change their nature and outlook; especially since new wealth and new opportunities have a more powerful effect on the spirit of women than on men.[5]

While Kiefer's observations betray something of an androcentric bias in his own time, he is correct that in ancient Rome women, at least those of the

Opposite: Roman Empire, first century CE. Donald T. Massey (illustrator) and Lesly F. Massey, 2015.

upper class, became the principal beneficiaries of the luxurious life. And by the first Christian century, the status of women in Roman culture as a whole had reached an advanced stage unrivaled by any era in ancient history, also influencing women throughout the empire. However, this new status for women was not without its problems.

Resources

As with other ancient cultures, we can learn a great deal about life in Rome from surviving literature as well as statuary, mosaics, and frescoes. The earliest Latin literature is dated around 230 BCE, when a Roman audience for the first time saw Greek drama adapted by Livius Andronicus. The height of Roman literature is considered to be the short period from 81 BCE to 17 CE. This begins with the works of Cicero, which include letters, orations, treatises, and philosophy. Historical writers of that era include Julius Caesar and Sallust. During the era of Emperor Augustus, there emerged great poetic works by Virgil and Ovid, and Livy produced a history of the Roman people. Then during the early imperial period, in which Christianity was born, the Stoic philosopher Seneca wrote various dialogues and letters, as well as a lengthy discourse on nature. Petronius produced the first Latin novel, called *The Satyricon*, and satirists like Martial and Juvenal wrote scathing but often humorous critiques of the sad state of Roman society. So, male Roman writers had much to say about the lives of women—in poetry and prose, history and fiction, from careful and critical analysis to exaggerated and biased satire.

The Roman Republic (458–30 BCE) and the early Roman Empire, dated from the rule of Augustus (27 BCE to 14 CE), are significant as the immediate background to the birth of Christianity. The emperors who followed Augustus were Tiberius (14–37 CE), Caligula (37–41), Claudius (41–54), Nero (54–68), Vespasian (69–79), Titus (79–81), Domitian (81–96), Nerva (96–98) and Trajan (98–117). Their rule parallels the birth and early expansion of the church and the writing of most of the documents that comprise the New Testament. Under both Nero and Domitian, Jews were expelled from various Roman cities and forced to relocate. Christians, at first perceived as a sect of Judaism, suffered periods of intolerance and persecution. Under the rule of Vespasian, with Titus as his military commander, Jerusalem was destroyed in 70 CE. Although Jews already lived in major centers all over the Empire as a result of the Diaspora, the destruction of Jerusalem marked a significant shift in centrality for both Jews and Christians.

Archaeological remains of this era are abundant in North Africa, Palestine, and Turkey, and throughout Europe as far as Great Britain. So, in a quest to understand womanhood in ancient Rome and possible influences of

Roman culture on the early church and New Testament documents, we have ample ancient resources from which to draw.

Early Legends

In her study of women in ancient Greece and Rome, Eva Cantarella devotes a chapter to the hypothesis put forth nearly a century ago that matriarchal systems existed in various areas of the Italian peninsula, specifically in Lombardy, Liguria, and Etruria.[6] These ideas, similar to arguments for matriarchy in ancient Greece, emerged from the connection of women with the earth through their roles in planting, harvesting, baking, making pottery, and weaving. Thus, families in proto-Italy have been assessed by some as either matrilocal or matrilineal, or both. However, as Cantarella argues, these structures and practices had nothing to do with leadership, political power, or male dominance of those communities. And it is clear that patriarchy was a deeply entrenched social paradigm in Italy long before the earliest records.

Nonetheless, it does seem that in the earliest Roman religion female figures were honored, and it is possible that this developed from legends of certain strong females in Rome's early or prehistory. Cults such as Mater Matuta of Satricum, Feronia of Mt. Soractus, and Fortuna of Praeneste all attest to the value of womanhood and the influence of strong women. Tanaquil, the beatified wife of Lucumo (Tarquinius Priscus), fifth king of Rome, is especially worthy of attention because of the stories told of her by Livy and Dionysius of Halicarnassus. Tanaquil was daughter of a powerful Etruscan family in Tarquinii, Etruria, and had ambitions of power. She thought her husband would make a good leader, but as the son of Demaratus, a Greek immigrant from Corinth, he would not be supported in Tarquinii where they lived. So at her insistence they relocated to Rome, which was not at the time dominated by a strong local aristocracy and therefore a fruit ripe for picking. On their arrival, so goes the legend, something bizarre happened. An eagle swooped down and snatched the hat from Lucumo's head, flew away, and then brought it back and placed it on his head again. Tanaquil interpreted this as an omen that her husband would become ruler. This began her reputation for prophetic abilities and her strong influence for several decades in pre–Republic Rome. She had four children. Her son Lucius Tarquinius Superbus became seventh and last king of Rome, and Arruns Tarquinius was a co-conspirator in the foundation of the Republic. Her daughter Tarquinia married Servius Tullius, who succeeded Tarquinius Priscus.[7]

A story also survives about the role of Tanaquil in the ascension of Servius. He was the son of a slave, raised under the care and protection of Tanaquil. While still a child, as he lay sleeping one day his head caught on fire. Tanaquil prevented those around from throwing water on him, and when he awoke the flames went out. Again, Tanaquil made a pronouncement. This prodigious phenomenon meant that young Servius would become a light to Rome. When her own husband was assassinated, she kept his death secret and installed Servius in his place. She told everyone that until the king returned, they should obey Servius.[8] According to Roman historian Rufus Festus, Tanaquil eventually became known as Gaia Cirillo, by which name she was deified in association with wedding customs and various domestic crafts practiced by women.[9]

Another legend from Rome's beginnings is called the "Rape of the Sabine Women," recorded by both Livy and Plutarch.[10] Set during the days of Romulus, the story involves an effort to procure wives from among a local population called the Sabines. Recognizing the threat of a rival contingent, the Sabines refused to allow their women to marry the Romans. Consequently, the Romans planned a festival called Neptune Equester and invited neighboring tribes that included the Caeninenses, Crustumini, Antemnates, and Sabines. At the festival Romulus gave a signal, at which the Romans attacked the Sabine men and absconded with a number of their women, no doubt both wives and daughters. Livy claims that no direct sexual assault took place, and that Romulus offered the women free choice of marriage as well as civic and property rights. The Romans did not keep their promise. However, when the Sabines later penetrated Rome to rescue their women, they found them to be content to remain. The women rushed forth to stop the fighting, pleading with the Sabine men not to shed blood over the matter.[11] So, ultimately Sabine women played a significant role in developing the population of Rome.

Social and Legal Status of Women

The earliest Roman law code is called the Twelve Tables, dating from about 450 BCE. This and later laws provided for the care and direction of every family by the *pater familias,* who was the oldest living male in a household. This individual had complete control of all family members, even life or death judgments. However, it should be noted that the concept of family in ancient Rome was very different from today's definition. Ulpian, writing in the early third century CE and a contributor to what became the Justinian Code, said that a family was a group of people under the authority of the pater familias [family father], both those derived by nature (meaning children and other subordinate relatives) and those subject to him by law (meaning wife and slaves, with no blood relation).[12] Those relationships were further defined by terms like *manus* (the hand) that described the nature of the husband's relationship to and control over the wife. The wife did not have the same measure of control over children as is common today. They were under the control of the husband. In fact, a common ritual after childbirth was for the infant to be presented at the feet of the father, who either recognized it by picking it up or rejected it by leaving it where it lay. A rejected child was then exposed to die. It might be tossed into the city drain or the river, or it might be simply abandoned to starve to death.[13] Most exposed infants were female, since male descendants were preferred. But even male offspring were subject to the authority of the pater familias until his death. Upon his death, custody of children was passed to the nearest male relative. Guardianship over females was also in force until the time of Diocletian in the late third century CE, but this eventually disappeared.

It is evident from Cantarella's summary of Etruscan women in the protoagricultural phase of Roman history that patriarchy was established long before the earliest records, and women were all subject to the authority of some male. Traditionally that was the father during childhood, then upon marriage authority switched to the husband, who exercised control over the wife and their children. Pomeroy states that the underlying principle of Roman legislation that placed women under the custody of men was the perception of female "weakness and light-mindedness."[14] There was never a time when Rome regarded women as truly equal to men, although there was a measure of equality in the laws before Augustus.

Under the rule of Augustus, two specific laws were enacted with the purpose of assuring marriage and associated ethics. They were the *lex Iulia de maritandis ordinibus* in 17 BCE and amendments in the *lex Papia Poppaeanuptialis* in 9 CE. Augustus ordered that men (ages 25 to 60) and women (ages 25 to 50) marry or remarry within the appropriate age group, and if possible they were to produce children. Freeborn women who had given birth to three children and freed women who had four children were liberated from male guardianship. One of the objectives was to help restore a declining population. For reasons not fully understood, there were fewer females than males. Some have concluded that the frequent exposure of female infants led to this crisis. Cantarella mentions the possibility of lead poisoning, since we have evidence that some of the commonly used cosmetics contained lead.[15] Giving birth to too many children at an early age may have caused a high mortality rate among young females. Some have also mentioned the use of contraceptives as a factor for a decreased number of pregnancies and childbirth, but the methods used then were likely not reliable enough to be a factor. Among the poor, too many children may have increased the economic burden. Among the elite, matrons may have preferred greater freedom to enjoy the luxuries of the new Rome. However, it is well known that the exposure (abandonment) of female infants was far more common than male infants.

Whatever the reasons, the population of Rome had declined to the extent that formal actions were taken to reverse the trend.

The laws enacted by Augustus were praised by some and opposed by most. A significant criticism was that the initial legislation created categories of individuals, rather than legal equality that before had been a pillar of Roman law. Cicero expressed resentment of the prohibition of marriage between patricians and plebeians, both being Roman citizens but of different social standing and influence.[16] Suetonius reported protests by the equestrians (mounted soldiers) because the new laws penalized young men who had not married and had not produced children.[17] It is more likely that their objection was that it deprived young men of affairs with older unmarried women, sexually experienced but not prostitutes. But the laws also affected inheritance and were perceived as punishing those who were unmarried and without children.[18] Even Julia, the daughter of Augustus, was not exempt from the new legislation. While married to Agrippa, she was tried for adultery with Sempronius Graccus and several other men. As a result most of the men were banished from Rome.[19] Although sentenced to death, Antonius was allowed to commit suicide. Julia herself was exiled to the island of Pandateria for five years. Dio Cassius provides a lengthy report of the response of Augustus to criticism and the amendments enacted in 9 CE.[20] Essentially, Augustus held his ground and passed on legislation that continued forward several centuries.

It is interesting that Roman women had no true given names. A male Roman citizen had three names: a family name (*cognomen*), the immediate father's name (*gens*), and a personal given name (praenomen). Females bore only the *cognomen* and the *gens*. When we see names such as Julia, Tullia, Cornelia, or Flavia, the name is actually the feminine form of the *gens*, the name of the father. It meant "daughter of Julius," or "daughter of Tullius." If there were two daughters, both would be referred to by the feminine form of the father's name, but designations were commonly applied to identify them, such as *prima* (first) and *seconda* (second), or *maior* (elder) and *minor* (younger), such as Cornelia Seconda or Flavia Maior.

Therefore, Roman women were defined by the men in their lives and were valued mainly as wives and mothers. Roman laws simply added definition and detail to the ancient norms. Although some women were allowed more freedom than others, there was always a limit, even for the daughter of an emperor. No matter how wealthy they were, because they could not vote or stand for office, women had no formal role in political matters. In general, women were not allowed to participate in the citizen assembly and could not hold a political office.[21] In reality, wives or close relatives of prominent men might exert political influence behind the scenes and therefore wield genuine, albeit informal, power.

On the positive side, Roman women were free to walk or ride about at will.[22] Women could be found attending all forms of public entertainment, including theatrical performances, chariot races, and the gladiatorial combats, and husbands welcomed the presence of their wives at banquets and celebrations.[23] Seldom were they restricted from social contact with other men. In public, the Roman matron was saluted by her husband as the mistress of his household.[24] The social life of upper class Roman women included being well informed in public affairs, current events, and politics. They had the liberty to conduct business, engage in financial enterprise on their own, and had legal recourse directly to the magistrates upon encroachment of their civil rights. But the degree of freedom a woman enjoyed depended largely on her wealth and social status.

Betrothal

Despite the advanced freedom among upper-class Roman women, old-world conventions thrived among the poor and in outlying areas many years after change in the city of Rome. It was unthinkable for a boy and girl to plan and arrange their marriage. The choice of partners for their children continued to rest with fathers, who for centuries before were accustomed to negotiating marriages of sons and daughters. As was the case in numerous other ancient cultures, professional matchmakers were sometimes enlisted to negotiate marriages on behalf of two families.[25] Roman girls were frequently married by the age of 15 and were forbidden to act independently of their father's will. Despite the requirement of their consent, marriages arranged by parents were expected to work out, and if true love developed it could be regarded as fortunate, but unusual and certainly not necessary. A mature woman likely had more of a say in a second marriage, or beyond.

The formal engagement of Roman couples consisted of the presentation of a ring, along with several other gifts for the bride, followed by a feast. The gifts, no doubt, arose over time out of the ancient bride-price, or earnest money (*coemptio*), that served as a deposit on the bride.[26] The ring, which may have been iron with gold plating, or solid gold for those who could afford it, was typically presented to the bride-to-be in the presence of friends and was slipped on the third finger of the left hand, a custom still practiced in most western cultures today. Aulus Gellius explained that this choice of fingers was due to its close connection to the heart, based on a delicate nerve which had been discovered in anatomical dissection.[27] Anatomy and physiology were rudimentary in those days and it may be that this explanation was simply invented. Nonetheless, this finger was given the honor of the ring that represented the heartfelt love on which ideally a marriage should be based. By these means the engagement was announced openly, and arrangements were begun for the wedding to follow months later. It seems, however, that such betrothals carried no actual legal obligations and were frequently broken, as they are today. Pliny regarded them to be among the numberless trifles which encumbered his society.[28]

Weddings

Plutarch provides a thorough treatment of the typical Roman marriage ceremony.[29]

The night before the wedding, the bride's hair was set in a crimson net. Then, on the wedding day she was dressed in traditional fashion. Carcopino describes it in these terms:

> A tunic without hem (*tunica recta*), secured round the waist by a girdle of wool with a double knot, the *cingulum herculeum*. Over this she wore a cloak or *pulla* of saffron color; on her feet sandals of the same shade; round her neck a metal collar. Her coiffure was protected by six pads of artificial hair (*seni crines*) separated by narrow bands, such as the Vestals wore during the whole period of their service; and over it she wore a veil of flaming orange—hence called the *flammeum*—which modestly covered the upper part of her face. On the top of the veil was placed a wreath, woven simply of verbena and sweet marjoram in the time of Caesar and Augustus, and later of myrtle and orange blossom.[30]

In this attire, the bride stood among her own people and welcomed the groom with his family and friends. The entire party proceeded to the atrium of the house, or to a special sanctuary, to offer a sacrifice to the gods, usually a pig, but sometimes a ewe or an ox. At this point, an optional part of the ceremony was affixing seals to the contract by witnesses, numbering as many as ten representing the two families. This custom also survives today.

An indispensable part of the ceremony, however, was the exchange of vows before the *auspex,* someone chosen to serve as the family augur. This also represents the transition of ancient customs into the new. In earliest Roman culture, the augur was a high-ranking priest who made predictions and gave advice by the interpretation of omens. He first examined the entrails of the sacrificial animal to assure its acceptability to the gods and the validity of the marriage. Then, the vows were stated in his presence. That this was the central factor is indicated by the record of the marriage of Cato and Marcia. This couple renounced all pomp and ceremony, summoned no witnesses or guests, and merely exchanged vows before Brutus as augur.[31]

After the vows, the guests burst into congratulations expressed as *bona fortuna* (good luck!). With that, the festivities began. At nightfall, the time came for the mother to bid farewell to her daughter, and the groom then escorted his bride to her new home, accompanied by a crowd of friends who marched by torchlight singing licentious songs to the music of flutes.[32] After the couple anointed and decorated the doorposts, the groom lifted the bride over the threshold, and their first night as a married couple began.

Marriage

Monogamy was the custom in archaic Italy, although there is ample evidence that married males engaged in relations with other women when they had the opportunity. It was expected also that a citizen male could engage in a relationship with one of his own slaves, and might have children by her, but a relationship with a female slave could never be considered legal marriage.

The Roman marriage contract was of two varieties. Under the old style, the wife was technically under the authority of the husband by a legal stipulation of their contract called *cum manu*.[33] This arrangement upheld the ancient system of tutelage under which all women fell, requiring that the bride pass from under the hand of her father to that of her husband. She was subject to her husband's almost absolute authority over her person and property. Yet, marriage did confer upon the wife the name and title of her husband. Having left her original *familia*, she became part of that of the husband and his relatives, and therefore she typically was not entitled to inheritance from her original family.

Although it was discouraged by Augustus, a second type of contract that modern scholars have called *sine manu* (without the hand) became very popular. Under this arrangement a marriage was socially acceptable but free of legal responsibility, and the wife remained the heir of her original family. Even with this arrangement, at first the wife had to be under the authority of some man, either a ward or guardian (*tutela*), chosen from among her relatives. But by the time of Hadrian this, too, passed away.[34] However, it seems that a woman with three children and a freed woman with four became legally independent, a status known as *sui iuris*. But this did not provide any greater social freedom.

Salvius Iulianus, who lived in the middle second century CE, claimed that a marriage could not be legally contracted if by constraint, but only by the consent of both parties. So, with the advancement of legislation, fathers lost their right to marry daughters off for political, social, or financial reasons without their consent.[35]

At some point in the first Christian century Roman women were considered in certain terms independent, the pater familias having become

158   Daughters of God, Subordinates of Men

theoretically obsolete.[36] A wife's personal property as well as any inheritance from her father remained in her control, completely independent of her husband. Only the dowry fell under his control and could be retained by him in the event of her disloyalty.[37] The *tutor optivus* enabled a father to leave his daughter free to choose her guardian, or to change it several times as she may desire for business reasons. Eventually, the power of pater familias would be diminished further by the change in laws governing inheritance. According to the ancient code of the Twelve Tables, a mother had no right of succession to a son who had died intestate. But under Hadrian (emperor from 117–138 CE) she was admitted, provisionally, as a legitimate heir by the *senatus consultum Tertullianum*. Later, under Marcus Aurelius (emperor from 161–180 CE), children became entitled to inherit from their mothers, regardless of the validity of the union from which they came.[38]

As early as Augustus, adultery by the wife was considered a public offense, and the pater familias held the authority to kill an offending female under his power. The husband did not have such power, but was obliged to divorce his wife for such an offense. The wife could also divorce an adulterous husband, but she was not obliged to do so. In most cases a wife would prefer tolerating infidelity to being divorced and without some measure of financial security. Augustus also initiated laws of *stuprum*, which made it a crime for a man to engage in sex with an unmarried upper-class woman or a widow, although intercourse with a prostitute was allowed. Women, at least those of the upper class, were severely punished for any sexual relations outside marriage. Suetonius reports that Augustus exiled both his daughter and his granddaughter for such conduct.[39] However, there is evidence that some women got around the laws of *stuprum* by registering with the local trade magistrates (*aediles*) as prostitutes, to whom such legislation did not apply.[40]

The Roman Matron

Carcopino expresses the opinion that the women of imperial Rome enjoyed a dignity and independence at least equal if not superior to those claimed by women in the modern West.[41] This is an exaggeration, as we have already seen. But certainly, the life of the Roman matron was far better than most women of antiquity. With the changes in marriage customs, women were freed from much of the structure of guardianship and restraint. Brides entered matrimony of their own free will and as the legal equals of their husbands. The wife was the mistress of her home, holding the keys to the storeroom and having charge of all the servants, male and female. She was queen in her own right, and while she may have had training in the art of housekeeping, she took full advantage of the status of manager and mistress. Stately leisure was a thing to be enjoyed by wealthy women, although it is important to note that this was provided by the labor of slaves and poorer classes, including women. And Plutarch claims that wealthy Roman matrons found it easy to dominate their husbands.[42]

Pomeroy begins her discussion of the Roman matron with a clear recognition of the almost unique merger of Hellenism and Roman culture to produce "the emancipated, but respected, upper-class woman."

> The Roman matron of the late Republic must be viewed against the background of shrewd and politically powerful Hellenistic princesses, expanding cultural opportunities for women, the search for sexual fulfillment in the context of a declining birthrate, and individual assertiveness characteristic of the Hellenistic period. The rest of the picture is Roman: enormous wealth, aristocratic indulgence and display, pragmatism permitting women to exercise leadership during the absence of men on military and governmental missions of long duration; and, as a final element, a past preceding the influence of the Greeks.[43]

Among the many women mentioned by various ancient writers, Cornelia Africana is often extolled as a paragon of matronly virtue and aplomb. She was the wife of Tiberius Gracchus Major, the son of Tiberius Sempronius Gracchus, a Roman Republican consul around 240 BCE. Cornelia bore 12 children, and after the death of Tiberius chose to remain a widow despite an offer of marriage from Ptolemy VIII. Only three of her children survived to adulthood, but of them Tiberius and Gaius were part of a line of significant figures in Roman politics and religion called the Gracchi.[44] Cornelia was educated in both Latin and Greek literature and had an astute understanding of Roman politics. She was actively involved in the reforms attempted by her sons, and they in turn used her reputation as a chaste and noble matron to their own political advantage. After their violent deaths, it appears that she retired from political life and received guests in a quiet villa away from the city. Although the authenticity of letters attributed to Cornelia is questioned by historians, if they are genuine she is among a small number of Roman women whose writings have survived. After her death, a marble statue of her was erected, but only the base is extant today. No doubt the details of her life were embellished or altered by later Roman historians.[45] But she was clearly embraced by the people of Rome and lauded for her virtue and social influence.

Osiek and Balch discuss the very complex system of relationships involved in patronage in the ancient Greco-Roman world.[46] Of special note is public patronage, whereby a wealthy man or woman might use their resources to support clubs, trade guilds, and religious associations, even to the extent of donating land or financing the construction of a building. In gratitude, the beneficiaries of this support would honor the patron with an inscription, statue, or a place of honor in meetings or civic administration. Examples include Livia, wife of Augustus; Eumachia, a widow in Pompei; Junia Theodora of Corinth; and Plancia Magna of Perga in Pamphylia. And, despite the fact that most of such patrons were male, it is interesting a female patron is mentioned by name in the New Testament. The Apostle Paul commends Phoebe, whom he describes as a *diakonos* (minister, servant) in the church in Cenchrea, as well as prostatis (patron).[47]

Greater Freedom

Circumstances determined that common and slave class women in ancient Rome were often illiterate. But contrary to the Greeks, the Romans never intentionally restricted their women from education. If matters of science, law, literature, or philosophy came into a Roman home, the wife was welcome to participate in it. Sallust says that Sempronia, wife of Decimus Brutus, was skilled in Greek and Roman literature, and was "distinguished by much refinement of wit, and much grace of expression."[48] Pliny also speaks highly of his wife's intellectual alertness and her love for literature.[49] And in terms of formal education, there is evidence that by the first century BCE, even among common people, there were schools for girls.[50]

Numerous champions of women's rights, such as Musonius Rufus, a first-century Stoic philosopher, claimed for women complete independence on grounds of moral and intellectual equality of the sexes.[51] The works of Musonius are only preserved in fragments, but he was known to Origen, an Alexandrian Christian writer in the early fourth century, who considered him to be a pre-Christian saint because of views that were so similar to those in the New Testament.[52] Musonius taught that wives should be dedicated to domestic duties, but that should not prohibit them from learning philosophy as well. He advocated equal access to education so that women could educate their children in the home. But in marriage he taught that the greatest love possible is between a husband and wife, and that they should love and support each other mutually.[53] Stephens summarizes:

> Musonius argued that there must be companionship and mutual care of husband and wife in marriage since its chief end is to live together and have children. Spouses should consider all things as common possessions and nothing as private, not even the body itself. But since procreation can result from sexual relations outside of marriage, childbirth cannot be the only motive for marriage. Musonius thought that when each spouse competes to surpass the other in giving complete care, the partnership is beautiful and admirable. But when a spouse considers only his or her own interests and neglects the other's needs and concerns, their union is destroyed and their marriage cannot help but go poorly.[54]

Osiek and Balch say that Musonius "stands as a lonely voice in his insistence that sexual fidelity should not operate on a double standard."[55]

With such encouragement, it seems that women in every quarter of the empire made a concerted effort to abandon traditionally female occupations and compete with men in every possible way. They studied law, political science, court procedure, international affairs, and philosophy. Others demonstrated their liberty by withdrawing their support of the various activities of their husbands. They voiced opinions openly and boldly, as if they were the masters of their houses, while bewildered husbands looked on in silence. They became open targets for the satirists, who were appalled by women who went out of their way to prove themselves the equals of men.[56] Juvenal predicted with trepidation: "No present will you ever make if your wife forbids; nothing will you ever sell if she objects; nothing will you buy without her consent."[57] Juvenal could not abide female intellectualism.

> Most intolerable of all is the woman who ... pardons the dying Dido and puts poets against each other, putting Virgil in the one scale and Homer in the other. The grammarians make way before her; the rhetoricians give in; the whole crowd is silenced.[58]

He further complains:

> I hate her who is forever poring over and studying Palaemon's treatise; who never violates the rules and principles of grammar; and skilled in antiquarian lore, quotes verses I never knew, and corrects the phrases of her friend as old fashioned, which men would never heed.[59]

And, Juvenal scorns women openly competing with men in tests of strength and agility, like Mevia, who "with spear in hand and breasts exposed, takes to pig sticking."[60] Some women, he reports, attended chariot races dressed in men's clothing, and others devoted themselves to fencing and wrestling. Likewise, the gluttonous table manners of some women incurred the criticism of Petronius, who describes Fortunata, the stout mistress of Trimalchio, gorged with food and staggering from intoxication.[61] Juvenal writes satirically of a woman who "eats giant oysters, pours foaming unguents into her unmixed *falernum*, and drinks out of perfume bowls while the roof spins dizzily round and every light shines double."[62]

With these liberties also came the opportunity for women to make themselves heard in terms of collective political voice. Laws enacted by Gaius Oppius (*lex Oppia*) in 215 BCE forbade women to wear excessive jewelry or colored clothing. Livy says that women rioted as a result and virtually demanded representation in any legislation which concerned them.[63] In 195, just 20 years later, that law was repealed because of demonstrations by women.[64]

Some have claimed that the natural result of feminism in Roman culture was the disintegration of gender roles in marriage and marriage itself. Considering that these shifts were a sudden anomaly in ancient paradigms, it was difficult for both men and women to adjust. Some women evaded maternal responsibilities for fear of losing their beauty. Many women refused to have children, using contraceptives or simply abstaining from sex as part of their reproach of male-oriented traditions. And it seems that for this reason alone numerous marriages at the end of the first and beginning of the second century were childless, including that of Trajan, Hadrian and Pliny.[65] Martial considered women worthy of praise if they bore as many as three children and exceptional if they had more.[66]

Tucker, expressing a view of most scholars in the nineteenth and early twentieth centuries, sees a principal cause of disintegration in Roman society in "the increasing demands of women, their increasing unwillingness to bear the natural responsibilities of matrimony, their extravagant expectations, and the impossibility of there being two masters in one house claiming equal authority."[67] This observation no doubt represents the point of view of most males in ancient Rome, but it also represents an androcentric bias that persists in the twenty-first century—a failure to recognize the possibility and value of genuine partnership between two individuals in marriage and gender equity in society.

It seems that many aristocratic couples slept apart, often in completely separate quarters. Petronius so indicates in his novel, in which Trimalchio boasts to his guests of the size of his house, including his wife's bedroom, which he calls "the nest of the she viper."[68] But it appears that where couples had such arrangements, one bedroom remained unused, and the husband slept in the chambers of the wife. Trimalchio must have slept with his wife Fortunata, for he complains of insomnia due to her snoring.

The liberties Roman husbands enjoyed in terms of sexual gratification outside marriage were viewed as upright and just. Cato greeted an acquaintance, whom he saw leaving a brothel, "proceed in your noble course."[69] Cicero states:

> But if there be anyone who thinks that youth is to be wholly interdicted from amours with courtesans, he certainly is very strict indeed. I cannot deny what he says; but still he is at variance not only with the license of the present age, but even with the habits of our ancestors, and with what they used to consider allowable. For when was the time that men were not used to act in this manner? When was such conduct found fault with? When was it not permitted? When, in short, was the time when that which is lawful was not lawful?[70]

With the emancipation of Roman women there occurred a parallel license for sexual activity, and the husbands did not like it. Sallust says that after the time of Sulla, women threw off all restraint of modesty.[71] It is clear that many women, especially those in Rome itself and other cities, would take the initiative in developing sexual relationships. Ovid states, "Chaste is she whom no one has asked; or be she not too countrified, she herself asks first."[72]

During the late first century BCE and into the first and second centuries CE there were various writers who wrote social and political satire. It was not comedic, but addressed perceived threats to the social order and continuity. They expressed all kinds of concerns, ranging from social-climbing foreigners to gluttony, marital unfaithfulness to greed and excess. Among such writers, Horace lived during the first century BC. But Seneca, Martial, and Juvenal's *Satires* all lived during the first Christian century and were contemporaries of the Apostle Paul. Juvenal is especially relevant, where "Book 2, Satire 6" is about decaying feminine virtue. Juvenal declared that a virtuous woman was difficult to find:

> Fall prostrate at the threshold of Tarpeian Jove, and sacrifice to Juno a heifer with gilded horns, if you have the rare good fortune to find a matron with unsullied chastity. So few are there worthy to handle the fillets of Ceres; so few, whose kisses their own fathers might not dread.[73]

It was not uncommon for a married woman to engage in affairs with numerous men and to employ various contraceptives to avoid pregnancy. Juvenal sarcastically advised husbands to give their wives some potion, lest they unknowingly become the father of an Ethiopian. And he further writes of one wife who, after being caught in adultery, made this defense:

> It was formerly agreed ... that you should do what you pleased, and that I also might have full power to gratify myself. In spite of your outcry and confounding heaven and sea, I am mortal.[74]

Horace also paints a grim picture of moral inequity of his day, finding no fault with male sexual freedom but blaming females for their abandonment of chastity:

> The times, fertile in wickedness, have, in their first place, polluted the marriage state, and thereby the issue and families. From this fountain, perdition being derived, has overwhelmed the nation and people. The virgin, marriageable, delights to be taught the Ionic dances, and at this time even is fashioned in her limbs, and cherishes unchaste desires from her infancy; for she courts younger debauchees when her husband is in his cups; nor has she any choice, to whom she shall privately grant her forbidden pleasures when the lights are removed, but, at the word of command, openly, not without the knowledge of her husband, whether it be a factor that calls for her, or the captain of a Spanish ship, the extravagant purchaser of her impurities.[75]

Sarcasm is evident also in the words of Seneca:

> Can one feel ashamed of adultery, now that things have come to such a pass that no woman keeps a husband at all, unless it be to pique her lover? Chastity

merely implies ugliness. Where will you find any woman so abject, so repulsive, as to be satisfied with a single pair of lovers, without having a different one for each hour of the day; nor is the day long enough for all of them, unless she has taken her airing in the grounds of one, and passes the night with the other. A woman is frumpish and old-fashioned if she does not know that adultery with one paramour is nicknamed "marriage."[76]

So, by the first century CE, the standards of morality in Roman culture were of concern to many, and it is not surprising that they, like many today, blamed feminism for all their social ills. Thus, the satirists were highly critical of women for conduct which their culture, and most of those before them, had reserved for men only.[77]

Divorce

Divorce already had become very common during the early empire, and eventually would reach epidemic proportions despite the efforts of Augustus to regulate behavior. His *Lex de ordinibus maritandis* in 18 BCE was intended to check the decline in birthrate by encouraging divorcees to remarry and to safeguard the wife's dowry.[78] But he allowed divorce for virtually any cause, provided the intentions were announced publicly. By the time of Juvenal, marriages among nobles were often shallow relationships, and many women were known to marry scores of men in succession as if collecting husbands had become a competitive sport.[79]

Although marriage *cum manu* placed the wife under the authority of the husband, custom restricted his power in order to provide some measure of stability in families and to prevent wives from being expelled from the household without significant blame, and only after investigation by a family council. In 307 BCE, the censors stripped a senator of his status for dismissing his wife without first seeking judgment of his domestic tribunal, and in 230 BCE another senator was rebuked by his fellows for putting away his wife for apparent barrenness.[80]

In succeeding generations, divorces became common and were obtained for trivial reasons, such as going outdoors without a head covering, stopping in the street to speak to a man, or attending the games without the husband's permission. Julius Caesar repudiated his second wife Pompeia for the simple reason that innocence was not enough to declare her chaste and faithful: "Caesar's wife must be above suspicion."[81] By this time, wives were accustomed to doing as they pleased, and such technicalities became mere excuses for men to divorce when they had no other practical means of exerting authority. Eventually, the institution of marriage was so disparaged that divorce became a whimsical component of matrimony, enacted by mutual consent. Valeria, a young divorcee and half-sister of the orator Hortensius, became the fifth wife of Sulla. Cicero, at age 57 and after 20 years of marriage, divorced Terentia, the mother of his children, and married the young and wealthy Publia.[82] Terentia seems to have born her fortune well, later marrying Sallust and after him Messalla Corvinus, and she died wealthy and vindicated.[83]

Augustus allowed divorce for virtually any grounds, provided the intentions were announced publicly. Through the *actio rei uxoriae* (application for publication of the dowry) a woman could reclaim funds or goods brought with her into the marriage in the form of a dowry. However, an appointed judge might grant to the husband maintenance for any children left in his care, and compensation for any damages caused by extravagance or misconduct on the part of the wife. But basically, the laws existed to safeguard the wife's dowry, which made her appealing to suitors and assured another marriage.

Juvenal offers a grim description of shallow relationships in his day:

> A rich wife with a covetous husband has all the widow's privileges. Why then does Sertorius burn with passion for Bibula? If you sift the truth, it is not the wife he is in love with, but the face. Let a wrinkle or two make their appearance, and the shriveled skin grow flaccid, her teeth get black, or her eyes smaller—"pack up your baggage," the freedman will say, "and march. You are become offensive. You blow your nose too frequently. March! And be quick about it! Another is coming whose nose is not so moist."[84]

Juvenal also depicts the extraordinary number of husbands collected by some women, as if it were a calculated objective:

> She leaves the doors so recently adorned, the tapestry still hanging on the house and the branches still green upon the threshold. Thus the number grows; thus she has her eight husbands in five years. A notable fact to record upon her tomb![85]

Seneca writes:

> Is any woman ashamed of being divorced, now that some noble ladies reckon the years of their lives, not by the number of consuls, but by that of their husbands, now that they leave their homes in order to marry others, and marry only in order to be divorced? Divorce was only dreaded as long as it was unusual; now that no report is without it, women learn to do what they hear so much about.[86]

And Martial declares with disdain that "she who marries so often does not marry; she is an adulteress by form of law."[87]

Osiek and Balch describe the concepts of honor and shame that were fundamental values in Mediterranean cultures. The male role was not just to dominate, but to maintain status, power, and reputation within a familial group. That especially involved providing protection and support of those less powerful, as well as showing hospitality to strangers. A female's role was to protect her sexual purity, for she in the eyes of males is "the mysterious gateway of birth and death."[88] So, a woman's sexual behavior had everything to do with maintaining honor for all her family, her husband in particular, or bringing upon them shame.

Beauty Aids

Various satirists dilate on the daily routine of wealthy Roman matrons. They are described as living a life of ease and self-indulgence, often spending the day doing little else but applying makeup, trying on clothes, and sitting among a troupe of attendants busying themselves over a lavish hairdo. Such matrons are described as waking up each morning to the piercing bark of a pair of scented and curled dogs that had slept at the foot of the bed. Their faces are still be smeared with a thin flour paste, applied the night before. They begin their day washing with scented water, followed by rinsing their mouths using a toothbrush with powders and pastilles to sweeten the breath. The process included enameling the teeth to cover stains or decay. The next step was a visit to the nearest bath house, accompanied by several attendants who carried fresh clothes. After bathing, they would enjoy a massage, and superfluous body hair was removed by scrubbing with a pumice stone or shaving with a razor.

The application of makeup was described as an elaborate process, comparable to that of any modern movie star or television celebrity. If the toiletries and makeup supplies were too many and too cumbersome to carry to the bath house, that process was taken up once back home. There, the matron would poise before a table of mirrors, wash basins, and an assortment of jars and bottles. Lees of wine or ocre mixed into a creamy paste became lipstick, and a powder was use to redden the cheeks.[89] Martial writes with biting sarcasm concerning the facade of his wife's makeup:

> Though, while you yourself, Galla, are at home, you are being dressed out in the middle of the Suburra, and your locks are prepared for you at a distance; though you lay aside your teeth at night with your silk garments, and lie stowed away in a hundred boxes; though even your face does not sleep with you, and you ogle me from under eyebrows which are brought to you in the morning; though no consideration of your faded charms, which belong to a past generation, moves you; though all this is the case, you offer me six hundred sesterces. But nature revolts, and, blind though she be, she sees very well what you are.[90]

In the early days of Roman history, even during the Republic, hairstyles were simple, consisting of a part in the middle with the hair gathered into a chignon at the back, or else flowing loose over the shoulders. But in imperial

Rome, particularly of women of the upper class, hairstyles became elaborate and complex. A woman trained at dressing hair and fitting wigs and hairpieces was called an ornatrix. She also was skilled in dying natural and artificial hair and all aspects of hair grooming and hygiene. For several reasons, baldness and thinning hair was a problem for both men and women in Roman society. Remedies of all sorts were concocted in the attempt to grow hair: oils, marrow from deer bones, bear and sheep fat, mixtures of pepper and rat excrement, all in vain. Therefore, many men and women wore wigs, even if they were ridiculed by those who did not require them. Wigs made from locks shorn from slave girls could be purchased near the temple of Hercules and the Muses in the Campus Martius. Ovid recorded an unexpected visit he paid to a female friend who, in haste to make her appearance, put her wig on backwards. He advised that women with scanty or missing locks should keep their doors guarded.[91] Juvenal ridiculed arranging hair in elaborate towers:

> So numerous are the tiers and stories piled one upon another on her head! In front you would take her for an Andromache; she is not so tall behind; you would not think it is the same person.[92]

Macrobius ridicules women who endured great pain for the sake of beauty. He describes a woman named Julia who commanded her ornatrix to pitilessly tear out any grey hairs she might find.[93] And the servants are described as suffering even more. Juvenal writes:

> If madam has an appointment and wishes to be turned out more nicely than usual, the unhappy Pescas who does her hair will have her own hair torn and the clothes stripped from her shoulders and breasts. "Why is this curl standing up?" she asks, and then down comes a thong of bull's hide to inflict chastisement for the offending ringlet![94]

A similar scene is described by Martial:

> One curl of the whole round of hair had gone astray, badly fixed by an insecure pin. This crime Lalage avenged with the mirror in which she had observed it and Plecusa, smitten, fell because of those savage locks![95]

In the past, historians assumed the satirists drew accurate descriptions of how things had come to be in Rome. But more recent scholarship tends to see these as gross exaggerations of reality, expressing genuine frustration and shame on the part of Roman males at the loss of control.

Dress and Head Covering

Despite all the changes in society, garments remained essentially the same through the Roman Republic and early empire. An undergarment made of linen was called a tunic—short for men, boys, and girls, and long for women. The outer garment worn by Roman citizens is described by Cowell as a "blanket" wrapped around the body and over the shoulders. The men's version of this was called a *toga*, and the women's version was a *stola*, with an added mantle (*palla*) very much like a heavy shawl that could be thrown over the shoulders or drawn over the head.[96] Those not of the citizen class wore a different kind of wrap.

Wealthy women might have a variety of garments, some even made of Indian or Egyptian cotton or Asian silk, rather than the local wool or linen, and these might be died in bright colors. The mantle might be decorated with fine embroidery, and she might carry a kerchief to wipe dust and perspiration from her brow. As described by Petronius, the noble lady would add to her ensemble a goodly number of jewels and ornamental earrings, a diadem in her hair, a choker around her neck, a pendant on her breasts, bracelets on each wrist, rings on her fingers, and at least a couple of Arabian ankle bracelets. She took in one hand her fan of peacock's feathers, to brush away flies, and in the other she held a sunshade. Or if she preferred, a servant would walk with her holding the sunshade over her head. Then, glistening in the sunlight, jangling with each step, and reeking of perfume, the fine lady strolled leisurely along streets and in gardens, challenging the critical eye of other women and stealing the smiles of male passersby.[97]

We commonly speak of veiling in the ancient world, but the term meant different things in different cultures. Among both Greeks and Romans, veiling was accomplished by drawing one portion of the outer garment over the top of the head. The purpose was not to cover the face, as in later Arabic custom, but to cover the head. According to Plutarch, it was the common custom for women to cover their heads, and men to uncover their heads, when going outside.[98] However, it would appear also that the head covering as a symbol of married status was abandoned by the wealthy matrons of this era. And Valerius Maximus, writing during the reign of Tiberius, said that one of the causes of divorce among Romans was a married woman daring to appear out of doors with nothing on her head.[99] There is reason to conclude that the head covering was even more important for priestesses than ordinary women. Vestal Virgins are consistently depicted with their heads covered, and Plutarch specifically mentions that fact because these women bore a burden of sanctity and dignity that demanded strict protocol in both demeanor and dress.[100]

Honorable Wives

There were women in Roman culture who maintained traditional roles and were held in high esteem for their morality. Seneca commended his mother

Helvia, stating respectfully that she had never followed the unchaste path of most women and never wore clothes that revealed the figure as though naked.[101] And Tacitus commends the German women for their noble degree of chastity and faithfulness to their own husbands, implying that the moral decadence of Rome was not pandemic.[102] And certainly it can be said that not all Roman marriages were bad, not even the majority. In describing the conditions of the Civil Wars, Appian begins by commenting on the remarkable examples of love of wives for their husbands.[103] In especially trying times when many nobles were placed on proscription lists and were either executed, exiled, or asked to commit suicide, great women of aristocracy stood out as hallmarks of devotion. Some had been the trusted confidants of their husbands, sharing in former political endeavors and choosing to remain by their sides in danger, even in fatal hours. Tacitus provides examples of such devotion. Under the reign of Tiberius, Sextia refused to survive her husband Aemelius Scaurus, who was forced to commit suicide in 34 CE. The same was true of Paxaea, who was wife of Pomponius Labeo.[104] Under Nero, the philosopher Seneca was sent the command of suicide, and his young wife Paulina opened her veins at his side. She was forcibly bandaged and saved at the order of Nero himself.[105] Also, late in the reign of Nero, Priscus and Gallus were accompanied into exile by their wives, the latter willfully leaving behind a fortune that was duly confiscated by the empire.[106] Pliny discusses at length the tragic circumstances in which Arria, wife of senator Caecina Paetus, proved a most loyal and devoted wife. With stoic control of her emotions, she nursed him through an almost fatal illness, only to be arrested with him for an alleged role in a revolt. When the fatal hour came in Rome before Claudius, she insisted on dying with her husband. She would not be dissuaded, and she drew a dagger from her cloak and plunged it into her chest. Then drawing it out again, she handed it to her husband and uttered the words, "It does not hurt, my Paetus."[107]

Pliny praises the wife of Macrinus, who lived with him in happiness for 39 years.[108] He also speaks favorably of his own wife, Calpurnia, actually his third, praising her for moral quality and sobriety: "How full of solicitude is she when I am entering upon any cause! How kindly does she rejoice with me when it is over!" He adds that when giving a public reading, she listens from behind the curtain and delights as she hears his praises. "She sings my verses and sets them to her lyre with no other master but love, the best instructor."[109] It is thought that Calpurnia was only 14 when they married, and Pliny was approaching 40. But she was indeed the love of his life. The now famous lines from one of his letters to her, written around 112 CE, bear out the deep affection:

> You say that you are feeling my absence very much, and your only comfort when I am not there is to hold my writings in your hand and often put them

in my place by your side. I like to think that you miss me and find relief in this sort of consolation. I, too, am always reading your letters, and returning to them again and again as if they were new to me—but this only fans the fire of my longing for you. If your letters are so dear to me, you can imagine how I delight in your company; do write as often as you can, although you give me pleasure mingled with pain.[110]

Pliny had sent her home from Bithynia to be with her aunt upon the death of her grandfather. While they were apart, Pliny died. Judith Harrington has published a novel entitled *Letters from Calpurnia, Pliny's Wife*. It is derived from manuscripts of Pliny's letters to Calpurnia that she discovered in the library of the Christian shrine, Meryemana Evi, located in the mountains above the ruins of Ephesus, in western Turkey. While fictitious, the work is well researched and offers insightful recreation of a voice history has never heard.

Besides testimonies like these, a great number of funeral inscriptions reveal the tender memories of departed wives from among the middle and lower classes. Kiefer reproduces these words from a tombstone erected during the days of the Republic:

> Short is my say, wander: stop and read it through. This poor stone covers a beautiful woman. Her parents called her Claudia. She loved her own husband unchangingly. She bore two sons. One she left behind on earth, the other buried in the earth's bosom. She spoke kindly and walked nobly, cared for her house and her spinning. I have finished. Go.[111]

From a later period these words are inscribed:

> She was the guardian spirit of my house, she was my hope and my only love. What I wished she also wished, what I shunned she shunned also. None of her inmost thoughts was ever hidden from me. She lacked no diligence in spinning wool, she was thrifty but she was generous in love to her husband. She tasted neither food nor drink without me. Good was her counsel, quick her mind, noble her repute.[112]

Women of Lower Classes

The life of luxury and leisure was only enjoyed by women of the upper class, since slaves and freed women continued to toil in the home and fields as if social change had passed them by. Wives of the poorer citizens and freed men were responsible for common household chores, as might be expected, and worked in spinning, weaving, and making clothes, and of course rearing children. Many also engaged in what might be called professions, either on their own or with their husbands. Many worked in the very important wool industry, weighing, selling, weaving, or making garments. Some were bakers.

Some worked in markets, selling fruit and vegetables, fish, various meats, and salt. Some were traveling merchants. Some made pottery. Some worked with metal, fabricating, and gilding.[113]

Female slaves were common, and they filled a variety of roles, by compulsion. They served in the houses of wealthy matrons. But they also worked on farms, and there is ample evidence that some slave women were wrestlers and some fought as gladiators. Many were prostitutes. Female slaves could not marry, and a conjugal relationship with a man was therefore considered to be without *cunnubium* or *matrimonium* (both referring to legal marriage). They had to be available for intercourse with the free male who headed the family, but any children they produced belonged to the father. A relationship between a female slave and a citizen was called *contubernium*.[114] Even a male and female slave could not be legally married. They had no legal status, and could neither hold or bequeath property, nor produce legitimate children. Either one, or both, could be sold and the relationship terminated as a matter of course. Ownership of the children of slaves, as legal *fructus*, was a matter debated by jurists on into the second century.[115] But a child of a slave belonged to the master of the house, if he was known to be the father.

Prostitution was legal in Rome and was officially regulated. Most prostitutes were slaves. While there were both male and female prostitutes, females were far greater in number. A variety of terms were used to describe prostitutes, but *scortum* was the most common. And the word *meretrix* seems to have described a higher class of prostitute, much the same as "call girl" in modern English vernacular. A *meretrix* was possibly comparable to the Greek hetaerae, although not so highly regarded as a class. Prostitutes feature in the works of Martial, Juvenal, and Ovid, especially the *Satyricon* by Petronius. The city of Rome had as many as 40 brothels, called *lupanaria* (from the term *lupa*, a she-wolf). By the fourth century CE some of the larger brothels were state owned and were considered tourist attractions.[116]

Religion

Religion and associated mythology bear a distinct Greek influence during Rome's prehistory, and also by the later artistic imitation of Greek forms. There is no Roman parallel to Hesiod's *Theogony*, since the Romans eagerly identified their own gods with those of the Greeks and reinterpreted Greek myths concerning the origins of deities. Therefore, the two cultures have essentially the same gods and goddesses, with different names. Rome's early myths and legends also have a dynamic relationship with Etruscan religion, which is less documented than that of the Greeks.[117]

There were two forms in which rites and rituals of traditional Roman religion were performed. One was domestic, involving reverence to the spirit of the family, hearth, and home. The *pater familias* served as family priest (*sacra familiae*), leading prayers and rites to the household and ancestral gods. The other was sponsored by the state and represented the devotion of the people to the gods of Rome. Like that of Greece, Rome had a pantheon of gods, both male and female, and a variety of ceremonies by which they could be honored and worshipped. The principal gods were Jupiter, Mars, Apollo, Mercury, and Neptune. The principal goddesses were Juno, Vesta, Minerva, Ceres, Diana, and Venus.

Cicero, writing about 45 BCE, presents a structured dialogue between Epicurean and Stoic philosophers on the nature of the deities and religion. He aligns himself more with the latter, and Book 2 of *De Natura Deorum* contains perhaps the earliest and best attempt in ancient literature to prove divine control over the universe and the providential care for humanity. Aristotle had already set forth evidence for divine existence, but Cicero personalized it. In essence, Cicero held the conviction that everything in the cosmos is under the direction and will of the gods, and Rome was supreme over other nations simply because of the piety of the people and their devotion to religious observances.[118] Temples, priests, priestesses, and sacred rites were provided by the state to this end. Ordinary individuals, male and female, were essentially observers in these rituals but supported them by their presence and offerings.

As in other areas of life, Roman women enjoyed freedom of religious expression and frequently held positions of honor and authority. Traditional Roman religion was different from that of the Greeks, however, in that there was little place for emotional release or individual expression. Prayers were confined to fixed formulas, and ceremonies were usually solemn and sedate.[119] There were certain festivals specifically for women, similar to the Athenian Thesmophoria, which were marked by frenzy and lewdness. The most prominent of these was the Bacchic cult, which at some point became open to male participants as well. The best information comes from Livy.[120] The festival involved drinking to the point of intoxication, Bacchus being the god of wine as well as licentious behavior, and typically culminating in a mad dash to the Tiber River, where participants threw torches into the water. Cantarella says that this "ritual represented a world turned upside down, an inversion of everyday life, a reversal of roles clearly revealed by the fact that the male participants dressed as women."[121]

And, just as the mystery religions played a significant role in changing the nature of Greek worship, so were exotic elements introduced into Roman religion in the same era. While it was the restricted social life of Greek women that demanded some means of emotional expression, it seems that the formal religion of Rome also engendered a craving for excitement. The Saturnalia, which the poet Catullus described as "the best of days," was a festival in honor of the god Saturn. It lasted several days and included a public banquet, followed by festivities and a carnival where social norms were commonly abandoned.[122] The best source of information on the Saturnalia is Macrobius, who describes it as a festival of light leading to the winter solstice.[123] This festival seems to have been the origin of the later celebration called *Dies Natalis Solis Invicti* (Birth of the Unconquerable Sun) held on December 25.

Towards the end of the first century BCE, there seems to have been a strong Roman apathy for the many cults and deities of their ancestors. Cicero wrote to his wife Terentia: "I only wish, my dear, to see you as soon as possible and to die in your arms, since neither gods, whom you have worshipped with such pure devotion, nor men, whom I have ever served, have made us any return."[124]

Pomeroy writes that "among the numerous cults developed by the Romans to enlist divine aid for practical purposes were those designed to uphold ideals for female conduct." A part of the genius of Roman organization is seen in categorizing, ranking, and labeling women according to desirable qualities, respectable conduct, marriage status, and social class.[125] Then, religious cults were created appropriate to each category. The best examples are the various cults of the goddess Fortuna, who is represented in numerous forms and cults. Symbolized by the ship's rudder, globe and cornucopia, the powers of Fortuna over womanhood were significant. The cornucopia especially was symbolic, in that it represented sexual maturity and fecundity, expected of the worthy Roman woman. Fortuna Virginalis was the patroness of girls who, when reaching puberty, traded the short *toga* for the long *stola* worn by a respectable woman. Upon marriage a bride then came under the care of Fortuna Primigenia, the patroness of *matronae* (matrons), childbirth, and motherhood. The cult of Fortuna Muliebris (Womanly Fortune) was founded to commemorate an incident in 491 BCE when Veturia and Volumnia, the mother and the wife of Coriolanus, met him at his camp with a delegation of women to stop his treasonous march against Rome.[126] And Fortuna Virilis was a cult associated with the sexual fortune of women, celebrated at or near the baths where men might be seen exposed. One of the earliest temples to Fortuna is located on the right bank of the Tiber outside the city. It is thought to date to the time of Servius Tullius, and might relate to the role of Tanaquil in bringing good fortune to her familial line of politicians and kings.

Fortuna was seen as the bringer of either good or evil, and therefore a fickle and unpredictable deity whose benevolence was never certain. She became a caricature of female capriciousness, and therefore the patron of the life of womanhood. Ovid, writing from exile, reflects ruefully on the "goddess who admits by her unsteady wheel her own fickleness; she always has its apex beneath her swaying foot."[127]

Mention should be made of the cult of Mater Matuta, an indigenous Latin goddess, who at some point became the equivalent of Aurora, the goddess of dawn, and also the Greek goddess Eos. But she was also associated with the sea harbors and ports. The cult was exclusively for women. It was practiced in several places, although the best known temple was at Satricum, located in antiquity on the bank of the Astura River some 60 kilometers southeast of Rome. But there was also one in Rome, located on the north side of the Forum Boarium, and the festival there was called the Matralia. According to legend it was constructed some time before 535 BCE by Servius Tullius, the sixth king of Rome, destroyed in 506 BCE, and then rebuilt by Marcus Furius Camillus in 396 BCE.[128]

Among the most revered deities, and appearing very early in Roman culture, was Vesta, the goddess of the hearth. She is a direct parallel to the Greek Hestia. The Vestal Virgins who were dedicated to service in the temple of Vesta were highly revered by the public.[129] These six nobly born young women were dedicated as early as age six and served for 30 years. They were sworn to chastity, ruled over by one chief Vestal, and were endowed with special exemptions and powers. They performed sacrifices on behalf of worshippers and offered prayers to Vesta. They also were the guardians of the sacred fire of the state, kept burning continually at their dwelling, the *Atrium Vestae*. An offense against any one of them in word or deed was punishable by death.[130] However, if a priestess of this order ever broke her vow of chastity, the penalty was to be buried alive by the Colline Gate after a solemn and dreadful procession.[131] This did happen a few times, but there is reason to think that the Vestals might have suffered the consequences of the misdeeds of others, as well as the misfortune of Roman society as a whole. When the economy suffered, or riots broke out, or a senator was murdered, a wayward Vestal must have been the cause and her punishment would make everything right.

Last, there was the cult of Bona Dea (the Good Goddess), considered by some to be a mystery cult, but it was actually an offshoot of an ancient state religion. It is commonly thought that her cult began in Magna Graecia along the southeastern coast of Italy, some time during the early or middle Republic, and eventually was given recognition as a state cult. The Bona Dea was associated with chastity and fertility in women, and also with healing and freedom from slavery. Many of her devotees were freed slaves and plebeians. She was also considered a protector from earthquakes and therefore the defender of the Roman state and people. Her rites allowed women the use of strong wine and blood sacrifice, things otherwise forbidden them by Roman tradition. Men were barred from her mysteries and the possession of her true name. She was identified as the wife, sister or daughter of the god Faunus, thus an equivalent or aspect of the nature goddess Fauna, who could prophesy the fates of women. In art she is identified by a scepter, vine leaves, wine, and a serpent, usually curled around her arm and sometimes holding a cornucopia.

The goddess had two annual festivals. One was held at her Aventine temple; the other was hosted by the wife of Rome's senior magistrate, the guests being a select group group of elite matrons and their female attendants. The cult in the city of Rome was led by the Vestal Virgins and the provincial cults by either virgin or matron priestesses.

Plutarch comments at length on the rituals to Bona Dea:

> It is not lawful for a man to attend the sacred ceremonies, nor even to be in the house when they are celebrated; but the women, apart by themselves, are said to perform many rites during their sacred service which are Orphic in their character. Accordingly, when the time for the festival is at hand, the consul or praetor at whose house it is to be held goes away, and every male with him, while his wife takes possession of the premises and puts them in due array. The most important rites are celebrated by night when mirth attends the revels and much music, also, is heard.[132]

Juvenal has an entirely different description, adding an orgiastic element to the rituals.

> The secrets of Bona Dea are well known. When the pipe excites them, and inflamed alike with the horn and wine, these maenads of Priapus rush wildly around, and whirl their locks and howl! Then, as their passions rise, how burning is their lust, how frantic their words, when all power of restraining their desires is lost. A prize is proposed, and Saufeia challenges the vilest of her sex and bears off the prize. In these games nothing is counterfeit, all is acted to the life; so that even the aged Priam, effete from years, or Nestor himself, might be enflamed at the sight. Then their lust admits of no delay. The woman appears in all her native depravity; and by all alike is the shout re-echoed from the whole den—"Now is the proper time. Let in the men!" But the adulterer still sleeps; so she bids the youth to put on the female hood and speed to the spot. If none can be found, they have recourse to slaves. If there is no hope of slaves, they will hire some water-carrier to come.[133]

Summary

Women of the Republic and early imperial Rome enjoyed considerable freedom compared to most other ancient cultures. They could walk about the streets at leisure, attend festivals and games, travel, and engage in business independently. Wealthy Roman matrons were certainly the beneficiaries of "the good life."

However, the degree of emancipation of Roman women has been exaggerated. It is clear that the concept of *pater familias* the rule of law and culture that bestows power upon the *pater familia* to deal with any and all issues relevant to members of his household persisted in many areas, even after its official demise, and the patriarchal definition of the Roman household continued to hold women to a station of subordination and inferiority. The ancient female cults were not structured to liberate women, but to patronize them by extolling their role as wives and mothers. Women were never granted true political voice or the opportunity to hold office. It is clear that Roman society suffered significant moral decay before and during the first century CE, and many writers unjustly pointed to uncontrolled women as the cause. Adultery and divorce were common, and many women reacted to attempts to regulate their behavior. In general, males in Roman society had a measure of sexual license not granted to women, and women were ridiculed and even punished for behavior that was customary for males. Besides this, within the class structure in the Roman world a large number of women were slaves, and the exploitation of slave women for sexual gratification was sanctioned. Slave women were denied even the basic right of marriage and possession of their own children.

Six

Mystery Cults

Numerous scholars have expressed dismay that there is much we do not know about the mysteries, and Pomeroy adds that it is challenging to understand why they gained such popularity.[1] Despite the lack of absolutes, we can only conclude that such cults provided what might have been missing from traditional worship, and therefore satisfied certain personal and social needs. We have no reason to think that the mysteries were the first experience or expression of emotion in religion, but it is evident that they represent a shift away from traditional rites, perhaps because of the impersonal nature of religion performed by priests on behalf of the people and the transactional motif of performing rituals simply to gain the favor of the gods. The mystery cults offered something else, something more, especially for women.

Barrett says that the mystery cults ranged in nature from licentious to the truly spiritual, which in simple terms offered something for everyone. Some appealed especially to Greek women because the rituals offered an occasion of freedom from seclusion. The licentious cults were popular among both women and men, but for different reasons. For women these cults addressed a deep psychological need to break free from social restraint and subordination to either husband or father.[2] And the mysteries typically welcomed participation by all classes of Rome's population, rich and poor, free and slave, and both men and women. The only exception to this was the cult of Mithras, which was exclusively for men and tended to attract soldiers and tradesmen. Representing trends in the first Christian century, Seneca speaks of the enthusiasm among Romans for the mystery cults because they offered excitement and adventure as an alternative to otherwise dull traditional forms of worship.[3] Therefore, the mysteries assist in our understanding of womanhood in the ancient Mediterranean world.

In *Ancient Mystery Cults*, Walter Burkert deals at length with the misinterpretation and stereotyping by historians over the last century.[4] Among numerous misconceptions is the notion that the mysteries were something new. In reality, the only cult that was truly new to the Greco-Roman world was Mithraism, emerging rather suddenly in the first century CE in Rome and spreading throughout the empire from there. But the god Mithras can be traced to Persia and Vedic India as early as the Bronze Age. All the other mystery cults were practiced hundreds of years before the emergence of Christianity, and all the deities except Isis and Mithras were connected to gods and goddesses of the regional pantheon.

Another misconception is that the mysteries were of foreign origin, often described as Asian or Oriental, imported to Greece and Rome with the return of troops from foreign engagements. An example of scholars who promoted this notion is Samuel Angus,[5] whose book *The Mystery-Religions* was first published in 1925. But this claim is only partially true. Egypt, the origin of the cult of Isis, is neither Asian nor Oriental, and communication with Egypt had become common for the Greeks as early as the fourth century from the exploits of Alexander. The cults of Demeter and Kore (Persephone) and the cult of Dionysus (god of wine and drama) are Greek in origin and merged into Roman culture along with the blending of the ancient pantheon of deities and traditional practices of worship and celebration. Neither can the Syrian Great Mother be considered Asian or Oriental, since Anatolia and Syria were part of the Mediterranean community of cultures. The goddess Cybele, associated with the Great Mother, is from Phrygia, which is in west central Anatolia and is also part of the Mediterranean-Aegean community.

A third stereotype is that the mystery cults represent a shift in religious outlook from realistic and pragmatic to the spiritual, particularly with regard to the concept of salvation. In reality, most of the mysteries began as nature cults, honoring deities that were believed to control the basic essentials of life for both families and communities. The wonder of the cult was essentially to enhance the sense that such deities were real by means of a personal experience. The concept of salvation common in the mysteries related to the initiation experience that brought renewed life and heightened awareness, as well as escape from the fates to some measure of control over personal future. Although there was an aspect of the afterlife in the Eleusinian Mysteries as well as Mithraism, the more common concept of salvation and spirituality in the mysteries is mundane compared to those in early Christian doctrine. Associations such as this appeared in some of the studies of the mysteries in the nineteenth and twentieth centuries, which were approached almost as Christian apologetics, viewing the mystery cults as part of a stream running steadily through history toward belief in one God.[6]

It should be noted also that the mysteries do not fit some definitions of religion, in that they were not mutually exclusive, had no unique claims of truth or validity, and for the most part did not adhere to a set of creeds or doctrines. Their adherents did not claim a patron deity as the one true god, or the one whose worship or teachings were the only way to experience divine

Six. Mystery Cults 179

presence. They may have competed for popularity, but they coexisted in a spirit of tolerance. And they were syncretistic, adopting ideas and practices from each other and from other ancient cults within the complex social structure and continuously evolving cultures of their day. It is also important to note a distinction between mystery cults and mysticism, the latter commonly referring to spiritual or contemplative dimensions in early and medieval Christianity. And also care should be taken not to confuse the mystery cults with what is commonly called magic or witchcraft, the ancient practice of spells and incantations, and the use of amulets and potions, all to manipulate both nature and spirits either for the benefit or to the detriment of humans. Some of the mystery cults, and some itinerant priests, employed such methods and devices, along with astrology, but these did not define the nature or purpose of the mystery cults.

There is also a common misunderstanding of terminology relevant to the mysteries. The term from which the very title of these cults is derived is the Greek word *musteria*, which to the modern reader conveys the idea of mystery (difficult to understand) and secrecy (information held by a few). In the New Testament, the Apostle Paul uses the term *musterion* in reference to thoughts, plans, or teachings revealed and instructed to believers that before were only in the mind of God: the mysterious plan for the salvation of Israel (Rom. 11:25), the mystery of God's wisdom (I Cor. 2:7), the mystery of the resurrection (I Cor. 15:51), the mystery of divine grace (Eph. 3:2), the mystery of Christ's relationship to the church (Eph. 5:2), and mystery of the nature of the Gospel message (Eph. 6:19). Therefore, Burkert argues that the emphasis on secrecy in modern parlance came from the New Testament, but the earlier use of various cognates of *musteria* (*muein, muesis*) actually refer to initiation. Therefore, mystery cults were "initiation" cults. This confusion may have come from Mycenaen Greek and antecedents to the secret elements in the Eleusinian cult. But it seems more likely that confusion arose when the term *musteria* was translated to the Latin *initia* (*initiare, initiatio*), from which came the English words "initiate" and "initiation." Nonetheless, while there were certain secret aspects to the mysteries, the primary element was initiation, rather than secrecy. That is more commonly expressed by the Greek term *teletai*.

The adjectives *aporrheia* (forbidden) and *arrheta* (unspeakable) are also used by various writers to describe matters pertaining to cult initiation that were considered to be secretive, despite their innocuous nature. Initiates were not to reveal to others what was done, said, and experienced.[7] And it is clear that many writers, themselves initiates in one or more of the cults, took these terms seriously and refrained from speaking openly and clearly about what they saw, heard, and experienced, either during intiation or from later instruction. Hence the initiates themselves perpetuated the modern idea of "mystery."

Another significant term is *orgion*, or the plural *orgia*, which evolved into "orgy" in English and has come to suggest group sexual debauchery. But the term simply means "rites" or "rituals." The Latin equivalent of *orgia* is *caerimoniae*, or in English "ceremonies." While some of the mysteries included wild frenzy, ecstasy, drunkenness, and even lewd and licentious behavior on the part of some participants, the term *orgia* was not intended to describe those specific activities. So, today references to "Bacchic orgy" conjur up specific images that do not justly represent the nature of the Bacchic cult or the mysteries as a whole.

The mystery cults had numerous features in common. First, they mostly operated on private membership and funding, and focused attention on the people rather than the state. Second, while they honored deities that were well known, they found more interesting methods of honoring them than traditional rituals and celebrations. They typically held their meetings at night, or in a dark cave, or in a darkened meeting hall, or even at a chosen place in the wide-open countryside, using torches or bonfires, music, singing, and dancing to create an intriguing atmosphere. Third, they were open to anyone, male or female, rich or poor, free or slave, and some offered positions of honor and leadership to people who would not have such opportunities in state religions. Fourth, most of the cult festivals and meetings were held one or two times a year, and there was little or no continual involvement or commitment. The significance of the festivals and meetings was enhanced by infrequency. Fifth, and perhaps most significant, all the mysteries focused on the experience of initiation and its impact on the initiate, which offered a personal and lasting sense of connection with the divine.

The principal mystery cults that we will examine in this chapter are those that became prominent in the Greco-Roman world in the centuries leading up to the birth of Christianity. These are the cult of Demeter and Kore (Penelope); the cult of Dionysus (god of wine and drama); the cult of Cybele, a syncretic mystery that included elements of the Syrian goddess Attargatis and the Great Mother, or the mother of the gods; the cult of Isis, which is Egyptian in origin; and Roman Mithraism.

The Eleusinian Mysteries

The Thesmophoria is not typically considered to be part of the mysteries, but is an ancient precursor. A comedy entitled *Thesmophoriazusae*, written by Aristophanes, was structured around this festival celebrated in honor of Demeter, goddess of grain and cultivation, and her daughter Persephone (also known as Kore). It was held in the fall each year, and it lasted three days. It commemorated the harsh summer months when, according to myth, the goddess abstained from her work in mourning for her daughter who was sequestered to Hades during that season. The name is derived from the plural noun *thesmoi* (laws) in reference to rules for working the land. Men were totally excluded from this festival, although they were expected to provide the necessary finances. Attendance was limited to married women whose spouses were Athenian citizens. Women bathed as preparatory cleansing for the ritual, and then slept in makeshift shelters outdoors. It was a time to get away from the house, the hearth, the husband, and the children.[8] The primary activity during this festival was burying pigs in the earth (or cravasses among rocks), then retrieving those that had been buried the year before and replanting them with seeds. It is likely that this was a magic ritual believed to make the seed germinate and grow. Spying on these procedures by men was met with harsh treatment. The ceremony had a secondary purpose, to promote fertility in the women who attended, and part of the preparation was sexual abstinence. When it was all over, they went back home very eager for sexual gratification, with husbands who were puzzled about the secretive activities but pleased at the results.

According to myth, the Eleusinian cult was instituted by Demeter herself. The Homeric "Hymn to Demeter" contains the following lines:

> And she revealed to them the celebration of her awesome rites, and taught them all her awesome mysteries which no one may transgress in any way, or inquire into or speak about, for great awe of the gods stops the voice. Blessed is the one of all the people on the earth who has seen these mysteries. But whoever is not initiated into the rites, whoever has no part in them that person never shares the same fate when he dies and goes down to the gloom and darkness below.[9]

The remains of the sanctuary of Demeter and Kore at Eleusis, about 20 miles from Athens, date back to the early Bronze Age. The site was abandoned around 1200 BCE at the end of the Mycenaean era and remained so until the eighth century. Then the site was reconstructed and used from that time until around 395 CE, when the Goths, led by Alaric, invaded the region.

The festival was actually planned and run by officials of the city of Athens and two families: the Eumolpidae, supposedly descendants of the mythical king Eumolpus, and the Kerykes, whose representatives played the role of *hierokeryx* (herald). Officials in the festival included the city magistrate, called the *basileus* (King Archon); a *dadoukos* (torchbearer); and the *hierophant* (the one who led the initiates and explained the secrets to them).

In preparation for the festival, the *hiera* (sacred articles) were transported in a procession from Eleusis to Athens. The procession was accompanied by a military guard called the *ephebes*.

The objects were carried by the priestesses in closed containers and kept from the eye of the public. It is thought that those articles included an head of grain (wheat, or more likely barley), since the festival involved the emergence of Persephone from the underworld to plant grain for the winter harvest. Hippolytus of Rome, a Christian theologian of the third century, was of this opinion also.[10]

The festival began on the fourteenth of the month of Boedromion (corresponding to the end of September or beginning of October) and lasted eight days. On the first day of the festival, the cult herald made a public invitation in the Agora at Athens to any Greek interested in being initiated into the mysteries. Barbarians and murderers were not welcome. That limitation changed during the Roman period; Augustus himself was initiated, as was Hadrian and other Roman officials well into the Christian era.

The second day of the festival was known as *Halade Mystai* (Initiates to the Sea). All those who chose to be initiated had to take a piglet down to the sea, wash it, and then sacrifice it as a ritual of purification. There were also lesser festivals at which initiates went through preparation and each was assigned a *mystagogos* (mentor, or coach) to help them through the process.

On the third day there was a sacrifice to the goddess in the city of Eleusis, and on the fourth day sacrifices were made to the god Asclepius. The latter, who was revered as the god of healing, was symbolized by the snake. Offerings to Asclepius were incorporated into the Eleusinian festivals in 421 BCE when a snake was brought to Athens from the Asclepian sanctuary in Epidaurus. On the fifth and sixth days of the festival, there were processions from the city of Athens to the sanctuary in Eleusis. One procession was led by the priesthood with the *hiera*, and the other procession included the *teletai* (initiates), with the statue of the Eleusinian god Iacchus (Bacchus) leading the way. Iacchus, the patron of initiates and torchbearer of the cult procession to and from Eleusis, was in mythology the son of Zeus and Demeter.[11]

What took place inside the sanctuary on the main day of the festival was kept secret. Pausanias wrote that he was told in a dream not to reveal anything about the interior of the sanctuary or the proceedings there,[12] but he does venture to say that there were "things done, things shown, and things said."[13] A description of the events is reconstructed from numerous sources by Kevin Clinton, summarized by Bowden.[14] He says that the initiates filed into the sanctuary, each wearing a hood and guided by a *mystagogue*. By flickering torchlight they could see toward the back of the cave a form like the goddess sitting on a rock. She was in deep sorrow and lamentation. They passed by and then proceeded to an area outside the Telesterion (the great hall of Eleusis), where they wandered about in confusion searching for Kore while a *hierophant* summoned her with the repeated sounding of a gong. Eventually she emerged from the cave guided by Eubuleus, the torchbearer who in myth led the way back from the underworld. She embraced Demeter, and then mother and daughter made their way into the Telesterion. After a time, the door opened and the *hierophant* stood silouetted against the bright light of thousands of torches inside held by the *epoptai,* the second year initiates or contemplatives. The initiates entered, dazzled by the brilliant light. Again they saw images of the goddesses with other significant deities all arrayed on a platform called the Anaktoron. Then when the ceremony was done, the new initiates were escorted out and the *epoptai* received a special vision, either given by the *hierophant* or enacted by those representing the deities. The revelation may have included the birth of a child, which represented *ploutos* (wealth), and the display of an ear of grain to symbolize the new harvest and the prospects of a profitable year.

Initiates participated in these cultic rituals only two times, first with the status of *mystes* and then second (presumably the following year) as *epoptes.* Only in the second year did they receive the revelation of the cult's secret meaning and purpose, and at least part of this revelation was not so much instructive in nature as spontaneous, meaning that it came to each initiate as a personal epiphany resulting from the powerful imagistic experience.

Some have speculated that drugs or alcohol were used to enhance the experience, especially the ecstasy, visions, and frenzy associated with other mystery cults. While wine drinking in excess was prominent in Bacchian cults, there is no evidence of any substances used in the Eleusinian cult. Bowden suggests that a more likely component in the powerful experience at Eleusis was special effects developed for Greek drama. Wandering around hooded in darkness, perhaps being spun around by the mentor, then suddenly brought into a large, brightly illuminated hall with illuminated figures representing deities, and multiple shadows, all combined to create a memorable experience. And there can be no doubt that the roles of Demeter and other deities were played by priests and priestesses, whose dramatic presence was enhanced by lights, shadows, colors, and music. Bowden concludes:

> At one level the Eleusinian Mysteries were an occasion on which the city of Athens honored the goddesses who guaranteed the harvests and the grain that the city needed in order to survive: sending out heralds to advertise the graciousness of the goddesses to other Greek cities and putting on sacrifices and processions in their names. But in the middle of these public festivities was a sequence of events in which the personal experience of the individuals was central. Behind the walls of the sanctuary at Eleusis they met the goddess and experienced her grace and power at first hand.[15]

Writers such as Pausanias and Herodotus provide information about numerous other cultic centers, very similar to the Eleusinian Mysteries where festivals and initiations were held and where Demeter and Kore were the honored deities. One is the mystery of Andania, a small city in the southwest region of the Peloponnese. There were also the mysteries of Arcadia, a region

184   Daughters of God, Subordinates of Men

in central Peloponnese. Lycosura, in the same region, had a sanctuary in honor of Despoina, the daughter of Demeter and Poseidon and sister of Arion, but statues there include Demeter, Artemis, and Arion. This cult gave attention to animals, rather than grain. Pausanias said that the Arcadians sacrificed from whatever animals they had, not by cutting the throats but instead by severing a limb.[16] The festival included dancing, as did the festival at Andania. And in Attica, mysteries were celebrated in a small town called Phyla where, similiar to Eleusis, the officials were drawn from the family of local priests. The cult of Demeter and Persephone also existed in Sicily and Italy as early as the eighth century BCE, but there is no evidence of initiation of the same nature as the Eleusinian Mysteries. And further east, in various regions of Asia Minor, there is evidence that simliar cults existed, even giving Demeter the title of Eleusinia. Cities such as Ephesus, Miletus, Smyrna, and Pergamum had cults honoring Demeter during the Hellenistic and Roman periods.[17] The rules of purity for the Priestess of Demeter Olympia at Cos were strict. She had to avoid contact with anything unclean, such as a corpse or a grave, and she was to avoid entering a house where someone had recently died. She was not to enter a house where a woman had recently given birth to a child, whether living or dead. And she was not to eat carrion.[18]

So, in this brief synopsis we can see the importance of the family of Eleusinian Mysteries, and the role of women as cult officials and initiates. This was an occasion on which the people of the city and countryside could honor the goddesses on whom they relied for the harvest of grain essential for their survival. But within the grand public event there was a series of processions and rituals in which the experience of individuals was of utmost importance. Within the sanctuary they met deities face to face, experienced divine presence and power in a memorable fashion, and then went away changed people.

The Mysteries of Samothrace

The sanctuary on the island of Samothrace was second only to the Telesterion at Eleusis in significance as a center of cult initiation in Greek culture. Dating to the seventh century BCE, at the time Greeks first settled the island, the sanctuary was dedicated to the *megaloi theoi* (the Great Gods). Herodotus says the island was taken over by the Greeks from local inhabitants whom he calls Pelasgians.[19] The importance of Samothrace is evident from frequent visits by Philip II of Macedon. It was there that Philip met his fourth wife, Olympias, daughter of King Neoptolemus I of Epirus, when both were initiated into the mysteries of Kabeiroi at the sanctuary of the Great Gods. She would become the mother of Alexander the Great.[20] The remains of three buildings similar to the Telesterion have been excavated at the site, and there are inscriptions in the area that suggest that only initiates were permitted. However, it seems that initiation was even more open than in other mystery cults, including even children.

The identity of the Great Gods is difficult to determine. Herodotus, whose reports have proved unreliable in many respects, says that Athenians derived from the Pelasgians a practice of making images of Hermes, displaying an erect phallus. This, he claims, is explained in a sacred story connected to the mysteries in Samothrace.[21] Such images have been found in Athens, but nothing from Samothrace supports it. Bowden finds an explanation by connecting the cult of Samothrace to several other cults, all related to the worship of gods called the Kabeiroi. Centers for this cult have been identified in the Egyptian city of Boetia, west of Thebes, and on several islands in the Aegean Sea, including Samothrace. Certain artwork on pottery has pointed to Dionysus and his son Pais as the Kabeiroi. Statements by other writers provide further clues to their identity. As is often the case, concerning secret matters of the mysteries, Pausanias is hesitant to be specific. But he ventures to say that in a certain city there were inhabitants called the Kabeiroi, and Demeter entrusted something to their keeping.[22] Apollonius of Rhodes, in his epic poem about Jason and the Argonauts, says that the cult of the Kabeiroi on Samothrace had four deities, whose cryptic names (Axieros, Axiokersa, Axiokersos, and Kasmilos) are actually Demeter, Persephone, Hades, and Hermes.[23] Excavations there reveal a number of other deities, including the Great Mother, the nature goddess Hecate (also Zerynthia), and the phallic god Kadmylos.[24] Therefore, we have reason to conclude that from pre-classical Greece there were numerous mystery cults in various centers that had elements in common with the Eleusinian Mysteries, including participation by women in various roles ranging from initiate to priestess.

The Cult of Dionysus

The god Dionysus, known as Bacchus to the Romans, appears along with the ancient Greco-Roman deities. The various myths of his birth and nurture in childhood are intriguing. In one story, he is said to be the son of Zeus and a mortal woman, Semele, daughter of King Cadmus of Thebes. Insisting that Zeus reveal himself to her in all his divine glory, she perished in the blaze of his transfiguration. Zeus then took the unborn child and stitched him to his thigh to develop. When he matured, Zeus sent him away to mythical Mount Nysa, located by various writers in Egypt, Anatolia, Libya, Ethiopia, or Arabia, where he was cared for by rain nymphs. It likely that these ancient speculations are the source of the assumption that his cult was of foreign origin. Other myths portray Dionysus as the son of Zeus and Demeter, or of Zeus and Persephone.

The play called *Bacchae* by Euripides, written toward the end of the fifth century BCE, draws from the Semele myth. Accompanied by Phrygian maenads, Dionysus comes in disguise to Thebes, the home of his mother. He is determined to make the Thebans pay for the insult, even by his mother's own sisters, of denying that he is the son of Zeus. As the play begins, he announces his intention to introduce Dionysian rites into the city and to demonstrate to King Pentheus, and to all Thebans, that he is indeed a god. The women have left their homes and are wandering, out of their minds in delirious celebration, in the wilderness of Cithaeron. Among the women are Semele's sisters, including Agave, mother of Pentheus, the current king. Former King Cadmus is still alive, and he and Teiresias are the only two men who have decided to participate in the rites of the new god. Pentheus denounces the new religion and the disorder it has brought to Thebes. Pentheus, thinking that Dionysus is the priest of the cult, has him thrown into prison. An earthquake destroys the palace and Dionysus emerges from the rubble unharmed. In the meantime, the maenads in the hills have gained supernatural powers, overpowered the king's army, and destroyed several villages. Dionysus invites Pentheus to see the women in their revelry, but insists that he go disguised as a woman. The maenads, including Agave, all still delirious, attack and kill the young king. Agave thinks she has killed a lion with her bare hands. When the ecstasy has passed, Cadmus explains what has happened, and father and daughter grieve together. By the end of the play, the city of Thebes is destroyed by its ruling party and by the exiling of its entire population, and the revenge of Dionysus has exceeded all reason. Thus two sides of Dionysus are revealed. First there is the god of wine and uninhibited joy. But there also is the god of bitter revenge and violence.[25] And as we have seen in other deities in various cultures, there is portrayed here the capricious and fickle nature that may be one of the reasons for the slow cultural rejection of traditional worship in the Greco-Roman world.

The earliest images of Dionysus show him bearded and robed, and therefore mature. He commonly holds a staff called a *thyrsus*. Later images show him as a youth, sensuous, and either naked or half-naked, and some sources describe him as womanly in appearance and manner.[26] The cult of Dionysus is commonly associated with wine, revelry, and ecstasy. Various images and paintings of Dionysus show on his head a garland of ivy and include a bull, a serpent, and of course, wine. He is often accompanied by satyrs, centaurs, the lecherous sileni, and a group of devoted women. Once thought by scholars to have developed late in Greco-Roman culture and imported from Asia, it is now clear that the worship of Dionysus dates from as early as 1500 to 1100 BCE by Mycenean Greeks. Celebrations were held three times each year, and for

Six. Mystery Cults 187

centuries only women took part. Later, men began to participate as well, and celebrations were held more frequently. Most of the celebrations took place in the wide open hills, not in a secluded sanctuary or darkened hall. But there was structure and organization, as indicated by an inscription from Torre Nova near Rome dating around 160 CE. The cult titles included priests, priestesses, statue-bearer, torchbearer, basket-bearers, chief and sacred herdsmen, and phallus-carriers.[27]

The theater of Dionysus in Athens just below the Acropolis dates to around 550 BCE, with later Roman overlay, and at its zenith it could seat over 15,000. This was the venue for theatrical performances, both tragedies and comedies, during the two major festivals to Dionysus, called the Dionysia and the Lenaea. The theater also included an altar for the sacrifice of animals during these festivals. In the late fourth century the cult became popular in Alexandria because of the interest Alexander had in Dionysus. It is said that Dionysus inspired Alexander to expand his influence to other lands.

One of the infamous events in the history of the cult was the Bacchanalia of 186 BCE, when it was brutally suppressed by the Roman Senate. Bacchic practices were declared forbidden and structures pertaining to the cult were dismantled. Women were still permitted to be bacchants, but men no longer could join them. There is reason to think that the cult had become a venue for politically and socially dangerous purposes, and the decree was primarily intended to prevent conspiracy. Livy, writing at the end of the first century BCE while Augustus was still in power, offers an account of what took place. He reports that the nocturnal gatherings of this cult were occasions for all kinds of licentious and criminal activity. He describes the noise of drums, cymbals, and loud screams that drowned out the cries of people being murdered. In a second part of his report, a Roman consul had discovered details of Bacchic activities from his mistress, a prostitute named Hispala. She recounts how the Bacchic cult developed and what she knew of the sordid crimes committed there. She reported that the cult had been changed by a woman named Paculla Annia, who began to initiate men and changed the ceremonies from day to night. As a result, the cult became something different and sordid. She described the frenzied behavior, men and women shrieking in madness, and matrons with desheveled hair running to the river with torches, thrusting them into the water and drawing them out again unquenched, because they were made of sulphur and lime. She said that whoever would not submit to defilement, or refused to violate others, became a victim and was executed.[28]

There was an official inquiry, many suicides, and some people were exiled as a result. Pomeroy says that thousands were sentenced to death, the women being handed over to husbands who by legal authority (*manus*) could kill them because of their inappropriate behavior. In some cases other relatives carried out the punishment.[29] However, Bowden says that because Livy's history has an explicit moral purpose, to demonstrate how far Roman moral values had gone awry, his report "should probably be dismissed as largely fictitious."[30]

The Senate's edict was not intended to abolish the cult, but to discourage the secret meetings of men and women, possibly because of the significant problem of marital infidelity that already plagued Roman society. It also was directed at politically dangerous alliances. Nonetheless, there is no reason to doubt that the cult was widespread, and because of the intentional use of wine as part of the rituals, inhibitions were diminished and libidinous and licentious behavior, at least on the part of some, naturally resulted. The fact that Dionysus is associated with disguises and masks might suggest also that attendees at such gatherings guarded their identity.

The Syrian Great Mother

Herodotus tells a story about a prince named Anacharsis from Scythia, north of the Black Sea, who visited Greece on his way home from exploring other lands. He sailed through the Hellespont and put in at Cyzicus, a port town of Mysia in Anatolia on a peninsula reaching out into the Sea of Marmara. There he witnessed a celebration of the mother of the gods. Although his people opposed adopting foreign customs, he vowed that if he reached home safely he would sacrifice to the Great Mother according to the manner of the Cyzicenes. Herodotus reports that he did so.[31] According to Apollonius, in his third century BCE poem "Argonautica," the cult was founded in Cyzicus by Jason.[32] The sanctuary was located on Mount Dindymon, and involved animal sacrifices, dancing, and music with flutes and drums.

However, other reports include the kind of wild and frenzied behavior that has come to be the stereotypical mystery cult festival. Lucian describes the Feast of the Torch (Fire) held in the Phrygian city of Hierapolis, located on hot springs in southwestern Anatolia. The ruins are adjacent to the modern town of Pamukkale in Turkey. He says the festival was attended by a multitude from various Syrian districts, and they brought with them images of deities for their own oblations. Among them were holy men, pipers, flutists, galli (a term used for priests in this particular cult), and a crowd of frenzied, frantic women.[33] Lucian reports that they cut down trees, erected them in the temple court and surrounded them with live sheep, goats, cattle, and birds, and on the branches hung garments and ornaments of gold and silver. The galli stood about gashing their arms and exposing their backs for others to lash with whips. Bystanders played flutes, beat drums, and sang either traditional sacred songs or words and melodies that came out spontaneously.

Some engaged in sexual activity as they were so inclined. As the atmosphere approached a crescendo, a holy man or a member of the crowd would be seized by frenzy and thrill the crowd with some form of self-mutilation. He describe how such a man would push through the crowd to the center of the court, screaming and tearing off his clothes. Then seizing a sword that was placed there for this very purpose, he would castrate himself and run through the streets with the severed members in his hand. Selecting a house as he ran, he would throw them inside. Then he would follow to plunder the house of female ornaments and garments.

Apuleius, through the lips of a character called Lucius, relates his role as a donkey in another frenzied ritual to the Syrian goddess. A priestess rode on his back, dresssed in special garb, while priests followed along lashing themselves until the ground was awash in blood. Lucius then served as the beast of burden to carry away the gifts showered upon the priests by the excited crowd for their provocative performance.[34]

By the late fifth century the cult of the Great Mother was introduced in Athens, and was held at first in the Agora. The festival was called the Galaxia and involved vegetarian offerings. The food eaten was a barley porridge. There is evidence of ecstatic worship in Athens associated with the Great Mother, perhaps not public but conducted by the attendants of the mother, called the Corybantes. Plato gives a description of the activities, which included music, dancing, and initiation rites.[35] Bowden says that iconography representing the Great Mother had reached a fixed form by around 500 BCE. She was often, but not always, depicted seated and holding a *phiale* (dish for offerings) in the right hand and a *typmanum* (drum) in the left. Sometimes a lion is at her side, or one on each side. No name of a traditional Greek or Roman goddess is associated with her, but instead the name Cybele. This appears to have come from the Phrygian cult of Mater Kubdeya, which became Meter Kybele in Greek.[36] This was particularly true of the cult of Syrian goddess Attargatis (Cybele) and her consort Hadad (Adad, Attis), the Syrian god of rain and storms. She is commonly identified with the Greek goddess Aphrodite, whose consort was Adonis.

Again, a Homeric hymn of unknown date and origin speaks of devotion and adoration of this goddess.

> Mother of all the gods and all mortals; sing of her for me, Muse, daughter of mighty Zeus, a clear song. She loves the clatter of rattles and the din of kettle drums, and she loves the wailing of flutes and also loves the howling of wolves and the growling of bright-eyed lions echoing hills and wooded hollows. And so farewell, goddess, I greet you and all other goddesses with my song.[37]

The cult was introduced to Rome in 205 BCE, where she was called *magna mater,* adapting the goddess to their own history as they had done with the traditional Greek pantheon. In this case it was her association with Mount Ida near the city of Troy that was significant, since legendary Anaeus, ancestor of Romulus, had come from Troy. It was prophesied that if the Mother Goddess were brought to Rome, with the cult would come the power to defeat and drive out all invaders. According to the poet Ovid, the power was associated with a sacred stone, brought from Mount Ida in Anatolia near Troy.[38]

A temple was constructed for Magna Mater on a Palatine Hill near the center of Rome and was dedicated in 191 BCE. Livy gives a detailed description of ceremonies in connection with the Syrian mother goddess, when hordes of women carried the image through the city to the temple of victory on the Palatine.[39] Although the cult was imported by the order of the senate, the Great Mother was served by a Phrygian priest and priestess, and no one of Roman birth was allowed to serve in the priesthood.

Clearly, some opposed such religions in Rome, and the cult was not actually made fully legal until the second century CE. Dionysius of Halicarnassus, writing in the first century BCE, stated firmly that these imported religious practices did not represent the reverent spirit of Roman tradition. Despite the stories of such among the gods, Romans did not practice such things as ritual castration, women mourning dead deities, ecstasy or Corybantic frenzy, reveling all through the night, secret mysteries, begging under the guise of religion, or men and women gathering together in temples, which were all things done by Greeks and barbarians.[40]

There is also evidence from Plato's *Republic* of travelling religious beggars, called *metragyrtai*, who went from place to place teaching or initiating people into the cult. These were looked upon with disfavor. Apuleius describes a eunuch who made a living going from village to village with a band of players performing music and dance.[41]

An interesting element of this cult was a consecration ritual for priests, called the taurobolium. Prudentius, a Roman Christian poet of the late fourth century, describes the ritual, which he finds blasphemous and repulsive: A huge pit was dug and over it was constructed a wooden floor, apparently in the form of lattice work, and pierced with small holes. A bull was led onto the floor and a spear thrust into its chest, so that a river of hot blood poured through the wooden floor and rained down on the initiate below. He describes how the initiate raised his face, so that his eyes were drenched and his tongue tasted the dark gory blood. When the ritual was complete, the initiate emerged, garments dripping, washed and born anew, prepared now for sacred service.[42] Bowden challenges a common claim that priests of this or any cult had to be eunuchs. The word gallus, used in associatiuon with devotees to the Great Mother, probably is derived from the root of gaul, and galatia, a romanized term for the people of middle Anatolia. While self-castration occurred in some of the festivals, it was not something required or connected to the priesthood. Martial, a Roman poet of the late first century, writes a rather sexually eplicit poem deriding Gallus, clearly a eunuch, whose only instrument for sexual activity is the tongue. He mentions Cybele, as if she is the object of sexual attention.[43]

The Mystery of Isis

The goddess known as Isis was significant in ancient Egypt, appearing as early as the Middle Kingdom (3100–2181 BCE). In mythology, Isis was both sister and wife to Osiris and the mother of Horus, the falcon-headed deity associated with national rulers. She was worshipped as the ideal mother and wife, goddess of nature and magic, patroness of slaves, artisans, and the poor, as well as the wealthy and powerful. Isis was also considered the guardian of children and the dead.

Plutarch's essay *On Isis and Osiris*, from the first century CE, is the most lengthy version of the myth concerning Isis. He relates how Osiris was murdered by his brother Seth. At a banquet held in honor of Osiris, Seth tricked Osiris into climbing inside a large chest. Then he closed the lid and thew him into the Nile. It drifted out to sea, and Osiris perished. In grief and despair, Isis set out in search for Osiris to give him a proper burial. The coffin drifted ashore in Byblos, on the Phoenician coast, and settled in the branches of a tree. Isis retrieved his body and brought it back to Egypt, where she hid it from Seth. But he found it, cut the body into 14 pieces, and scattered them all over Egypt. Isis, accompanied by her sister Nephthys, again set out on a search. They retrieved all but the phallus, which had been swallowed by a fish. Then drawing from all her powers, Isis resurrected Osiris.[44]

There is much more to the myth, but this will suffice to reveal why Isis was significant to Egypt. Isis as protector of Osiris represents the divine protection of the Egyptian pharaoh, and her ability to restore rule even in the face of attack by enemies. There is also a possible link with the recovery of power by the Egyptians after a time of rule by the Hyksos kings. And it should be noted that in Egypt Osiris had a major cult in the city of Abydos in Upper Egypt, which included a celebration of accomplishments, victories in battle, and a reinactment of his restoration to life. An inscription from the second century CE, supposedly a copy of an earlier one in the temple of Hephaestus in Memphis, extols the goddess Isis and declares her scope of power and influence.

I am Isis, the mistress of every land, and I was taught by Hermes, and with Hermes I devised letters, both the sacred [hieroglyphics] and the demotic, that all things might not be written with the same letter.

I gave and ordained laws for human beings, which no one is able to change.
I am eldest daughter of Kronos. I am wife and sister of King Osiris.
I am she who finds fruit for humans. I am mother of King Horus.
I am she that is called goddess by women. For me was the city of Bubastis built.
I divided the earth from the heaven. I showed the paths of the stars.
I ordered the course of the sun and the moon. I made strong the right.
I brought together woman and man.
I appointed to women to bring their infants to birth in the tenth month.
I ordained that parents should be loved by children.
I laid punishment upon those disposed without natural affection toward their parents.
I made with my brother Osiris an end to the eating of human beings.
I revealed mysteries unto human beings. I taught humans to honor images of the gods.
I consecrated the precincts of the gods. I broke down the governments of tyrants.
I made an end to murders. I compelled women to be loved by men.
I made the right to stronger than gold and silver.
I ordained that the true should be thought good.
I devised marriage contracts. I assigned to Greeks and barbarians their languages.
I made the beautiful and the shameful to be distinguished by nature.
I ordained that nothing should be more feared than an oath.
I have delivered the plotter of evil against other humans into the hands of the one he plotted against.
I established penalites for those who practice injustice. I decreed mercy to suppliants.
I protect righteous guards. With me the right prevails.
I am the Queen of rivets and winds and sea.
No one is held in honor without my knowing it.
I am the Queen of war. I am the Queen of the thunderbolt.
I stir up the sea and I calm it. I am in the rays of the sun.
I inspect the courses of the sun. Whatever I please, this too shall come to an end.
With me everything is reasonable. I set free those in bonds.
I am the Queen of seamanship. I make the navigable unnavigable when it pleases me.
I created walls of cities.
I am called the Lawgiver [Thesmophoros. a classical epithet of Demeter].
I brought up islands out of the depths into the light.
I am Lord [note masculine form] of rainstorms.
I overcome Fate. Fate hearkens to me. Hail, O Egypt, that nourished me![45]

In Greece, from the fifth century onwards there was a curiosity about Egypt. That is evident in the works of Herodotus, Diodorus, and others, but is understandable in light of the significance of Egypt to Alexander and the founding of the city of Alexandria in 331 BCE. During the Hellenistic era and the Ptolemaic Dynasty, the people of mainland Greece embraced Egyptian culture and religion. During that time Athens became the site of the first temple to Isis in Greece. From there the cult spread rapidly through the eastern Mediterranean and into Asia Minor, although the consort of the imported Isis was Sarapis, commonly understood to be the reincarnation of Osiris. By the end of the second century BCE, Isis reached Italy as well. The earliest temples were in Puteoli (105 BCE) and Pompeii (80 BCE). Apuleius reports that the college of priests of Isis was established in 80 BCE.[46] However, Bowden points out that there is no evidence of public cults of Isis in Rome before 43 BCE, but that year marked a pact of Octavian, Marc Antony, and Marcus Lepidus that included establishing a temple of Isis and Sarapis, reflecting ties with Egypt from the time of Julius Caesar.[47]

The cult of Isis did not display all the elements of the mysteries. Animals were not killed for the purpose of a scared meal, but killed, wrapped in linen, buried in a pit, and left to rot, similar to the burial of piglets in the Thesmophoria. At first, when Isis came to Greece and Rome, the priests were Egyptian, but in time locals were appointed also. There were both priests and priestesses and certain other roles (like basket-bearers) that were held only by women.

The term *mystes* (initiate) is not used in connection with the cult of Isis, but there was an initiation ceremony. There were also references to sacred articles and robes. Apuleius describes a procession in honor of Isis in the city of Corinth, in which both male and female initiates shined brightly in their linen robes. Women with anointed hair covered with a transparent veil and men with their head cleanly shaved made noise with sistrums of bronze, silver and gold.[48]

However, the depth of the initiation experience is revealed in the story of Lucius, the character in the novel *Metamorphoses* by Apuleius. Lucius is a traveler from Algeria, in north Africa, with an insatiable desire for knowledge of the secret things. While trying to perform a spell that will change him into a bird, he is accidentally transformed into a donkey and carries a priestess on his back during a procession connected to the cult of the Great Mother. In the final book of that story, Lucius finds restoration and fulfilment as an initiate of the Isis cult. He is dressed in a new linen robe and escorted into the temple of Isis in Corinth for initiation. He will not say what took place there, but he says:

I reached the boundary of death, and set foot on the threshold of Proserpina, and then I returned, carried through all the elements, in the middle of the night I saw the sun blazing with bright light; I approached the gods below and the gods above face to face, and worshipped them from nearby.[49]

Devotees of Isis appear to be more connected to the cult after initiation than those in most other mysteries. And it should be noted that the cult of

Isis was in ways more than a mystery cult. She had a temple on the Campus Martius in Rome, and also one at Pompeii, with frescoes representing key elements of practice. But the cult also included sacred books, written in hieroglyphics, and the priests and initiates wore Egyptian-styled clothing. So, being an initiate involved taking on some form of Egyptian identity and continuing to learn secrets of the cult. This no doubt provided an exotic appeal, and there must have been something remarkable about the experience of initiation. It was especially appealing to women. The role of *sacerdos* (cult minister) was open to women as well as men.

Needless to say, many Romans did not like their wives participating in such cults, believing that they were being deceived and exploited. It is likely that many of the reports and stories, much like the satires, were either exaggerated or fabricated as instruments of traditional restoration. Flavius Josephus, first-century Jewish historian, tells a story about a woman in Rome named Paulina, wife of Saturninus. A younger man named Decius Mundus, of the equestrian order, fell deeply in love with Paulina and tried desperately to seduce her with gifts and promises of wealth. She was supremely virtuous and declined. Heartbroken, he decided to starve himself to death. But a freed woman named Ide, apparently from the household of his father, intervened and offered, for a sum of money, to create a ploy to get Mundus one night with Paulina. Knowing that Paulina was a devotee of Isis, Ide bribed a priest at the temple to convince Paulina that the god Anubis had requested her to play the part of the god's bride in the common annual ritual of sacred marriage. Her husband agreed that such would be an honor. So, when the time came, in the place of Anubis was Mundus, who enjoyed Paulina's affections the entire night. A few days later Mundus came to see her and told her that he was Anubis in disguise. She then told her husband, who took the matter to the emperor Tiberius. The result was banishment for Mundus, execution for Ide and the priests, and demolition of the temple of Isis.[50]

Speaking directly about the Isis cult, Juvenal warns men to beware of women who are religious fanatics, filling the house with worshipers of some foreign deity and allowing the cult minister, whom he describes as a large obscene eunuch, to make predictions of the future and then ask for gifts in return for his protection. Juvenal says disparagingly that if so bidden by their priest, such gullible women were prepared to go down to the Tiber and plunge through the ice, and then crawl on bleeding knees, naked and shivering, half way across Rome, all to atone for sleeping with their own husbands on a sacred day. Or if so bidden by an Egyptian goddess, they would journey to the source of the Nile just to bring back water to sprinkle on the steps of the temple. Why, he asks, would such foolish women think that a god would speak to them?[51]

As noted previously, the works of satirists such as Juvenal are an exaggeration of reality. Such is the nature of satire. But their descriptions reveal the tension in Roman culture relevant to the shifts in the status and behavior of women, primarily that of wealthy matrons, and the dissatisfaction among men who feared losing their dominant position over women.

Roman Cult of Mithras

Mithraism was truly the latecomer among the mysteries, emerging in Rome during the first century CE and lasting into the fourth century. And it can be described appropriately as foreign in origin, with elements that trace to Persia and even Indian Vedism. But in the form that arose in Rome, it was somewhat unique and seems to have then spread rapidly to other parts of the empire. It had similarities to other cults, in particular those of Dionysus and Isis, but as Bowden points out there are no surviving myths about the god Mithras. Traditionally, Mithras is said to be associated with covenant and oath, therefore a judicial presence and protector of truth. But Mithras is also seen as the guardian of cattle, the harvest and the waters, all sources of food and sustenance in Persia. We do know that the cult was exclusively for men, and there is iconic evidence of the cult all over Europe and into Great Britain. It was very popular among soldiers, merchants, and tradesmen, which may explain the rapid spread. Some scholars have stated that the elaborate initiation rites and the exclusion of women were serious handicaps in competing with the other mysteries.[52] However, the cult lasted well into the fourth century, outlasting most of the earlier mystery cults.

The cult was practiced in a cave or hall designed to resemble a cave, called the Mithraseum—small compared to the halls and temples of other mysteries. They were rectangular and had seating along both long sides. Opposite the entrance there was typically a cult image called the tauroctony, a relief sculpture of Mithras killing a bull with a sword or dagger. Near the entrance there were also typically two statues of young men (Cautes and Cautopates) holding torches, one upright and the other lowered, and on the ceiling various representations of the illuminaries (sun, moon, stars, and planets), and even consellations (signs of the zodiac). In their meetings, the initiates ate meat and drank wine. During the intiation the subject was stripped naked, blindfolded, hands tied behind his back, forced to kneel before a sword-bearing official, and ultimately forced to lie prone on the floor. Besides the initiation, there were also seven grades of ascension, much like the modern Free Masons and other fraternal orders. As with the Isis cult, Mithraism involved an ongoing participation, regular meetings, and instruction in great secrets represented by the cult. The purpose and objectives, along with sacred documents and further instruction, are not known. But evidence suggests matters pertaining to astrology, and Bowden notes that the various elements in the tauroctony correspond to constellations running fron Taurus to Scorpio, Mithras being the sun itself.[53]

Summary

Bowden, whose book is wonderfully written and illustrated, comments frequently that so many questions are unanswered and there is so much we do not know. Yet, we do have some idea of what the mystery cults were about, the reason for their popularity, and their relevance to our understanding of womanhood in the ancient world. Bowden also says that while some scholars in the past have drawn a likeness between Christianity and the mystery cults, more recent scholarship is inclined to see Christianity as a mystery cult.[54] There are certain similarities, and participation by women is an important one. What took place on Pentecost in Jerusalem when the church was born may have resembled certain mystery cults in terms of excitement, enthusiasm, and even ecstasy. There are mentions of glossolalia on that occasion, and later on in the Corinthian church, but on a broad scale there was little to compare Christian gatherings with the mysteries, certainly not in terms of frenzy and debauchery. Osiek and Balch point out the stark contrast between a Mithras cult meeting and a Sunday assembly in a Christian house church.[55] The Mithras cult was not open to women, and the gathering place would have been a cave or dark hall, secluded from public view. In contrast, the house church would have been open to all, visible from the street, and the meals, the practice of Eucharist (communion), songs, and prayers were in no way secretive. These Christian assemblies included women, children, slaves, and guests.

With the exception of Mithraism, the mystery cults challenged traditional patriarchy in a limited but significant way, by compounding the cultural tension that already existed due to unjust structures such as slavery and the subordination of women. But that was not their purpose. In the mystery cults, initiates discovered a strong personal sense of divine presence, combined with a cathartic and liberating emotional experience. Burkert concludes that cults of this sort, especially in the Greek culture, may have been a decisive invention for an important purpose. "Mysteries were initiation rituals of a voluntary, personal, and secret character that aimed at a change of mind through experience of the sacred."[56] So, somewhere in the polarities of light and darkness, agony and ecstasy, open outdoors and secluded caverns, quiet contemplation and pulsating music, solitude and pressing frenzied crowds, initiates to the mystery cults found something—an experience that, while changing nothing in the world around them, still made a difference.

Conclusions

We have discussed the major cultures of the ancient Near East and Mediterranean perimeter, including Mesopotamia, Egypt, Greece, and Rome, as well as Judaism and the mystery cults. Combined, these cultures and subcultures provide the broad-based backdrop for the birth of Christianity. The reason for reaching back as far as Mesopotamia and Egypt is to better understand the beginnings of Judaism, out of which Christianity was born, and also to discover influences on the Hebrew sacred texts that are still revered by Christians and form the major part of the Bible. The present objective is to identify specific cultural influences on the New Testament with regard to the status of women and the meaning of womanhood, and their impact on the church.

The influence of the ancient world on modern Christian tradition is undeniable. The best known examples pertain to Christmas (such as the date December 25, tree decorations, lights, garlands, Saint Nicolas) and Easter (rabbits, eggs, lilies, and the very name Easter derived from the goddess Ashtarte). Here we see practices derived from ancient social and religious customs, some totally unrelated to Christianity, whose origin and purpose are long forgotten.

There are other examples that represent some kind of association of the early church with the mystery cults. After the time of Constantine, terms derived from *musterion* (mystery) that were used in connection with the mystery cults came to be applied to Christian rituals, such as communion and baptism, which later would be designated sacraments.[1] Eusebius refers to Christians as initiates (*mystai*) and prophets as *mystagogoi*, both adopted from Eleusinian cult terminology.[2] Bowden says that the carrying of a statue of the Virgin Mary through the streets is a relic of processions in ancient festivals where the Mother Goddess was so carried.[3] Such practices demonstrate the durability of folk customs, and also might suggest their emotional rather than intellectual importance in community life. Some customs, however, may have begun with a distinct intellectual objective. Blundell sees in the beatification of the Virgin Mary an attempt to provide the church a sense of what virgin Greek goddesses offered, referring specifically to a feminine connection with God that was without sexuality, and therefore nonthreatening to both men and women.[4]

It is commonly known that various marriage customs in the modern West can be traced to the Romans, including the veil, as described in a previous chapter. Engagement and wedding rings were probably a remnant of the older *coemptio* (earnest money) that served as a deposit on the bride.[5] The choice of the third finger of the left hand is also Roman, the reasons for which were explained by Aulus Gellius.[6]

However, determining direct influences on the writers of the New Testament is a different matter. Some Christians deny the possibility of influence from either secular or religious sources on any biblical writer or document, simply because that conflicts with certain views of inspiration. It has become common in recent years, especially among conservative Christians, to refer to the Bible as "God's Word," a loaded term that ignores the human element in composition and implies some degree of literalism, such as inerrancy, authority, and thematic unity of all biblical documents. Such preconceptions often lead to untenable conclusions and are contrary to all we have learned about how the Bible was produced and transmitted through history.

We are aware of Paul's rabbinical education and evidence in his doctrine that he had studied and absorbed ideas already conceived by certain Greek philosophers.[7] We also are aware of his encounters with Epicurean and Stoic philosophers during his travels (Acts 17:18) and his challenge of certain elements of Greek philosophy (I Cor. 1:18–31). That is also evident in deutero-pauline teachings, an example found in Colossians 2:8.[8] Perhaps the most obvious connection of Paul with the Greek mind is found in his frequent instructions concerning bearing fruit and ethical living, often presented as exhortations to conclude his epistles.[9] Betz notes that this ethical focus resembles the convictions of Menander and Xenophon.[10] Barnhart also argues that Paul was influenced by Plato. For Barnhart, I Corinthians 13 "reads like a redaction of passages from the *Symposium*."[11] In Luke's account of Paul's discourse on the "unknown god," delivered on the Areopagus in Athens,[12] Paul drew from the Cretan poet Epimenides with the statement "by Him we live and move and have our very being,"[13] and he also quoted the Cilician poet Aretas, who said that men are the offspring of God.[14] He added that the true God "made the world and all things therein." In this he conflicted with the Stoics, whose pantheism placed Zeus within the cosmos as the organizer, but not at the beginning as creator. This perhaps illustrates Paul's attempt to blend Greek philosophy with rabbinic Judaism.

Naturally, within the immediate first-century context, Judaism would have provided the strongest and most significant influences on writers of the

New Testament, since most were Jews (Luke being the only certain exception). But considering the syncretism of both religion and culture that is evident in the environment out of which Christianity emerged, we must consider a variety of possible influences, including terminology and writing style, theological and philosophical concepts, ethical mores, social structures, and traditional religious practices. Bowden says that "the ideas of early Christianity may have owed much to Greek thought, but its practices owed much to Jewish rituals."[15]

In the present study, our concern is specifically related to the New Testament teachings concerning womanhood and the status of women. And the evidence of cultural influence is strong. As we move toward conclusions, it is important first to review how Christianity began.

The Jesus Movement

New Testament spokesmen claim Jesus Christ as their authority, either by recollection of his teachings and deeds, or in the case of Paul, by revelation (Gal. 1:12).[16] Moreover, the New Testament church claims Christ as its founder and author, and the source of its religious doctrines and way of life. As worded by Goguel, the Christian church is without a doubt the direct outcome of the life and ministry of Jesus Christ.[17] Jesus's own ministerial thrust is expressed in the Lukan version of his synagogue message in Nazareth, based on Isaiah's vision of an era of ministry to the outcast and oppressed of society.

> The Spirit of the Lord is on me, because he has anointed me to proclaim good news to the poor. He has sent me to proclaim freedom for the prisoners and recovery of sight for the blind, to set the oppressed free, to proclaim the year of the Lord's favor.[18]

His personal identity with this prophecy is suggested by his comment after the reading: "This day is the scripture fulfilled in your hearing." This, writes Vigeveno, was "the revolutionary manner of Jesus."[19] He spoke out against social injustice and moral evil of every description, but avoided the cynicism and recalcitrant spirit of many philosophers and rebels of his day. He despised exploitation of the poor in the name of justice and lashed out far more harshly at religious hypocrisy than at the sins of the common people.[20]

Rauschenbush describes Jesus as a builder of a new social order,[21] and in their discussion of empowerment in family relations, Jack and Judith Balswick compare Jesus to Karl Marx as an originator of utopian ideology.[22] It must be noted, however, that while Jesus's message can be described as revolutionary in form, content, and implications, it also assumes that his followers will always live in world of injustice, political domination, poverty, and oppression. Jesus did not challenge slavery or Rome's discriminatory social order, nor did he call for social or political revolution. He taught his followers to "give to Caesar what is Caesar's, and to God what is God's" (Mark 12:17). Bart Ehrman explains this in terms of the eschatological expectation in Jesus. He says that for Jesus "society, with all its conventions, was soon to come to a screeching halt, while the Son of Man arrived from heaven in judgment on the earth." Jesus was preparing people for the destruction of the current society and the revelation of something new.[23]

Shailer Matthews points to fraternity as the functional principle of love towards mankind that undergirded the message of Jesus. He further asserts that the times and places where people "have come most under the influence of the words and life of Jesus have been those in which institutions at variance with fraternity—branding, polygamy, the exposure of children, slavery, drunkenness and licentiousness—have disappeared."[24] That, of course, is somewhat idealistic, since it is not true of all areas where Christianity has spread nor even true of all Christian communities, and we cannot ignore the fact that the Christian world participated in slavery for centuries. But he is correct that the ministry and message of Jesus represents the noblest of ethics. Cullmann describes this principle at work in the lives of early Christians as the means whereby the example of Christ continued to influence the world after his departure.[25]

For precisely these reasons, women held a position of high esteem in the life and ministry of Jesus, and it becomes abundantly clear that Jesus held a view of women quite contrary to the predominant views in his day.[26] In the Johannine tradition, there is a story of Jesus conversing with a Samaritan woman about living water (John 4:1–42) and another story of how Jesus defended a woman who was about to be stoned to death for adultery (John 7:53–8:11). The Lukan record includes a unique story of the anointing of Jesus, here by a woman with a bad reputation, whom Jesus defended in response to criticism. He said "she has done a good thing" (Luke 7:36–50). He allowed a woman with a uterine hemorrhage to touch his garment, against common taboos and avoidance of defilement (Mark 5:25–34). He approved the choice of Mary of Bethany to engage in dialogue with him, rather than assisting her sister Martha in domestic chores (Luke 10:38–42). Jesus accepted financial support from women who followed him in his ministry (Luke 8:1–3), which was unprecedented in his day. He lauded a widow who gave all she had to a temple treasury for alms (Luke 21:1–4). Women were with him at his crucifixion when virtually all the men had fled (Mark 15:40–41). And all four Gospels acknowledge women as the first to observe and report the empty tomb (Matthew 28:1–10, Mark 16:1–8, Luke 24:1–10, John 20:1–2).

Certainly in whatever sense Jesus sought to minister to social need and proclaim the principles of justice, mercy, and love, so he sought to encourage and elevate women.[27] Many scholars have noted the special kindness toward women which all the Gospels attribute to Jesus, and which must be carefully noted in the light of his mission.[28] From the very start women were responsive to his teachings and devoted to his person.[29] Pratt comments that "women of all ranks in society found in him a benefactor and friend, before unknown in all the history of their sex."[30]

The Synoptics offer various glimpses into the ministry of Jesus that are more readily accepted by scholars than certain elements of the fourth Gospel, and which reflect something of Jesus's opposition to traditional attitudes toward women. Bo Reike correctly notes that the Lukan writer emphasizes the attention given by Jesus to Samaritans, women, and other groups that were either despised or exploited.[31]

The Synoptic divorce material is of great scholastic interest, partly because of the differences in detail between Matthew and Mark.[32] It is possible that the occasion for these statements was an attempt by Jewish leaders to draw Jesus into the debate between the schools of Hillel and Shammai concerning the grounds for divorce suggested in Deuteronomy.[33] But in all three Synoptics, Jesus is presented as concerned with promoting marital fidelity, not with grounds for divorce. He clearly attacks traditional divorce practices, particularly the inclination of many male Jews to interpret Mosaic divorce laws for personal advantage. And while none of the accounts overtly extends to women the right to divorce an adulterous husband, Jesus attacks the customary bias toward men that is evident in contemporary laws and ethical traditions.[34] The insertion of the "except for fornication" phrase by Matthew, which is not in the Markan parallel, is an effort on the part of the writer to portray Jesus as siding with the school of Shammai, and is indicative of the strong influence of Judaism on this writer.

It is interesting also that in the long discourse on divorce in Matthew 19, Jesus appeals to the priestly creation story, rather than the Yahwist story of Adam and Eve,[35] and then shifts to Genesis 2:24 to support the concept of marital devotion and oneness.[36] Jesus seems careful to avoid the implications of the Adam and Eve story that served as the basis for traditional rabbinic teachings on the subordination of women. Witherington also stresses that in discussing sexual sins Jesus seems to redirect attention from women, who generally bore the brunt of accusation and punishment in Jewish society, to men who are duly responsible for controlling their aggressive passion.[37] Therefore, the implication emerging from the Gospels is that Jesus was opposed to all forms of injustice against women, including those extensions of patriarchy evident in religion. The Synoptic Gospels also report statements by Jesus to his disciples in opposition to dominance, as exhibited by the rulers of the nations, in favor of leadership that is demonstrated by service and humility.[38]

The Earliest Church

It is no surprise then that the earliest Christian community, a limited group of people who had been taught by Jesus himself, included women. As Scroggs words it, we cannot "explain the prevalence and equality of women in the earliest church if such attitudes were not initiated by Jesus himself."[39] Luke estimates the number of disciples as about 120 (Acts 1:15), including Mary the mother of Jesus, his brothers, and others identified only as "the women." As is often the case in ancient literature, the names of the women in this group were not as important as the names and attributes of the men. Although not mentioned, Mary Magdalene was surely among the number. From John 20:1 in particular, she is remembered by Christians in general as the first evangelist who alone ran to tell Peter and John of the empty tomb.

The Jesus movement began with those initial disciples, joined by a much larger number of converts who lived in the area and others who had come to Jerusalem from various parts of the empire for the Feast of Pentecost (Acts 2). The earliest example of a house church is that of Mary of Jerusalem, mother of John Mark (Acts 12:12). And the earliest persecution of Christians was from the local Jewish community, of which Saul of Tarsus was a part. It is evident that Jews did not see the movement as separate from their own community until at least the middle of the second century. Therefore we have to conclude that early persecution of Christians was considered by the Jews to be a matter of discipline and correction. The Christians, on the other hand, saw themselves as persecuted.[40] This led to a scattering of the followers of Jesus to other places, such as Samaria, coastal towns like Joppa and Gaza, and northward to Damascus (Acts 8:1-2). Most of the key leaders, including Peter and the other Apostles, remained in and around Jerusalem.

Some of these early converts also remained committed to the synagogue and the laws and customs of Judaism. Convinced that gentiles who identified with them also needed to embrace the Laws of Moses, specifically circumcision, a number of self-appointed representatives of the Jerusalem church went to Antioch to teach and promote this opinion. They recoiled at the discovery that gentile converts continued to dine with pagan friends and eat meats offered to idols. So, along with insisting on circumcision, they also tried to prohibit other practices that they found offensive. The result was the Jerusalem Council (Acts 15) attended by Paul, Barnabas, and others as delegates from the church in Antioch, in an attempt to work out an amicable solution. Those issues continued to be debated for several years, as is evident from their discussion by Paul in his epistles to the church in Corinth and Rome, and from Galatians we gather that the matter created something of a rift between Paul and the leaders of the Jerusalem church.

Prior to that meeting, Paul and Barnabas had traveled to Cyprus and then to Asia Minor establishing churches. After the Jerusalem Council they split up, Barnabas returning to his home in Cyprus with his relative John Mark. Paul selected Silas and pushed through Asia Minor westward into Greece. In Paul's mission endeavors, many women were converted in various cities—in Philippi a merchant named Lydia; in Thessalonica a number of wives of leading men (*gunaikon te ton proton*); in Berea honorable Greek women; in Athens a woman named Damaris, among others; and in Corinth a woman named Priscilla and her husband, Aquila. Some were converted from Judaism and others from Greco-Roman traditional religions that Paul summarily called "idol worship" (I Thessalonians 1:9). No doubt some of these converts had been initiates in one or more mystery cults, but we have no record of that.

Travel was relatively easy at that time, due to the Pax Romana (Roman peace), both by ship and road. Many Christians, like Priscilla and Aquila (tentmakers) and Lydia (purple fabric merchant) traveled on business and converted others wherever they went. In this rapid expansion of Christianity, women played a variety of roles. Evidence from Paul's correspondence with the church in Corinth indicates that women prayed and prophesied in the assembly (I Corinthians 11 and 14). At the conclusion of his letter to the church in Rome, Paul named several women who were significant leaders in various roles—Priscilla, already mentioned, who was clearly involved in evangelism and church leadership, and Phoebe, whom he calls a both a *diakonos* (minister, servant, deacon) and a *prostatis* (Latin *patron*, sponsor, financial supporter). He mentions also Mary, his colleague who had worked very hard for the benefit of the Christians there. Junia and Andronichus, perhaps husband and wife, are said to have been believers before Paul, at some point "fellow prisoners," and "notable among the apostles." Tryphaena, Tryphosa, and Persis are all referred to as Paul's "co-workers" for the Gospel. And Julia, the mother of Rufus, is described by Paul as "like a mother to me also."[41]

Within a matter of two decades, Christians were assembling in house churches all over the Roman Empire. Gatherings were presided over by the leader of the household, whether male or female. If they were formerly Jewish, or casually attached to a synagogue, they might have had access to portions of the Hebrew scripture translated into Greek (the Septuagint, produced in Alexandria, late second century BCE). If so, they read selections at their assemblies, just as it was done in the synagogue.[42] In time, various Christian epistles and tractates were written and were circulated among churches, also read aloud for all to hear.

The elements of the Christian house church were modeled after the Roman family cult, combined with the format for Jewish special meals and celebrations in the home. But the most remarkable element of the church was that, like most of the mystery cults, there was a sense of freedom for women from social structures like patriarchy. Likewise, it is clear from certain statements of Paul that he opposed the practice by many married men of sexual relations with prostitutes or female slaves, and his comments echo the teachings of Musonius Rufus, his Roman contemporary.[43] His advice was that each man should have his own wife, and each wife her own husband. So among the earliest Christians a higher standard of moral conduct was expected, and in marriage a spirit of equity and mutual respect was encouraged. Paul said it best in his epistle to the Galatians: "There is neither Jew nor Greek, slave nor free, male nor female, for you are all one in Christ Jesus" (Galatians 3:28).

The Reversion

Stambaugh and Balch state unreservedly that there was an egalitarian spirit in these earliest Christian house churches, with women sharing leadership. But within a few years various rules were imposed that reverted to traditional patriarchy.[44] By the end of the first century, something had changed. Looking at the nature of the church by the fourth century, Cantarella writes:

> But it is not by chance that the fall of the Empire coincided with the reemergence of misogyny, to which the teachings of the Church fathers also made a significant contribution. The ground women had won was lost; women were once again pushed back to the "female" world, characterized, as always, by subservience.[45]

In light of the teachings of Jesus, and what we know of the participation of women in the earliest Christian community, we have to ask what brought about this staggering reversal of practice and doctrine. This was more than a casual trend. It was intentional and directive, initiated by church leaders in order to control the behavior of women and maintain a patriarchal structure, both at home and in the life of the church, as it was in the surrounding culture. The reversal to patriarchy, and the determination of future Christian doctrine on the status of women, hinges primarily upon seven key texts in the New Testament, reproduced here in full from the New International Version. It would be beneficial to read them carefully before proceeding with this final chapter:

> **I Corinthians 11:3–16** But I want you to realize that the head of every man is Christ, and the head of the woman is man, and the head of Christ is God. Every man who prays or prophesies with his head covered dishonors his head. But every woman who prays or prophesies with her head uncovered dishonors her head—it is the same as having her head shaved. For if a woman does not cover her head, she might as well have her hair cut off; but if it is a disgrace for a woman to have her hair cut off or her head shaved, then she should

Conclusions

cover her head. A man ought not to cover his head, since he is the image and glory of God; but woman is the glory of man. For man did not come from woman, but woman from man; neither was man created for woman, but woman for man. It is for this reason that a woman ought to have authority over her own head, because of the angels. Nevertheless, in the Lord woman is not independent of man, nor is man independent of woman. For as woman came from man, so also man is born of woman. But everything comes from God. Judge for yourselves: Is it proper for a woman to pray to God with her head uncovered? Does not the very nature of things teach you that if a man has long hair, it is a disgrace to him, but that if a woman has long hair, it is her glory? For long hair is given to her as a covering. If anyone wants to be contentious about this, we have no other practice—nor do the churches of God.

I Corinthians 14:33–35 For God is not a God of disorder but of peace—as in all the congregations of the Lord's people. Women should remain silent in the churches. They are not allowed to speak, but must be in submission, as the law says. If they want to inquire about something, they should ask their own husbands at home; for it is disgraceful for a woman to speak in the church.

Ephesians 5:22–24 Wives, submit yourselves to your own husbands as you do to the Lord. For the husband is the head of the wife as Christ is the head of the church, his body, of which he is the Savior. Now as the church submits to Christ, so also wives should submit to their husbands in everything.

Colossians 3:18 Wives, submit yourselves to your husbands, as is fitting in the Lord.

I Timothy 2:9–15 I also want the women to dress modestly, with decency and propriety, adorning themselves, not with elaborate hairstyles or gold or pearls or expensive clothes, but with good deeds, appropriate for women who profess to worship God. A woman should learn in quietness and full submission. I do not permit a woman to teach or to assume authority over a man; she must be quiet. For Adam was formed first, then Eve. And Adam was not the one deceived; it was the woman who was deceived and became a sinner. But women will be saved through childbearing—if they continue in faith, love and holiness with propriety.

Titus 2:2–9 Likewise, teach the older women to be reverent in the way they live, not to be slanderers or addicted to much wine, but to teach what is good. Then they can urge the younger women to love their husbands and children, to be self-controlled and pure, to be busy at home, to be kind, and to be subject to their husbands, so that no one will malign the word of God.

I Peter 3:1–6 Wives, in the same way submit yourselves to your own husbands so that, if any of them do not believe the word, they may be won over without words by the behavior of their wives, when they see the purity and reverence of your lives. Your beauty should not come from outward adornment, such as elaborate hairstyles and the wearing of gold jewelry or fine clothes. Rather, it should be that of your inner self, the unfading beauty of a gentle and quiet spirit, which is of great worth in God's sight. For this is the way the holy women of the past who put their hope in God used to adorn themselves. They submitted themselves to their own husbands, like Sarah, who obeyed Abraham and called him her lord. You are her daughters if you do what is right and do not give way to fear.

To some, these texts may sound all the more authoritative when read as a unit. To others they may sound all the more offensive. But reading them together helps to emphasize the significance of these texts within the New Testament and the enormous dilemma the church faced in the late first and early second century with regard to the status of women. They also emphasize the challenge for Christians in resolving gender issues in our present time. That challenge involves determining the reason for these statements and the reason the documents that contain them were included in the corpus of Christianity's sacred literature.

The Reason

Being associated with the Jews made life all the harder for Christians, since Jews already were considered by Rome to be a recalcitrant and rebellious people, looked on with serious disfavor. Claudius expelled Jews from Rome in 49 CE, allegedly because they were constantly rioting and resisting Roman laws.[46] When Christianity came to Rome, there were at least a dozen synagogues in the city, and it is likely that this is where the gospel message was initially preached there. But it is also likely that this led to a clash between the synagogues that prompted action against them by Claudius. Aquila and Priscilla were among the Jewish Christians who were expelled from Rome at that time, and from there they went to Corinth where they first met Paul (Acts 18:2). Then in 54 CE the new Emperor Nero allowed Jews, and Christians with them, to return to Rome.

The first documented case of official persecution of the Christians by the Roman government took place at the instigation of Nero. The trigger was a great fire that broke out in Rome in 64 CE, destroying portions of the city and resulting in local economic devastation. Suetonius reports that the fire was set on the order of Nero himself, possibly as a means of ridding the city of a poorly constructed section of apartments.[47] The report of Tacitus is different, claiming that Nero was away at the time, in Antium, and could not have been responsible. Tacitus also wrote that upon his return Nero provided food and supplies, and opened gardens and public buildings to assist those displaced by the fire. Looters and arsonists were said to have spread the flames by throwing torches and hindering measures to halt the fire. Nevertheless, the result was an official reaction against Christians.[48] The details remain a matter of debate due to these and other conflicting reports. And there is no evidence that it involved or led to any retaliation outside the city of Rome.

However, within a couple of years after that event, Paul was arrested in Jerusalem and went through a series of trials. Because of his Roman citizenship, he insisted on a hearing before the emperor. Eventually he was brought

Conclusions 207

to Rome where he resided under house arrest (Acts 21–28). According to Ignatius, writing around 110 CE, Paul was executed, but no mention is made of Rome.[49] Tradition has it that both Paul and Peter were martyred there.

In 66 CE a contingent of zealous Palestinian Jews initiated a revolt, holding up in Jerusalem. That resulted in a war that lasted four years. In 69 CE Vespasian was called back to Rome to become emperor, and left his son Titus in command. In 70 CE Titus destroyed much of Jerusalem and demolished the temple. Those Christians still there scattered, and Jerusalem was never again the hub of Christianity.

Eusebius, in his famous history of the church, reports a persecution in Lyons in 170 CE that began with mob violence, including assault, looting, and the stoning of known Christians.[50] There are numerous individuals and small Christian groups that were executed at various times and places as well. During the reign of Marcus Aurelius, Polycarp, bishop of Smyrna and allegedly a pupil of John the Apostle, was executed sometime between 155 and 180 CE, and Justin was beheaded along with several of his pupils around 165 CE. With the deaths of Polycarp and Justin, the term "martyr" came to be applied to Christians who died for their faith. A group of 12 North African Christians were so martyred in Silla, Numidia, in 180 CE. And Perpetua, a young Christian noblewoman, along with her pregnant servant Felicity and several others, were executed by sword in Carthage in 203. This is commonly associated with the reign of Septimius Severus, but there are conflicting reports about his disposition toward Christians.

The first empire-wide persecution took place under Maximinus Thrax, who ruled from 235 to 238 CE, although only church leaders were sought out. It was not until Decius, known as Trajan (emperor from 249 to 251 CE) that there was an official persecution of Christian laity. Christians were given the opportunity to avoid punishment by publicly offering sacrifices or burning incense to Roman gods and were accused by the Romans of impiety when they refused. That in turn was punished by arrest, imprisonment, torture, and execution.

Therefore, beginning as early as 49 CE, many Christians lived in fear of persecution and death, circumstances that waxed and waned in intensity and was typically in specific locations, but endured for nearly three centuries. In these circumstances they were compelled to assess how they might survive without renouncing faith in Jesus Christ. The question was how to give to Caesar what was due Caesar, and to God what they were compelled by faith to offer God. The answer that came from various writers was to be good law-abiding citizens and comply with customs and traditions, neither offending nor causing trouble, but at the same time remaining true to core elements of faith. That objective was the reason for the teachings represented in the seven texts reproduced above.

Explanations and Solutions

Only in the last half century, prompted by the feminist movement, has there been a critical reexamination of these passages in light of ancient history. Scholars of the stature of Elizabeth Schüssler Fiorenza and Rosemary Radford Ruether, whose hallmark works were produced in the early 1980s, and numerous others more recently, have brought to light facts that point to an explanation. With the explanation, there also was sought a solution to the problem of gender inequity that persists today.

Admittedly, some early feminist writers were on the right track but were motivated also by their commitment to biblical authority. That led occasionally to rather frantic and faulty exegetical methods. For example some interpreted *kephale* (head) in I Corinthians 11 as meaning "source" instead of "authority" in order to lessen the appearance of a domination hierarchy in marriage.[51] Others have explained the prohibition of women to speak in I Corinthians 14 as addressed only to women in the first part of the Christian assembly, allegedly attended by "uninitiated and unlearned unbelievers." The problem, it is argued, is that women were asking too many questions and were disrupting the order and flow of the service.[52] This is based on the assumption that the church in Corinth had two parts to the assembly, which in fact was a much later development where the "mass of catechumens" was held separately from the "mass of the faithful," who alone were allowed to take the Eucharist.

With a similar objective, many exegetes have exaggerated the implications of the pronoun *allelon* in Ephesians 5:2 to suggest a mutual submission and partnership between husbands and wives. The purpose of this strategy was to remove patriarchal overtones from these texts, and to extract from the New Testament a unified doctrine of gender equity. Such arguments, while misguided, have placated some church women.

Other scholars and clerics have resorted to the patronizing jargon of the ancient Greeks, and also the ministers who opposed the Women's Suffrage Movement in the late 1800s, to persuade women to feel honored in their station of subordination. This was essentially the claim that women are special creatures of God who exert a positive influence on the world by nurturing children and loving their husbands, and as such are intended to be protected, pampered, and cared for by men. Most women have reacted strongly against this approach also.

The seven texts reproduced above have been critically examined by innumerable commentators and exegetes, including most feminist scholars who seek solutions to gender inequity still prevalent in Christianity. For the present, comments will focus on a few important points to demonstrate the origin of these statements. First, it must be noted that Paul is not the author of most of these statements. In recent years Paul has been labeled a misogynist by some feminists, who saw him as the singular source of the New Testament doctrine of female subordination. But Paul can only be credited with I Corinthians 11, and the authors of the rest of these statements are unknown. The conclusion of scholarship today is that the I Corinthians 14:33–35 is an interpolation from a later writer, and not the words of Paul. The books of Ephesians and Colossians were written by a disciple of Paul, a deutero-paulist, who represented certain developments in theology in the next generation. The same is true of the Pastoral Epistles (I and II Tim. and Titus), whose author writes in the name of Paul and reflects a level of structure and order in the church that developed later.

Admittedly, some Christians dismiss the opinions and conclusions of biblical scholars as mere sophistry, irrelevant to their beliefs simply because these texts are in the Bible. No matter who wrote them, they are viewed as inspired, authoritative, and indisputable, a broad and sweeping determination derived essentially from II Timothy 3:16–17. However, evidence is strong and clear that these key texts reflect well-established cultural norms and structures, and were written in an effort to persuade Christians to comply, against the groundwork laid by Jesus and the earliest church.

It has been demonstrated in the previous chapters that all cultures in Christianity's milieu were patriarchal, with complex social structures rooted in male domination. Egyptian culture and all Mesopotamian subcultures were patriarchal. And from their records we learn that women were perceived by men as mysterious, possessors of uncanny knowledge, earthy, sensual, desirable, and valuable, yet physically weak, emotionally erratic, unruly, and vengeful. Women were enigmatic, both desired and feared by men. Therefore they had to be dominated and controlled.

From this world emerged the Hebrews, ancestors of Judaism, who viewed woman as the "divine afterthought," created for the benefit, pleasure, and the service of the man. The Greeks, following Aristotle, defined males as form and spirit, characterized by intellect and reason, and females as matter and emotion, and therefore inferior, requiring supervision, and existing primarily for reproduction. The Romans had similar views of women, although allowing them a more complex role in society, defined in terms of managing the household, educating children, and representing the honor of the husband in public. Roman women, primarily wealthy matrons, were allowed more public freedom than Greek wives, but if that freedom was not exercised with dignity and loyalty the result was the husband's shame. So, in all these cultures, women remained to one degree or another under the control of men. All of these cultures discouraged polygyny in favor of variations of sequential monogamy, and they all also allowed sexual privileges for men that were discouraged, if not forbidden, in women. Even in the mystery cults, which arose in the Greco-Roman era, where women had significant freedom of expression and participation, there remained a cultural structure of male dominance, and female participation offered only an occasional experience that was counter to the realities of their world.

Of the New Testament texts reproduced above, the clearest connection to the immediate socio-political context is I Peter 3:1–6. Fiorenza states simply that this household code offers readers a strategy for survival amidst trials and persecutions. Slaves and wives had to prepare to suffer for being Christians, but they could diminish their suffering by conforming "to the customs and ethos of the pagan household and state."[53] This particular statement pertains to Christian women with non-Christian husbands.

This is correct, but the life suggested by the writer of I Peter is more than mere survival, or keeping a low profile and staying quiet and invisible in order to avoid persecution. It is more than passive compliance. Rather, it is an evangelistic technique, no doubt derived from the teachings of Jesus: "You are the light of the world; a city on a hill cannot be hidden" (Matt. 5:14). The writer proposes that compliance with established customs can be utilized by Christian women to demonstrate the admirable Christian ethos by active participation in benevolence, servitude, and willing compliance with social and state interests. Thus when good works and compliant natures are seen, the observers might be won to Christ.

Bruce Winter offers a thorough discussion of this and related texts in *Seek the Welfare of the City*, deriving his title from Jeremiah 29:7, as well as from Greco-Roman sources.[54] His stated objective is to demonstrate that Christians of the first-century Greco-Roman world "were taught to embrace this tradition in order to help sustain and enhance the life of the cities in which they lived." He emphasizes that the term *politeia* is not about politics in the sense that modern Westerners think of it, but "public life." He challenges scholars who see the early Christians as ambivalent towards the city and Roman Empire and simply wanted to avoid upsetting the government.[55] And he argues convincingly that the writer of I Peter saw Christians as people of dual citizenship—citizens of the heavenly city of God (Heb. 11:10), as well as responsible residents in the Roman Empire. Paul taught something similar in Romans 13:1–7, although the subordination of wives and slaves is not included in his statement. But Christian duty to the state is all the clearer in I Peter if the entire section is read.

To paraphrase, the writer pleads with his audience to live as if they are foreigners and exiles, to maintain good conduct so that if any one accuses them of being lawbreakers, their mode of life will demonstrate that they are in fact good law-abiding citizens (I Peter 2:11–12). Then, as a conclusion he exhorts them not to live in fear, but always to be prepared to defend their beliefs with a spirit of gentleness and respect. And, he reminds them to keep

Conclusions

their consciences clear to put to shame anyone who wrongly accuses them. It is better to suffer for being a good citizen and a devout Christian, than to suffer for breaking laws or customs (3:14–17). Therefore, the reasoning behind the household code in the middle of this long text in I Peter is to demonstrate how best to live and survive, and how to win others to Christ, under harsh social conditions, persecution, and the threat of death. This writer also appeals to Hebrew legends of the patriarchs in Genesis, referring to Sarah's obedience to Abraham, whom she called Lord (*kurios*).

The same objective lies behind the household codes in Ephesians 5 and Colossians 3. These codes had been structured by Roman law, based on the format presented by the Greek philosopher Aristotle. Arius Didymus, first century BCE Stoic philosopher and instructor of Augustus, summarized the domestic ethics taught by Aristotle:

> A man has the rule of his household by nature, for the deliberative faculty in a woman is inferior, in children it does not yet exist, and in the case of slaves, it is completely absent.[56]

Therefore, family structure formulated and codified by the Greeks and enforced by the Romans was adapted by unnamed New Testament writers in I Peter, Ephesians, and Colossians and passed on to Christians. The advice to women and slaves in Christian households is compliance and resignation to the ancient patriarchal paradigm, as well as Roman social order, to avoid creating conflict and to make a positive impression. It is significant that the wording of Galatians 3:28 ("there is neither Jew nor Greek, slave nor free, male nor female") is also the format for Colossians 3:11, which introduces the household code there. But the "male and female" is excluded, and the wording is "there is no Gentile or Jew, circumcised or uncircumcised, barbarian, Scythian, slave or free, but Christ is all, and is in all."

Of course, not all Christians in the late first and early second century felt the immediate threat of persecution, so such instructions were not totally about survival. Further, not all households among them had slaves, or were led by a male. There were many women and men who lived independently. However, whether free or slave, male or female, all Christians were under the obligation to exemplify the spirit of Christ and to win others by example as well as teaching. Thus, all Christian women and slaves became heirs of these prescriptions for compliance. And in turn, these familial relationships became the model for church relationships, which included evidence of female subordination in church. David Balch sees these codes as a conservative reaction against progressive possibilities for women in the Jesus movement and early Pauline churches.[57]

Concerning I Corinthians 14:34–5, the suggestion that wives can learn all they need to know from their husbands is also a Greek and Roman view mentioned in previous chapters. A similar suggestion appears in I Timothy 2:9–15, although here the writer appeals to other social norms as well. Ehrman calls attention to the similarities of these two texts, noting that neither was written by Paul.[58] We have seen in previous chapters that various writers, both Greek and Roman, described the dress of courtesans, prostitutes, and women of questionable character, which clearly was different from the mode of dress by honorable and respectable wives. This is noteworthy, not because Christian women were held to the highest standards of appearance and conduct, but because the content and wording is derived from earlier sources. The writer also draws from Jewish tradition by appealing to Genesis 2. First he asserts that the subordination and submission of Christian wives follows the order of creation, and second he associates woman's place with Eve's role in the Fall. Thus, the writer appeals to Hebrew myth as the theological basis for female subordination. Further, as was the case with the Pandora myth in Greco-Roman culture, woman is blamed for all the problems of the world, and her subordinate status is part of her punishment. Last, this writer also defines the Christian woman's purpose and value in terms of bearing children, a concept also derived from earlier cultural perspectives.

Concerning the dress codes in I Timothy 2, Winter points out the similarities with discussions of dress, jewelry, and makeup by numerous Greco-Roman writers, and in the reversion to patriarchal structure in the early church, the public perception of Christian wives becomes all the more important.[59] Concerning this, Clement of Alexandria, a Christian writing around 200 CE, is critical of women who wear gold, dye their hair, and paint their eyes, all to attract the gaze of others. This he says is not the behavior of good wives, but of courtesans. And if you were to remove all the dye, the ornaments, and the fabric, you would not find a godly woman but a fornicator and adulteress occupying the shrine of the soul.[60]

The text in Titus 2:2–9 also needs explanation. First, it is part of another version of the household codes and includes some of the ethical and social mores already discussed, especially about subordination of wives and devotion to domestic duties. But the stated objective is not to promote behavior that is of itself ethically good and right, but compliance with the traditional paradigms so that "no one will malign the word of God." A second point of interest is that this text draws from a long-standing custom in ancient cultures that older women teach younger women the ways of life, domestic chores, marriage, and motherhood.

Admittedly, the one text in this group that is generally accepted as Pauline, I Corinthians 11, reflects a clear appeal to contemporary custom for what is proper in the Christian assembly. It is possible that Paul experienced a degree of culture shock when he traveled west into Macedonia and Achaia. He saw customs and behavior there which he had not seen before. But what distinguishes this text from the others is that Paul recognizes that women are praying and prophesying in the assembly, and he does not challenge that. The matter on which Paul urges social compliance is the head covering, which he states is a symbol of marriage status, and he illustrates his concern with the reference to cropping the hair. In previous chapters it was pointed out that in both Greek and Roman culture the head covering was highly symbolic of a wife's subordinate relationship to her husband. It is also worthy of mention that in various places an adulteress would be shamed by having her hair cropped short.[61] And for that reason, Paul states that if a married Christian woman chooses to be in public without a head covering, she dishonors her husband and may as well have her hair cropped like an adulteress.

While little will be said on this, we must acknowledge the male-oriented leadership that appears in the Pastorals (I Tim. 3:1–12; Titus 1:5–9). Fiorenza expresses certainty that this does not represent a formal hierarchy in the church at this point, but certainly the groups are delineated by age. Also, the church in these epistles is considered to be the household of God, and therefore maintains a patriarchal format.[62]

A final text, not included in the ones listed earlier, is the comparison of husband and wife to Christ and the church in Ephesians 5:25–27.

> Husbands, love your wives, just as Christ loved the church and gave himself up for her to make her holy, cleansing her by the washing with water through the word, and to present her to himself as a radiant church, without stain or wrinkle or any other blemish, but holy and blameless.

Osiek and Balch point out that despite the connection of this comparison to the household codes immediately before it, the thrust of the metaphor is directed more to the church than to married couples.[63] The writer reminds them of the incomparable sacrifice, glorification, and resulting worthiness of the one whom they serve as spiritual Lord (*kurios*) in a material world ruled by the emperor. However, the purpose and application to the husband, no doubt, is to promote deeper love on the part of husbands for their wives, rather than simply viewing them as bearers of children and wards in the household. This is expressed by the term *agape*, a word that conveys commitment, devotion, and self-sacrifice, and is emblematic of Christian ethics throughout the New Testament. But to compare this to Christ's love for the church elevates the requirement for a husband to virtual divinity. If anything, this wording might have been chosen to remind husbands of the social responsibility of provision and protection they owe to those in their households, who are considered weaker and inferior to the husband, and therefore to earn the level of honor that was important to males in their culture.[64] But nothing in the metaphor removes or diminishes the substance of the code that relegates the wife to subordination and inferiority. If anything, it strengthens it.

Summary

The spirit and message of the Gospel of Jesus Christ are opposed to all forms of injustice, including domination, persecution, slavery, racism, classism, abuse, exploitation of the weak, and subordination of women. Jesus himself treated women with dignity and respect, and the details of his ministry suggest his opposition to traditional paradigms of dominance. A strong movement toward the freedom and equity of women is evident in the earliest Christian community, where women held positions of influence and leadership in the church (evangelist, prophetess, minister/deacon, patron, apostle, and some would say elder/pastor as well).

However, at some point in the first century there began a reversion to patriarchy in churches. Based on I Corinthians 11, Paul himself made suggestions along this line and therefore to a degree compromised the ideals expressed in Galatians 3:28. Later writers, whose teachings are represented by the above key texts, were even more forceful concerning female subordination, and represent a broader effort to comply with the patriarchal norms and structures of the Greco-Roman culture. In time, their teachings were interpreted by the church as binding precepts on all Christians everywhere.

This leads the modern Christian to further conclusions. Advice by mostly unnamed New Testament writers to comply with Roman law is not justification of political tyranny; admonition to slaves to submit to their masters is not justification of slavery; admonition to wives to be submissive to husbands is not justification of patriarchy and male domination; and statements discouraging women from speaking in church, teaching men, or praying or prophesying without a head covering, is not justification for denying women positions of leadership in church. These are relics from antiquity that do not measure up to the ethics of Jesus or the spirit of the Gospel.

Appendix 1: Periods of Ancient Mesopotamian History

Prehistory	**Before 3200 BCE** Semites and Sumerians arrive and settle, begin to farm, herd, and trade.
Proto-Dynasty	**3200–2300 BCE** First definitive writing, first Dynasty of Ur and royal cemetery.
Old Akkadian	**2300–2100 BCE** Sargon the Great and first Semitic Empire. 2100–2000 BCE. Kingdom of Ur.
Old Babylonian and Assyrian	**2000–1600 BCE** Earliest rival kingdoms in Babylon and Assyria. Hammurabi unites region. Cultural development and emergence of Akkadian language.
Middle Babylonian	**1600–1100 BCE** Invasion of Kassites. Early ancestors of Israel migrate into southern Levant. Mittani (Indo-Europeans) invade northern Mesopotamia.
Middle Assyrian	**1300–1000 BCE** Assyria takes control of northern Mesopotamia, establishes Ashur as capital. Israelites settle in Egypt, become enslaved, then Moses leads Exodus; conquest of Canaan by 1200 BCE. From 1100 BCE nomadic Aramaeans and Chaldeans overrun Mesopotamia.
Neo-Assyrian	**1000–609 BCE** Nineveh becomes capital, invasion of surrounding territories under Asarhaddon and Ashurbanipal. End of Israel's monarchy, division into Israel

	(north) and Judah (south). Israel conquered by Assyria and disappears.
Neo-Babylonian	606–539 BCE
	Nebuchadnezzar conquers Assyria, invades and exiles Israel's population. A generation of Israelites live in Mesopotamia.
Persian	539–330 BCE
	Cyrus defeats Babylon, consolidates entire region. Frees Israel to return and rebuild Jerusalem and temple.
Seleucid	330–130 BCE
	Alexander conquers Persia and begins Hellenization. Seleucid rulers control Mesopotamia.
Parthian	129 BCE–224 CE
	Mesopotamia controlled by Parthian rulers (the Arsacid Dynasty) and diminishes in political, military, and social significance.

Appendix 2: Periods of Ancient Egyptian History

Pre-Egypt	4000–3200 BCE Naqada culture, primitive oval mud huts; simple hunting, fishing and agriculture; gold and silver jewelry, pottery, magic, adoration of Mother God; tribal conflicts; scorpion King(s); copper, papyrus, linen, connection with Levant cultures; buildings of unbaked bricks; boats with sails.
Dynasty 0	3050 BCE Menes unifies upper and lower Egypt; hewn stone houses, tools, and vessels; many deities depicted with human body and animal head. Pharaoh becomes a god-king.
Early Period	Dynasties I and II, 3050–2813 BCE Hieroglyphics; basins to control floods, canals for irrigation; Egypt one state, officials a distinct class.
Old Kingdom	Dynasties III–VI, 2686–2345 BCE Imhotep priest, architect, physician; Khufu, great pyramids and Sphinx at Giza; limestone statues; first bronze; first great dam; Queen Meresankh III (high priestess of Toth).
Late Old Kingdom and First Intermediate Period	Dynasties VII–XIa, 2345–2055 BCE Regional competition; cult of Osiris; drought, famine, civil disorder.

218   Appendix 2

Middle Kingdom	**Dynasties XIb–XIII, 2055–1750 BCE** Domesticated cats; tombs with two floors; model boats with painted figurines (gifts for the dead); cultural exchange with Mesopotamia.
Second Intermediate Period	**Dynasties XIV–XVII, 1750–1550 BCE** Social unrest; secularization; Hyksos rule in Avaris; horse and chariot introduced; Egyptian vassals in Thebes; Ahmose I expels Hyksos; reunification.
New Kingdom	**Dynasties XVIII–XX, 1550–1140 BCE** Thutmose I builds first tomb in Valley of Kings; conquest of other lands; Hittite invasion and later expulsion; Books of the Dead; pyramid building ceases; Hatshepsut's expedition to Punt (Somalia), Akhenaten and Nefertiti, Tutankhamen; Thutmose III obelisks at Heliopolis; Rameses II and battle of Kadesh; Mernenptah's Victory Stela (earliest mention of Israel); iron replaces bronze; collapse of grain production.
Third Intermediate Period	**Dynasties XXI–XXV, 1090–715 BCE** Weakening of central power; Sheshonq conquers Jerusalem; Ethiopians overrun Egypt; Assyrians conquer Egypt, and many exiled, then return.
Saite Period	**Dynasty XXVI, 672–525 BCE** Reunited under Psammetic I; Ahmose II peaceful reign; settlements of Diaspora Jews in Elephantine.
Classical Era	
Late Period	**Dynasties XXVII–XXXI, 525–332 BCE** Persian domination; canal from Mediterranean to Red Sea.
Hellenistic Period	**Macedonian and Ptolemaic rulers, 332–30 BCE** Alexander the Great conquers Egypt
Roman Period	**Caesars, 30 BCE–395 CE**

Expanded from timeline by Cyril Aldred, *The Egyptians* (London: Thames and Hudson, 1961), p. 11.

Appendix 3:
Key Events in Ancient Judaism
(dates approximate)

1800 BCE	Pre-Israelite clans migrate from Mesopotamia to Haran in Syria, then into southern Levant (Canaan)
1400 BCE	el-Amarna letters (the Hapiru: Abdiherpa, king of Urusalem)
1300 BCE	Egyptian presence in Canaan (Stela of Bet-Shean)
1250–1230 BCE	Exodus, sojourn in Sinai, Law of Moses, tabernacle, and invasion of Canaan
1200–1050 BCE	Judges and periodic conflicts with local tribes
1040 BCE	Samuel (prophet and judge)
1030–933 BCE	Monarchy (Saul, David, Solomon; earliest collections of documents, temple)
933 BCE	Division of Israel and Judah (separate lines of kings; prophets oppose idolatry)
722 BCE	Israel conquered by Assyria, and disappears
606–589 BCE	Invasions by Nebuchadnezzar, destruction of Jerusalem and Israel's deportation to Babylon
539 BCE	Defeat of Babylonians by Persians
538 BCE	Cyrus allows the Jews to return to Jerusalem and altar is reestablished
520–515 BCE	Temple rebuilt by Zerubabel, Haggai and Zekariah (prophets)
458 BCE	Ezra reads the Torah
445–432 BCE	Nehemiah in Jerusalem
440–400 BCE	Diaspora Jews settle in Egypt (Elephantine papyri)
323–64 BCE	Seleucid Dynasty (Hellenization)
250–130 BCE	Septuagint produced in Alexandria
167–160 BCE	Maccabean revolt
140–16	Hasmonean Dynasty

63	Civil war in Judea and Roman intervention
73–4	Herod the Great (Idumean, installed by Romans); rebuilds temple
4 BCE–39 CE	Herod Antipas (tetrarch of Galilee and Perea); Jesus of Nazareth and birth of Christianity
66–73 CE	First Jewish-Roman war
70 CE	Destruction of temple by Roman general Titus

Appendix 4: Outline of Ancient Greek History

Paleolithic, Mesolithic and Neolithic Periods
Transition from a nomadic "hunter-gatherer" lifestyle to settled village life and agriculture.

The Bronze Age: 3000–1100 BCE
The Minoan civilization came to power on the island of Crete, superseded by the Mycenaean civilization on the mainland of Greece.

The Early Iron Age: 1100–900 BCE
The Mycenaean civilization wanes. Dorians invade southern Greece. Displaced Greek-speaking peoples move into Asia Minor.

The Geometric Period: 900–700 BCE
Development of the Greek polis, including Athens, Corinth, and Sparta. Trade with other Mediterranean cultures. Colonies are established in Italy and Sicily. Writing develops; epic poems produced.

The Archaic Period: 700–480 BCE
Prosperity of city-states and colonies. Political, religious, philosophic and artistic development. Persia dominates Greek cities in eastern Aegean and Asia Minor. Persians invade mainland Greece in 490 and 480 BCE. Athens leads a league of Greek states against the Persians.

The Classical Period: 480–323 BCE
Prolific literature, drama and art. Athens increases in wealth and power and develops democratic government. The Delian League becomes the Athenian Empire. Kimonian and Periklean building programs, including the Parthenon and other temples on the Acropolis. Peloponnesian War (431–404 BCE) and the defeat of Athens. Rise of Macedonia under Philip II, and ultimate conquests by Alexander the Great.

The Hellenistic Period: 323–31 BCE
Death of Alexander, and empire divided into three ruling dynasties: Seleucids in Asia Minor, Ptolemies in Egypt, and the Antigonids (Macedonian) in Greece. Hellenization (language, art, architecture, literature, athletics) throughout areas of control. Athens is center of philosophy in Greece, rivaled by Alexandria in Egypt.

The Roman Period in Greece: 31 BCE–323 CE
Rome engulfs Hellenistic kingdoms. Octavian (Augustus) becomes first emperor. Achaia becomes a Roman province. Rome adopts and perpetuates much of Greek learning, arts, and religious centers (with earlier merging of traditional myths and pantheon of deities).

Adapted from Kevin T. Glowacki, www.stoa.org/athens/essays/history.html.

Appendix 5: Outline of Ancient Roman History

Beginnings of Rome (c. 753–616 BCE)
Legends of Alba Longa, early Latins settle on the Palatine, foundation of Rome and rule of Romulus, Numa Pompilius, Tullus Hostilius, and Ancus Marcius.

Later Kings (c. 616–510 BCE)
Legends of the Etruscan kings, Tarquinius Priscus, Servius Tullius, and Tarquinius Superbus; development of symbols of power; appearance of soothsayers ; development of public works, such as walls, water conduits, and sewage; construction of temples.

Early Republic (c. 510–343 BCE)
Struggle against ruthless control; struggle for political stability, economic balance, and common justice.

Conquest of the Italian Peninsula (c. 343–264 BCE)
Visions of expansion; a consolidated army of Rome sets about to gain territory about the Tiber River, eventually overpowering and pacifying the confederacy of Latin towns and granting citizenship to those who cooperate.

Conquest of the Mediterranean World (c. 264–133 BCE)
The First Punic War against Carthage marks Rome's initial foreign campaign. Rome develops a fleet of ships for sea battle and proves victorious at Mylae in 260 BCE. An invasion of North Africa is not successful. The Second Punic War (218–201 BCE) includes Hannibal's invasion of Italy. In 201 at the battle of Zama, Scipio is victorious over Hannibal. Carthage becomes a province, and Rome wins Spain and all islands in between Italy and Carthage.

Fall of the Republic (c. 133–31 BCE)
This period is defined by external war and internal civil strife, summarized by the names and stories of various rulers of Rome as a republic (either consuls,

tribunes, or dictators); first the Gracchi brothers (Tiberius and Gaius), Marius and Sulla, Pompey, Julius Caesar, Marc Antony and his consort Cleopatra, and Octavius (Augustus), who then declares himself emperor.

Early Roman Empire (31 BCE–100 CE)
Octavian is given title Augustus by the senate and becomes *pontifex maximus* (high priest) and *imperator* (emperor). He is succeeded in this role by a long line of emperors. Those during the first Christian century are Tiberius (14–37), Caligula (37–41), Claudius (41–54), Nero (54–68), Galba (68–69), Otho (69), Vitellius (69), Vespasian (69–79), Titus (79–81), Domitian (81–96), Nerva (96–98), and Trajan (98–117).

Adapted from *Outlines of Roman History* by William C. Morey (New York: American Book, 1901); retrieved January 2015, http://www.forumromanum.org/history/.

Chapter Notes

Abbreviations: Used in notes for certain multivolume works, classical libraries (Greek and Latin), and other ancient primary sources. **BCL**—Bohn's Classical Library; **CH**—Code of Hammurabi; **DM**—Herbert Danby's Mishnah; **EBT**—Epstein's Babylonian Talmud; **ISBE**—International Standard Bible Encyclopedia; **LCL**—Loeb Classical Library; **NBD**—New Bible Dictionary; **NSHERK**—New Schaff-Herzog Encyclopedia of Religious Knowledge; **PG**—Patrilogia Graeca; **TDNT**—Theological Dictionary of the New Testament

Introduction

1. I Corinthians 11:2-16; I Corinthians 14:33-35; Ephesians 5:22-24; Colossians 3:18; I Timothy 2:9-15; Titus 2:4; I Peter 3:1-7. These will be discussed in the final chapter.
2. Ephesians 5, Colossians 3, and I Peter 3, as referenced in note 1, above.
3. James Dunn, "The Household Rules in the New Testament," in *The Family in Theological Perspective*, ed. S. Barton (Edinburgh: T & T Clark, 1996), p. 62.
4. Michelle Zimbalist Rosaldo and Louise Lamphere, eds., *Women, Culture and Society* (Stanford: Stanford University Press, 1974), p. 17.
5. Ibid., pp. 67-87.
6. David Mace and Vera Mace, *Marriage East and West* (Garden City, NY: Doubleday, 1960), pp. 30-31.
7. Joan Morris, *The Lady Was a Bishop* (New York: Macmillan, 1973), p. 105. See also E. C. McLaughlin, "Equality of Souls, Inequality of Sexes: Women in Medieval Theology," in *Religion and Sexism*, ed. R. R. Reuther (New York: Simon and Schuster, 1974), pp. 229-230.
8. Walter Wagner, "The Demonization of Women," *Religion in Life* XLII (Spring 1973), p. 56.
9. *Book of Enoch*, Book I (Book of the Watchers), 7:1-2. See Wagner, "The Demonization of Women," p. 62.
10. David Buss, *The Handbook on Evolutionary Psychology* (New York: Wiley, 2005), p. 5.
11. Nancy Chodorow, *The Reproduction of Mothering: Psychoanalysis and the Sociology of Gender* (Berkeley: University of California Press, 1999).
12. Mary Van Leeuwen, *My Brother's Keeper: What the Social Sciences Do (and Don't) Tell Us about Masculinity* (Downer's Grove, Ill.: InterVarsity Press, 2002), p. 146.
13. Elizabeth Schüssler Fiorenza, *In Memory of Her* (New York: Crossroad, 1992), p. 11.
14. Zainab Bahrani, *Women of Babylon* (London: Routledge, 2001), pp. 14-27.
15. Sarah Pomeroy, *Goddesses, Whores, Wives and Slaves: Women in Classical Antiquity* (New York: Schocken, 1975).
16. Bahrani, *Women of Babylon*, pp. 14-27. See also Maude Glasgow, *The Subjugation of Woman and the Traditions of Men* (New York: M. I. Glasgow, 1940), p. 94; G. A. de Moubray, *Matriarchy in the Malay Peninsula* (London: George Routledge and Sons, 1931), p. 37; and Johann Bachofen, selections published as *Myth, Religion and*

Mother Right (Princeton: Princeton University Press, 1967).
17. Carol R. and Melvin Ember, *Cultural Anthropology* (New York: Appleton-Century-Crofts, 1973), pp. 185–209.
18. Rosemary R. Ruether, *Liberation Theology* (New York: Paulist Press, 1972), p. 95f.
19. "Matriarchy," *Encyclopedia Britannica*, Vol. XV (London: William Benton, 1964), p. 93.
20. Bahrani, p. 18.
21. Alister E. McGrath, *Christian Theology: An Introduction* (Oxford: Blackwell, 2001), p. 110.
22. Fiorenza, *In Memory of Her*, p. xv.
23. Pomeroy, *Goddesses, Whores, Wives and Slaves*, p. xv.
24. Fiorenza, p. xxiv.

Chapter One

1. Jean Bottéro, *Everyday Life in Ancient Mesopotamia*, trans. Antonia Nevill (Baltimore: Johns Hopkins University Press, 2001), p. ix. This is a collection of essays first published in *L'Histoire* and gathered by Bottéro in this significant work, with contributions also from André Finet, Bertrand Lafont, and Georges Roux.
2. Samuel Noah Kramer, *History Begins at Sumer: Thirty-Nine Firsts in Recorded History* (Philadelphia: University of Pennsylvania Press, 1988).
3. Zainab Bahrani, *Women of Babylon*, pp. 130–32.
4. Ibid., p. 133.
5. Ibid., p. 141–60.
6. Thorkild Jacobsen, *The Harps That Once...: Sumerian Poetry in Translation* (New Haven: Yale University Press, 1987), p. 141.
7. Ibid., p. 21.
8. Rivkah Harris, "Inanna-Ishtar as Paradox and a Coincidence of Opposites," *History of Religions* 30 (1990), pp. 261–278; see also Harris, *Gender and Aging in Mesopotamia* (Norman: University of Oklahoma Press, 2000), p. 163.
9. Bahrani, p. 150.
10. Epic of Gilgamesh, Assyrian International News Agency Books Online http://www.aina.org/books/eog/eog.pdf. And Epic of Gilgamesh, Penguin Classics, Andrew George trans. http://www.cidmod.org/sidurisadvice/Gilgamesh.pdf
11. Bahrani, pp. 155–158.

12. Morris Jastrow, "The Descent of Ishtar into the Netherworld," *The Civilization of Babylonia and Assyria* (Philadephia: J. B. Lippincott Company, 1915), Academy for Ancient Text, retrieved May, 2014, http://www.ancienttexts.org/library/mesopotamian/ishtar.html.
13. Stephanie Dalley, *Myths from Mesopotamia* (New York: Oxford, 1989), p. 158.
14. Ibid., p. 305.
15. James B. Pritchard, *Archaeology and the Old Testament* (London: Oxford University Press, 1958), pp. 206ff.
16. G. R. Driver and J. C. Miles, *The Babylonian Laws, Vol. I* (London: Oxford University Press, 1952), pp. 41–45.
17. Leonard W. King, trans., *The Seven Tablets of Creation* (1902), retrieved July 2014, http://www.sacred-texts.com/ane/stc/index.htm.
18. Herodotus, *The History of Herodotus*, Vol. I, ed. and trans. George Rawlinson (New York: D. Appleton and Company, 1885), pp. 178–200.
19. George Roux, "Did the Sumerians Emerge from the Sea?" in Bottéro, *Everyday Life in Ancient Mesopotamia*, pp. 7–8.
20. Roux, "The Great Enigma of the Cemetery at Ur," in Bottéro, p. 25.
21. The ziggurat is a pyramid tower with a rectangular base and flat top, designed for worship, and no doubt the kind of tower mentioned in Genesis 11:1–9. Besides the Ziggurat of Ur, other remains include the Ziggurat of Aqar Quf, near Baghdad; Chogha Zanbil in Khūzestān, Iran; and Sialk, near Kashan, Iran, which is the oldest, dating from around 2800 BCE.
22. Roux, "Did the Sumerians Emerge from the Sea?" in Bottéro, p. 22.
23. Gwendolyn Leick, *Mesopotamia: The Invention of the City* (London: Penguin, 2001).
24. Roux, in Bottéro, pp. 30–40.
25. Leick, *Mesopotamia: The Invention of the City*, p. 116.
26. Ibid., pp. 269–70.
27. Amelie Kuhrt, *The Ancient Near East: c. 3000–330 B.C.*, Vol. 2 (London: Routledge, 1995), p. 251.
28. Herodotus I, 185.
29. Roux, "Semiramis: The Builder of Babylon," in Bottéro, p. 142.
30. Bahrani, p. 122.
31. Michelle Marcus, "Art and Ideology in Ancient Western Asia," in Jack Sasson

Chapter Notes—One 227

et.al. eds. *Civilizations of the Ancient Near East.* (New York: Charles Scribner's Sons, 1995), pp. 2487–2502.
32. Bahrani, p. 125.
33. Megan Cifarelli, "Gesture and Alterity in the Art of Ashurnasirpal II of Assyria," *Art Bulletin* 80 (1998): 210–228.
34. Bahrani, p. 130.
35. Letha Scanzoni and Nancy Hardesty, *All We're Meant to Be* (Waco: Word Books, 1974), p. 41.
36. S. A. Cook, *The Laws of Moses and the Code of Hammurabi,* Vol. I (London: John Murray, 1878), p. 71; E. A. Wallis Budge, *Babylonian Life and History,* second edition (London: The Religious Tract Society, 1925), p. 165; Charles Seltman, *Women in Antiquity* (London: Thames and Hudson, 1956), pp. 30–32.
37. *Code of Hammurabi* 117, trans. L. W. King, retrieved July 2014, http://eawc.evans ville.edu/anthology/hammurabi.htm.
38. Ibid., 118.
39. Ibid., 119.
40. Ibid., 127.
41. Ibid., 133–35.
42. Ibid., 136.
43. Ibid., 209.
44. Ibid., 210.
45. Ibid., 213–14.
46. Ibid., 180.
47. Ibid., 150.
48. Ibid., 162.
49. Ibid., 163.
50. Ibid., 179.
51. Ibid., 178.
52. Ibid., 181–82.
53. Ibid., 183–84.
54. The letters of Nimmuria to Dusratta and Kallima-Sin in the Tel-Amarna Tablets provide details. See Morris Jastrow, *The Civilization of Babylonia and Assyria* (Philadelphia: J. B. Lippincott Company, 1915), p. 346.
55. Cook, *The Laws of Moses,* p. 78. A similar gift in later Hebrew culture was called the *mohar,* which Laban consumed, incurring the anger of his daughters, Leah and Rachel (Gen. 31:15). The Chaldee term also appears in the Hebrew vocabulary as *nadin,* a large gift presented to a harlot; *Gesenius' Hebrew and Chaldee Lexicon,* trans. Samuel P. Tragelles (Grand Rapids, MI: Wm. B. Eerdmans, 1964), p. 535.
56. Herodotus I, 196.
57. *Code of Hammurabi,* 144.
58. Ibid., 145–47.

59. Marten Stol, "Private Life in Ancient Mesopotamia," *Civilizations of the Ancient Near East,* Vol. 3, ed. Jack M. Sasson (New York: Charles Scribner, 1995), pp. 489–90.
60. Cook, p. 77.
61. Stol, p. 486.
62. Bottéro, p. 117.
63. Budge, *Babylonian Life and History,* p. 165; Cook, p. 102.
64. *Code of Hammurabi,* 148–49.
65. Ibid., 128.
66. G. Driver and J. Miles, *The Assyrian Laws* (Oxford: Clarendon Press, 1935).
67. Martha T. Roth, *Law Collections from Mesopotamia and Asia Minor* (Atlanta: Scholars Press, 1995), p. 169.
68. *Code of Hammurabi,* 159–61.
69. Ibid., 151.
70. Ibid., 156–7.
71. Ibid., 170–77.
72. Bahrani, p. 53.
73. Ibid., Plate 3, p. 53.
74. Bottéro, p. 98.
75. Bahrani, pp. 44–45.
76. Robert D. Biggs, "Medicine, Surgery, and Public Health in Ancient Mesopotamia," in *Civilizations of the Ancient Near East,* Vol. 3, ed. Jack M. Sasson (New York: Charles Scribner and Sons, 1995), p. 1917.
77. Bottéro, p. 104.
78. Jane R. McIntosh, *Ancient Mesopotamia: New Perspectives* (2005), pp. 273–75, https://books.google.com/books?id=9veK7E 2JwkUC&printsec=frontcover&dq=isbn:157 6079651&hl=en&sa=X&ei=686_VPKxLYyc Nr76g9gP&ved=0CB8Q6AEwAA#v=one page&q&f=false.
79. *Code of Hammurabi,* 129.
80. Ibid., 130.
81. Ibid., 132.
82. Bertrand Lafont, "The Ordeal," in Bottéro, pp. 199–209.
83. Bottéro, p. 116.
84. *Code of Hammurabi,* 153–57.
85. Ibid., 137–39.
86. Ibid., 141–43.
87. William W. Hallo and J.J.A. Van Dijk, *The Exaltation of Inanna* (New Haven: Yale University Press, 1968), pp. 22–25.
88. Julia Assante, "The Kar.kid/harimtu, Prostitute or Single Woman? A Reconsideration of Evidence," *Ugarit-Forschungen* 30 (1998): 5–96.
89. *Epic of Gilgamesh* VII, iii, 6.
90. Leick, *Mesopotamia: The Invention of the City,* pp. 124–25.

91. Marc Van De Mieroop, *A History of the Ancient Near East* (Malden, MA: Blackwell, 2004), pp. 45–46.
92. Leick, p. 57.
93. Bottéro, p. 94.
94. Leick, p. 57.
95. Bottéro, p. 107–111.
96. Ibid., p. 107.
97. Bahrani, p. 137.
98. Leick, p. 92.
99. Joan G. Westenholz, *Legends of the Kings of Akkade: The Texts* (Winona Lake, IN: Eisenbrauns, 1997), pp. 39–41.
100. Leick, pp. 128–30.
101. Van De Mieroop, pp. 262–3. See also Leick, p. 236.
102. Daniel Schwemer, "Magic Rituals: Conceptualization and Performance," in *The Oxford Handbook of Cuneiform Culture*, eds. Karen Radner and Eleanor Robson (Oxford: Oxford University Press, 2011), p. 434.
103. Bahrani, pp. 122–23.
104. *Code of Hammurabi*, 49, 100–107.
105. Ibid., 110.
106. Ibid., 119.
107. Leick, p. 182.
108. Joan G. Westenholz, "Tamar, Qedeša, Qadištu, and Sacred Prostitution in Mesopotamia," *Harvard Theological Review* 82 (1989), pp. 245–265.
109. Herodotus I, 199.
110. Laurentino Jose Afonso, "Prostitution," *Encyclopedia Judaica*, Vol. XIII (Jerusalem: Keter, 1974), p. 1244.
111. Bottéro, p. 95.
112. Gerda Lerner, "Origin of Prostitution in Ancient Mesopotamia," *Signs: Journal of Women in Culture and Society* 11, No. 2 (Winter, 1986): 236–254.
113. Dalley, *Myths from Mesopotamia*, p. 305.
114. Julia Assante, "The kar.kid/harimtu, Prostitute or Single Woman?"
115. Stephanie Lynn Budin, *The Myth of Sacred Prostitution in Antiquity* (New York: Cambridge University Press, 2008), p. 1.
116. Budin, p. 20.
117. Morris Silver, "Temple/Sacred Prostitution in Ancient Mesopotamia Revisited: Religion in the Economy," *Ugarit-Forschungen* 38 (2006): 631–663. Retrieved January 21, 2015, https://www.google.com/?gws_rd=ssl#q=Morris+Silver%2C+Temple%2FSacred+Prostitution+in+Ancient+Mesopotamia+Revisited.
118. Budin, p. 68.
119. Herodotus I, 93.
120. Herodotus II, 35–36.
121. Herodotus III, 97.
122. Herodotus IV, 104.
123. Herodotus IV, 117.
124. Herodotus IV, 180.
125. Budin, p. 71.
126. Budin, p. 89.
127. Lucian, *The Syrian Goddess* 6, trans. Herbert A. Strong and John Garstang, 1913, http://www.sacred-texts.com/cla/luc/index.htm.
128. Budin, p. 103.
129. Leonard King, *Another Version of the Creation of the World by Marduk*, lines 9–40, pp. 132–7. Retrieved on-line http://www.sacred-texts.com/ane/stc/index.htm.
130. King, trans., *Another Version of the Creation of the World by Marduk*, lines 9–40, pp. 132–37.
131. Leick, p. 2.
132. Leick, p. 84.
133. Bottéro, p. 118.
134. Joseph Campbell, *The Hero with a Thousand Faces* (Princeton, N.J.: Princeton University Press, 1949).
135. *Epic of Gilgamesh* III, 12.
136. Glasgow, *The Subjugation of Woman*, p. 89.
137. Information from ancient Sumerian, Assyrian and Persian cultures presents essentially the same picture; Simone de Beauvoir, *The Second Sex*, ed. and trans. H. M. Parshley (New York: Bantam, 1961); Charles Seltman, *Women in Antiquity* (London: Thames and Hudson, 1956).
138. Lerner, p. 253.
139. Gwendolyn Leick, *Sex and Eroticism in Mesopotamian Literature* (London: Routledge, 1994), p. 65.

Chapter Two

1. Barbara Watterson, *Women in Ancient Egypt* (Gloucestershire: Amberley, 2011), p. 13.
2. One of seven fragments of a stela known as the Royal Annals, dating from the Old Kingdom of ancient Egypt. This particular fragment is housed in the Antonio Salinas Archaeological Museum in Palermo, Italy. Five fragments are held in the Egyptian Museum in Cairo, and one is held in the Petrie Museum in London.
3. Cyril Aldred, *The Egyptians* (London: Thames and Hudson, 1961), p. 9.

Chapter Notes—Two

4. Genesis 12:10–20.
5. Abraham's visit to Egypt (Genesis 12:10ff.) has little significance. But the later residence in Goshen (Wadi Tumilat) by the "sons of Israel" (Genesis 44–50) and their subsequent period of captivity (Exodus 1–2) implies significant Egyptian influence on the Hebrews.
6. Alan R. Schulman, "Potiphar," *Encyclopedia Judaica*, Vol. 13, p. 933–34.
7. G. Ernest Wright, *Biblical Archaeology* (Philadelphia: Westminster, 1962), p. 56.
8. Marc Van De Mieroop, *A History of Ancient Egypt* (West Sussex: Wiley-Blackwell, 2011), Sources in Translation 10.1, p. 254; Lawrence Bradt, *Reading the Old Testament: An Introduction* (New York: Paulinist Press, 1984), p. 163.
9. University of Toronto, The Tumilat Project 1978–85, directed by John Holladay.
10. Isis and Osiris are discussed in chapter 6 in connection with mystery cults in the Roman Era.
11. Herodotus II, 37.
12. Margaret A. Murray, *The Splendour That Was Egypt* (London: Sidgwick and Jackson, Ltd., 1949), p. 181.
13. Pierre Montet, *Everyday Life in Egypt*, trans. H. R. Maxwell-Hyslop and Margaret S. Drower (London: Edward Arnold Publishers Ltd., 1958), p. 30.
14. Aldred, *The Egyptians*, p. 53.
15. A. M. Blackman, "priest, priesthood," *Encyclopedia of Religion and Ethics*, ed. J. Hastings (Edinburgh: T & T Clark, 1908–26), p. 298.
16. Murray, *The Splendour That Was Egypt*, p. 181.
17. Gay Robins, *Women in Ancient Egypt* (Cambridge: Harvard University Press, 1993), p. 156.
18. Barbara Watterson, *The Gods of Ancient Egypt* (London: B. T. Batsford, 1984), pp. 62ff.
19. Robins, p. 21.
20. Ibid., p. 27.
21. Watterson, 2011, p. 116.
22. I. E. Edwards, *Hieratic Papyri in the British Museum* I (London: Trustees of the British Museum, 1965), p. 25, pl. 11, no. 2.
23. Robins, p. 48.
24. Van De Mieroop, p. 145.
25. Drower, pp. 35–36; Aldred, p. 167.
26. A. H. Sayce, *The Egypt of the Hebrews* (London: Rivington, 1895), p. 57.
27. Robins, p. 54.
28. Watterson, 2011, p. 31.
29. Robins, p. 27.
30. Ibid., p. 30.
31. Alan R. Schulman, "Diplomatic Marriage in the Egyptian New Kingdom," *Journal of Near Eastern Studies* 38 (1979), pp. 177–93.
32. Herodotus II, 35.
33. J. Gardner Wilkinson, *The Manners and Customs of the Ancient Egyptians*, Vol. I (London: John Murray, 1878), p. 316.
34. Richard B. Parkinson, *Voices from Ancient Egypt; An Anthology of Middle Kingdom Writings* (London: British Museum Press, 1991), p. 110.
35. Papyrus Brooklyn 35.1446. See Marc Van De Mieroop, *A History of Ancient Egypt*, p. 119.
36. Watterson, 2011, p. 39.
37. Robins, p. 136.
38. Sarah B. Pomeroy, *Women in Hellenistic Egypt: From Alexander to Cleopatra* (Detroit: Wayne State University Press, 1990).
39. Papyrus Grenfell I; See Naphtali Lewis, *Greeks in Ptolemaic Egypt* (Oxford University Press, 1986), pp. 88–103.
40. Instructions of Amenhotep, 28 Retrieved on-line http://www.touregypt.net/instructionofamenemope.htm
41. Miriam Lichtheim, *Ancient Egyptian Literature: The Old and Middle Kingdoms*, Vol. II (Berkeley: University of California Press, 1976), pp. 146–49.
42. Montet, p. 45.
43. Miriam Lichtheim, *Ancient Egyptian Literature: The Old and Middle Kingdoms*, Vol. I (Berkeley: University of California Press, 1973), p. 69.
44. Lichtheim, Vol. II, pp. 182–93.
45. Jaroslav Cerny, "Consanguineous Marriages in Pharaonic Egypt," *Journal Egyptian Archives* (40, 1954), pp. 23–9.
46. Miriam Lichtheim, *Ancient Egyptian Literature: A Book of Readings*, Vol. III (Berkeley: University of California Press, 1980), pp. 127–28.
47. Watterson, 2011, p. 56; see Papyrus Louvre 7846; Papyrus Berlin, 13614.
48. P. W. Pestman, *Marriage and Matrimonial Property in Ancient Egypt* (Leiden: E.J. Brill, 1961), pp. 7–19.
49. Diodorus I, 27, i and I, 80, iii [LCL, *Loeb Classical Library* (London: William Heinemann, 1917–1946)].
50. Ibid., p. 86.
51. Robins, p. 26.

52. James Henry Breasted, *A History of Egypt* (London: Hodder and Stoughton, 1951), p. 85.
53. Montet, *Everyday Life in Egypt*, p. 50.
54. Aldred, p. 43.
55. Montet, p. 51.
56. Lichtheim, Vol. II, p. 207.
57. Genesis 39:7–20.
58. Tale of Two Brothers (Pap. d'Orbiney); Available untranslated on-line https://archive.org/stream/papyrusdorbineyb00br itrich#page/n5/mode/2up. See Susan T. Hollis, *The Ancient Egyptian Tale of Two Brothers: The Oldest Fairy Tale in the World*, Oklahoma: University of Oklahoma Press, 1996.
59. Maxims of Ani, II, 13, 17 in Isaac Meyer, *Maxims of the Scribe Ani Also Known As the Papyrus of Bulak*, Kessinger Legacy reprint, 2010. Instruction of Ptahhotep, 18, Battiscombe G Gunn, trans. London, 1906. Retrieved on-line http://www.gutenberg.org/files/30508/30508-h/30508-h.htm#chap02; *Instruction of Ptahhotep* 18.
60. Robins, p. 68–70.
61. Lichtheim, Vol. II, p. 137.
62. Ibid., p. 136.
63. Robins, pp. 79–80.
64. Lichtheim, Vol. II, p. 108.
65. Robins, p. 88.
66. Lichtheim, Vol. II, p. 169.
67. B. J. Kemp, "The City of el–Amarna as a Source for the Study of Urban Society in Ancient Egypt," *World Archaeology* 9 (1977): 123–39; "The City of el–Amarna as a Source for the Study of Urban Society in Egypt," in *Acts of the First International Congress of Egyptology*, ed. W. Reineke (Berlin: Akademie-Verlag, 1979), pp. 369–70. "Tell el-'Amarna," in *Ancient Centres of Egyptian Civilization*, eds. H. S. Smith and R. M. Hall (London: Egyptian Education Bureau,1983), pp. 57–72; "A model of Tell el–Amarna," *Antiquity* 74 (2000), pp. 15–16.
68. Patrick J. Houlihan, *The Animal World of the Pharaohs* (Cairo: American University in Cairo Press, 1996); A. Lucas and J. R. Harris, *Ancient Egyptian Materials and Industries* (Mineola, NY: Dover Publications, 1999).
69. Winifred S. Blackman, "Some Social and Religious Customs in Modern Egypt," *Bulletin de la Société Geographie d'Égypte* XIV (1926), p. 48. See also Blackman, *The Fellahin of Upper Egypt* (Cairo: American University in Cairo Press, 2000).
70. Cyril Aldred, *Tutankhamun's Egypt* (London: British Broadcasting Corporation, 1972), p. 9; cf. Drower, p. 42.
71. Lichtheim, Vol. I, p. 170.
72. B. J. Kemp, *Ancient Egypt: Anatomy of a Civilization* (London: Routledge, 1989), pp. 257–58.
73. Wilkinson, *The Manners and Customs of the Ancient Egyptians*, p. 316.
74. Watterson, 2011, p. 33.
75. W. A. Ward, "Non-royal women and their occupations in the Middle Kingdom," in *Women's Earliest Records from Ancient Egypt and Western Asia*, ed. B. Lesko (Atlanta: Scholar's Press, 1989), p. 35.
76. Robins, p. 111.
77. Henry G. Fischer, *Egyptian Women of the Old Kingdom and of the Heracleopolitan Period* (New York: Metropolitan Museum of Art, 1989), p. 14–15.
78. P. Berlin 3033, known as the Westcar Papyrus, dates from Egyptian Dynasty IV and contains five tales, told in the court of Cheops by his sons, about miracles performed by priests and magicians.
79. For possible interpretations, see Miriam Lichtheim, *Ancient Egyptian Literature*, Vol. I, pp. 215–22.
80. Exodus 1:15–21; 2:7.
81. Watterson, 2011, p. 49.
82. Wendy Buonaventura, *Serpent of the Nile: Women and Dance in the Arab World* (Northhampton, MA: Interlink, 2010), p. 13.
83. Robins, p. 122.
84. Montet, pp. 70–74.
85. E. A. Leonard, "St. Paul on the Status of Women," *Catholic Biblical Quarterly* XII (July 1950), p. 311.
86. W. M. F. Petrie, *Social Life in Ancient Egypt* (London: Constable, 1924), pp. v–vi.
87. Wilkinson, p. 316.

Chapter Three

1. *Mishnah*, Baba Batra 14b–15a, in *The Mishnah*, trans. Herbert Danby (London: Oxford University Press, 1974), p. 799ff. (Herbert Danby's *Mishnah* hereafter abbreviated *DM*.)
2. Emil Schurer, *A History of the Jewish People in the Age of Jesus Christ*, Vol. I, new English edition, eds. G. Vermes and F. Millar (Edinburgh: T & T Clark, 1973), pp. 76–79.
3. *Avot* of R. Natan 2:9.
4. *Jerusalem Talmud*, Ketubot 16b–17a.
5. Shabbat 21b.
6. *Babylonian Talmud*, Gittin 90a.

7. Rachel Biale, *Women and Jewish Law* (New York: Shocken Books, 1984).
8. Genesis 11:28, 31; 15:7.
9. Nathan M. Sarna, "Genesis," *Encyclopedia Judaica*, Vol. 7 (Jerusalem: Keter, 1973), pp. 388–90.
10. For possible sources of the Pentateuch, see Artur Weiser, *Introduction to the Old Testament*, trans. D. M. Barton (London: Darton, Longman and Todd, 1961), pp. 81–124.
11. George Tavard, *Women in Christian Tradition* (Notre Dame, IN: Notre Dame Press, 1973), pp. 11–14.
12. Weiser, *Introduction to the Old Testament*, p. 100.
13. Exodus 18:4; Deuteronomy 33:7, 26, 29; Psalms 121:1–2; 146:3,5. See Ruth Tiffany Barnhouse and Urban T. Holmes III, *Male and Female: A Christian Approach to Sexuality* (New York: Seabury Press, 1976), p. 18.
14. Helmut Thielicke, *The Ethics of Sex*, trans. John W. Doberstein (New York: Harper & Row, 1964), p. 4.
15. Genesis 2:23.
16. Michael L. Rosenzweig, "A Helper Equal to Him," *Judaism* 35, no. 3 (1986), pp. 277–80. But it appears in Psalms 16:8 and 23:5, suggesting "in the presence of," "adequate," or "suitable."
17. Barnhouse and Homes, *Male and Female*, p. 19.
18. Tavard, *Women in Christian Tradition*, pp. 11–14.
19. quoted by Tavard, p. 14.
20. K. H. Graf, Julius Wellhausen, Abraham Kuenen, Samuel Driver (all of the nineteenth century), and Otto Eisfeldt, W. O. E. Oesterley, Theodore Robinson and C. H. Dodd (of the first half of the twentieth century). Paul Tillich sees the Genesis Fall as historicized myth, a symbolic expression of the state of things from the standpoint of the writer. Two possible human experiences reflected in the story are: 1) the sexual awakening in adolescence, with sexual feelings and the consequent sense of guilt; and 2) the human desire for forbidden knowledge and the resulting guilt. See Tillich, *Systematic Theology* (Chicago: University of Chicago Press, 1951–63), Vol. II, p. 34 and Vol. III, p. 73.
21. John Skinner, "Genesis," *International Critical Commentary* (Edinburgh: T & T Clark, 1969), pp. 51ff. E. F. Kevan, "Genesis," *The New Bible Commentary*, ed. F. Davidson (London: The InterVarsity Fellowship, 1967), p. 80.
22. Tavard, p. 14ff. Some feminists have argued that a female religion among prebiblical Semites did not just fade away, but was the victim of centuries of persecution and suppression by advocates of a new religion where male deities were supreme. The Adam and Eve myth was contrived to support and propagate this religion. See Merlin Stone, *The Paradise Papers* (London: Virago, 1979).
23. Paul S. Fiddes, "Woman's Head is Man," *The Baptist Quarterly* 31, no. 8 (1986), p. 376.
24. Genesis 2:24; a point noted by Jesus in criticizing rabbinic attitudes toward marriage and divorce (Matthew 19:1ff).
25. Genesis 3:14ff. However, a number of scholars recognize that suffering and subjection are not presented here as a curse of God, but God's prediction of the suffering she will experience because of human sin and the tyranny of man; e.g., J. Skinner, *A Critical and Exegetical Commentary on Genesis* (Edinburgh: T & T Clark, 1910), p. 82; S. R. Driver, *The Book of Genesis* (London: Methuen, 1904), p. 49. Traditionalists typically appeal to this account for a divine ordinance of female subjection, but there is none. See Joyce Baldwin, "Women's Ministry," *The Role of Women*, ed. Shirley Lees (Leicester: Inter-Varsity Press, 1984), pp. 170–73.
26. Irvin A. Busenitz, "Woman's Desire for Man: Genesis 3:16 Reconsidered," *Grace Theological Journal* 7:2 (1986), pp. 203–12; Scanzoni and Hardesty, *All We're Meant To Be*, p. 35.
27. Biale, *Women and Jewish Law*, pp. 123–24.
28. Ibid., pp. 13–14.
29. Ancient city of Ebla, Syria. See Hans H. Wellisch, "Ebla: The World's Oldest Library," *Journal of Library History* 16.3 (Summer 1981), pp. 488–500.
30. Bezalel Porten, "History," *Encyclopedia Judaica*, Vol. 8, p. 574.
31. Leviticus 25.
32. I Peter 3:6–7.
33. Genesis 21:9–10.
34. Genesis 29:9–35; 34:11–12.
35. Children of Jacob (whose name became Israel): from Leah (Reuben, Simeon, Levi, Judah, Issachar, Zebulun, and Dinah); from Rachel (Joseph and Benjamin); from Leah's handmaid Zilpah (Gad and Asher);

from Rachel's handmaid Bilhah (Dan and Naphtali); all born in Padden-aram. Rachel died after giving birth to Benjamin. Genesis 29:32–30:24; 35:16–26. Joseph's two sons, Ephraim and Manasseh, became two of the Twelve Tribes of Israel (Levi and Joseph were excluded).

36. Anson Rainey, "Shasu or Habiru: Who Were the Early Israelites?" *Biblical Archeology Review* 34 (November 2008).

37. Porten, "History," p. 574.

38. Carol A. Redmount, "Bitter Lives: Israel In and Out of Egypt," in *The Oxford History of the Biblical World*, ed. Michael D. Coogan (New York: Oxford University Press, 1999), p. 98.

39. Porten, pp. 574–75.

40. Exodus 1:8–3:16.

41. G. Ernest Wright. *Biblical Archaeology* (Philadelphia: Westminster, 1962), pp. 54–60; John Gray, *Archaeology of the Old Testament World* (London: Thomas Nelson, 1962), pp. 76–77.

42. From leaving Egypt to the fourth year of Solomon's reign is 480 years, according to I Kings 6:1. Cf. Judges 11:26; Acts 13:19.

43. Porten, p. 574.

44. Marc Van De Mieroop, *A History of Ancient Egypt*, p. 210.

45. Compare Exodus 20 to Deuteronomy 5; see the divorce law in Deuteronomy 24 and the covenant sections in Deuteronomy 27–28.

46. Exodus 15:20–21.

47. Judges 4:4ff.

48. Ruth 1–4.

49. I Samuel 1:2–2:10.

50. Biale, p. 19; *Mishnah*, Berakhot 20a–20b.

51. I Kings 18–21; Proverbs 7:6–23; I Samuel 28:7–25; Proverbs 19:13; Ezekiel 23:45.

52. Proverbs 18:22; 31:28; Ecclesiastes 25:9; 26:1–2.

53. I Kings 11:1–4.

54. *Babylonian Talmud*, Erubin 100b, in *The Babylonian Talmud*, ed. Isidore Epstein (London: Soncino, 1935–1948), Mo'ed III, p. 697. (Epstein's *Babylonian Talmud* hereafter abbrev. *EBT*).

55. *Babylonian Talmud*, Nedarim 20a (*EBT*, Nashim III, pp. 56–57).

56. John 4:27; Luke 7:39.

57. Louis Finkelstein, *The Pharisees: The Sociological Background of Their Faith*, second edition (Philadelphia: The Jewish Publication Society of America, 1940), p. 47.

58. *Mishnah*, Ketuboth 9:4 (*DM*, p. 258).

59. *Mishnah*, Niddah 5:7 (*DM*, p. 751); Masser Sheni 4:4 (*DM*, p. 79); Ketuboth 4:1 (*DM*, p. 249).

60. Josephus, *Antiquities of the Jews*, IV, viii, 15, in *The Life and Works of Flavius Josephus*, trans. William Whiston (Grand Rapids: Kregel, 1967), p. 97.

61. Proverbs 19:14; Tobit 6:17; *Babylonian Talmud*, Mo'ed Katan 18b (*EBT*, Mo'ed VIII, p. 118).

62. *Babylonian Talmud*, Kiddushin 29b (*EBT*, Nashim VIII, p. 142).

63. *Mishnah*, Yebamoth 6:6 (*DM*, p. 227).

64. Biale, p. 61.

65. *Mishnah*, Baba Batra 10:4 (*DM*, p. 380).

66. *Mishnah*, Kiddushin 2:1 (*DM*, p. 323).

67. Hebrew *arash*, Exodus 22:16; Deuteronomy 22:23–28. The English terms "betrothed" and "espoused" carry much the same idea.

68. Henri Daniel-Rops, *Daily Life in the Time of Jesus*, trans. Patrick O'Brien (New York: Hawthorn, 1962), p. 142.

69. Biale, pp. 46–8.

70. Ben-Zion Schereschewsky, Ketubah, *Encyclopedia Judaica*, Vol. X, p. 926; *Mishnah*, Ketuboth 7:6 (*DM*, p. 255).

71. *Mishnah*, Ketuboth 5:5 (*DM*, p. 252).

72. Exodus 21:10; *Babylonian Talmud*, Ketuboth 47b (*EBT*, Nashim II, p. 273).

73. *Mishnah*, Ketuboth 5:5 (*DM*, p. 252).

74. Bedclothes spotted with blood from the breaking of the hymen upon the first occasion of intercourse. This was unreliable, but an ancient custom nonetheless. See Deuteronomy 22:14–21. This is still practiced in modern times in some African tribes and among some Muslim bedouins. See C. F. Keil and F. Delitzsch, *Biblical Commentary on the Old Testament: The Pentateuch*, Vol. III (Grand Rapids, MI: Eerdmans, 1959), p. 411.

75. *Mishnah*, Ketuboth 1:5–10 (*DM*, p. 246); David Mace and Vera Mace, *Marriage East and West*, pp. 43–44.

76. Deuteronomy 22:21–29; Biale, pp. 239–255.

77. Proverbs 12:4; 19:13; 25:24.

78. Ecclesiasticus 25:13.

79. George Foot Moore, *Judaism in the First Centuries of the Christian Era*, Vol. II (Cambridge, MA: Harvard University Press, 1946–1948), p. 122.

80. C. Caverno, "Polygamy," in *International Standard Bible Encyclopedia*, Vol. IV,

ed. James Orr (Grand Rapids: Eerdmans, 1955), pp. 2416–67.
81. Deuteronomy 25:5–10.
82. Genesis 38:8–10.
83. Leviticus 18:16; 20:21.
84. Matthew 22:23ff.
85. Biale, pp. 102–112.
86. John 4:7ff.
87. Samuel P. Tragelles, trans., *Gesenius' Hebrew and Chaldee Lexicon* (Grand Rapids, MI: Eerdmans, 1964), p. 525.
88. *Protevangelium of James* 16; Retrieved on-line http://www.gnosis.org/library/gosjames.htm. See Deuteronomy 22:23; Daniel-Rops, *Daily Life in the Time of Jesus*, p. 142.
89. *Mishnah, Sotah* 9:9 (*DM*, p. 305).
90. David M. Feldman, "Chastity," *Encyclopedia Judaica*, Vol. V (Jerusalem: Macmillan, 1971), p. 363.
91. Biale, p. 183; see Leviticus 18:1–19.
92. Mace and Mace, pp. 43–4.
93. *Babylonian Talmud*, Yebamoth 61 v (*EBT*, Nashim I, p. 409). See also Biale, pp. 190–192.
94. Laurentio Jose Afonso, "Prostitution," *Encyclopedia Judaica*, Vol. XIII, p. 1244; see I Kings 3:16–27.
95. Tragelles, p. 249. See also Numbers 25:1–2; Jeremiah 3:6; Ezekiel 6:9; and Hosea 4:12.
96. Genesis 38:14; Joshua 2:1ff.
97. I Kings 3:14ff.
98. *Sifra*, Kedoshim 7:1–15.
99. Leviticus 19:29; 21:7–9.
100. Deuteronomy 22:13–21.
101. Proverbs 7:7–27; 2:16; 6:24–25; I Kings 22:38; Isaiah 23:16; Jeremiah 3:3.
102. Moshe David Herr, "Prostitution," *Encyclopedia Judaica*, Vol. XIII, p. 1244–5; Tosefta, tem. 4:8.
103. *Babylonian Talmud*, Kethuboth 64b (*EBT*, Nashim III, p. 387).
104. Afonso, p. 1244.
105. W. O. E. Oesterley and T. H. Robinson, *Hebrew Religion, Its Origin and Development* (London: Society for Promoting Christian Knowledge, 1952), p. 61.
106. W. O. E. Oesterley and T. H. Robinson, *A History of Israel*, Vol. II (London: Oxford University Press, 1957), pp. 217–227.
107. J. H. Hertz, ed., *The Pentateuch and the Haftorahs* (London: Soncino Press, 1975), p. 850. Since the early 1800s, scholars typically have dated Deuteronomy in the seventh century BCE, written for the purpose of religious reforms initiated by Josiah (641–609).
108. Leviticus 21:7; 22:13; Numbers 30:10; Deuteronomy 22:19.
109. *Mishnah*, Yebamoth 14:1 (*DM*, p. 240).
110. *Mishnah*, Gittin 9:10 (*DM*, p. 321).
111. Gittin 90a–b.
112. B. Cohen, "Concerning Divorce in Jewish and Roman Law," *Proceedings of the American Academy for Jewish Research* XXI (1952): 3–34.
113. Ecclesiasticus 25:26.
114. *Mishnah*, Nedarim 11:12 (*DM*, p. 280); Ketuboth, 5:5, 7:2–10 (*DM*, pp. 252–55).
115. Ibid.
116. Matthew 5:31–2; 19:3–12; Mark 10:1–12, Luke 16:18.
117. Josephus, *Antiquities of the Jews* XV, vii, 10; XVIII (Whiston, *The Life and Works*, pp. 462, 541); cf. Mark 6:17–19.
118. Schereschewsky, *Encyclopedia Judaica*, p. 927.
119. Oesterly and Robinson, *A History of Israel*, Vol. II, pp. 217–27; cf. *Babylonian Talmud*, Kiddushin 29a (*EBT*, Nashim, III, p. 140).
120. Ecclesiasticus 39:1–3.
121. Aaron Demsky, "Education," *Encyclopedia Judaica*, Vol. VI, p. 386.
122. *Babylonian Talmud*, Yoma, 66b (*EBT*, Mo'ed V, p. 311); *Mishnah*, Sofah 3:4 (*DM*, p. 296).
123. *Mishnah*, Nedarim 4:3 (*DM*, p. 269).
124. *Babylonian Talmud*, Kiddushin 34a (*EBT*, Nashim, VIII, pp. 140, 167).
125. *Babylonian Talmud*, Megillah 18a (*EBT*, Nashim VIII, p. 422).
126. *Babylonian Talmud*, Peshashim 62b (*EBT*, Mo'ed IV, p. 313).
127. Leviticus 19:27.
128. *Mishnah*, Kiddushin 1:7 (*DM*, p. 322); *Babylonian Talmud*, Berakoth 20b (*EBT*, Zera'im I, p. 122). See Biale, pp. 10–43.
129. Kenneth H. Maahs, "Male and Female in Pauline Perspec¬tive: A Study in Biblical Ambivalence," *Dialogue & Alliance* 2, no. 3 (Fall 1988), p. 17; E. S. Gerstenberger & W. Schrage, *Woman and Man*, trans. Douglass Stott (Nashville: Abingdon, 1981), p. 23.
130. Leviticus 15:19ff.; *Mishnah*, Niddah (*DM*, pp. 745–57).
131. Leviticus 12:6–8; 14:1–32; *Mishnah*, Kerithoth 2:1 (*DM*, p. 564).
132. Clarence J. Vos, *Women in Old Tes-*

tament Worship (Delft: Verenigde Drukkerijen Judels & Brinkman, 1968).
133. Deuteronomy 16:16; Exodus 23:17; 34:23.
134. Shmuel Safrai, "Temple," *Encyclopedia Judaica*, Vol. XV, p. 966.
135. Leviticus 1:4; 3:2; Safrai, *Encyclopedia Judaica*, pp. 966-7.
136. *Babylonian Talmud*, Hagigah 16b (*EBT*, Mo'ed VIII, p. 109).
137. *Babylonian Talmud*, Megillah 23a (*EBT*, Mo'ed VIII, p. 140).
138. S. E. Johnson, "Asia Minor and Early Christianity," in *Christianity, Judaism and Other Greco-Roman Cults*, ed. J. Neusner (Leiden: Brill, 1975); cf. Elisabeth Schüssler Fiorenza, *In Memory of Her* (London: SCM, 1983), p. 250.
139. W. M. Ramsay, *Asiatic Elements in Greek Civilization: The Gifford Lectures in the University of Edinburgh, 1915-16* (London: J. Murray, 1928), p. 267; cf. p. 268, fn. 1.
140. H. L. Strack, "Synagogue," *The New Schaff-Herzog En¬cyclopedia of Religious Knowledge*, Vol. XI (Grand Rapids, MI: Baker, 1953), p. 214.
141. W. Bacher, "Synagogue," in *A Diction¬ary of the Bible*, Vol. IV, ed. James Hastings (ed.), (Edinburgh: T and T Clark, 1902) p. 640.
142. Philo Judaeus, quoted by John Stanley Glen, *Pastoral Problems in First Corinthians* (Philadelphia: Westminster Press, 1964), p. 135. A similar view was expressed by Jesus ben Sirach around 180 BCE: "because of her we all die" (Ecclesiasticus 25:4).
143. Ephesians 5:22-24; Colossians 3:18-25; I Peter 3:1-7.
144. *Jerusalem Talmud*, Berakoth 7:18. See Fiorenza, p. 217.
145. Biale, p. 147ff.
146. Ben Witherington, *Women in the Ministry of Jesus* (Cambridge: University Press, 1984), pp. 1-10. See also Louis Jacobs, "Women," *Encyclopedia Judaica*, Vol. XVI, p. 626.

Chapter Four

1. Xenophon, *Oeconomicus* 7:30.
2. Sarah B. Pomeroy, *Goddesses, Whores, Wives, and Slaves* (New York: Schocken, 1975), pp. xv-xvii.
3. M. L. West, *Hesiod: Theogony* (Oxford: Clarendon Press, 1966). Jasper Griffin, "Greek Myth and Hesiod," in *The Oxford History of the Classical World*, eds. J. Boardman, J. Griffin and O. Murray (Oxford: Oxford University Press, 1986), p. 88.
4. Oceanus, Coeus, Crius, Hyperion, Iapetos, Theia, Rhea, Themis, Mnemosyne, Phoebe, Tethys and Cronus.
5. Pomeroy, p. 2.
6. Hesiod, *Works and Days* 60-105.
7. Aristophanes, *The Thesmophoriazusae* 786 (LCL III, p. 199).
8. Hesiod, *Theogony* II 585-612, online version trans. Hugh G. Evelyn-White (1914), http://www.sacred-texts.com/cla/hesiod/theogony.htm.
9. Sue Blundell, *Women in Ancient Greece* (Cambridge, MA: Harvard University Press, 1995), pp. 25-46.
10. *Theogony* II, 886-926.
11. Homer, *Iliad* 2: 224-305 [trans. E. V. Rieu, 1950, revised by Peter Jones and D. C. H. Rieu (London: Penguin Books, 2003)].
12. Blundell, p. 27.
13. "Hymn to Artemis," *The Homeric Hymns*, trans. Jules Cashford (London: Penguin Books, 2003), p. 108.
14. *Iliad* 21:483-4.
15. Pausanias 3:16:7-10, in *Description of Greece*, trans. W. H. S. Jones, http://www.theoi.com/Text/Pausanias3B.html.
16. "Hymn to Aphrodite," *Homeric Hymns* 5:25-30, Cashford, p. 86.
17. Blundell, p. 32.
18. "Hymn to Pythian Apollo," *Homeric Hymns* 3:325-55, Cashford, pp. 45-46.
19. Pausanias 2:38:2.
20. Aristophanes 973-76.
21. Pausanias, 5:16:1-5.
22. *Iliad* 14:213.
23. *Theogony* 201.
24. Hippolytus 443-448.
25. Euripides, *Andromache* 289ff.
26. *Homeric Hymns* 2:401-3.
27. Blundell, pp. 40-41.
28. Carl G. Jung, "The Psychological Aspects of the Kore," in *The Archetypes and the Collective Unconscious*, ed. Sir Herbert Read, et al., trans. R. F. C. Hull (New York: Bollingen, 1959), pp. 182-203. Also Jung, "Psychological Aspects of the Mother Archetype," *Archetypes*, pp. 75-110.
29. Blundell, pp. 42-43.
30. Pollux, *Onomasticon* I, 23.
31. Pomeroy, p. 17.
32. *Iliad* 3:432-36.
33. *Iliad* 3:146-160.
34. *Iliad* 6:429-32.

35. Homer, *Odyssey* 9–10, trans. Richmond Lattimore (New York: Harper & Row, 1965).
36. Blundell, pp. 52–53.
37. *Iliad* 22:472.
38. Pomeroy, p. 46.
39. Andromache and Hecuba in the *Iliad* and Penelope in the *Odyssey*.
40. George Toumbouros, "The Laws of Ancient Greece," in *Parallel Legislation*, Vol. I (Munich: Suddeutscher Verlag Press, 1959), p. 41.
41. J. P. Mahaffy, *Social Life in Greece* (London: Macmillan, 1877), p. 146.
42. *Odyssey*, trans. Samuel Butler, http://classics.mit.edu/Homer/odyssey.html.
43. Eva Cantarella, *Pandora's Daughters* (Baltimore: Johns Hopkins University Press, 1987), p. 41.
44. Plutarch, *Lives*: Solon 17. See P. Rhodes, "The Reforms and Laws of Solon the Wise: An Optimistic View," in *Solon of Athens: New Historical and Philological Approaches*, eds. J. Blok and A. Lardinois (Leiden: Brill, 2006).
45. For an exhaustive discussion of slavery under Solon's polity, see André Bonnard, *Greek Civilization*, trans. A. L. Sells (London: Allen and Unwin, 1957), pp. 115–126.
46. Bonnard, p. 127–28.
47. Mahaffy, *Social Life in Greece*, pp. 147–48. Although the origin of monogamy is controversial, Bonnard contends that among the Greeks it was adopted only in the early classical period and was in fact an unfavorable trend contributing to the degradation of women in general, pp. 128–30.
48. T. G. Tucker, *Life in Ancient Athens* (London: Macmillan and Company, 1907), p. 52.
49. The term *kyrios* is also used in the New Testament to describe the relationship of Jesus Christ to believers and the relationship of husband to wife (I Peter 3:6).
50. Plutarch, *Lives*, Solon XXI (LCL I, p. 463).
51. Plutarch, *Moralia* 144A (LCL II, p. 331).
52. Dio Chrysostom VII, 64–80 (LCL I, p. 323–31).
53. Plutarch, *Moralia* 90B (LCL II, p. 25–27).
54. Herodotus V, 18 (LCL III, p. 19); Lysias, *On the Murder of Eratosthenes*, 23, 39–41 (LCL, p. 15, 23).
55. Lysias, *Against Simon* 6ff. (LCL, p. 75).
56. Xenophon, *Oeconomicus* VII, 23–34 (LCL, pp. 421–425).
57. Wilhelm A. Becker, *Characles: Illustrations of the Private Life of the Ancient Greeks*, trans. F. Metcalfe (London: Longmans, Green and Co., 1895), p. 462–98.
58. Aristophanes, *The Thesmophoriazusae* 797 (LCL III, p. 201).
59. Athenaeus, *The Deipnosophists* XII, 20C, D (LCL V, pp. 293ff.). Phylarchus, a contemporary of Aretus of the third century BCE, has no surviving works.
60. Plutarch, *Moralia* 775, D, E (LCL X, p. 23).
61. Plutarch, *Moralia* 140D (LCL II, p. 311).
62. Mary R. Lefkowitz and Maureen B. Fant, *Women's Life in Greece and Rome*, third edition (Baltimore: Johns Hopkins University Press, 2005), pp. 83ff.
63. Cantarella, *Pandora's Daughters*, p. 43.
64. Euripides, *Andromache* 595–600 (LCL II, p. 461).
65. Herodotus I, 94 (LCL I, p. 123).
66. Strabo, *Geography* XI, 14, 16 (LCL V, p. 341). Modern scholars have come to question the nature of cult prostitution, suspecting that we have misunderstood it.
67. Plato, *Laws* VI, 281C, D (LCL IX, p. 489).
68. Cornelius Nepos, "Preface," *On the Great Generals of Foreign Nations* 1–8 (LCL, p. 369–70).
69. Plutarch, *Moralia* 139C, 140D (LCL II, pp. 305, 311).
70. Plutarch, *Moralia* 142D (LCL II, p. 321).
71. Thucydides II, 45 (LCL I, p. 341).
72. Plutarch 242 E, F (LCL III, p. 475).
73. Sophocles, *Antigone*, trans. R. C. Jebb, http://classics.mit.edu/Sophocles/antigone.html.
74. Euripedes, *Medea*, trans. E. P. Coleridge, http://classics.mit.edu/Euripides/medea.html.
75. Euripides, *Iphigeneia at Aulis* 1393 (LCL I, p. 131).
76. Plato, *Republic*. See Mahaffy, *Social Life in Greece*, pp. 274–5.
77. Bonnard, *Greek Civilization*, p. 130. See also G. W. Botsford and E. G. Sihler, eds., *Hellenic Civilization* (New York: Octogon, 1965), pp. 340–45, on a political demonstration by women in Athens sometime between 431 and 404 BCE.
78. Aristotle, *Metaphysics* 986.

79. Plato, *Republic* 5:451–461; see Lefkowitz and Fant, *Women's Life*, pp. 41–47.
80. Plato, *Laws* 773–76.
81. Aristotle, *Politics* 1259–1277. See Blundell, pp. 186–87.
82. Holger Thesleff, *The Pythagorean Texts of the Hellenistic Period* (Åbo: Åbo Akademi, 1965), pp. 142–5. Full quote in Pomeroy, pp. 134–36.
83. Elizabeth Shüssler Fiorenza, "Breaking the Silence: Becoming Visible," in "Women: Invisible in Church and Theology," Elizabeth Schüssler Fiorenza and Mary Collins, eds., *Concilium 182: Religion in the Eighties* (Edinburgh: T & T Clark, 1985), p. 5.
84. Xenophon, *Memorabilia* II, 2, 4 (LCL, p. 107).
85. Plutarch, *Moralia* 13F (LCL I, p. 65ff.).
86. Xenophon, *Oeconomichus* II, 13; VII, 5 (LCL, pp. 389, 415). See Pausianus IV, 19, 6 (LCL II, p. 277).
87. Xenophon, *Memorabilia* II, 6, 36 (LCL, p. 145).
88. Xenophon, *Oeconomicus* VII, 11 (LCL, pp. 417).
89. Plutarch, *Moralia* 13F (LCL I, p. 65f.).
90. Dio Chrysostom VII, 80 (LCL I, p. 331).
91. Dio Chrysostom VII, 80 (LCL I, p. 331).
92. Xenophon, *Oeconomicus* II, 12 (LCL, pp. 387–89).
93. Plutarch, *Moralia* 138–46 (LCL II, pp. 299–343).
94. Ibid., 140, A (LCL II, p. 309).
95. Ibid., 139, D (LCL II, 305).
96. Ibid., 185, D (LCL III, p. 93); *Lives*, Themistocles 5 (LCL II, p. 53).
97. Euripides, *Iphigeneia at Aulis* 725 (LCL I, p. 69).
98. Xenophon, *Oeconomicus* VI–X (LCL, p. 443).
99. Plutarch, *Moralia* 140, E (LCL II, 311).
100. Xenophon, *Oeconomicus* III, 12 (LCL, p. 385).
101. Lysias, *On the Murder of Eratosthenes* 30ff. (LCL, p. 19).
102. Becker, *Characles*, p. 497.
103. Plutarch, *Moralia* 291, F (LCL IV, p. 177).
104. Lysias, *On the Murder*, 19ff. (LCL, p. 13); Aristophanes, 479–500 (LCL III, p. 173).
105. Dio Chrysostom VII, 143–51 (LCL I, pp. 369–73).
106. Ibid.
107. Ibid.
108. Xenophon, *Oeconomicus* VII, 5 (LCL, p. 415).
109. Xenophon, *The Banquet* II, 9.
110. Mitchell Carroll, *Greek Women* (Philadelphia: Rittenhouse, 1908), p. 299; Plato, *Laws* VII, 804, E (LCL X, p. 57).
111. Plutarch, *Moralia* 145, C (LCL II, p. 339).
112. Plutarch, *Moralia* 145, E (LCL II, p. 341).
113. Oxyrhynchus papyrus, fragments 98 and 132, dating from around 200 CE.
114. Bonnard, *Greek Civilization*, pp. 86–100.
115. Blundell, pp. 82–91.
116. Carroll, pp. 300ff.
117. Pomeroy, pp 137–38.
118. Frederick C. Grant, *Hellenistic Religions* (New York: Liberal Arts Press, 1953), p. xxi.
119. Pollux, *Onomasticon* I, 23.
120. Herondas, *Mime* IV.
121. Blundell, p. 162; see Aeschylus, *Libation Bearers* 306–478, and the mourning of Electra and a group of women at the tomb of Agamemnon.
122. Blundell, p. 161–63.
123. Didorus Siculus 16:26:6.
124. Herodotus VIII, 41. See Blundell, p. 161.
125. Thomas Egbert James, "Prostitution," *Encyclopedia Britannica*, Vol. XVIII (London: William Benton, 1964), p. 597.
126. James Donaldson, *Woman: Her Position and Influence in Ancient Greece and Rome, and Among Early Christians* (London: Longman, Green and Co., 1907), p. 292.
127. I Corinthians 6:16–18; 7:2; II Corinthians 12:21.
128. Plutarch, *Moralia* 140, B (LCL II, p. 309); 144, B, D (LCL II, p. 333ff.); Dio Chrysostom, VIII 133; 42 (LCL I, p. 363–69).
129. Dio Chrysostom, VII, 133–42 (LCL I, pp. 363–69).
130. Athenaeus, *The Deipnosophists*, XIII, 577 (LCL VI, p. 115).
131. Athenaeus, *The Deipnosophists*, XIII.
132. Plutarch, *Pericles* 24.
133. Athenaeus, *The Deipnosophists* XIII. See Friedrich Hauck and Seigfried Schultz, *Theological Dictionary of the New Testament*, Vol. VI, ed. G. Friedrich (Grand Rapids, MI: Eerdmans, 1968), p. 580.

134. Seneca, *De Consolatione ad Helviam Matrem*, 16:5.
135. G. Davis, "Clothes as Sign," in *Women's Dress in the Greek World*, eds. L. Llewellyn-Jones and Sue Blundell (London: Duckworth, 2002), pp. 228–38.
136. Blundell, p. 35.
137. Paul LaCroix, *History of Prostitution*, Vol. I, trans. Samuel Putnam (Chicago: Pascal Covici, 1926), p. 239.
138. Strabo, *Geography* VIII, 6:20 (LCL IV, p. 189ff.).
139. Herodotus, *The Histories* I, 199, http://en.wikipedia.org/wiki/Herodotus; see Merrill F. Unger, *Archaeology and the New Testament* (Grand Rapids, MI: Zondervan, 1962), p. 243.
140. Stephanie Budin, *The Myth of Sacred Prostitution in Antiquity* (Cambridge: University Press, 2008).
141. Ann Pippin Burnett, "Servants of Peitho: Pindar fr. 122 S," *Greek, Roman, and Byzantine Studies* 51 (2011): 49–60; Athenaeus XIII: 573–74.
142. Budin, pp. 140–41.
143. Budin, p. 7.
144. Third century letter from Philadelphia (Papyrus Cairo Zen 3:59451). See Budin pp. 168–71.
145. Strabo, *Geography* XII 3:34.
146. Budin, p. 173.
147. Herodotus V, 22 (LCL III, p. 23).
148. M. N. Tod, "Macedonia," *International Standard Bible Encyclopedia*, Vol. III (Grand Rapids, MI: Eerdmans, 1939), p. 1956.
149. Mitchell Carroll, *Greek Women* (Philadelphia: Rittenhouse, 1908), p. 133.
150. Pomeroy, pp. 120–25.
151. Plutarch, *Alexander* 2:4–5.
152. E. M. Blaiklock, *From Prison in Rome: Letters to the Philippians and Philemon* (Grand Rapids, MI: Zondervan, 1964), p. 47.
153. J. B. Lightfoot, *St. Paul's Epistle to the Philippians*, twelfth edition (London: Macmillan, 1898), pp. 55–57.
154. Acts 16:13, 15; 14:4, 12.
155. Sophocles, *Oedipus at Colonus* 348 (LCL I, p. 179). See Carroll, pp. 365ff.
156. Blundell, pp. 92–94; Pomeroy, pp. 142–43.
157. Thucydides, *The History of the Peloponnesian War* I, 6, trans. Richard Crawley, http://classics.mit.edu/Thucydides/pelopwar.1.first.html.

158. Kenneth Clark, *The Nude; A Study of Ideal Art* (New York: Pantheon, 1956), p. 21.
159. Blundell, p. 94.
160. Plato, *Republic* 452.
161. Pomeroy, p. 145–46.
162. Hugh Bowden, *Mystery Cults of the Ancient World* (Princeton: University Press, 2010), fig. 8, p. 14.

Chapter Five

1. Eva Cantarella, *Pandora's Daughters* (Baltimore: Johns Hopkins University Press, 1987), p. 119.
2. F. R. Cowell, *Everyday Life in Ancient Rome* (London: B. T. Batsford Ltd., 1961), p. 13.
3. Livy, *History of Rome* (*Ab urbe condita libri*) 39:6.
4. Appian, *Civil Wars* 1:1–7.
5. Otto Kiefer, *Sexual Life in Ancient Rome*, trans. Gilbert Highet and Helen Highet (London: George Routledge and Sons, Ltd. 1941), p. 43.
6. Cantarella, pp. 101–12.
7. Livy 1:34, Dionysius 3:47.
8. Livy 1:41.
9. Giovanni Boccaccio, *Famous Women*, trans. Virginia Brown (Cambridge, MA: Harvard University Press, 2001), pp. 94–95.
10. Plutarch, *Parallel Lives* 2:15–19.
11. Livy 1:9–13
12. Ulpian, *Digests* (the Code of Justinian) 50:16:195:2, http://www.archive.org/stream/digestofjustinia01monruoft/digestofjustinia01monruoft_djvu.txt.
13. Cantarella, p. 115; Mary R. Lefkowitz and Maureen B. Fant, *Women's Life in Greece and Rome*, third edition (Baltimore: Johns Hopkins, 2005), pp. 94–95.
14. Sarah B. Pomeroy, *Goddesses, Whores, Wives, and Slaves* (New York: Schocken, 1975), p. 150.
15. Bruce W. Winter, *Roman Wives, Roman Widows* (Grand Rapids, MI: Eerdmans, 2003), pp. 39–58; see also Cantarella, pp. 128–29.
16. Cicero, *de Republica* 2:37, 63; Winter, pp. 50–1.
17. Suetonius, *Augustus* 34:2.
18. Dio Cassius 54:16, 1–2; 56:1, 2.
19. Seneca, *On the Brevity of Life* 4:5; *On Benefits* 6:1–2.
20. Dio Cassius 55 and 56.
21. Gellius 5:10, 19.
22. Livy 5:25.

23. Cornelius Nepos, *Lives* (LCL preface, p. 26ff.); Cowell, *Everyday Life*, pp. 170–178.
24. J. P. V. D. Balsdon, *Roman Women* (London: The Bodley Head, 1962), p. 45.
25. Plutarch, *Lives* "Marcus Cato," XXIV, 2–4 (LCL II, pp. 375–77). Pliny, *Letters*, I, 14 (LCL I pp. 49–53).
26. Pliny, *Natural History* XXXIII, 28 (LCL IX, p. 25); Juvenal, VI, 25 (LCL, p. 85).
27. Gellius X, 10; see also Jerome Carcopino, *Daily Life in Ancient Rome* (New Haven: Yale University Press, 1962), p. 81.
28. Pliny, *Letters* 1:9 I, ix (LCL I, p. 31).
29. Plutarch, *The Roman Questions* 20: 101–108.
30. Carcopino, *Daily Life in Ancient Rome*, p. 81.
31. Juvenal, VI, 224; Lucian, *Pharsalia* II, 370–71. See Carcopino, p. 83.
32. T. G. Tucker, *Life in the Roman World* (New York: Macmillan, 1922), p. 299.
33. Tucker, p. 289.
34. Gaius I, 145; cf. Carcopino, p. 76.
35. Plutarch, *Lives,* "Marcus Cato" XXIV, 2–4 (LCL II, pp. 375–77); Pliny, *Letters* I, 14 (LCL I, pp. 49–53).
36. Gaius III, 17 on the patria potestas (pater familias), the code that in earlier times protected the supreme power of the father of a family.
37. Gellius XVII, 6 (LCL III, pp. 223–25).
38. Carcopino, p. 76.
39. Suetonius, *Augustus* 101.
40. Tacitus, *Annals* 2:85:1.
41. Carcopino, p. 53.
42. Plutarch, *Moralia* 198D (LCL III, p. 177–79).
43. Pomeroy, p. 149.
44. Plutarch, *Life of Tiberius and Gaius Gracchus* I:5.
45. Emily Hemelrijk, *Matrona Docta: Educated Women in the Roman Elite from Cornelia to Julia Domna* (London: Routledge, 1999), pp. 193–96. See also Bella Vivante, ed., *Women's Roles in Ancient Civilizations* (Westport, CT: Greenwood Press, 1999).
46. Carolyn Osiek and David L. Balch, *Families in the New Testament World* (Louisville: Westminster John Knox, 1997), pp. 48–54.
47. Romans 16:1–2.
48. Sallust, *Conspiracy of Catiline* 25 (LCL, p. 43).
49. Pliny, *Letters* 4, 19 (LCL I, p. 333).
50. Dionysius of Halicarnassus, XI, 28; Cowell, pp. 39–40; Kiefer, *Sexual Life*, p. 11.
51. Lefkowitz and Fant, pp. 50–54.
52. Cora E. Lutz, ed., *Musonius Rufus: The Roman Socrates,* Yale Classical Studies 10 (London: Oxford University Press, 1947); see Origen, *Against Celsius* 3:66.
53. Musonius Rufus, *Lectures* XII:1–6; XIIIA:4–5; XIV:5–6, trans. Cora Lutz, https://sites.google.com/site/thestoiclife/the_teachers/musonius-rufus/lectures.
54. William O. Stephens, "Musonius Rufus" 6, *Internet Encyclopedia of Philosophy*, http://www.iep.utm.edu/musonius.
55. Osiek and Balch, p. 63.
56. Juvenal VI, 246–64, 300–05 (LCL, pp. 103–107); Petronius, *Satyricon* 67, 70–76 (LCL, p. 126, 132–52).
57. Juvenal VI, 121–130 (LCL, p. 101).
58. Ibid., 398, 456 (LCL, pp. 117–21).
59. Ibid., 450ff. (LCL, p. 121).
60. Ibid., 246–64 (LCL, p. 103–105).
61. Petronius, *Satyricon* 67, 70–6 (LCL, pp. 126, 132–52).
62. Juvenal VI, 300–305; 425–33 (LCL, p. 107).
63. Livy 34:1 (LCL I, p. 413–14).
64. Pomeroy, pp. 178–80.
65. Pliny the Younger, *Letters* IX, 36; Juvenal VI, 268; Petronius 41, 77; cf. Carcopino, p. 90–91.
66. Martial XI, 53 (LCL II, p. 277).
67. Tucker, *Life in the Roman World*, p. 292.
68. Petronius 41, 77. See also Pliny the Younger, *Letters* IX, 36; Juvenal VI, 268 ff. (LCL, p. 105).
69. Horace, *Satires*, I, 2c (LCL, p. 21).
70. Cicero, *Oration for M. Caelius* XX, Bohn's Classical Library III (London: George Bell and Sons, 1900–1905) pp. 268ff.
71. Sallust, *Conspiracy of Catiline* XIII (LCL, p. 23).
72. Ovid, *The Amores* I, 8, 44 (LCL, p. 351).
73. Juvenal VI, 50 (LCL, p. 87).
74. Juvenal VI, 500 (LCL, p. 133).
75. Horace, *Odes* III, 6 (LCL, p. 201–203).
76. Seneca, *On Benefits* III, 16 (LCL III, p. 157).
77. Sallust, *Conspiracy of Catiline* XIII (LCL, p. 23); Horace, *Odes* III, 6 (LCL, p. 201–203); Ovid, *The Amores* I, 8, 44 (LCL, p. 351); Tacitus, *The Germans*, 17–19 (LCL I, p. 157–59); Juvenal, VI, 500 (LCL, p. 133).
78. Suetonius, *The Lives of the Caesars* II, 34 (LCL I, p. 177–79).
79. Juvenal VI, 1421 (LCL, p. 95); Seneca, *On Benefits* III, 16 (LCL III, p. 157).

80. Valerius Maximus II, 9, 2; Gellius X, 15; see Carcopino, pp. 95–96.
81. Plutarch, *Lives,* "Caesar" × (LCL VII, p. 467).
82. Plutarch, *Lives,* "Cicero" 41 (LCL VII, p. 187).
83. Jerome, *Against Jovinianum* I, 48; Pliny, *Natural History* VII, 49 (LCL II, p. 613).
84. Juvenal VI, 1421 (LCL, p. 95).
85. Juvenal VI, 224ff. (LCL, p. 101).
86. Seneca, *On Benefits* III 16 (LCL III, p. 157).
87. Martial, *Epigrams* VI 36 (LCL IV, p. 203).
88. Osiek and Balch, pp. 38–40.
89. Ovid, *Art of Love* III, 211; Juvenal II, 93; Martial IX, 37; see Carcopino, p. 168.
90. Martial, *Epigrams* IX, 37 (Bohn's Classical Library); see also LCL II, p. 97–99.
91. Cowell, p. 64.
92. Juvenal VI, 501–504 (LCL, p. 125).
93. Macrobius II, 5, 7.
94. Juvenal VI, 487–93 (LCL, p. 123).
95. Martial, *Epigrams,* II, 66 (LCL I, p. 147).
96. Cowell, pp. 68–72.
97. Petronius 66; Carcopino, p. 170. See Cowell, p. 65, on the common complaint by men of women wearing too much perfume.
98. Plutarch, *Roman Questions* 14; *Moralia* 267.
99. Valerius Maximus 6:3, 10.
100. Plutarch, *Lives,* 1.
101. Seneca, *Helvia* XVI (LCL II, p. 471).
102. Tacitus, *The Germans* 17–19 (LCL I, pp. 157–59).
103. Appian, *The Civil Wars* IV, 36 (LCL IV, p. 203).
104. Tacitus, *Annals* VI, 29 (LCL, p. 203).
105. Ibid., XV 62–64 (LCL, pp. 317–19).
106. Ibid., XV, 71 (LCL, p. 329).
107. Pliny, *Letters* III, 16 (LCL I, p. 249).
108. Ibid., VIII, 5 (LCL II, p. 103).
109. Ibid., IV, 19 (LCL I, p. 333).
110. Pliny, *Letters* LX (Harvard Classics, 1909–14).
111. Kiefer, *Sexual Life,* p. 27.
112. Ibid.
113. Lefkowitz and Fant, pp. 223–24.
114. Cantarella, pp. 114–15; Kiefer, pp. 49–50.
115. *Digest* 7, 1, 68 and 22, 1, 28.
116. Thomas A. McGinn, *The Economy of Prostitution in the Roman World: A Study of Social History and the Brothel* (Ann Arbor:

University of Michigan Press, 2004), pp. 167–168.
117. John North, *Roman Religion* (Oxford: Oxford University Press, 2000), pp. 4–6.
118. Marcus Tullius Cicero, *De Natura Deorum (On the Nature of the Gods),* Book 2, trans. Francis Brooks (London: Methuen, 1896), http://oll.libertyfund.org/titles/539.
119. James Donaldson, *Woman:Her Position and Influence in Ancient Greece and Rome, and Among Early Christians* (London: Longman, Green and Co., 1907), p. 93.
120. Livy 39:13–5.
121. Cantarella, p. 127.
122. Catullus 14:15; see John F. Miller, "Roman Festivals," *The Oxford Encyclopedia of Ancient Greece and Rome* (Oxford University Press, 2010), p. 172.
123. Macrobius, *Saturnalia* 1:1, 8–9.
124. Cicero, *Letters to Friends* 14:4, trans. Evelyn Shuckburgh, http://en.wikisource.org/wiki/Letters_to_friends/14.4.
125. Pomeroy, p. 206.
126. Livy 2:40.
127. Ovid, *Ex Ponto* 4:3.
128. Livy, *History of Rome* 5:14.
129. W. Warde Fowler, *Social Life at Rome in the Age of Cicero* (London: Macmillan, 1908), pp. 18–19.
130. Tucker, p. 115.
131. Plutarch, *Lives* 18:1.
132. Plutarch, *Lives,* "Caesar," XI, 3ff. (LCL VII, pp. 463–65).
133. Juvenal VI, 316–41 (LCL, p. 109).

Chapter Six

1. Sarah B. Pomeroy, *Goddesses, Whores, Wives and Slaves* (New York: Schocken, 1995), p. 76.
2. C. K. Barrett, *The New Testament Background: Selected Documents* (New York: Harper and Row, 1961), pp. 91–100.
3. Seneca, *Of a Happy Life* 26.
4. Walter Burkert, *Ancient Mystery Cults* (Cambridge, MA: Harvard University Press, 1987).
5. Samuel Angus, *The Mystery-Religions: A Study in the Religious Background of Early Christianity* (1925; repr. New York: Dover Publications, 1975), p. 12. See also James Donaldson, *Woman: Her Position and Influence in Ancient Greece and Rome, and Among the Early Christians* (London: Longmans, Green and Co., 1907).

6. Angus, p. 43.
7. Burkert, pp. 7–9.
8. Sue Blundell, *Women in Ancient Greece* (Cambridge, MA: Harvard University Press, 1995), pp. 163–65.
9. "Hymn to Demeter," *Homeric Hymns* 2:474–82, trans. Jules Cashford (London: Penguin, 2003), p. 51.
10. Hippolytus, *Refutation of Heresies* 5:8, 39–40.
11. Confusing mythological associations, some derived from Aristophanes, *Frogs* 342.
12. Pausanias 1:38, 7.
13. Pausanias 8:25, 7.
14. Hugh Bowden, *Mystery Cults of the Ancient World* (Princeton: University Press, 2010), pp. 41–42; Kevin Clinton, "The Sanctuary of Demeter and Kore at Eleusis," in *Greek Sanctuaries: New Approaches*, eds. Nanno Marinatos and Robin Hagg (London: Routledge, 1993), pp. 118–19.
15. Bowden, p. 48.
16. Pausanias, 8:37, 8.
17. Bowden, pp. 68–77; Strabo 14:1, 3; Herodotus IX, 97.
18. Frederick C. Grant, *Hellenistic Religions* (New York: The Liberal Arts Press, 1953), p. 26.
19. Herodotus II, 51.
20. Plutarch, *Alexander*, 2:1.
21. Herodotus II, 51.
22. Pausanias, 9:25, 6.
23. Apollonius, *The Argonautica* 1:917, trans. R.C. Seaton, http://classics.mit.edu/Apollonius/argon.html.
24. Karl Lehman, *Samothrace, A Guide to the Excavations and the Museum*, Thessalonika, 1998.
25. Euripides, *The Bacchae*, http://classics.mit.edu/Euripides/bacchan.html.
26. Walter F. Otto, *Dionysus Myth and Cult* (Bloomington: Indiana University Press, 1995).
27. Bowden, p. 128.
28. Livy 39:8 and 13.
29. Pomeroy, p. 154.
30. Bowden, p. 127.
31. Herodotus IV, 7.
32. Apollonius, *The Argonautica* 1:1079–1152.
33. Lucian, IV (LCL, pp. 339–411); Grant, *Hellenistic Religions*, p. 117.
34. Apuleius, *Metamorphoses* (also called *The Golden Ass*) 8:27–28; Grant, p. 121–22.
35. Plato, *Euthydemos* 277.
36. Bowden, p. 85.
37. "Hymn to the Mother of the Gods," *Homeric Hymns* 14, trans. Jules Cashford, p. 113.
38. Ovid, *Fasti* 4:264–72.
39. Livy, XXXIX, 13–17 (LCL XI, p. 251).
40. Dionysius of Halicarnassus, *Roman Antiquities* 2:19.
41. Apuleius, *Metamorphoses*, 8:24–9:4.
42. Prudentius, *Peristephanon* 10:1011–50. See Barrett, pp. 96–97.
43. Martial 3:81.
44. Plutarch, *Morals* 4, *On Isis and Osiris*, 13–19.
45. The Cyme inscription, found in Asia Minor, can be dated to the second century CE, the most complete of the various Isis aretalogies. See http://www.haverford.edu/relg/faculty/amcguire/relg221b/femaledivine.htm.
46. Apuleius, *Metamorphoses*, 11:30.
47. Bowden, p. 161.
48. Apuleius, 9:10.
49. Apuleius, 11:23.
50. Josephus, *Jewish Antiquities* 18:66–80.
51. Juvenal, VI, 515–541 (LCL, pp. 125–27).
52. F. R. Cowell, *Everyday Life in Ancient Rome* (New York: Putnam, 1961), p. 192; James Moffatt, *The First Epistle of Paul to the Corinthians* (New York: Harper, n.d.), p. 149.
53. Bowden, p. 187.
54. Bowden, p. 24. See Martin Goodman, *The Roman World: 44 BC–AD 180* (London: Routledge, 1997), p. 315.
55. Carolyn Osiek and David L. Balch, *Families in the New Testament World* (Louisville: Westminster John Knox, 1997), pp. 30–31.
56. Burkert, p. 11.

Conclusion

1. Hugh Bowden, *Mystery Cults of the Ancient World* (Princeton: Princeton University Press, 2010), p. 45; Justin, *Apology* 1:66.
2. Eusebius, *Demonstratio Evangelica* (*Proof of the Gospel*) 1:10, 32; 3:4, 48; 4:7, 1.
3. Bowden, pp. 8–9.
4. Blundell, p. 46.
5. Pliny, *Natural History*, XXXIII, 28 (LCL IX, p. 25); Juvenal VI, 25 (LCL, p. 85).
6. Gellius, X, 10; also the English word "matrimony" from the Latin *matris munia*, "duties of the mother."
7. W. J. Conybeare and J. S. Howson, *The*

Chapter Notes—Conclusion 241

Life and Epistles of St. Paul (Grand Rapids, MI: Eerdmans, 1959), pp. 282–283.
   8. Alister E. McGrath, *Christian Theology: An Introduction* (Oxford: Blackwell, 2001), pp. 224–225.
   9. Romans 12–15; Galatians 5–6; I Thessalonians 5; I Corinthians 5–10.
   10. Hans Dieter Betz, *Paul's Letter to the Churches in Galatia* (Philadelphia: Fortress, 1979), pp. 291, 299.
   11. Joe E. Barnhart, "Plato's Symposium and Early Christianity," *The Journal of Higher Criticism* II, no. 2 (Fall, 2005): 12–18.
   12. Acts 17:22–31.
   13. Diogenes Laertius, *Lives of Philosophers* 1:112.
   14. Acts 17:28. The same words appear in the *Hymn of Cleanthes*, a Stoic from Assos.
   15. Bowden, p. 24.
   16. For this section, see also Lesly F. Massey, *Women in the Church: Moving Toward Equality* (Jefferson, NC: McFarland, 2002), pp. 9–16.
   17. Maurice Goguel, *Jesus and the Origins of Christianity*, Vol. I (New York: Harper Torchbooks, 1960), p. 18.
   18. Luke 4:18–19; cf. Isaiah 61:1, "The Spirit of the Lord is upon me, because he anointed me to preach the gospel to the poor. He has sent me to proclaim release to the captives, and recovery of sight to the blind, to set free those who are downtrodden, to proclaim the favorable year of the Lord."
   19. H. S. Vigeveno, *Jesus the Revolutionary* (Glendale: G/L Publications, 1972), pp. 5–12.
   20. Matthew 23:1ff.; cf. Ezekiel 22:29; Ecclesiastes 5:8.
   21. W. Rauschenbush, "Jesus the Builder of the New Society," in *Great Lives Observed Jesus*, ed. Hugh Anderson (Englewood Cliffs, NJ: Prentice Hall, 1967), p. 126. See also Vigeveno, *Jesus the Revolutionary*, pp. 5–12.
   22. Jack O. Balswick and Judith K. Balswick, *The Family: A Christian Perspective on the Contemporary Home*, third edition (Grand Rapids, MI: Baker, 2007), pp. 280–81.
   23. Bart D. Ehrman, *The New Testament: A Historical Introduction to the Christian Writings*, fourth edition (New York: Oxford University Press, 2008), pp. 407–408.
   24. Shailer Matthews, "Jesus' Philosophy of Social Progress," in *Great Lives Observed Jesus*, ed. Hugh Anderson, p. 122; See Matthews, *The Social Teaching of Jesus, An Essay in Christian Sociology* (New York: Macmillan, 1897), pp. 191–97.
   25. Oscar Cullman, *The Early Church*, ed. A. J. B. Higgens (London: SCM Press, 1956), p. 195.
   26. Ben Witherington, *Women in the Ministry of Jesus* (Cambridge: University Press, 1984), pp. 125–131.
   27. Albrecht Oepke, "gune," *Theological Dictionary of the New Testament*, Vol. I, ed. G. Kittel (Grand Rapids, MI: Eerdmans, 1969), p. 784; Leonard Swidler, "Jesus Was a Feminist," *South East Asia Journal of Theology* XIII, 1 (1971): 102–104.
   28. Henri Daniel-Rops, *Jesus in His Time*, trans. R.W. Millar (London: Eyre and Spottiswoode, 1956), p. 252.
   29. Martin Debelius, *Jesus*, English edition (London: SCM, 1963), p. 54.
   30. D. M. Pratt, "Women," in *International Standard Bible Encyclopedia*, Vol. V (Grand Rapids, MI: Eerdmans, 1955), p. 3102.
   31. Bo Reike, *The Gospel of Luke*, trans. R. Mackenzie (Richmond: John Knox Press, 1962), p. 63.
   32. Charles C. Ryrie, *The Role of Women in the Church* (Chicago: Moody, 1978), pp. 40–49. The "except for fornication" clause in Matthew 5:32 and 19:9 has been the source of debate in church doctrine concerning grounds for divorce and remarriage. The clause does not appear in Mark 10:11 or Luke 16:18 and is generally considered to be the writer's insertion to accommodate a Jewish audience.
   33. *Babylonian Talmud*, Gittin IX:10.
   34. Matthew 19:4–9; Mark 10:3–12; Matthew 5:31–2; Luke 16:18; cf. Deuteronomy 24:1ff.
   35. Genesis 1:27.
   36. Matthew 19:5–6.
   37. Witherington, *Women in the Ministry of Jesus*, pp. 18–28.
   38. Mattthew 20:26; Mark 10:43; Luke 22:26.
   39. Robin Scroggs, "Women in the New Testament," *The Interpreter's Dictionary of the Bible*, supp. vol. (Nashville: Abingdon Press, 1976), p. 967.
   40. Claudia Setzer, *Jewish Responses to Early Christians: History and Polemics, 30–150 C.E.* (Minneapolis: Fortress, 1994).
   41. Romans 16:1–15. See also Lesly F. Massey, *Women and the New Testament: An*

Analysis of Scripture in Light of New Testament Era Culture (Jefferson, NC: McFarland, 1989), pp. 41–57.

42. The Ethiopian eunuch, encountered by Philip along the road from Jerusalem to Gaza, had in his possession a scroll of Isaiah. See Acts 8:26–40.

43. I Corinthians 6:9–10; 7:1–8.

44. John E. Stambaugh and David L. Balch, *The New Testament in Its Social Environment* (Philadelphia: Westminster, 1986), pp. 55, 106.

45. Eva Cantarella, *Pandora's Daughters* (Baltimore: Johns Hopkins, 1987), p. 178.

46. Suetonius, *Claudius* 25.

47. Suetonius, *Nero* 38.

48. Tacitus, *Annals* 15:38; Cassius Dio, *Roman History* 62:16–17.

49. Ignatius of Antioch, *Letter to the Ephesians*, 12.

50. Eusebius, *Ecclesiastical History* 5:1, 7.

51. Paul S. Fiddes, "Woman's Head is the Man," *The Baptist Quarterly* 31, 8 (1986): 370–83.

52. Letha Scanzoni and Nancy Hardesty, *All We're Meant To Be* (Waco: Word, 1975), pp. 96–8.

53. Elizabeth Schüssler Fiorenza, *In Memory of Her* (London: SCM, 1983), p. 261.

54. Bruce Winter, *Seek the Welfare of the City: Christians as Benefactors and Citizens* (Grand Rapids, MI: Eerdmans, 1994), p. 1; see also Tacitus, *Annals* 12:53.

55. Winter, pp. 3, 13, 200. See also Wayne A. Meeks, *The First Urban Christians: The Social World of the Apostle Paul* (New Haven: Yale University Press, 1983) and *The Origins of Christian Morality: The First Two Centuries* (New Haven: Yale University Press, 1994).

56. Arius Didymus, *Household Codes* 41–44, trans. David Balch, in Osiek and Balch, *Families in the New Testament World*, p. 119.

57. Carolyn Osiek and David L. Balch, *Families in the New Testament World* (Louisville: Westminster John Knox, 1997), p. 30; see David Balch, *Let Wives Be Submissive: The Domestic Code in I Peter* (Chico: Scholars Press, 1981), pp. 143–51.

58. Ehrman, *The New Testament*, p. 410.

59. Bruce Winter, *Roman Wives, Roman Widows* (Grand Rapids, MI: Eerdmans, 2003), p. 119.

60. Clement, *Paidagogos*, III:2.

61. Dio Chrysostom, *Orations* 64:3; Tacitus, *Germania*, 19; Athenaeus, *The Deipnosophists* 12:27; Aristophanes, *The Thesmoriazusae* 838.

62. Fiorenza, pp. 288–89.

63. Osiek and Balch, p. 121.

64. Ehrman, pp. 411–12.

Bibliography

Ancient History

Aldred, Cyril. *The Egyptians*. Third edition. London: Thames and Hudson, 1998.
_____. *Tutankhamun's Egypt*. London: British Broadcasting Corporation, 1972.
Angus, Samuel. *The Mystery-Religions: A Study in the Religious Background of Early Christianity*. New York: Dover Publications, 1975. First published London: Murray, 1925.
Archer, Gleason L. *A Survey of Old Testament Introduction*. Revised edition. Chicago: Moody, 1974.
Bahrani, Zainab. *Women of Babylon*. London: Routledge, 2001.
Barrett, C. K. *The New Testament Background: Selected Documents*. New York: Harper and Row, 1961.
Becker, Ernest. *Escape From Evil*. New York: Free Press, 1975.
Becker, Wilhelm A. *Charicles: Illustrations of the Private Life of the Ancient Greeks*. Frederick Metcalfe (trans.). London: Longmans, Green, 1895.
Benedict, Ruth. *Patterns of Culture*. Boston: Houghton Mifflin, 1959.
Biale, Rachel. *Women and Jewish Law*. New York: Shocken, 1984.
Blummer, H. *The Home Life of the Ancient Greeks*. Ahie Zimmern (trans.). London: Cassell, 1893.
Blundell, Sue. *Women in Ancient Greece*. Cambridge, MA: Harvard University Press, 1995.
Boadt, Lawrence. *Reading the Old Testament: An Introduction*. New York: Paulist Press, 1984.
Bonnard, André. *Greek Civilization*. A. L. Sells (trans.). London: George Allen and Unwin, 1957.
Botsford, G. W., and E. G. Sihler (eds.). *Hellenic Civilization*. New York: Octogon, 1965.
Bottéro, Jean. *Everyday Life in Ancient Mesopotamia*. Antonia Nevill (trans.). Baltimore: Johns Hopkins University Press, 2001.
Bowden, Hugh. *Mystery Cults of the Ancient World*. Princeton: Princeton University Press, 2010.
Breasted, James H. *A History of Egypt*. London: Hodder and Stoughton, 1951.
Bright, John. *A History of Israel*. London: SCM Press, 1966.
Brun, Henry J. *Women of the Ancient World*. New York: Richards Rosen Press, 1976.
Budin, Stephanie. *The Myth of Sacred Prostitution in Antiquity*. New York: Cambridge University Press, 2008.
Budge, E. A. Wallis. *Babylonian Life and History*. Second edition. London: Religious Tract Society, 1925.

244 Bibliography

Burkert, Walter. *Ancient Mystery Cults.* Cambridge, MA: Harvard University Press, 1987.
Burrows, Miller. *More Light on the Dead Sea Scrolls.* New York: Viking Press, 1958.
Cantarella, Eva. *Pandora's Daughters.* Baltimore: Johns Hopkins University Press, 1987.
Carcopino, Jerome. *Daily Life in Ancient Rome.* New Haven: Yale University Press, 1962.
Carroll, Mitchell. *Greek Women.* Philadelphia: Rittenhouse Press, 1908.
Contenau, George. *Everyday Life in Babylonia and Assyria.* London: Edward Arnold Publishers, 1954.
Coogan, Michael D., and Mark S. Smith (eds.). *Stories from Ancient Canaan.* Louisville: Westville John Knox Press, 2012.
Cook, R. M. *The Greeks Till Alexander.* London: Thames and Hudson, 1961.
Cook, S. A. *The Laws of Moses and the Code of Hammurabi,* 2 vols. London: John Murray, 1878.
Cooney, Kara. *The Woman Who Would Be King: Hatshepsut's Rise to Power in Ancient Egypt.* New York: Crown, 2014.
Cowell, F. R. *Everyday Life in Ancient Rome.* London: B. T. Batsford, 1961.
Culver, Elsie Thomas. *Women in the World of Religion.* Garden City: Doubleday, 1967.
Dalley, Stephanie. *Myths from Mesopotamia.* New York: Oxford, 1989.
Davidson, A. B. *Old Testament Prophecy.* Edinburgh: T & T Clark, 1903.
Deissmann, Adolf. *Light from the Ancient East.* L. R. M. Strachan (trans.). Grand Rapids, MI: Baker, 1965.
de Moubray, G. A. de C. *Matriarchy in the Malay Peninsula and Neighbouring Countries.* London: George Routledge, 1931.
de Vaux, Roland. *Ancient Israel, Its Life and Institutions,* John McHugh (trans.). Second edition. London: Darton, 1965.
Dill, Samuel. *Roman Society from Nero to Marcus Aurelius.* London: Macmillan, 1919.
Donaldson, James. *Woman: Her Position and Influence in Ancient Greece and Rome, and Among the Early Christians.* London: Longmans, Green, 1907.
Driver, G. R., and Miles, J. C. *The Assyrian Laws.* Oxford: Clarendon Press, 1935.
_____. *The Babylonian Laws, I and II.* Oxford: University Press, 1952.
Earl, Donald. *The Age of Augustus.* New York: Crown, 1968.
Edersheim, Alfred. *Sketches of Jewish Social Life in the Days of Christ.* London: Religious Tract Society, n.d.
Ehrman, Bart D. *The New Testament: A Historical Introduction to the Christian Writings.* Fourth edition. New York: Oxford University Press, 2008.
Ember, Carol R., and Melvin Ember. *Cultural Anthropology.* New York: Appleton-Century-Crafts, 1973.
Ferguson, John. *The Heritage of Hellenism.* New York: Science History Publications, 1973.
Finkelstein, Louis. *The Pharisees: The Sociological Background of Their Faith.* Second edition. Philadelphia: Jewish Publication Society of America, 1940.
Fischer, Henry G. *Egyptian Women of the Old Kingdom and of the Heracleopolitan Period.* New York: Metropolitan Museum of Art, 1989.
Fowler, W. Warde. *Social Life at Rome in the Age of Cicero.* London: Macmillan, 1908.
Friedlander, Ludwig. *Roman Life and Manners Under the Early Empire,* 4 vols. London: George Routledge, 1928.
Giaznelli, Giulio (ed.). *The World of Classical Athens.* New York: Putnam's, 1970.
Glasgow, Maude. *The Subjection of Women and the Traditions of Men.* New York: Maude Glasgow, 1940.
Gollaher, David L. *Circumcision: A History of the World's Most Controversial Surgery.* New York: Basic Books, 2000.
Goodenough, E. *Jewish Symbols in the Greco-Roman Period,* 10 vols. New York: Pantheon, 1956.

Grant, Frederick C. *Hellenistic Religions: The Age of Syncretism.* New York: Liberal Arts Press, 1953.
Gray, John. *Archaeology of the Old Testament World.* London: Thomas Nelson, 1962.
Guthrie, W. K. C. *The Greeks and Their Gods.* London: Methuen, 1950.
Hale, W. H. (ed.). *The Horizon Book of Ancient Greece.* New York: American Heritage, 1965.
Halliday, W. R. *The Pagan Background of Early Christianity.* London: Hodder and Stoughton, 1925.
Hallo, William W., and J. J. A. Van Dijk. *The Exaltation of Inanna.* New Haven: Yale University Press, 1968.
Hauer, Christian E., and William A. Young. *An Introduction to the Bible.* Upper Saddle River, NJ: Prentice-Hall, 1998.
Hayes, John L. *A Manual of Sumerian Grammar and Texts.* Aids and Research Tools in Ancient Near Eastern Studies, second revised edition. Malibu: Undena Publications, 2000.
Hedlund, Mary F., and H. H. Rowley (trans. and eds.). *Atlas of the Early Christian World.* London: Thomas Nelson, 1958.
Hemelrijk, Emily. *Matrona Docta: Educated Women in the Roman Elite from Cornelia to Julia Domna.* London: Routledge, 1999.
Jacobsen, Thorkild. *The Harps That Once...: Sumerian Poetry in Translation.* New Haven: Yale University Press, 1987.
Jastro, Morris. *The Civilization of Babylonia and Assyria.* Philadelphia: J. B. Lippincott, 1915.
Keller, Werner. *The Bible as History.* Joachim Rehork (ed.); William Neil and B. H. Rasmussen (trans.). New York: William Morrow, 1981.
Kemp, B. J. *The City of Akhenaten and Nefertiti: Amarna and Its People.* London: Thames and Hudson, 2012.
_____. *Ancient Egypt: Anatomy of a Civilization.* London: Thames and Hudson, 1989.
Kiefer, Otto. *Sexual Life in Ancient Rome.* Gilbert and Helen Highet (trans.). London: George Routledge, 1941.
Kitchen, Kenneth A. *On the Reliability of the Old Testament.* Grand Rapids, MI: Eerdmans, 2003.
_____. *Ramesside Inscriptions, Historical and Biographical,* 6 vols. Oxford: B. H. Blackwell, 1975–1983.
Kramer, Samuel Noah. *The Sumerians: Their History, Culture and Character.* Chicago: University Press, 1964.
_____. *History Begins at Sumer: Thirty-Nine Firsts in Recorded History.* Philadelphia: University of Pennsylvania Press, 1988.
Kuhrt, Amelie. *The Ancient Near East: c. 3000–330 B.C.,* Vol. 2. London: Routledge, 1995.
La Croix, Paul. *The History of Prostitution.* Samuel Putnam (trans.). 3 vols. Chicago: Pascal Covici, 1926.
Leick, Gwendolyn. *Mesopotamia:The Invention of the City.* London: Penguin, 2001.
_____. *Sex and Eroticism in Mesopotamian Literature.* London: Routledge, 1994.
Lesko, Barbara S. *Women's Earliest Records from Ancient Egypt and Western Asia.* Atlanta: Scholars Press, 1989.
Lichtheim, Miriam. *Ancient Egyptian Literature: The Old and Middle Kingdoms,* Vol. I. Berkeley: University of California Press, 1973.
_____. *Ancient Egyptian Literature: The New Kingdom,* Vol. II. Berkeley: University of California Press, 1976.
_____. *Ancient Egyptian Literature: The Late Period,* Vol. III. Berkeley: University of California Press, 1980.

Lindsay, Jack. *Leisure and Pleasure in Roman Egypt*. London: Frederick Muller, 1965.
Llewellyn-Jones, Lloyd, and Sue Blundell (eds.). *Women's Dress in the Ancient Greek World*. London: Duckworth, 2002.
Lukas, Jan. *Pompeii and Herculaneum*. London: Spring Books, 1966.
Mace, David, and Vera Mace. *Marriage East and West*. New York: Doubleday, 1960.
Mahaffy, J. P. *Social Life in Greece*. London: Macmillan, 1877.
McGrath, Alister E. *Christian Theology: An Introduction*. Oxford: Blackwell, 2001.
Mireaux, Emile. *Daily Life in the Time of Homer*. Iris Sells (trans.). London: Allen and Unwin, 1959.
Montet, Pierre. *Everyday Life in Egypt*. H. R. Maxwell-Hyslop and Margaret Drower (trans.). London: Edward Arnold, 1958.
Moore, George Foot. *Judaism in the First Centuries of the Christian Era*, 3 vols. Cambridge, MA: Harvard University Press, 1946-8.
Murray, Margaret A. *The Splendour That Was Egypt*. London: Sidgwick and Jackson, 1949.
Nash, Ernest. *Pictorial Dictionary of Ancient Rome*. New York: Praeger, 1961.
Neil, J. *Everyday Life in the Holy Land*. London: Church Mission to the Jews, 1930.
Nemet-Nejat, Karen Rhea. "Women in Ancient Mesopotamia." In *Women's Roles in Ancient Civilizations: A Reference Guide*, ed. Bella Vivante. Westport, CT: Greenwood Press, 1999.
Nock, A. D. *Early Gentile Christianity and Its Hellenistic Background*. New York: Harper and Row, 1964.
Oesterley, W. O. E., and T. H. Robinson. *Hebrew Religion, Its Origin and Development*. London: Society for Promoting Christian Knowledge, 1952.
_____. *A History of Israel*, Vol. II. London: Oxford University Press, 1957.
Økland, Jorunn. *Women in Their Place: Paul and the Corinthian Discourse of Gender and Sanctuary Space*. Journal for the Study of the New Testament, Supplement Series 269. London: T & T Clark International, 2004.
Oppenheim, A. Leo. *Ancient Mesopotamia*. Chicago: University of Chicago Press, 1964.
Osiek, Carolyn, and David L. Balch. *Families in the New Testament World*. Louisville: Westminster John Knox, 1997.
Parkinson, Richard B. *Voices from Ancient Egypt: An Anthology of Middle Kingdom Writings*. London: British Museum Press, 1991.
Pestman, P. W. *Marriage and Matrimonial Property in Ancient Egypt*. Leiden: E. J. Brill, 1961.
Pfeiffer, C. F. *Between the Testaments*. Grand Rapids, MI: Baker, 1959.
_____. *The Dead Sea Scrolls*. Grand Rapids, MI: Baker, 1962.
Pomeroy, Sarah B. *Goddesses, Whores, Wives and Slaves*. New York: Schocken, 1995.
_____. *Women in Hellenistic Egypt: From Alexander to Cleopatra*. Detroit: Wayne State University Press, 1990.
Pritchard, James B. *Archaeology and the Old Testament*. London: Oxford University Press, 1958.
Ramsay, W. M. *Asiatic Elements in Greek Civilization: the Gifford Lectures in the University of Edinburgh, 1915-16*. Second edition. London: J. Murray, 1928.
Rawlinson, George (ed. and trans.). *The History of Herodotus*. New York: D. Appleton, 1885.
Rawson, Beryl (ed.). *Marriage, Divorce and Children in Ancient Rome*. Oxford: University Press, 1991.
Reineke, W. (ed.). *Acts of the First International Congress of Egyptology*. Berlin: Akademie-Verlag, 1979.
Ringgren, Helmer. *Israelite Religion*. David Green (trans.). London: Society for Promoting Christian Knowledge, 1966.

Robins, Gay. *Women in Ancient Egypt*. Cambridge, MA: Harvard University Press, 1993.
Roth, Martha T. *Law Collections from Mesopotamia and Asia Minor*. Atlanta: Scholars Press, 1995.
Sasson, J. M., J. Baines, G. M. Beckman, and K. S. Rubinson (eds.). *Civilizations of the Ancient Near East*. New York: Scribner's, 1995.
Sayce, A. H. *The Egypt of the Hebrews*. London: Rivington, 1895.
Schurer, Emil. *A History of the Jewish People in the Age of Jesus Christ*. G. Vermes and F. Millar (trans.). New English edition, Vol. I. Edinburgh: T & T Clark, 1973.
Smith, H. S., and R. M. Hall (eds.). *Ancient Centres of Egyptian Civilization*. London: Egyptian Education Bureau, 1983.
Smith, J. M. Powis. *The Origin and History of Hebrew Law*. Chicago: University Press, 1931.
Stembaugh, John E., and David L. Balch. *The New Testament in Its Social Environment*. Wayne Meek (ed.). Philadelphia: Westminster, 1986.
Stendahl, Krister. *The Bible and the Role of Women: A Case Study in Hermeneutics*. Emil T. Sanders (trans.). Philadelphia: Fortress, 1966.
Tarn, W. W. *Hellenistic Civilization*. Second edition. London: Edward Arnold, 1930.
Tavard, George H. *Woman in Christian Tradition*. Notre Dame, IN: University of Notre Dame Press, 1973.
Tcherikoves, Victor. *Hellenistic Civilization and the Jews*. Philadelphia: Jewish Publication Society of America, 1959.
Thomson, George. *Studies in Ancient Greek Society*. London: Lawrence and Wishart, 1949.
Toumbouros, George. *Parallel Legislations*, Vol. II. Munich: Suddeutscher Verlag Press, 1959.
Tucker, T. G. *Life in Ancient Athens*. London: Macmillan, 1907.
_____. *Life in the Roman World*. New York: Macmillan, 1922.
Unger, Merrill F. *Archaeology and the New Testament*. Grand Rapids, MI: Zondervan, 1962.
Van De Mieroop, Marc. *A History of Ancient Egypt*. West Sussex: Wiley-Blackwell, 2011.
_____. *A History of the Ancient Near East*. Malden, MA: Blackwell, 2004.
Vivante, Bella (ed.) *Women's Roles in Ancient Civilizations: A Reference Guide*. Westport, CT: Greenwood Press, 1999.
Vos, Clarence J. *Women in Old Testament Worship*. Delft: Verenigde Drukkerijn Judels und Brinkman, 1968.
Watterson, Barbara. *Women in Ancient Egypt*. Gloucestershire: Amberley, 2011.
Winter, Bruce. *Roman Wives, Roman Widows*. Grand Rapids, MI: Eerdmans, 2003.
_____. *Seek the Welfare of the City*. Grand Rapids, MI: Eerdmans, 1994.
Wolff, Hans Walter. *Anthropology of the Old Testament*., Margaret Kohl (trans.). London: SCM, 1974.
Wright, Frederick Adam. *Feminism in Greek Literature from Homer to Aristotle*. New York: E.P. Dalton, 1923.
Wright, G. Ernest. *Biblical Archaeology*. Philadelphia: Westminster, 1962.
Young, Edward J. *An Introduction to the Old Testament*. Revised edition. London: Tyndale, 1960.

Journals and Essays

Asmussen, J. P. "Bemerkungen zur Sakralen Prostitution im Alten Testament." *Studia Theologica* XI (1959): 167–192.
Assante, Julia. "The kar.kid/harimtu, Prostitute or Single Woman? A Reconsideration of Evidence." *Ugarit-Forschungen* 30 (1998): 5–96.

Busenitz, Irvin A. "Woman's Desire for Man, Gen. 3:16 Reconsidered." *Grace Theological Journal* 7 (Fall 1986): 203-212.
Cerny, Jaroslav. "Consanguineous Marriages in Pharaonic Egypt." *Journal of Egyptian Archives* 40 (1954): 23-29.
Cifarelli, Megan. "Gesture and Alterity in the Art of Ashurnasirpal II of Assyria." *Art Bulletin* 80 (1998): 210-228.
Franklin, Doris. "Impact of Christianity on the Status of Women." *Religion and Society* 32 (June 1985):43-55.
Harris, Rivkah. "Inanna-Ishtar as Paradox and a Coincidence of Opposites." *History of Religions* 30 (1990): 261-278.
Kemp, B. J. "A Model of Tell el-Amarna." *Antiquity* 74 (2000): 15-16.
_____. 1977. "The City of el-Amarna as a Source for the Study of Urban Society in Ancient Egypt," *World Archaeology* 9 (1977): 123-39.
Leonard, E. A. "St. Paul on the Status of Women." *Catholic Biblical Quarterly* XII (July 1950): 311-320.
Lerner, Gerda. "The Origin of Prostitution in Ancient Mesopotamia." *Signs: Journal of Women in Culture and Society* 11 (Winter 1986): 236-254.
McKeating, Henry. "Jesus ben Sira's Attitude to Women." *The Expository Times* 85 (December 1973): 85-87.
Rosenzweig, Michael L. "A Helper Equal to Him (Gen. 1:27; 2:18-24)." *Judaism* 35 (Summer 1986): 277-280.
Rowley, H. H. "Israel's Sojourn in Egypt." *Bulletin of the John Rylands Library* 22 (1938): 243-290.
Schulman, Alan R. "Diplomatic Marriage in the Egyptian New Kingdom." *Journal of Near Eastern Studies* 38 (1979): 177-93.
Shideler, Mary McDermott. "Male and Female Created He Them." *Religion in Life* 43 (Spring 1974): 60-67.
Stockton, Eugene D. "The Woman: A Biblical Theme." *Australian Journal of Biblical Archaeology* 1.6 (November 1973): 106-112.
Wagner, Walter. "The Demonization of Women." *Religion in Life* XLII (Spring 1973): 56-74.
Westenholz, Joan G. "Tamar, Qedeša, Qadištu, and Sacred Prostitution in Mesopotamia." *Harvard Theological Review* 82 (1989): 245-265.

Commentaries

Billerbeck, Paul, and H. L. Strack. *Kommentar zum Neuen Testament aus Talmud und Midrash.* Munchen: C. H. Beck, 1956.
Driver, S. R. "A Critical and Exegetical Commentary on Deuteronomy." *International Critical Commentary.* Third edition. Edinburgh: T & T Clark, 1965.
Hertz, J. H. (ed.). *The Pentateuch and Haftorahs.* Second edition. London: Soncino Press, 1975.
Keil, C. F., and F. Delitzsch. *Biblical Commentary on the Old Testament: The Pentateuch,* 3 vols. Grand Rapids, MI: Eerdmans, 1959.
Skinner, John. "Genesis." *International Critical Commentary.* Edinburgh: T & T Clark, 1969.

Feminist Works

Barnhouse, Ruth Tiffany, and Urban T. Holmes III (eds.). *Male and Female.* New York: Seabury Press, 1976.
Chafe, William H. *Women and Equality.* New York: Oxford University Press, 1977.

Chodorow, Nancy. *The Reproduction of Mothering: Psychoanalysis and the Sociology of Gender*. Berkeley: University of California Press, 1999.
Christ, Carol P., and Judith Plaskow (eds.). *Womanspirit Rising: A Feminist Reader in Religion*. San Francisco: Harper and Row, 1979.
Collins, Patricia Hill. *Black Feminist Thought: Knowledge, Consciousness and the Politics of Empowerment*. New York: Routledge: 1990.
Cone, James H. *For My People: Black Theology and the Black Church*. Johannesburg: Skotaville, 1985.
Fiorenza, Elizabeth Schüssler. *In Memory of Her*. London: SCM, 1983.
Fiorenza, Elizabeth Schüssler, and Mary Collins (eds.). "Women: Invisible in Church and Theology." *Concilium 182: Religion in the Eighties*. Edinburgh: T & T Clark, 1985.
Lees, Shirley (ed.). *The Role of Women*. Leicester: Inter-Varsity Press, 1984.
Massey, Lesly F. *Women and the New Testament: An Analysis of Scripture in Light of New Testament Era Culture*. Jefferson, NC: McFarland, 1989.
_____. *Women in the Church: Moving Toward Equality*. Jefferson, NC: McFarland, 2002.
Rosaldo, Michelle Zimbalist, and Louise Lampere (eds.). *Women, Culture and Society*. Stanford: University Press, 1974.
Ruether, Rosemary Radford. *Liberation Theology*. New York: Paulist Press, 1972.
_____. *Religion and Sexism*. New York: Simon & Schuster, 1974.
_____. *Sexism and God-Talk*. London: SCM, 1983.
Scanzoni, Letha, and Nancy Hardesty. *All We're Meant to Be*. Waco: Word, 1975.
Stendahl, Krister. *The Bible and the Role of Women: A Case Study in Hermeneutics*. Emile T. Sanders (trans.). Philadelphia: Fortress Press, 1966.
Witherington, Ben. *Women in the Earliest Churches*. Cambridge: University Press, 1988.
Young, Pamela Dickey. *Feminist Theology/Christian Theology: In Search of Method*. Minneapolis: Fortress, 1990.

Theology

McGrath, Alister E. *Christian Theology: An Introduction*. Oxford: Blackwell, 2001.

Lexicons, Grammars and Word Studies

Brown, Frances, S. R. Driver, and Charles A. Briggs (eds.). *A Hebrew and English Lexicon of the Old Testament*. Oxford: Clarendon, 1957.
Gesenius, F. N. *Hebrew and Chaldee Lexicon*. Samuel P. Tregelles (trans.). Grand Rapids, MI: Eerdmans, 1957.

Classical Sources

Bohn's Classical Library. London: George Bell and Sons, 1900–1905.
Danby, Herbert (trans.). *The Mishnah*. London: Oxford University Press, 1974.
Epstein, Isidore (ed.). *The Babylonian Talmud*. London: Soncino, 1935–1948.
Kittel, Rudolf (ed.). *Biblia Hebraica*. Stuttgart: Privilegierte Wurttembergische Bibelanstalt, 1949.
The Loeb Classical Library. London: William Heinemann, 1917–1946.
Septuagint with Apocrypha: Greek and English. London: Samuel Bagster, 1851.
Whiston, William (trans.). *The Life and Works of Flavius Josephus*. Grand Rapids, MI: Kregel, 1967.

Online Resources

Epic of Gilgamesh, summary by Richard Hooker.

Jastrow, Morris. "The Descent of Ishtar into the Netherworld." *The Civilization of Babylonia and Assyria*, 1915. Retrieved May 2014. http://www.ancienttexts.org/library/mesopotamian/ishtar.html.
Juvenal. *Satires*. Retrieved January 2015. http://www.tertullian.org/fathers/juvenal_satires_00_eintro.htm.
King, L. W. (trans.). *Code of Hammurabi*. Retrieved July 2014. http://eawc.evansville.edu/anthology/hammurabi.htm.
King, L. W. (trans.). *The Seven Tablets of Creation*. Retrieved July 2014, http://www.sacred-texts.com/ane/stc/index.htm.
Livy. *The History of Rome*. Retrieved December 2014. http://mcadams.posc.mu.edu/txt/ah/Livy.
Lucian. *The Syrian Goddess*. Herbert A. Strong and John Garstang (trans.). 1913. Retrieved November 2014. http://www.sacred-texts.com/cla/luc/index.htm.
McIntosh, Jane R. *Ancient Mesopotamia: New Perspectives*. ABC-CLIO, 2005. Retrieved January 2015. https://books.google.com/books?id=9veK7E2JwkUC&printsec=frontcover&dq=isbn:1576079651&hl=en&sa=X&ei=686_VPKxLYycNr76g9gP&ved=0CB8Q6AEwAA#v=onepage&q&f=false.
Musonius Rufus. *Lectures*. Cora Lutz (trans.). Retrieved January 2015. https://sites.google.com/site/thestoiclife/the_teachers/musonius-rufus/lectures.
Silver, Morris. "Temple/Sacred Prostitution in Ancient Mesopotamia Revisited: Religion in the Economy." *Ugarit-Forschungen* 38 (2006): 631–663. Retrieved January 2015. https://www.google.com/?gws_rd=ssl#q=Morris+Silver%2C+Temple%2FSacred+Prostitution+in+Ancient+Mesopotamia+Revisited.
Stephens, William O. "Musonius Rufus (c. 30–62 CE)." *Internet Encyclopedia of Philosophy*. Retrieved January 2015. http://www.iep.utm.edu/musonius.
Thompson, James C. *Women in the Ancient World*. Retrieved November 2014. http://www.womenintheancientworld.com.

Index

Abram (Abraham) 22, 57, 90
Abydos 191
Acca Larentia 147
Achilles 119
Adam 5, 87-9
Addu-Guppi 26
Adonia festival 117
Adonis 116-17, 189
adultery 36-38, 100-3, 121, 132
Aeneas 147
Aeschylus 126
Agamemnon 119
Agave 186
Ahhotep 63
Akiva 102
Akkadians 23
Alexandria 143-4, 187, 192, 203
Amarna 75
Amat-Mamu 46
Amenemope 68
Amenhotep IV (Akhenaten) 54, 63, 93
Amorites 22
Amose I 63
Amun 59, 62
An, Anu 41
Andromache 120, 128
anthropology 7
Antigone 127
Antisthenes 134
Aphrodite 111, 116, 140, 189
Apocrypha 85
Apollo 114
Apollonia (Senmonthis) 68
Apollonius 188
Appian 149, 169
Apuleius 189-90, 193
Aristophanes 127-8
Aristotle 130
Arius Didymus 211
Arria 169

Arsinoe II 144
art 16-7, 144-5
Artemis 113-15
Arthryte 62
Asclepius 182
Asenath 57
Ashtarte 60, 197
Ashur-Sharrat 28
Ashurbanipal 20, 23, 44
Ashusikildingira 24
Aspasia 128, 139
Assyrians 23
astrology 196
Aten 63, 93
Athaliah 95
Athena 113-14, 126
Atum 59
Augustus (Octavius) 153-4, 157-8, 164-5, 182
auletrides 139
Aulus Gellius 155, 198
Aurora 174
auspex (augur) 156 Baal 60

Babylon 23
Bacchus 172, 180, 182
Balawat, Gates of 29
Bastet 61
Bathsheba 95
Bedouin 90
Berериah 105
betrothal 86, 97, 155-6
Biale, Rachel 86, 89, 108
Bible, authority of 5
bitter water 37, 100
Bona Dea 174-5
bondage 93
bride price 31, 91, 121
Briseis 119
brothel 171

251

Bubastis 61
Budin, Stephanie 140
Burkert, Walter 177

Cairo Museum 55
Calpurnia 169
Calypso 120
Canaan, Canaanites 88, 91
capax 67
Chaldees 87, 90
Chamaeleon 140
childbirth 36, 74, 78, 131, 153, 162
Christianity 196–214
Christmas 197
Chryseis 119
church 202
Cicero 150, 154, 162, 172–3
circumcision 93
Cleopatra VII 144
Clytemnestra 126, 143
coemptio (earnest money) 155, 198
contraceptive 36, 74
Coptic 55
Corinth 141, 208
Cornelia Africana 159
Cornelius Nepos 125
corveé labor 80
Cybele 178, 191 dancing 78–80

Deborah 94
Deir el-Medina 68, 72, 75
deities 40–2, 61–2, 111–18, 172
Demeter 49, 112–13, 117, 178, 180–1
Demotic 55
Deuteronomy 94, 201
Diaspora 85, 106, 150
Dike 112
Dinah 91
Dio Chrysostom 123, 131, 138
Diodorus 21, 26, 55, 71
Dionysus (Bacchus) 143, 178, 185–8
divorce 38–9, 72–3, 86, 102–3, 133–4, 164–6, 201
dowry 31, 164
Draco 121
dress 81, 167–8, 212
Dumuzi 19, 25, 41–2, 102–3
dwellings 74

Easter 197
Ebla Tablets 90
ecstasy (frenzy) 183, 188, 190
education 103–5, 129, 134–5, 160–1
Eirene 112
Electra 127
Eleusis, Eleusinian 117, 178, 180–4

Enheduanna 39, 44
Enki (Ea) 51
Enlil 19, 41
Ennigaldinanna 44
Enoch 9
Enuma Anu Enlil 44
Enuma Elish 49–50
epoptai 182–3
Eridu 22, 50
Erinna 135
Erinyes (Furies) 126
Erishkigal 19
Eros 116
eschatology 6, 200
Eubuleus 182
Eunomia 112
Euphrates 15
Euripides 128, 186
Eusebius 207
Eve 5, 8–9, 87–9, 96
Exodus 58, 93 Fall 87, 89, 96

Fauna 174
Fayyum (Crocodilopolis) 61
Felicity 207
fellahin 75
feminism 10–12
Fiorenza, Elizabeth Schüssler 12, 14, 208
fishing 75
fornication 103, 201
Fortuna 173
Fortunata 162
Freud, Sigmund 93 Gaia 111

Galaxia 189
gallus 188, 190–1
Genesis 9, 15, 57, 83, 87, 90–2
Gennesaret 75
Gilgamesh 18, 20, 40, 51
Gipar 43
Goshen 58
Gracchi 159
Great Mother 188
grooming 81, 166
Gula 33, 36
gynaeconitis 123

Hadrian 158, 182
hair 81, 166–7, 213
Hammurabi 20, 30–9, 53
Hannah 94–5
Hapiru (Habiru) 58, 91–3
Haran 90
harem 71
Harrington, Judith 170
Hathor 60–61

Index

Hatshepsut 54, 64, 93
Hebrew 83, 88, 90–3
Hecataeus 55
Hekunsig 25
Helen of Troy 119
Heliopolis 59
Hellenism 142, 144
Helvia 169
Hephaestus 191
Hera 112–16
Hermopolis 59
Herodotus 21, 32, 47, 55, 61, 66, 109, 140, 188
Herondas 136
Hesiod 109, 111, 123
Hestia 112–4
hetaerae 124, 133, 138–9
Hierapolis 188
hieratic 55
hierodule 141–2
hieroglyphs 55
hierophant 181–3
Hillel 86, 102, 201
Hispala 187
Hittites 54
home 115
Homer 109, 118–21
homosexual 100
Horace 163
Horus 60
household codes 5, 210–11
Hurrians 92
Hyksos 54, 64, 92

idolatry 101
incest 69
infant exposure 153
inheritance 157–8
Instruction of Any 72–3
Iphigeneia 127
ish, ishah 88
Ishtar (Inanna) 17, 26, 41–2
Isis 60–1, 178, 191–5
Isitemheb 62

Jerusalem 86, 99, 102, 108, 150, 196, 207
Jesus ben Sirach 103–4
Jesus of Nazareth 96, 99, 103, 108, 199–201
jewelry 168
Jezebel 95
Joseph 57–58, 91–2
Julia 154
Julius Caesar 150, 164, 193
Jung, Carl 117–18
Justinian Code 152
Juvenal 150, 161, 163, 165, 167, 175, 194

Kabeiroi 184
Kadesh 54
kephale 208
ketubah 103
Khenerit 62
Khufu 54
Kiefer, Otto 149

Lamashtu 36
Laodice 143
Leah 91
lesbian 100, 134
Levant 90
levirate marriage 94, 99
Livia 160
Livy 149, 150–1, 161, 172, 187, 190
love 169–70, 200, 213
Lucian 188
Lucius 189
Lydia 143, 203
Lysias 123
Lysistrata 127

Macedonia 142–3
Macrobius 167, 173
Maglu Texts 44
Magna Graecia 174
make-up 81, 166
Manetho 57
manus 152, 157, 164, 187
Marcus Aurelius 158
market 77
marriage 30–4, 69–73, 96–8, 157–8, 162, 171
Martial 150, 163, 165–7, 191
Mary Magdalene 202
Mary, mother of Jesus 202
Mary of Bethany 200
matchmaker 97, 131, 155
Mater Matuta 151, 174
matriarchy 7, 12, 52, 112
Maximinus Thrax 207
Medea 127
medicine 36, 78
megaloi theoi (Great Gods) 184–5
Megiddo 80
Memnon, Colossi of 65
Menes (Narmer) 54
menstruation 73, 105–8
Meptum 37
Merneptah (Merenptah) 58
Metis 114
metragurtai 190
Mezuzah 106
Midrash 86
midwife 35, 78, 104
Miriam 92, 94
Mishnah 85, 95, 105

misogyny 71, 209
Mithras 177-8, 195-6
monogamy 32, 71, 122, 157, 209
monotheism 93, 104
Moses 68, 78, 92-4
Mott, Lucretia 10
mourner 78-79, 136
musician 78-79
Musonius Rufus 160-1, 204
musterion 179, 197
mystagogos 182
Mystery cults 177-96
mystes (initiate) 183, 193

naditu 45-46
Naomi 94
Naqada 54
Naucratis 55
Nausicaa 120
Naville, Edouard 58
Nebuchadnezzar 23
Nefertari 63
Nefertiti 54, 65
Neferura 64
Nephthys 191
Nero 206
Nile 76
Ninbanda 24
Nineveh 23
Ningal 25, 44
Ninhursag 41
Ninlil 41
Nitocris 26
nudity 35, 144-5
nursing (breast-feeding) 74, 78-9, 92

Odysseus 114, 119-21
oikos 122, 127, 130
Olympias 143, 184
Onnes 26-27
orgy 180
Osiris 60, 191
Ovid 150, 163, 173

Paculla Annia 187
Palermo Stone 55
Pales 147
Panathenaea 113, 136
Pandora 8, 112, 212
Parthenon 113
pater familias 152, 172
patriarchy 5, 9-12, 29, 32, 59, 90, 105, 109, 112, 118, 122, 151, 153, 176, 201, 204, 209, 214
patronage 159
Paul 7, 130, 137, 143, 163, 198, 202-3, 209
Paulina (wife of Saturninus) 194
Paulina (wife of Seneca) 169

Pausanias 114, 116, 182, 184-5
Pax Romana 203
Peitho 138
Pelluciae of Amun 62
Penelope 120-21
Pentateuch 94
Pentecost 202
Penthelia 62
Perictione 130
Perpetua 207
persecution 202, 206
Persephone (Kore) 49, 116, 178, 180
Petrie, Flinders 58
Petronius 150, 161-2
Philo Judaeus 107
Phoebe 160, 203
Pinder 140
Pithom 58-59
Plancia Magna 160
Plato 125, 129, 190
Pliny 156, 160, 169-70
Plutarch 123-6, 131, 138, 156, 159, 175, 191
politeia 210
Pollux 118, 135
Polycarp 207
polygamy 71, 90
Pomeroy, Sarah 11, 13, 109
Pompeia 164
Potiphar 57-58, 72
priestess 61, 136, 193
Priscilla 203
prophetess 62
prostitution 31, 40, 46-9, 101-2, 125, 136-8, 147, 171
prytaneion 136
Ptahhotep 69
Pu-abi 25
Pythagorus 128
Pythia 136

qadishtu 46
Qumran 85

Ra 60
Raamses 58
rabbi, rabbinical 83, 104
Rachel 91
Rahab 101
Rameses II 58, 93
religion 40-9, 61-3, 105-7, 135, 171-5, 177-8, 201
Remus 147
Rhea 112
Rhea Silvia 147
ring 155
Romulus 147, 190
Ruether, Rosemary Radford 208

Rufina 106
Ruth 94, 99

Sabine women 152
sacerdos 194
Sadducee 99
Sallust 150, 162
Salvius Iulianus 157
Samaritan woman 200
Samarra 23
Sammuramat 27
Samothrace 184–5
Sappho 134–5
Sarah 90
Sarapis 193
Sargon 23, 43
Satamun 66
Satan 8
Saturnalia 172–3
Scorpion King 54
scribe 77
Semele 185–6
Semiramis 26
Semite 21, 75, 90–1
Sempronia 160
Seneca 139, 150, 163, 165, 177
Septimius Severus 207
Septuagint 85
servants 57, 77
Set (Seth) 60, 191
sex, sexuality 33, 62, 165–6
Shamhat 52
Shammai 86, 102–3, 201
Sheftu (Teti) 67
Shema 95, 105
Shiduri 52
shrine, family 74
singing 61
skirt 29
slavery 6, 28, 30–2, 90, 121, 170–1, 200
Socrates 129, 134
Solomon 95
Solon 122, 138
Sophists 129
Sparta 124–5
Stanton, Elizabeth Cady 10
Steinem, Gloria 11
stelae 55
Strabo 57, 141
stuprum 158
Suetonius 154, 206
Sumer, Sumerians 22
synagogue 104, 106–8, 206

Tacitus 206
Tale of the Two Brothers 71

Talmud 85, 101
Tanakh 83, 85, 88, 96, 104
Tanaquil 151–2
Tarquinia 151
taurobolium 190
Taweret 60
Tefillah 106
Telesterion 182, 185
Terentia 165, 173
Thalassa 111
Theodosius 64
Theogony 111–13
Thesmophoria 49, 127, 172, 180, 193
Thucydides 126
Thutmoses III 93
Tigris 15
Tihenut 67
Tiy 64, 66
tokens, of virginity 98
Torah 86, 105–6
Trajan (Decius) 207
Troy 116, 119, 126, 190
tutela (guardian) 157

Ulpian 152
Ur 22, 24–26, 90
Ur-Nammu, Code 20
Uruk 22
Utnapishtim (Ziusudra) 51

Valerius Maximus 168
Valley of the Kings 75
veil 33, 139, 164, 168, 198, 213
venereal disease 36
Vesta (Vestal virgins) 168, 174–5
Virgil 150
Virgin Mary 198
virgin, virginity 33, 98, 113

wedding 156
Wernero 67
widow 94, 99, 200
wife (matron) 70, 109, 116, 154–5, 158–60, 212
wig 81
witchcraft 179
Women's Suffrage 208
Woolley, Leonard 24
work 76–77
worship 177
worthy woman 95

Xanthippe 134
Xenophon 109, 128, 131, 134

Yahweh, Yahwist 87, 89, 94, 201

Ziggurat 22–3, 41

www.ingramcontent.com/pod-product-compliance
Ingram Content Group UK Ltd.
Pitfield, Milton Keynes, MK11 3LW, UK
UKHW041934140426
5217IPUK00014B/480